LA MUCULUFA II

Excavation and Survey 1988–1991
The Castelluccian Village and Other Areas

ARCHAEOLOGIA TRANSATLANTICA
XII

A Series in Mediterranean Archaeology

edited by

Tony Hackens
Professor of Classical Archaeology
Université Catholique de Louvain, Louvain-la-Neuve

R. Ross Holloway
Professor of Central Mediterranean Archaeology
Brown University, Providence

Published with the support of Brown University and the Fonds Abbé Mignot
pour l'archéologie classique a l'Université Catholique de Louvain.

PUBLICATIONS D'HISTOIRE DE L'ART ET D'ARCHEOLOGIE
DE L'UNIVERSITE CATHOLIQUE DE LOUVAIN — LXXV

LA MUCULUFA II

Archaeologia Transatlantica
XII

Excavation and Survey of the Regione Siciliana
Soprintendenza ai Beni Culturali ed Ambientali di Agrigento
in Collaboration with Brown University

by

Brian Evans McConnell

with the collaboration of John Chervinsky, Susan S. Lukesh, Laura Maniscalco,
Melissa Moore, Nancy Peterson, Alfredo Riedel, Angela Rovida

CENTER FOR OLD WORLD
ARCHAEOLOGY AND ART
BROWN UNIVERSITY
PROVIDENCE, RHODE ISLAND

DEPARTEMENT D'ARCHEOLOGIE
ET D'HISTOIRE DE L'ART
COLLEGE ERASME
LOUVAIN-LA-NEUVE, BELGIUM

1995

To William Lawrence

Contents

Foreword

The present volume completes the publication of the researches carried out at La Muculufa by the Soprintendenza ai Beni Culturali ed Ambientali of Agrigento in collaboration with Brown University between 1982 and 1991. Beginning in 1988 the director of the excavations has been Brian E. McConnell, the major author of this volume. Previously the excavation was directed by the undersigned assisted by Martha S. Joukowsky in charge of field operations and Susan S. Lukesh in charge of processing and analysis of the excavated materials. The many debts of the American excavators and staff are acknowledged in Prof. McConnell's preface. Still it must be emphasized that the excavations were the direct fruit of the vision of Prof. Ernesto D. Miro, Soprintendente ai Beni Culturali, and the continued support of his successor Dott.ssa Graziella Fiorentini.

The result of the work at La Muculufa has been the documentation of a village dating to the later third millennium B.C. and of a federal sanctuary connected with it. Never before have the remains of a settlement of the Castelluccian Culture or a Castelluccian sanctuary been recorded so thoroughly. Never before has the function of such sanctuary within the geographical boundaries of its influence, in this case the Salso River Valley from Caltanissetta on the north to Licata at the mouth of the Salso on the south, been established so clearly. Rarely has Castelluccian domestic architecture received such careful study. And the radiocarbon dates from La Muculufa fix the chronology of this period of Sicilian history for the first time on the basis of physical evidence. Moreover, the study of the mass of exquisitely decorated display pottery from the Sanctuary by Prof. Lukesh has led to the identification of a towering personality among the potter-painters of the third millennium in Sicily, the La Muculufa Master, see "The La Muculufa Master and Company: The Identification of a Workshop of Early Bronze Age Castelluccian Painters" in *Revue des Archéologues et Historiens d'Art de Louvain* 24 (1991).

The Sanctuary at La Muculufa has been published in Holloway, Joukowsky, Lukesh and others, "La Muculufa, The Early Bronze Age Sanctuary: The Early Bronze Age Village, excavations of 1982 and 1983" in *Revue des Archéologues et Historiens d'Art de Louvain* 23 (1990). The chamber tombs of the site were studied by George Parker,

"The Early Bronze Age Chamber Tombs at La Muculufa" in *Revue des Archéologues et Historiens d'Art de Louvain* 18 (1985) and a burial cave is published by Brian E. McConnell and Gabriella Morico, "La Muculufa (Butera, Caltanissetta) stazione siciliana dell'Età del Bronzo Antico, prima parte: La Muculufa un anfratto per sepoltura del Bronzo Antico, seconda parte da Cleto Corrain e Mariantonia Capitanio, Alcuni resti scheletrici umani da 'La Muculufa'" in *Archivio per l'Antropologia e la Etnologia* 120 (1990). Other preliminary publications are summarized in Prof. McConnell's Introduction.

The speedy completion of an excavation publication is a goal that too often remains unfulfilled. Prof. McConnell and his collaborators faced not only the rigors of summer excavation below the shadeless pinnacle of La Muculufa but carried out their analysis of the material during the difficult period of transition in the Licata Museum between its former and present location. Although the shades of the ancient villagers and guardians of the Sanctuary of La Muculufa may well have looked with bemusement on our labors, theirs was part of the cultural ascent of Sicily and the Mediterranean, and in an island where the glories of that ascent are so present, theirs was by no means a modest step upward.

R. Ross Holloway

Preface and Acknowledgements

This monograph presents a comprehensive account of explorations at the site of La Muculufa along the lower valley of the Salso River by the Superintendency for Cultural and Environmental Resources of the the Provinces of Agrigento and Caltanissetta, Sicily from 1988 to 1991, and it complements the studies on work at this site from 1982 to 1987 already published as a volume by R. Ross Holloway and his collaborators in the Revue des Archeologues et Historiens d'Art de Louvain 23, 1990, p.11–67.

Inasmuch as research since 1988 has focused on the Castelluccian village, the present volume seeks to provide a comprehensive treatment of this part of the site, and it incorporates in expanded form several preliminary publications. In particular, discussion of the excavation and architecture of the hut structures in the village appeared as an article in the American Journal of Archaeology 96, 1992, p.23–44, and that of the geophysical survey and subsequent excavation during the summers of 1990 and 1991 appeared in the form of a paper presented at the symposium "Social Dynamics of the Prehistoric Central Mediterranean" held at the Fifty-seventh Annual Meeting of the Society for American Archaeology (Pittsburgh, Pennsylvania, April 8–12, 1992). A full bibliography of publications related to La Muculufa appears at the end of this chapter.

Many studies appear here for the first time. The chapter on Castelluccian ceramics by Laura Maniscalco and those on the terracotta, stone, bone and other finds provide a full presentation and evaluation of the materials found both within the context of the architectural remains, and those found outside of significant prehistoric archaeological strata. A report by Prof. A. Riedel on animal bones recovered from the area of the Castelluccian crevice burial excavated in 1987 and 1989 and published previously (B.E. McConnell, G. Morico, C. Corrain and M. Capitanio, "La Muculufa (Butera, Caltanissetta), stazione siciliana dell'Età del Bronzo Antico," Archivio per l'Antropologia e la Etnologia 120, 1990, p.115–150) is presented in this volume. Special attention should be given to the physio-chemical studies of Castelluccian pottery presented in this volume, inasmuch as little prior materials research has been performed to date on prehistoric Sicilian ceramics. Finds pertaining to the historical phases of La Muculufa's occupation document the full range of cultural resources present at the site and place the countryside of south-central Sicily in the perspective of developments at other major centers. It is unfortunate, though inevitable, that not all of the excavated materials could be catalogued and studied either for lack of funds and personnel or for lack of time and space; nevertheless, it can be stated that no major constituent element of the excavated assemblages has remained untreated and that each class of material is a qualitatively significant sample. A catalogue and concordance of all finds which have been studied appears as an appendix.

Research at La Muculufa has been performed as a collaborative project between the Superintendency for Cultural and Environmental Resources of Agrigento and Caltanissetta, Sicily and the Center for Old World Archaeology and Art of Brown University. Administration of the site has passed since to the Superintendency for Cultural and Environmental Resources of Caltanissetta, which became an entity in January of 1992. Funding for this project was provided both by the Sicilian Regional government and by the Center for Old World Archaeology and Art of Brown University. Support for the costs of labor and for the transport, storage, and conservation of excavated materials was provided by the Department of Cultural and Environmental Resources (Assessorato ai Beni Culturali ed Ambientali) of the Sicilian Regional government. Thanks are owed to G. Fiorentini, Superintendent of the Superintendency for Cultural and Environmental Resources of Agrigento for her support of this research, as well as to R. Panvini, project director for the Agrigento Superintendency and now for the Superintendency of Caltanissetta, and Excavation Assistants L. Scicolone, (1988–89) and G. Profumo (1991) for their wholehearted commitment to the preparation and management of the fieldwork. Thanks are also owed to Arch. Angelo Di Franco and other personnel of the Agrigento Superintendency at Licata. Special acknowledgement is owed to Arch. Pietro Meli, director of the development project for the new museum complex in the Badia Grande at Piazza S. Angelo, Licata, for access to the facilities during the course of restoration, as well as for the hospitality and assistance offered by the Licata Archaeological Society of which he is president. Members of the Licata Archaeological Society and especially A. Mazerbo, F. Todaro, and Arch. G. Cavaleri provided helpful collaboration both during the excavation campaigns and at other times throughout the year. Employees of the Agrigento superintendency and workmen of the excavation-contractors V. Ortega (1988 and 1991) and G. Gristina (1989) carried out the excavation and conservation work with efficiency and skill.

Fieldwork from 1988 to 1991 was directed by Brian E. McConnell in collaboration particularly with Laura Maniscalco McConnell. Funding for the university group was provided by the Center for Old World Archaeology and Art of Brown University. Thanks are owed to R. Ross Holloway, M.S. Joukowsky and R. Winkes for their encouragement and support. Participants in the field campaigns include: (1988) B.E. McConnell (group director), L. Bellanca (illustrator), I.V. Maiore (assistant archaeologist); (1989) B.E. McConnell (group director), L. Maniscalco (archaeologist), C. Catanzaro (illustrator), M. Chesson (assistant); (1990) B.E. McConnell (group director), B.W. Bevan (geophysical surveyor), N.E. Peterson (assistant); (1991) B.E. McConnell (mission director), L. Maniscalco (archaeologist), P. Barrett (illustrator), S. Jay (illustrator), O. Doonan (assistant), A. Rovida (assistant archaeologist), and P. Lucchesi (illustrator).

Special thanks are owed to the Notaio Dott. Giuseppe Navarra and to his family for their friendship in every campaign and for their hospitality to the mission especially during the summer of 1989, as well as to Sig.ra Angela Guida and to her family for permission to excavate on their property.

Many individuals have offered helpful advice and made special arrangements for the special studies presented in this monograph. In particular, M.S. Balmuth (Tufts University) made arrangements with H. Lechtmann (Massachusetts Institute of Technology) for the petrographic study of Castelluccian ceramics; the direct assistance of M. Geselowitz and I.K. Whitbread are acknowledged, as well. Thanks are owed to P.M. Dott. Luigi Infantino of the Regional Authority for Mines (Corpo Regionale delle Miniere) for his generous advice and assistance in the library and archives of the Regional Minerals Agency (Ente Regionale Mineraria) at Caltanissetta. The authors, whose individual contributions are cited separately, acknowledge the library and research services of their respective institutions; Brian E. McConnell is particularly grateful for the use of library facilities at Brown University, the Istituto d'Archeologia of the Università degli Studi di Catania, Columbia University, and the University of Michigan—Ann Arbor.

The illustrations in this monograph were prepared by P. Barrett, L. Bellanca, C. Catanzaro, S. Crapanzano, A.K. Goodheart, S.T. Jay, K. Klaiber, M.J. McConnell, L. Merra, S. Mortellaro, and N.E. Peterson. The photographs were prepared by G. Cavaleri, N. Leonnet and by the various authors.

This monograph offers a full view of what was once a very important settlement in Castelluccian Sicily, yet most of the archaeological remains at La Muculufa remain to be excavated. It is an awesome reality that the crest looks down upon the excavation in the same way it looked down upon its Early Bronze Age inhabitants whose remains are being excavated. Despite the fragility manifest in constant weathering and the kind of systematic demolition so evident in clandestine excavation and in the quarrying of nearby Monte dei Drasi, time stands in La Muculufa's favor, thanks in large part to the legal measures taken by the Sicilian Regional government to protect it, and even today La Muculufa stands as a stage more majestic and significant than any of the individual actors who have played their parts upon its slopes.

Bibliography of Publications Related to La Muculufa

R.R. Holloway, "Primi Saggi di Scavo a "La Muculufa" (Butera)," Sicilia Archeologica 52–53, 1983, p.33–44.

R.R. Holloway, "Scavi archeologici alla Muculufa e premesse per lo studio della cultura castellucciana," Atti della seconda giornata di studi sull'archeologia Licatese e della zona della bassa valle dell'Himera, Licata 1985, p.69–90.

R.R. Holloway, "Scavi archeologici del periodo castellucciano a La Muculufa (Butera)," Kokalos 30–31, 1984–85, p.483–88.

R.R. Holloway, The Archaeology of Ancient Sicily, London, 1991, p.24–26.

R.R. Holloway, M.S. Joukowsky, S.S. Lukesh, "Mining La Muculufa," Archaeology 41, 1988, p.40–47.

R.R. Holloway, et al., La Muculufa, The Early Bronze Age Sanctuary: the Early Bronze Age Village, Excavations of 1982 and 1983, Providence and Louvain-la-Neuve, 1990 = Revue des Archeologues et Historiens d'Art de Louvain 23, 1990, p.11–67, including: R. R. Holloway, M.S. Joukowsky and S.S. Lukesh: "The excavation"; S.S. Lukesh: "Pottery"; J.L. Leurquin: "Chipped Stone Industry"; R.R. Holloway: "Worked Bone Amulets"; B.E. McConnell: "La Muculufa after the Bronze Age"; K. Cruz-Uribe: "The Mammalian Fauna"; J. Buckley and A. Long, "Reports of C14 Analysis"; and L. Costantini: "Report of Vegetal Remain Collected in Castelluccian Strata of the Village in 1988."

M.S. Joukowsky, "L'industrie de la pierre et du materiel de broyage au debut de l'age du bronze à la Muculufa, en Sicile," L'Anthropologie 91, 1987, p.273–82.

S. S. Lukesh, "The La Muculufa Master and Company: The Identification of a Workshop of Early Bronze Age Castelluccian Painters," Revue des Archéologues et Historiens d'Art de Louvain 24, 1991.

B.E. McConnell, "The Castelluccian Village at La Muculufa (Licata, Sicily)," paper delivered to the Ninetieth General Meeting of the Archaeological Institute of America (abstract) American Journal of Archaeology 93, 1989, p.276–77.

B.E. McConnell, "La Muculufa," Bibliografia Topografica della Colonizzazione Greca in Italia Meridionale e nelle Isole Tirreniche, VIII Naples-Pisa, 1991, p.424–425.

B.E. McConnell, "L'insediamento medievale alla Muculufa (Butera, CL)," Atti del Congresso 'L'Età di Federico II nella Sicilia Centro-Meridionale,' Gela, 8–9 December, 1990, p.229–33.

B.E. McConnell, "La Muculufa (Butera, CL): the 1989 and 1990 Field Seasons," paper delivered to the Ninety-second General Meeting of the Archaeological Institute of America (abstract) American Journal of Archaeology 95, 1991, p.306–307.

B.E. McConnell, "The Early Bronze Age Village of La Muculufa and Prehistoric Hut Architecture in Sicily," American Journal of Archaeology 96, 1992, p.23–44.

B.E. McConnell, "La Muculufa (Butera, CL): indagini di scavo e ricerche dal 1988 al 1991," Atti del VIII Congresso Internazionale di Studi sulla Sicilia Antica, Palermo, 18–23 April, 1993, forthcoming in Kokalos.

B.E. McConnell, G. Morico, C. Corrain and M. Capitanio, "La Muculufa (Butera, Caltanissetta), stazione siciliana dell'Età del Bronzo Antico," Archivio per l'Antropologia e la Etnologia 120, 1990, p.115–150.

B.E. McConnell and B.W. Bevan, "Spatial Analysis of a Castelluccian Settlement in Early Bronze Age Sicily," paper presented to the symposium "Social Dynamics of the Prehistoric Central Mediterranean," Fifty-seventh Annual Meeting of the Society for American Archaeology (Pittsburgh, Pennsylvania, 8–12 April, 1992), forthcoming in J. Morter, J. Robb and R. Tykot, eds., Social Dynamics of the Central Mediterranean.

G. Parker, "The Early Bronze Age Chamber Tombs at La Muculufa," Revue des Archéologues et Historiens d'Art de Louvain 18, 1985, p.9–33.

G. Pottino, "Monumenti funerari della prima e media età del bronzo nella Sicilia centro meridionale," Sicilia Archeologica 14, 1981, p.73–86.

With the exception of the following works all abbreviations for bibliographical references follow those given in the American Journal of Archaeology 90, 1986, p.384–94:

Atti Licata II = Atti della seconda giornata di studi sull'archeologia Licatese e della zona della bassa valle dell'Himera, Licata, 1985.

La Muculufa I = R.R. Holloway, et al., La Muculufa, The Early Bronze Age Sanctuary, The Early Bronze Age Village, Excavations of 1982 and 1983, Providence and Louvain-la-Neuve, 1990, Revue des Archeologues et Historiens d'Art de Louvain 23, 1990, p.11–67.

I – THE EXCAVATION

Introduction

The Salso River valley extends for 110 kilometers from the southern coast of Sicily into the island's interior heartland. Called also the Southern Himera, as it was in Antiquity, this river is the traditional division between eastern and western Sicily, a division regarded as that between the territory of indigenous Sicel and Sican peoples[1]. Roughly twenty kilometers inland from the river's mouth at Licata rises the crest now called La Muculufa in the territory of Butera, Caltanissetta (Plate 1.1). During the Middle Ages this crest was called Mocluse and it seems likely that this toponym has its origin in the era of the Arab emirs who ruled Sicily from the Ninth century A.C. through the Norman conquest in A.D. 1086[2].

Archaeological exploration along the crest of La Muculufa has revealed a prehistoric settlement composed of a terraced village on the south-eastern slope below the crest, a necropolis of chamber tombs along central portion of the crest, and an open-air sanctuary on a large natural terrace at the crest's eastern end, as well as other traces of occupation in historic times (Plate 1.2). The prehistoric settlement appears to belong exclusively to the Castelluccian culture which heralds the appearance of the Sicilian Early Bronze Age in the third millennium B.C. and which witnesses the crystallization of many of the Island's traditionally indigenous cultural features which were preserved to the time of the arrival of Phoenician and Greek colonists[3]. Inasmuch as the Castelluccian culture is found across roughly two-thirds of the island, the position of La Muculufa along the river Salso is particularly significant, and the stratigraphic and spatial complexity of the site along with the rich quality of the ceramic, stone and other artifacts recovered there seems to confirm this. Excavation in 1982 and 1983 identified the location, cultural context, and general condition of structures in a limited area of the village (Plate 1.2, zone F) and devoted particular attention to the study of Castelluccian ceramics in the wider context of ceramic production in Early Bronze Age Sicily. Excavations conducted through 1987 on a natural terrace at the eastern extremity of the crest (Plate 1.2, zone T) revealed a rich deposit of Castelluccian ceramics, animal-bone and charcoal roughly 4 m deep associated with traces of stone walls and terracotta hearth-surfaces which pertained to the open-air sanctuary[4].

Beginning in 1988 the program of fieldwork focused specifically upon the physical structure and the history of

---

[1] No ancient author states specifically that the Salso/Southern Himera river divided the territories controlled, at least in the historical tradition, by the Siculi and the Sicani; however, this conclusion can be inferred reasonably from the texts of Thucydides (VI.2) and Diodorus Siculus (V.2 and V.8); cfr. also Livy, XXIV.6.7). For modern interpretations of the literary evidence see: Luigi Bernabò Brea, La Sicilia prima dei Greci, (Milano 1958), p.174, and E. Manni, "'Indigeni' e colonizzatori nella Sicilia Preromana," in 'Assimilation et résistance à la culture gréco-romaine dans le monde ancien = Travaux du VIème Congrès International d'Etudes Classiques. Madrid, Septembre 1974, Paris, 1976, p.181–211, esp. p.185ff., reprinted in Sikelika kaì Italika, Scritti Minori di Storia Antica della Sicilia e dell'Italia Meridionale, vol. 1, Rome, 1990, p.97–137, esp. p.103ff. G. Navarra gives the most complete discussion of this matter in Città Sicane Sicule e Greche nella Zona di Gela, Palermo, 1964, p.44–45 citing F. Cluverio, Sicilia Antiqua, Lugduni Batavorum, 1916, I, XVII, p.215–216.

[2] The Latin name 'Mocluse' is given in a list of ten centers conquered by Roger d'Hautville in the Count's official chronicle written by Gaufredo Malaterra. See B.E. McConnell, "L'insediamento medievale alla Muculufa (Butera, CL), Atti del Congresso 'L'età di Federico II nella Sicilia Centro Meridionale,' Gela, 8–9 December, 1990, p.229–33; B.E. McConnell, "La Muculufa after the Bronze Age," in La Muculufa I, p.49–56. It is possible that the name 'La Muculufa' is derived from the common arab toponym 'magaruca' meaning 'infertile land' and 'mahruqa' meaning 'burned' in reference to the land; cf. G.B. Pellegrini, "Terminologia geografica araba in Sicilia," Annali dell'Istituto Orientale di Napoli, Sezione Linguistica 3, 1961, p.109–201, here 138. Discussion of a possible twelfth century reference to La Muculufa as the *casale* 'Michalchilfe' and of medieval remains found at La Muculufa during the 1989 and 1991 excavation campaigns appears on pages 33–34 of this volume.

[3] The term Castelluccian was coined by Luigi Bernabò Brea for the culture first identified by Paolo Orsi at the turn of the centry as the "primo periodo siculo"; cf. P. Orsi, "La Sicilia preellenica," Atti della Società italiana per il progresso delle scienze, XII Riunione, Catania, 1923, Città di Castello, 1923, p.1–35, esp. p.8–15; idem, "La necropoli sicula di Castelluccio (Siracusa)," BPI, 18, 1892, p.1–34 and p.67–84; Bernabò Brea (supra n.1) 13. Regarding the Castelluccian culture see L. Bernabò Brea, "Eolie, Sicilia e Malta nell'età del bronzo," Kokalos, 22–23, 1976–77, p.33–110, esp. p.43–46, and S. Tusa, La Sicilia nella preistoria, Palermo, 1983, p.263–360. R. R. Holloway prefers to include the preceding "Eneolithic" or "Copper Age" cultures into a more widely encompassing notion of the Early Bronze Age; cf. Italy and the Aegean, 3000–700 B.C., Louvain-la-Neuve and Providence, 1981, p.24.

the village. Trial trenches excavated during the summer of 1988 were opened out during the 1989 campaign to reveal a 300 square-meter section of one of the terraces upon which the village was built. By the end of the 1989 campaign it was possible to discern the remains of at least four huts—Hut No. 1 on a lower terrace, and on a terrace higher up the hillslope Hut Nos. 2, 3 (upper and lower), and 4, as well as traces of other structures in at least three stratified phases. Inasmuch as this area covered only a small fraction of the entire village and because a large portion of the surface in this area had been disturbed by plowing, a geophysical survey of the area immediately northeast of the excavation zone was conducted in June of 1990 by Dr. Bruce Bevan (Geosight, Pitman, NJ) in order to ascertain the subsurface conditions of the archaeological deposit and to guide future fieldwork. Excavation during a brief, three-week campaign in August of 1991 confirmed the findings of the survey and established a basis for the analysis of the topography of the Field excavation zone and the layout of the Castelluccian village (Plate 2).

Geological and Natural Setting

The Salso river basin covers roughly 2,002 square-kilometers, and it is the second largest river basin in Sicily in terms of length and breadth (the Simeto river basin is the largest). In geological terms, the Salso passes through the large Tertiary sedimentary basin which dominates over 5000 square kilometers in central-southern Sicily between the Platani and Gela rivers and which consists of six major levels of deposition, the earliest deposits of which date to the Mesozoic period and the latest to the Middle and Upper Pliocene (Plate 3.2). Clays of various form constitute over half of the sediments found in this basin, and a chalky sulphurous series appears across roughly twelve percent of the area, particularly in the south. The generally low permeability of the soil (less than thirty percent, except in sandy deposits where it can reach over fifty percent) has led to high erosion and the creation of a landscape marked by deep gullies and lofty crags[5].

La Muculufa is defined by the Salso river which passes along its northern and western flanks from Isola Finnuta to Isola dei Cuti. The eastern and southern sides are delimited by the Torrente della Pietrosa which flows into the Salso at Isola dei Cuti and the Torrente Brigadieri which flows into the Salso at Isola Finnuta by way of the Vallone Valentino. The crest of La Muculufa is formed primarily from strata in the chalky sulphurous series of the Upper Miocene, including calcareous rock of travertinoide type, saccarious gypsum and white marl, which have been set vertically in a tortured process of deformation. Debris from the decomposition of these strata fills the crags of the crest and the upper slopes of its northern and southern flanks, while older clays (argille brecciate) mark the lower slopes. The erosion of these soft strata undercuts the rock above, causing large blocks to have fallen to the slopes below[6].

The soil on the surface is composed primarily of clay and silt which is light grayish in color and which contains many stones. In the cultivated areas, stones are frequently about 15 cm in size; in uncultivated areas, the stones are about 15–100 cm in size. Thistles and other spiny plants cover the ground-surface, but there are almost no woody shrubs in the area. The Corpo Forestale of the Italian government has for many years now been engaged in a program of re-forestation, primarily of pine and eucalyptus trees, along the northeastern flank of La Muculufa and in Contrada Suor Marchesa to the southeast.

The region is rural with the distance between structures of over one kilometer, and there are no industries in the vicinity except for a quarry which is rapidly eliminating Monte dei Drasi on the other side of the Salso opposite La Muculufa from the skyline. A sulphur mine was opened on the western flank of La Muculufa in 1876 and functioned continuously until its closure in the late 1960s. The abandoned masseria Pietrapiccola, the farmstead owned most recently by the Bruscato family, and the Casa

---

[4] Fieldwork in the area of the eastern terrace (Zone T) between 1985 and 1987 is discussed in La Muculufa I, 14–18. Smaller projects performed during the 1989 excavation campaign are discussed on page 19 of this volume.

[5] T. Rocco, "Gela in Sicilia. Un singolare campo petrolifero," Rivista Mineraria Siciliana, 10, 1959, p.167–88; R. Coltro, "Le formazioni siciliane nel quadro della sistemazione idrogeologica," Atti del Convegno Nazionale su l'Idrologia e la sistemazione dei piccoli bacini, Roma, 6–7 giugno 1969, p.327–36, esp. p.334f.; R. Coltro and V. Ferrara, "Contributo alla conoscenza della dissestabilità del bacino del fiume Salso o Imera meridionale," Cassa per il Mezzogiorno, Ripartizione attività per le regioni, Quaderno n.53., Acireale, esp. p.9, 33ff., and 51.

dei Cipressi are the only structures along La Muculufa's southern flank. Agriculture is dedicated primarily to grain

and in recent years to grape-growing, but much of the land remains idle or devoted to pasture[7].

The effect of this landscape in conjunction with the climate and the passage of the seasons can be quite striking[8]. On a clear day in the fall or the spring, the distant cone of Mt. Etna rises above the horizon as it is seen from the eastern terrace. The craggy crest of La Muculufa itself is visible to the surrounding region for kilometers, and it seems likely that the strangely attractive form of the crest and the availability of fresh water both from the Salso river and from temporary springs which are said to have flowed out of the crest's crevices drew people there to settle[9].

The Campaigns of 1988 and 1989

The Castelluccian village was discovered along the southern flank of the crest in a field which opens out across a

---

[6] L. Baldacci gives the following geological description of La Muculufa together with Monte dei Drasi in Descrizione Geologica dell'Isola di Sicilia, Memorie Descrittive della Carta Geologica d'Italia, Roma, 1886, p.263–264: "... Ad Est di questi colli [Monte rosseddo] si vede spiccare sulle argille tortoniane la cresta del monte Drasi (378m) che è costituito da un enorme banco di gesso diretto N.E.-S.O. e inclinato fortemente a S.E.; sotto di esso spuntano a N.O. i tripoli concordanti col gesso. La cresta del monte Drasi si vede traversare l'Imera, il cui letto in quel punto è quasi strozzato, e va a costituire sulla sponda sinistra di quel fiume il monte Muculufa dove esiste un'importante solfara.

"Solfara Muculufa.—L'inclinazione degli strati gessoso-solfiferi è affatto opposta a quella del monte Drasi, cioè verso N.O.: questa inclinazione che è assai forte (quasi verticale) all'affioramento diminuisce in profondità fino a circa 40°. I tripoli spuntano lungo tutto l'affioramento nel versante S.E.; su essi posa un banco di calcare siliceo perculiato di 50 o 60 metri di potenza, sul quale viene lo strato solfifero che ha una potenza variabile da 5 a 20m ed è coperto da un banco di 30m di arenazzolo. Sull'arenazzolo vengono poi dei potenti gessi cristalini e balatinati, che sembra vadano ad immergersi sotto le argille mioceniche mentre invece non sono che posati su esse: il minerale solfifero contiene da 17 al 18% di zolfo." See also G. Castaldo and G. Stampanoni, Memoria Illustrativa della Carta Mineraria d'Italia, Memorie per servire alla descrizione della Carta Geologica d'Italia, Vol. 14, Roma, 1975, p.161–73, esp. p.166.

The closest area studied in geological detail lies just southwest of La Muculufa in contrada Passarello; cf. L. Ogniben, Le «argille brecciate» siciliane con i rilievi di dettaglio di Grottacalda (Valguarnera, Enna), Passarello (Licata, Agrigento), Zubbi (S. Cataldo, Caltanissetta), Istituto di Geologia e Mineralogia, Università di Padova, Memorie, v.18, 1954, esp. p.21–40. A summary of this important monograph, but without illustrations, appears as L. Ogniben, "'Argille scagliose' ed 'Argille brecciate' in Sicilia," Bollettino del Servizio Geologico d'Italia, 75, 1953, p.281–289. Thanks are owed to Prof. R. Cristofolini and Prof. A. Pezzino (Istituto delle Scienze della Terra, Università degli Studi di Catania) and to Dott. P.M. Luigi Infantino (Corpo Regionale delle Miniere, Caltanissetta, Ente Regionale Mineraria) for their help in this research, as well as to Prof. C. Corrain (Dipartimento di Biologia, Universitàdi Padova) who obtained a rare original copy of Ogniben's monograph.

A similar geological situation has been described recently in the publication of results of an archaeological survey in the territory of Pietraperzia; cf. S. Tusa, "Functions, resources and spatial organisation in the Pietraperzia territory (Enna—Sicily) between the Copper and Bronze Ages," in E. Herring, et al., eds. Papers of the Fourth Conference of Italian Archaeology, London, January 1990, The Archaeology of Power, Part 1, London, 1991, p.27–41.

---

[7] Description based on B.W. Bevan, "A Geophysical Survey at La Muculufa," (unpublished field report 17 July 1990) p.2–3 and on information obtained from the Corpo Regionale delle Miniere, Ente Regionale Mineraria, Caltanissetta. Maps of the sulphur mine, which was opened as property of the Conte D'Almerita Tasca and closed following a serious collapse under the administration of the company SO.CHI.MI.SI. appear from 1876 to 1968 under the name 'Macalufa' (sic).

[8] The aesthetic impact of the landscape is described eloquently in the decree of the Sicilian Regional government which declared La Muculufa a natural reserve (Gazzetta Ufficiale della Regione Siciliana, Parte I, N.56, 2–6): "... salendo alla collina, gli elementi che ne compongono l'aspetto geo-morfologico-naturalistico offrono sempre uno spettacolo suggestivo e, comunque, vario ora il pinnacolo di roccia isolato e forato da numerose tombe preistoriche, ora il fotto cespuglio della palma nana, ora la piccola foresta preistorica dei finocchi selvatici dagli steli secchi, ora l'improvvisa visione delle pendici della collina coi bei fabbricati rurali e le masserie; ... I vestiti delle stagioni avvolgono la «Muculufa» rappresentandola ognivolta diversa: le mattine d'inverno la bruma del fiume ne avvolge e circonda la base e sul cielo di pallido azzurro la cresta rocciosa appare navigare sul mare della nebbia; la verde veste della primavera con metamorfosi lenta diviene il mantello dorato dei grani d'agosto: il brullo terreno d'ottobre recando la tavolozza di tutte le terre, prelude al nuovo ciclo."

[9] Traces of natural springs cut in the rock may be seen at various points along the crest, one of which lies quite close to the village.

wide, natural terrace and which gently rises at a slope of twenty-four percent (approximately fourteen degrees above the horizontal) to the rocky crest which then hurls itself upward in a series of tormented crags to a maximum elevation of 391 meters above sea-level (msl). The elevation of the field itself is roughly 300 msl, and it is divided by a stone wall into two properties, one which until recently had been plowed for the cultivation of wheat and the other to the east which had never been cultivated. The archaeological deposit in the western property was found beneath an average 80 cm of plowed humus and a clayey soil mixed with smaller pebbles.

Although the precise limits of the Castelluccian village have not been established, it is estimated that the settlement extended between 25,000 and 30,000 square meters on the basis of sherd scatter, previous excavation and traces of prehistoric structures already visible on the surface. It appears that the village did not extend beyond the edge of the field's natural terrace—a test-pit measuring 4.0 x 2.0 meters and dug to a depth of 1.0 meters in the field of a terrace downslope from the Castelluccian village revealed no significant amount of cultural remains; sterile soil appeared beneath the plowed humus. Perhaps this level ground served the Castelluccian village as an area of cultivation.

Methodology

Before proceeding with a description of the remains, it is worth noting the system of reference and measurement employed. The excavation in all campaigns utilized a grid-plan of squares measuring five meters along each side. The grid was marked with meter-coordinates increasing to the East and to the South in order to indicate the precise planimetric location of all finds. Elevation measurements were made with respect to specific datum points which had been selected during the 1982 campaign and marked with metal stakes set in cement[10].

Throughout this monograph the following terms will be used: zone, area, and portion. The term 'zone' refers to a component of the site—excavation zone F (Field) refers to the Castelluccian village (identified as 'zone V' in La Muculufa I) and other structures in the field below the crest, zone T (Terrace) to the Castelluccian sanctuary (identified as 'zone S' in La Muculufa I) and structures of historical date on the terrace at the eastern end of the crest, and zone N (Necropolis) to the necropolis of rock-cut chamber tombs which are found along the central part of the crest. An 'area' is a contiguous excavation within an excavation zone, while a 'portion' is a sub-division of an area which ideally corresponds to actual archaeological features. A system of alphanumerical coding for the portions was devised by Dr. Susan Lukesh in order to facilitate the interpretive classification of horizontal measurements. Portions were created in a decimal hierarchy as the excavation progressed and as the natural arrangement of features gradually emerged from the artificial arrangement of excavation squares (e.g., portions F132 and F133 were both subdivisions of the larger portion F130 which had been defined at the outset of the excavation).

The area of Hut No. 1

The first evidence of structural remains in the village (Hut No. 1) had been found in portions F10–60 excavated in 1982 and 1983, and it consisted of a terracotta surface on a gravel foundation with fragments of burned wall daub[11]. A goal of the 1988 excavation campaign was to re-examine the remains of this structure in the context of expanded excavation in this area. Although the backfill and

---

[10] The elevation reference points for 1988 were Point 00 (310.9 msl) and Point 10 (309 msl), while in 1989 Point 10 was used for all measurements pertaining to the prehistoric village. During the 1991 campaign, instead, Point 40 (312.4 msl) was used as a depth datum for portions F170, F180, F190 and F200 (for the latter portions, an intermediate point had to be used in order to calculate the depth to point 40), while Point 10 continued to be used as the datum reference for work in portions F70, F110 and F130. All elevation measurements in this monograph are given in respect to Point 10 and expressed with thte words 'meters' written out. Measurements of length and height are expressed using abbreviations.

One of the technical problems which beset the project was the redefinition of the excavation grid. Between the campaigns of 1982/83 and 1988 the field had been replowed and virtually no trace of the previous excavation grid remained, except for a single stake later identified as 112E, 106S. Discrepancy also arose between the grid used for the geophysical survey and that employed for the excavation in 1991. The indications given on the geophysical survey map were only approximate, especially since the geophysical survey grid (for reasons of time) had been laid out along the sloping ground-surface and not surveyed in a horizontal plane. Effort was made to lay out the surveyed excavation grid in conjunction with the grid established in 1989 which was fairly well preserved within the fenced excavation area, but the coordination was never truly precise.

the protective covering installed over these remains in 1983 was removed and the terracotta floor surfaces were cleaned, the form of this structure did not become significantly clearer. It was discovered, however, by extending the excavation to the east and west that the structure had been built on a level area filled in behind a terrace wall formed from an outcrop of bedrock running roughly East-West. Finds recovered during the clearing included small ceramic fragments, bits of wall-daub and a globular cup (Cat. No. 191, 102–107E 106–111S, -1.83) which had been placed against the northern side of the terrace wall. Animal bones were also found in the floor of Hut No. 1.

In order to examine the terrace upon which Hut No. 1 had been constructed, the excavation area was expanded to the west in portion F100 and to the east in Trench F110. These portions were further subdivided and extended to the south in portions F120 and F114, respectively. To the East, in Portion F110, the stretch of natural rock outcrop which had been utilized to create the southern edge of the terrace was found to continue. In the fill behind this outcrop, there were found numerous terracotta spindle whorls and burnt soil which seemed to have been deposited in order to create a level ground surface. A line of stones perhaps from a wall running from NW to SE was found between 106–111E/107–112S. Along the alignment of grid-line 107E a series of stones seemed to mark the line of a wall with other, smaller stones along 108.5S between 109.5–112E which may have served as a support. Nearby, a large pit had been filled with ceramics, bones and spindle whorls, all of which had been burned together with their soil matrix. The interpretation of this pit is not clear.

To the Northwest of Hut No. 1, a surface of packed pebbles and soil in portion F102 at ca. -1.40 meters indicated what may be the line of a path ascending the slope in a gentle rise from West to East. A poorly preserved surface with traces of terracotta flooring and several fragments of wall daub was also found in portions F102 and F120 at roughly the same elevation as Hut No. 1. A radiocarbon date of 3680 ±100 b.p. calibrated to 2200–1940 B.C. was obtained from charcoal recovered from soil which rested upon this surface in F102 (97–102E,

108.5–111S, -1.38– -1.52). This date corresponds to two dates obtained in connection with Hut No. 1 during the 1982 campaign (cf. Appendix I, Nos. 1, 2 and 4)[12].

During the 1983 excavation campaign, terracotta flooring had been found at a higher level than that of Hut No. 1. This flooring was found in 1988 to extend across portions F101 and F102 at elevations ranging around -0.70 meters. Although it clearly belonged to a subsequent phase in terms of stratigraphy, the exact nature of this flooring was not apparent. No trace of a wall was found, although traces of burning and fragments of wall-daub and pottery, some of which seemed to be in situ, suggest that it was once part of a structure. A bit of cupriferous metal was also found on the terracotta flooring, but it was not clear whether the metal fragment actually belonged to the Castelluccian context because it was found near a disturbance resembling that caused by a mechanical shovel in portion F101[13]. Other enigmatic surfaces were noted in portion F102 at -0.83 and -1.00 meters.

Preliminary Trenches

The excavation in 1988 proceeded with the opening of test trenches measuring 4.0 x 2.0 meters oriented N-S/E-W. The placement of the trenches was based upon subjective, judgmental selection according to the lay of the terrain and the apparent position with respect to the archaeological deposits discovered in portions F10–60 in 1982 and 1983. Trench F70 was opened to the east of the prior excavation area, while Trench F80 was opened upslope on what was presumably another level area. Efforts were made during the course of the 1988 campaign to enlarge each trench as time and manpower would permit. Trench F70 was enlarged to cover an area approximately

---

[11] This structure is described as an ovoid hut in R.R. Holloway, "Scavi archeologici alla Muculufa e premesse per lo studio della cultura castellucciana," in Atti Licata II, p.79 and pl. 32, figs. 1–2; cf. idem in La Muculufa I, p.12.

[12] The calibrated radiocarbon dates (one sigma) most likely fall in the following ranges: 1—F25L60 (Hut No. 1), 2204–1684 BC (92% probability), 2—F25L60 (Hut No. 1), 2338–1690 BC (95% probability), and 4—F102, 2199–1916 BC (96% probability). See Appendix I of this volume.

[13] It is not entirely clear whether the fragments of metal belong to the ancient stratum or to a disturbance of the soil noticed a few centimeters away in the western balk of the trench. Bronze finds in Sicily during the Copper and Early Bronze Ages are extremely rare; cf. Tusa (supra n.2) p.204–205 with fig. 4, p.318 with fig. 36 and p.377, n.53, and L. Bernabò Brea, "Eolie, Sicilia e Malta nell'età del bronzo," Kokalos 22–23, 1976–1977, p.61 and p.100, Fig. A.

15 x 10 m, while F80 reached a maximum extension of 5 x 10 m. The positions of these trenches and the extension of the excavation at the end of the 1988 campaign are shown in Plates 4 and 6.

Portion F70

Portion F70 revealed the poorly preserved remains of a structure at roughly the same elevation as the lower pavements in portion F102. In portion F74 a terracotta pavement was found at an elevation of -1.00 meters. Traces of terracotta flooring were discovered in portion F74 around 104.5E, 117S and 104.5E,118.5S, but it was not possible to distinguish related wall structures before the end of the season. The fact that this pavement was part of a hut was clearly indicated by the yellowish soil mixed with baked clay and traces of burning and by the many fragments of Castelluccian ceramics, wall-daub and stone grinders which were found on it, including an extraordinary fragment of a jug or an amphora painted along the rim in the form of an abstract face (Cat. No. 93, 117–121E, 96–101S, bd. -1.00, Plates 16.3 and 30). Expansion of the excavation along the floor in F74 revealed that the structure of which it was part lay immediately below a terrace wall (this wall sustained the terrace upon which Hut Nos. 2, 3 (lower) and 4 to be discussed below had been created). Continued digging in this area in 1991 between 113–115.5E and 86.5–88S from -0.485 to -0.715 meters depth did not reveal traces of the structure's wall, except for a series of stones bonded with limestone bits set in an irregular arc which probably defined the wall of a hut along its western side[14].

Portions F80, F130 and F160

The northwestern corner of portion F70, F71 and portion F80 revealed remains resting at a higher elevation than those in portion F74. The expansion of these trenches together with portions F130, F140 and portion F160 into a full excavation zone during the summer of 1989 showed that the area was defined by a terrace over 10 meters wide which had been created between terrace walls constructed in stones of various dimensions set where possible among the natural limestone outcrops of the mountain. The upper terrace wall was preserved for only a short stretch (taken as a whole it was 6.5 meters long and 0.70 meters wide), while the lower wall presented greater definition and seemed to continue to the west into the upper portion of trench F30 which had been excavated in 1983. Within this terrace at least four structures—Hut No. 4, Hut No. 2 and Hut Nos. 3 (upper) and 3 (lower)—were found in stratigraphic sequence (Plates 4, 13.1 and 13.2).

Hut No. 4

This structure was defined in 1989, although elements of it had been excavated in 1988. Within portion F71, in the area around point 112E/91S two strata of Castelluccian ceramics could easily be distinguished. The higher one was sealed beneath a ground surface (battuto) marked by bits of limestone at 1.43 meters (or the level of Hut No. 3, upper) and itself consisted of a packed ground surface measured at roughly 1.15 meters (or the level of Hut No. 3, lower). Beneath this stratum, still more Castelluccian ceramics were found resting on the terracotta floor of Hut No. 4 at 0.95 meters. Although the eastern limit of this structure was not easily discernable, it appears that Hut No. 4 measured at least 3.0 x 2.4 meters and was delimited by a single line of stones 30 cm thick. The terracotta floor, which was 6 cm thick, had been fired red, probably by conflagration, and a circular depression measuring 17 cm in diameter by 10 cm in depth was located at the center. The walls of the structure seem to have been set upon a layer of stones which served as a foundation.

Other Structures

It is most likely that Hut No. 4 was contemporary with traces of other wall-structures to the East. One feature consisted of a tight circle of stones between 114.5E and 91–92S which on the basis of much carbon found within it may have served as a hearth. Two stone alignments, a western one measuring 1.30m and an eastern one 1.70 m in length, may have served as foundations for Hut No. 3 (lower), although the connection was not clear in the stratigraphy along the southern side of Hut No. 3 (lower) between the wall of that structure and the wall of Hut No. 4. Excavation between 118–120E and 89–91.5S during the 1991 campaign revealed a level of burned soil between

---

[14] It is necessary to correct the identification of stone bits used both in wall construction and in the preparation of ground surfaces at the site. Whereas this material was identified as gypsum (marna) in B.E. McConnell, "The Early Bronze Age Village of La Muculufa and Prehistoric Hut Architecture in Sicily," American Journal of Archaeology, 96, 1992, p.23–44, it actually consists of decomposed limestone.

0.66 and 0.45 meters, and at 0.35 meters a level of compact soil may indicate an ancient ground-surface.

Hut No. 2

During the 1988 excavation campaign Trench F80 reached an average depth of 80 cm and yielded a great quantity of ceramic and daub fragments. The enlargement of Trench F80 in 1989 revealed a circular structure (Hut No. 2) approximately eight meters in diameter (Plates 5 and 13.3). It was delimited by a wall-socle of stones packed with limestone bits which was 30 cm thick and preserved for a length of 5.5 m along its northern side. The wall-socle of Hut No. 2 seems to have been set upon and to have used as a foundation a portion of the wall around Hut No. 4 in portion F71, the floor of which lay approximately 26 cm lower. Approximately half of the hut's total area, that along the southern side, seemed to have been lost to erosion and/or plowing. Stones and wall-daub which apparently had been employed in the construction of the northwestern portion of the hut wall were found heaped by the plow in disarray in portion F83[15]. Plow-marks were still visible at the bottom of the stratum of humus.

Along the interior of the wall-socle there appeared a bench composed of earth with bits of limestone sprinkled on the surface which rose approximately 16 cm from the central floor-level and achieved a maximum width of 0.85 meters. An exploratory cut in the bench measuring 1.30x1.10 m revealed no noticeable substructure. The interior edge of the bench had been given a terracotta covering seven centimeters in thickness, and pieces of this covering were found scattered across the hut floor. Whereas the stone wall-socle lay in a circle, the interior border of the bench lay in an ellipse thus giving the floor an estimated measurement of 4.8 m East-West by 4.5 m North-South. A deposit of heavily burnt soil with many daub fragments and ceramic sherds was found along and on top of the bench (Plate 13.4), and it appears that the structure had been destroyed by a violent conflagration.

A stone vespaion served as a foundation for the hut's floor, and a portion of the floor's original terracotta surface was discovered, as well. A hole measuring approxi-

mately 30 cm in diameter by 24 cm in depth was found in the floor next to the bench along the northern side of the hut, and it presumably served as a setting for a post which was part of the superstructure for the hut roof. The area immediately around this hole was dark indicating that the post may have burned; carbon was also found in the hole. A similar though less well defined dark area along the eastern side of the bench may indicate the location of another post. At precisely the center of the structure, a curious terracotta element (S89/112) was found set into the floor. It seemed to be the circular base of a ceramic vessel which had been broken off and left in situ, measuring 23 cm in diameter, 2.2 cm in wall thickness, and reaching a depth of 8.5 cm beneath the surface. Although an actual whole vessel may have once been set in the floor, it seems more likely that the terracotta element had been created and set in place in order to hold the central post of the hut's superstructure and to keep it from contacting moisture in the soil which might cause it to rot[16].

The deposit of finds and materials fallen from the superstructure was found along the northern side of Hut No. 2 sloping at an angle to the south, probably along the plane cut by plowing. Originally, it appeared that the deposit within the hut wall consisted of two strata: a higher one between ca. 1.25 and 1.15 meters, and a lower one between 1.15 and 1.04 meters. The discovery of the bench suggested that there was in reality a single destruction stratum sealed at varying elevations across the bench and the floor, and a detailed examination of the find-spots seems to confirm this simpler explanation. At the southern side of Hut No. 2, a lens of sherds between 106.5–110E and 91–97S packed up to a level of 1.15 meters seemed to have been compressed by plowing and by the excavation itself to the level of the bench. Between this lens and the bench on the northern side of the structure a deposit of fallen wall daub rose to an elevation of 1.40 meters.

A stratigraphic section dug in 1988 on the exterior of the hut wall in portion F84 revealed a sequence of two levels (Plate 6). The upper level lay at an elevation of 1.86 meters, and it was associated with the two portions of walls set at right angles to each other between 105–110E and 86–90S in portion F81 and with Hut No. 3 (upper).

---

[15] Most of these stones were eventually removed with the exception of an arc of stones which seemed to belong to a small section of terracotta flooring at the edge of the plow-line.

[16] Thanks are owed to G. Castellana for this suggestion. In addition, a base such as this has no parallel among the ceramics found at this site.

Between 1.50 and 1.42 meters elevation, a great many fragments of daub and large fragments of ceramics were found in 1989, including *corno fittile* Cat. No. 218 at 1.42 meters. Among the finds recovered in 1988 between 1.57 and 1.47 meters in association with Hut No. 2 were fragments of an incised ware (Cat. No. 172 incised rim fragment F82 107–110E 93–96S third cut to 2.43 meters, Cat. No. 173 incised fragment F82 107–110E 93–96S third cut to 2.43 meters) which has been identified at several sites in southern Sicily as a ceramic of Tarxien culture of the Maltese archipelago. It is just as likely, however, that this is an incised version of painted reticulate designs which are amply documented among the painted Castelluccian wares[17].

One of the most striking features of Hut No. 2 is the sheer number of materials, especially ceramics, which were recovered. There were at least 36 pedestal bowls, 19 jars, 4 pithoi, 2 bowls and 2 cups. The fact that much of the structure and the deposit within it were damaged by the plow suggests that there had once been even more. As suggested by Laura Maniscalco in her analysis of the ceramics, Hut No. 2 may have served as the storeroom of a local potter. She also notes the discovery in situ at ca. 1.15 meters of a pedestal bowl (Cat. No. 2) and next to it a carinated pitcher(Cat. No. 85) in what appears to be a typical combination. Within Hut No. 2 a shell necklace (Cat. No. 411) was found in stratigraphic association with a pedestal bowl (Cat. No. 4) from which it may have fallen.

Outside the area of the hut a thin layer of of limestone bits which was roughly 5 cm thick in the soil defined the ground surface associated with this structure. The level of this surface seemed to correspond to that of the bench in such a way that the actual floor of Hut No. 2 lay slightly below it. Although the wall socle along the western side of Hut No. 2 had been destroyed by plowing, a terracotta phallus (*corno fittile*) was found along what seemed to have been its exterior in portion F83 (Cat. No. 218 104.6E, 94.6S, 1.42 meters). This same limestone-bit surface extended to the East into the area of Portion F130 in such a way as to provide a stratigraphic association with Hut No. 3 (lower). Traces of this surface along the exterior of Hut No. 2 in Portion F84 (Plate 6, sections a–a' and d–d', Level 1) were found together with charcoal which yielded a radiocarbon date of 3790 ±60 b.p. calibrated to

2292–2129 B.C. (cf. Appendix I, No. 3) which may most likely be associated with the floruit of Hut No. 2.

While the remains of Hut Nos. 2 and 4 could be distinguished clearly, the remains of two huts found in Portion F130 were so fragmentary and situated in such a way that they were distinguished simply as No. 3 (lower) and No. 3 (upper). Further excavation in this area may reveal, however, that they belong to separate structural contexts.

Hut No. 3 (lower)

The outline of this structure was given both by an extensive area of terracotta flooring and by the line of stones which formed its wall-socle (Plate 7.1). Little of the wall socle was preserved except for a line of three stones 1.20 m long and 0.20 m wide on the northeastern edge of the hut and a single stone along its western side. The structure seems to have been constructed in an area partially dug out of the hillside along its northern side to level the area at 1.20 meters. Larger stones found immediately beneath the floor-level of this structure along its southern side probably formed part of the foundation. Many rounded cobbles (grinding stones?) had been deposited along the exterior of the wall socle, as well as a series of *corni fittili* and a fire-dog (Cat. Nos. 216, 221, 236 (*alare*, or brazier), and 222). The exterior of Hut No. 3 (lower) was associated with the same layer of limestone bits which defined the ground surface associated with Hut No. 2 on its western side.

The plan of the structure followed that of a circle divided in half and drawn apart with a length of 6.6 m and a width of 4.6 m. Two post-holes measuring (A) 13 cm in diameter and 15 cm in depth at 116E/87.5S and (B) 10 cm in diameter and 15 cm in depth at 114.7E/88.4S define the radii around which the respective eastern and western ends of the structure were laid out. Charcoal recovered from the eastern hole (A) offered a radiocarbon date (terminus ad quem) for the structure of 3990±60 b.p. calibrated to between 2574 and 2427 B.C. (cf. Appendix I, No. 5).

Hut No. 3 (upper)

Consisting of a single stretch of stones set in two rows roughly 2.8 m long and 0.45 m wide, the wall of Hut No. 3 (upper) was associated with a floor surface defined by a stratum of ash and ceramic and daub fragments which had fallen over an area measuring 1.00 m E-W by 0.50 m N-

---

[17] Cf. S.S. Lukesh in La Muculufa I, p.31.

S and onto a layer of limestone gravel roughly 5cm thick at 1.54 meters, or 34 cm above the remains of Hut No. 3 (lower). The layer of limestone gravel seemed to rest on a fill of ceramics and soil which covered the remains of Hut No. 3 (lower), especially in portion F131 (Plates 7.2, 14.1 and 14.2).

The fact that the line of the wall seemed to follow that of the lower structure in portion F135 suggests that the upper structure followed the plan of the lower one, although it should be noted that the construction of the upper wall socle was notably more robust than that of the lower one. Two *corni fittili* (Cat. Nos. 219 and 220 at 1.70 meters depth at 115.81E/83.61S were also found immediately to the North of Hut 3 (upper) at the elevation of the upper structure (but nevertheless in planimetric correspondence to those found along the exterior of its lower counterpart).

In portion F132 between F116–117.2E and 85–87S, a piece of carbonized wood 20 cm long and 6 cm in diameter was found at an elevation of 1.80 meters in the context of burnt soil. A narrow trunk such as this could have been placed in the post-hole found in the terracotta flooring of Hut No. 3 (lower) found nearby. A portion of this wood sent for radiocarbon analysis provided a date of 3960±70 b.p. which was calibrated to between 2568 and 2329 B.C. (cf. Appendix I, No. 6). This date confirms, and is statistically indistinguishable from, the one obtained from the post-hole in the floor of Hut No. 3 (lower).

The wall of Hut No. 3 (upper) seemed to lose its definition in a mass of stones and Castelluccian ceramics at its western end in the portion which was defined for its disturbance as F134 (Plate 14.1). Although the wall did seem to curve inward into the hillside, perhaps beneath the wall defined as the upper terrace wall, removal of the mass of stones revealed a small vessel (Cat. No. 137) at floor level thus indicating that the stones had simply collapsed there.

Despite this confusing situation, a stratigraphic layering of finds could be identified as well in portion F134. One group was discovered clustered in association with collapsed stones and wall daub roughly 15 cm thick between 1.49 and 1.43 meters. Beneath this layer was a stratum of brown soil without ceramics roughly 30 cm thick which lay on top of another layer of finds between 1.19 and 1.27 meters which rested in turn on the pavement of

terracotta of Hut No. 3 (lower). There was noticeably less wall daub in this portion, however, than in portion F133.

Despite its proximity and similar elevation there seems to be no structural connection between the wall of the upper hut and the upper terrace wall, which lay at an unusually high elevation with respect to the structures in portion F130. The difference in size between the smaller stones of the hut wall and the larger boulders of the terrace wall further distinguishes them. It may be the case that this so-called terrace wall actually belonged to a structure because stones which appeared to belong to a floor foundation were discovered at 1.85 meters in portion F131; also, many ceramics and flint fragments were found by it between 2.19 and 1.85 meters.

Structural Conservation

Until a permanent program of conservation could be initiated, the hut structures were preserved by placing a nylon net mesh across the terracotta floor, by backfilling soil removed by the excavation into the excavation area, and by setting stone supports to reinforce delicate wall-structures. Before covering them, the terracotta floors and the border along the bench were treated with Acryloid B-72 in a solution under ten percent with paint thinner (45% toluene) and alcohol. A low brick wall was erected along the southern side of Hut No. 3 (lower) in order to sustain the soil beneath the structure. The test cut in the bench of Hut No. 2 was filled with soil mixed with gypsum in order to match the appearance of the bench. The entire excavation area was enclosed in a wire fence, and drainage ditches were dug to protect the site from damage by water flowing along the ground surface.

Other projects (Terrace zone, Rock-crevice burial)

Other projects were completed also on the eastern terrace (Plate 1.2, zone T and Plate 12) and around the opening of a natural crevice which had been used for burial at one of the entrances to the necropolis (Plate 1.2, zone N and Plate 14.3). Fieldwork during the 1989 campaign completed the removal of the balk between trench portions T60 and T70/80 (15–16N, 9–17E), and a portion measuring 4 m by 2 m (T130, 8–10N, 6–10E) was excavated to a depth of 60 cm beneath the ground surface. Unfortunately, the archaeological deposit in portion T130 had been rendered illegible by the fall of rocks from the crest in antiquity, and it was possible only to remove the remaining portions of the 2.28 m deep deposit of soil, Castelluccian ceramics, bone fragments, and bits of carbon which had already been identified in the trench balk.

The remaining portion of the circular structure found in zone T in 1982 between 2–6E/13–15S was cleaned: it measured 1.15 meters in width and consisted of boulders set along the interior and exterior faces with stones on the interior. Another wall appeared roughly 0.80 meters below this one: it was 0.50 meters wide and preserved for a length of 1.10 meters. In association with this latter wall there was found an almost flat stone with a concave area for the insertion of a post, perhaps as the base for a support of a roof. At -11.40 meters in T130 there was found what appeared to be a double row of stones set in the Castelluccian deposit. This corresponds to the terrace wall in fine polygonal stone masonry ca. 0.30m thick which was found during the campaign of 1987[18]. A series of medieval rubbish pits filled with stones and pottery sherds and characteristic of muslim occupation were found also in T60[19].

Stratigraphy and Chronology

La Muculufa offers fundamental new data for the chronology of the Early Bronze Age in Sicily. The series of 17 radiocarbon dates from the Terrace zone and six dates from the Field zone (see Appendix I) now place the Castelluccian culture squarely in the second half of the third millennium B.C. While the relatively tight clustering of dates in each respective zone does not permit a wide internal chronology at the site, the presence of several strata and the variety in ceramic style does suggest that the Castelluccian settlement at La Muculufa had more than a single phase.

At least three building-phases can be identified at the site, and the possibility that structures were built and rebuilt on a seasonal basis should not be ruled out. On the upper terrace of the village it was possible to distinguish at least three stratigraphic levels. Hut No. 4 and the traces of walls emerging from the balk beneath the southern portion of Hut No. 3 (lower) constitute the earliest level. A stratigraphic section cut between Hut No. 4 and Hut No. 2 between 111–112E and 95–96S from 1.04 to 0.85 meters elevation defined the stratigraphic relation between the two. The surface of gypsum bits which seems to extend across the entire area of the terrace joins Hut No. 2 and Hut No. 3 (lower) in a second level, and it covers Hut No. 4. The third level is given clearly by the wall remains of Hut No. 3 (upper) and by the upper surface of gypsum bits in portion F84 and wall alignments in portion F81. On the lower terrace, instead, a succession of only two stratigraphic levels could be identified to any degree: one associated with Hut No. 1, and the other associated with a surface in terracotta which had been noticed in portion F103. Excavation in portions F70 and F110 during the 1991 campaign did not succeed in linking the two areas with a single stratigraphic section.

The radiocarbon dates obtained from the analysis of samples recovered in 1988 refer to the first phase on the lower terrace and to the second phase on the upper terrace, but all of the dates are relatively close, and they correspond to those obtained from the Castelluccian deposit in zone T at the eastern end of the crest. One should not, however, try to associate the stratigraphy of the village with the stratigraphy of the Castelluccian deposit in the Terrace zone because the latter stratification seems due to the specific circumstances of this location, and in particular to the fall of rock from the crest.

It appears, therefore, that despite the existence of separate construction phases, there is presently no evidence to indicate a particularly long period of prehistoric occupation at the site. The absolute chronology of calibrated radiocarbon dates from La Muculufa accords well with what we know from cross-cultural, relative chronologies in the Aeolian islands, the Maltese archipelago and in the Aegean region[20], although none of these associations are based on a great number of actual imports and they tell us more about the outset of the Sicilian Early Bronze Age than they do about its actual length[21]. The appearance of an unusual dish perhaps created in imitation of an Early Helladic ware (Cat. No. 121) in this context would take on greater significance in lengthening the Castelluccian presence at La Muculufa (see discussion by L. Maniscalco in this volume). One estimate regarding the duration of

---

[18] For an illustration of this wall see La Muculufa I, p.21, figure 19.

[19] Pit A at 13–14N, 6–7E, dug from -11.39 to -11.91; Pit B at 15–16N, 7–8E.

the entire Castelluccian Early Bronze Age is at least four hundred years[22], and the stratigraphy of a deposit of ceramics found in contrada Ciavolaro at Ribera suggests a chronology of roughly six hundred years from the latter Third millennium to the sixteenth and possibly the fifteenth centuries B.C.[23]. The long duration of the Castelluccian culture throughout the island of Sicily is an indicator of its conservative character, and further exploration at La Muculufa may well produce evidence for the later phases of the Early Bronze Age.

[20] The Castelluccian culture is contemporary with the Capo Graziano culture of the Aeolian islands, with both the Tarxien Temple and Tarxien Cemetery phases of the Maltese prehistoric culture sequence, and with the earliest Mycenaean imports in the West; cf. L. Bernabò Brea, "Eolie, Sicilia e Malta nell'età del bronzo," Kokalos, 22–23, 1976–1977, p.33–110; R.R. Holloway, Italy and the Aegean 3000–700 B.C., Louvain and Providence, 1981, p.44. For a recent re-dating of the beginning of the Capo Graziano culture in the Aeolian islands to the end of the Third millennium B.C. and its attribution to the Early Helladic III cultures of the Aegean, see L. Bernabò Brea, Gli Eoli e l'inizio dell'età del bronzo nelle isole Eolie e nell'Italia meridionale: archeologia e leggende, Annali del Seminario di studi del mondo classico, Quaderno N. 2, Istituto Universitario Orientale, Napoli, 1985, p.13.

[21] Direct association between Castelluccian Sicily and both the Tarxien and Tarxien Cemetery cultures of Malta can be made in terms of cross-cultural finds and in more general terms of architecture; cf. L. Bernabò Brea, "Abitato Neolitico e Insediamento Maltese dell'Età del Bronzo nell'Isola di Ognina (Siracusa) e i Rapporti fra la Sicilia e Malta dal XVI al XIII sec. a.C.," Kokalos, 12, 1966, p.40–69, E. Procelli, "Il complesso tombale di Contrada Paolina e il problema dei rapporti tra Sicilia e Malta nella prima età del bronzo," Bollettino d'Arte, n.s. 9, 1981, p.83–110, esp. p.104–106, and S. Tusa, "The Megalith Builders and Sicily," Journal of Mediterranean Studies, 1, 1991, p.267–285. Calibrated radiocarbon dates from the Maltese archipelago place the Tarxien Temples between 3300/3000 and 2500 B.C. and the Tarxien Cemetery phase after 2500 B.C. ; cf. C. Renfrew, "Malta and the Calibrated Radiocarbon Chronology (with an Appendix by Jane M. Renfrew)," in C. Renfrew, ed. Problems in European Prehistory, Edinburgh, 1979, p.255–261, although the cultural associations of some of the dated materials have been challenged (cf. Procelli, op. cit. this note, 104 and 108, n.98).

[22] S. Tusa, La Sicilia nella Preistoria, Palermo, 1983, p.288.

The Geophysical Survey of 1990[24]

Bruce W. Bevan

Given the great extent of the village, the fact that its remains could not be observed on the surface due to plowing, and the relatively high cost of excavation, it was decided to perform a geophysical survey across the Field excavation zone. The goal of the survey was to describe the sub-surface topography in such a way as to have a general view of the layout of the village and to permit the excavation of the cultural remains with greater efficiency. Subsequent excavation during the summer of 1991, in fact, proved that the site was far more complex than a geophysical survey alone could show.

Methodology

The geophysical survey used a Geonics Ltd. EM38 electromagnetic induction meter to measure the soil's electrical conductivity and magnetic susceptibility[25]. The two measurements which are made by this instrument can allow the stoniness of the soil and its thickness to be estimated.

Three rectangular areas were surveyed (Plate 2). The main survey area measured 65 m East-West by 45 m North-South between 105–170E and 30–75S in what appeared to be the center of the village (Plate 13.6). Surveys were also performed in smaller strips. One to the east between 160–180E and 25–31S. The other one to the southwest of the main survey area; it was outside the excavation grid and measured 6 by 20 meters. For each area,

[23] The association of Capo Graziano II ceramics with pottery of the Castelluccian 'Naro-Partanna' styles leads G. Castellana to date the latter to the sixteenth and fifteenth centuries B.C.; cf. Un Decennio di Ricerche Preistoriche e Protostoriche nel Territorio Agrigentino, show cat. Agrigento—Museo Archeologico Regionale, 16 June–30 September 1990, p.48. This association is, so far, the principal grounding for the chronology of the latter part of the Castelluccian culture. Note that the Naro and Partanna variants of Castelluccian ceramics are now considered to be separate ceramic styles; cf. discussion by L. Maniscalco in this volume.

[24] This is an edited version of B.W. Bevan, "A Geophysical Survey at La Muculufa," unpublished field report, 17 July 1990 [B.E.McC.].

tape-measures were laid along opposite sides of the rectangle. A cord was then stretched between the two tape-measures. This cord had painted bands at 1.00 meter intervals along it; traverses were guided by this cord and measurements were usually made with a spacing of 1.00 meters (the only exception was the northeast area). Since a distance of 1.00 meters could readily be estimated from this cord, three lines could be surveyed before the cord was moved parallel for another set of measurements. Measure-

---

[25] The EM38 is about a meter long, and it looks much like a carpenter's level. It is a member of a general class of instruments called electromagnetic induction meters. Other instruments can detect deeper objects than the EM38 can, but the depth range of the EM38 seemed well-suited to the site. The Geonics EM38 was designed primarily to measure the electrical conductivity of the earth. The unit of electrical conductivity is the millisiemens per meter, abbreviated mS/m. By changing a switch on the instrument, the EM38 can also measure the magnetic susceptibility.

Magnetic susceptibility quantifies how well the earth conducts a magnetic field; it is the magnetic analog of electrical conductivity. In SI (System International) measurements, magnetic susceptibility is a pure number, without a unit name. Susceptibility values are much less than one, so it is easier to write them by multiplying them by 1000. The average value of susceptibility was about 0.8 parts per thousand (ppt), or 0.0008 in SI units.

In general, rock is rather poor as both an electrical and as a magnetic conductor, while soil is usually a good conductor of both electricity and magnetism. Iron and iron-containing minerals usually have a high magnetic susceptibility. Iron minerals, such as magnetite, can accumulate in the soil; in some types of rock, such as the limestone found here, there is only a low concentration of magnetic minerals.

The measurement of magnetic susceptibility will allow differences in the stoniness or thickness of the soil to be determined. Cultural practices can also increase the magnetic susceptibility of the soil. Ceramics have a high susceptibility and other fired earth features such as stoves can also be easy to detect with this measurement. Organic soil can also be higher in magnetic susceptibility than other soils, so refuse pits can sometimes be detected.

The EM38 measures the electrical conductivity of the earth to a depth of about 1.5 meters. Archaeological features can have a higher or lower conductivity than the surrounding earth, and therefore their locations underground can sometimes be estimated with this instrument. For example, stone and sand usually have a low conductivity, while clay and dark, organic soil can have high conductivity. In principle, a buried terrace could be traced as a line of low conductivity over the stone wall; the conductivity could be higher on the slope above (and possibly below) the wall where a thicker layer of soil has accumulated.

ments were recorded in a Metrosonics dl-712 data logger, a rugged hand-held computer[26].

All conductivity measurements were made with the bar of the instrument at a height of 0.3m, while susceptibility measurements were made at a height of 0.6m[27]. A total of 7103 spatial measurements of conductivity and susceptibility were made over the period of 3–7 June 1990. During that time, the weather was generally sunny and warm; while there was intermittent rain and lightning on June 6, the site was otherwise dry.

Due to the low values of electrical conductivity and magnetic susceptibility at this site, normally insignificant variations in the EM38 caused its measurements to be somewhat variable. It appears most likely that changes in temperature caused the calibration of the EM38 to drift during the measurements. This undesirable effect was readily corrected by removing all linear changes in the measurements along each traverse. When the linear drift of the EM38 was corrected, a smoothing operation replaced each measurement by the average of that measurement and the eight adjacent measurements surrounding it and centered on it[28]. The measurements of electrical conductivity were much less affected by the drift of the EM38 than were the measurements of magnetic susceptibility. A simple grid smoothing of the data does not help enough,

---

[26] This logger can store 1167 measurements, along with their date and time. When the memory of the logger filled, the data were dumped to another computer and recorded on magnetic disks. The data logger does not record the coordinates of each measurement; it simply records the sequence number of each measurement. Later, a computer program was used to covert these sequence numbers to grid coordinates. The primary advantage of the data logger is that the measurements can be recorded with greater precision than would be possible by writing down the readings on the analog meter.

[27] The accuracy of the measurements of the EM38 is about 1 mS/m. The average measurment at this site was in the range of 7–8 mS/m. Because of the stones on the surface, the EM38 could not always be set directly on the soil; variable height caused readings to be irregular. Stiff weeds at the site also kept the instrument from the surface. Therefore, the EM38 was lifted to a height of 0.3m in order to minimize unimportant variability in the measurements. The measurements were corrected for this elevation.

For the susceptibility measurements, the EM38 was lifted to an elevation of 0.6m above the earth. At this elevation, any magnetic materials in the earth cause the measurement of apparent susceptibility to decrease. The susceptibility measurements were adjusted for the effect of this elevation.

but by subtracting the average measurement on each east-west line from each measurement on those lines, undesirable striations are almost completely removed. This same smoothing operation was applied to the conductivity data from the two small grids which were later surveyed. While the cause of this shift in the conductivity readings is probably again due to temperature changes within the instrument, the shift is quite small, and it is within the specifications of the instrument.

Survey results

Initial evaluation of the survey data indicated that a distinctive change was to be found within the earth. In Plate 2, the areas shown with hatching vertical to the survey base-line mark the approximate locations where there may be relatively few stones in the earth; it is also possible that the soil could have a greater content of clay or organic matter in those areas. Hatching oblique to the survey base-line indicates locations where there might be a greater density of stones in the earth; it is also possible that the soil is sandier at those locations or that bedrock is at a shallower depth there. The broad line marks a distinct geophysical boundary. Both the conductivity and the susceptibility are much lower on the east (right hand) side of the line. It is therefore possible that a band of stone is to be found on the east side of the line. There are some locations where one measurement (susceptibility or conductivity) shows an anomaly but the other measurement does not; however, there is no location where an area with a high magnetic susceptibility matches an area with low electrical conductivity (or vice versa), and therefore the two measurements are moderately well correlated[29].

On June 3, 1992, informal measurements of conductivity were made along the northwestern side of the field near the base of the crest in a search for possible chamber tombs hidden by the soil. While these measurements suggested that the conductivity of the rock could be in the vicinity of 1.5–2 mS/m, no distinct high conductivity anomalies were detected. Additional measurements on bedrock suggested that its magnetic susceptiblity could be about 0.11ppt. Both of these values are much lower than the average measurements during the geophysical survey, which were a conductivity of about 7.5 mS/m and a susceptibility of 0.8 ppt. Further measurements were made of the susceptiblity of two rock samples using a Geoinstruments model JH-8 magnetic susceptibility meter, but neither rock gave a measurable reading. This suggests that their susceptiblity is less than 0.05 ppt.

Additional measurements were made on the backdirt pile from previous excavations. This indicated a magnetic susceptibility of 0.55–0.7 ppt, somewhat less than the average above. The conductivity, however, was only about 3.1 mS/m, much lower than the average found during this survey. It appears likely that the topsoil here has quite a low conductivity; it is possible that the soil from the archaeological strata also has a low conductivity.

The geophysical stratification of the soil was estimated in one area where there was a high conductivity anomaly. A resistivity sounding was made, and it indicated that the resistivity of the earth decreases with depth; this means that the conductivity increases with depth[30]. This could be due to an increasing clay content, more moisture, or an accumulation of conductive soil minerals (such as salts) at greater depths. At the depth of 1.5–2.0 meters, the conductivity of the soil could be greater than 20 mS/m, while the soil at the surface could have a conductivity of only about 4 mS/m.

---

[28] The contour mapping of this data was done with the package of programs called Surfer from Golden Software (Denver, Colorado). The smoothing was done with a subprogram of that package called Grid, using a 3x3 measurement average and a center weight of unity. Several of the one-point anomalies were caused by grid stakes; while the metal-containing stakes were generally removed before the survey approached them, some remained to cause anomalies. These one-point anomalies were individually smoothed before using the program Grid.

[29] This correlation is confirmed by the tendency for conductivity and susceptibility to increase and decrease together. Expressed in mathematical terms based on a visual evaluation of the data the correlation is: conductivity = 10.17 x susceptibility - 0.75.

---

[30] The resisitivity sounding was done with four earth-contacting electrodes equally spaced along a line; this is the Wenner configuration. A series of measurements were made keeping the midpoint of the four electrodes at one point while increasing the spacing between each of the electrodes. With a greater spacing between the electrodes, the electrical current from the resistivity meter goes deeper into the earth and resistivity is measured at a greater depth. Due to the dry soil here, salty water was poured around each electrode in order to improve the contact with the earth, but the unwatered electrodes appear to have allowed an adequate contact.

The small rectangular area at the northeastern corner of the main grid between 160–180E and 25–31S was surveyed with measurements at a spacing of 0.5m; only conductivity measurements were made. The terrain in this area had not been plowed, and there were traces of stone hut-structures visible on the surface, including one which measured 3.5m E-W by 7.0m N-S with a wall in a double row of stones 1.20 m thick. A distinct band of low conductivity in the northeast corner of this grid was noted. There is a topographic dropoff on the east side of this low conductivity anomaly, and it is possible that this linear anomaly is caused by the stones of a terrace wall. This anomaly, however, is approximately perpendicular to the linear anomaly of the large grid. While the reason for this is not known, the anomalies appear to be separate and independent, and they do not seem correlate with the pattern of stones visible on the surface.

Additional measurements were made along the strip to the west of the main survey area. This area was selected because there appeared to be a concentration of grinding stones at the surface which might indicate the presence of a hut. The geophysical data, however, reveal little about this area. While the greater variability on the western side of the strip may be the result of small features indicating human occupation, this side of the grid is also closest to the road which goes to the site. The grading of the road shifted soil downhill, and it is possible that clumps of soil from the road grading are the cause of small geophysical anomalies.

It appears likely that the measurements of magnetic susceptibility are a better indicator of buried features at this site than are the measurements of electrical conductivity; however, the maps of electrical conductivity and magnetic susceptibility are rather similar. The geophysical patterns are rather different on the two sides of the property boundary. On the northerly, unplowed side the patterns are smaller and more complex. The geophysical lineament which seems to mark a terrace is only apparent on the northern, unplowed side of the property line. Larger-area anomalies, about 5–8m in size, are most evident on the southern side of the property line. It is possible that plowing has obliterated the small, shallow features which the EM38 might be detecting on the north side of the property boundary, but it is possible also that the additional stoniness at the surface there causes a greater variability in the measurements.

By the end of the 1990 season it was still uncertain what the geophysical pattern of a hut might be. If a hut depression were filled with earth containing few stones, high conductivity and high susceptibility would be expected. Pavements on the hut floors, probably too thin to be detected with a conductivity survey, might nevertheless give an anomaly of high magnetic susceptibility, for ceramic fragments and burnt earth likely to be found in association. One should bear in mind, however, that a geophysical survey cannot identify cultural strata, nor can it ascribe a cultural or chronological context to the features indicated by the anomalies. It was concluded that one or two excavations should be tried on each type of geophysical anomaly and that it might be worthwhile to check one of the areas where only conductivity or only susceptibility indicated an anomaly.

The Campaign of 1991

Trenches were opened during a brief excavation campaign in August of 1991 around two anomalies with low susceptibilty and conductivity: Trench F170 between 120–125E and 45–50S, and Trench F180 between 135–140E and 55–60S. In the area between these anomalies (about 10 meters or roughly the area equivalent to the width of the terrace of Huts 2 and 3) the geophysical survey had indicated an anomaly of high susceptibility/conductivity, and here another excavation area was opened: Trench F190 between 130–135E and 47.5–50S. Further upslope, in an area of high susceptibility and conductivity another trench was opened: Trench F200 between 128.5–131E and 39–41.5S. All of the trenches were connected in the course of the excavation and opened to the widest area possible given the available time and manpower (Plate 8.1).

In Trench F180 the cultural deposit began at roughly 0.40 meters beneath the ground surface. Immediately it appeared that an area of fallen rock had created the anomaly of low susceptibility and conductivity. This mass of rock may have fallen from a terrace wall discovered at the northern end of the trench which consisted of a double row of large stones set as orthostates and which appeared to continue to the west in the geophysical survey as a line of low conductivity and susceptibility.

The prehistoric architectural remains brought to light were of a notable consistency. In the lowermost area of the excavation, a wall roughly 6.0 meters long was found running from south-southwest to north-northeast between 132–133E and 62.5–61.5S from 3.09 to 3.00 meters; it separates portions F182 and F183. Constructed in a Castelluccian technique with large stones set vertically in the soil together with smaller stones and limestone bits, it seems to have served as a fencing or small terrace wall. This wall seems to have been interrupted by the first of two medieval inhumation burials (Burial 1) which were also found in portion F182 (Plate 14.4).

To the northwest of this wall a gravel surface was found at 40 cm beneath the surface. At the eastern end of the wall there were found several *corni fittili*, a fire-dog (Cat. No. 235), and a large quantity of Castelluccian ceramics and other finds at 2.42 meters. Other features in portion F182 included a semicircle of stones found at 3.15 meters between 135–136E and 60–62S, and a series of three medieval rubbish pits filled with dark soil and stones located between 136.5–137.5E and 61.5–62.5S from 2.44 to 2.16 meters. It is likely that these pits were related culturally to the two inhumation burials. A gravel surface was found between 134–134.5E and 55.5–56S at 3.02 meters. This surface which descended to 2.09 meters between 137–140E and 60.5–62.5S stratigraphically covered a poorly preserved terracotta pavement between 130–131.5E and 60–62.5S as well as the long Castelluccian wall which separated portions F182 and F183.

Very consistent remains of a hut were noted also in portion F181 at a depth between 2.49 and 2.26 meters, or roughly 1.50 meters beneath the present ground-surface, out of range of the EM38. Above this level at roughly 2.83 meters, an arc of stones was noticed between 50.5 and 51.5S. Unfortunately, the arc never seemed to have a great consistency—the stones were loosely packed and not associated with any clear ground-surface or flooring—and it was eventually removed. This wall, however, once may have been part of a structure, and it was associated with a great many ceramic fragments, chipped stone tools and other finds.

The area indicated by an anomaly of high susceptibility and conductivity in portion F190 proved to be the poorly preserved floor of an oval hut defined by bits of terracotta pavement and the rough outline of a stone wall-socle. At 4.22 meters around the point 130E/50S traces of a

pavement in terracotta and a great quantity of Castelluccian ceramics were found beneath masses of fallen stone.

In portion F171, a deposit of compact yellow-brown soil with ash and many fragments of wall daub and ceramics appeared at 7.43 meters. At 7.34 meters a surface with limestone bits was found. Unfortunately, the definition of this deposit was not clear, and it may have fallen from above just as the soil and the many large stones which were found in the superficial stratum throughout this area.

Immediately above this area, in the western half of portion F200, an area of fallen wall daub extended between 122–124E and 40–42S, while a small area of terracotta pavement with stones around it was found between 120–122E and 37.5–40S. This wall was associated with a packed surface of burned soil with traces of carbon between 126–130E and 37.5–40S at 7.06 meters (roughly 1.0 meters below the current ground surface).

The western and eastern halves of portion F200 were separated by an alignment of stones between 125–130E and 36–40S similar to that which separated portions F182 and F183. Between 130–132.5E and 35–37.5S and 6.94–6.86 meters, a ground-surface in limestone bits was found.

In the eastern part of portion F200 a stratigraphic sounding was opened in an area where a pit had been located between 131.5–132.5E and 35.5–36.5S. After digging out the pit between 6.86 and 6.64 meters, a test-pit 1.71 m deep was created between 130–132.5E and 37.5–40S from 6.64 to 5.98 meters (Plate 8.2). Four distinct surfaces of beaten earth and limestone bits were revealed:

6.64 to 6.49 meters, grey soil with limestone bits,

6.49 to 6.44 meters, grey soil with limestone bits (a ground-surface?),

6.44 to 6.28 meters, dark grey-brown soil with ash,

6.28 to 6.16 meters, grey soil with limestone bits,

6.16 to 5.98 meters, dark brown soil with stones.

It appeared that the archaeological deposit continued beneath this last elevation. Over the lowermost stratum, there lay a thick stratum of burned soil with many ceramic fragments.

Comparing Survey and Excavation Data

Re-evaluation of the survey data in light of the results of the 1991 excavation produced the following findings[31]. The most distinctive anomaly within the excavation was the area of unusually low magnetic susceptibility and electrical conductivity near point 120E/50S. Excavation there in portion F172 revealed a concentration of large boulders and an outcrop of bedrock which suggests that the unexcavated susceptibility low which forms a line heading toward the northeast corner of the survey area is likely also to be a dense concentration of stone. This concentration of stone probably is the terrace wall which delimited the northern side of the terrace which included the hut in portion F190. The linear susceptibility low indicates that the wall is near or slightly downhill from the area of stones, although the geophysical evidence is weak. There is a distinct northeast trend for the rock alignments and a tendency for some susceptibility anomalies to be aligned in that direction. Clusters of small rocks would not have been detected by the survey.

It is possible that the floor surface with few stones found in F190 correlates with the susceptibility high that is there. On the other hand, the deep deposit found at F181 has no susceptibility anomaly. The feature in area F181 lies in an area of distinctly low conductivity. While it is possible that the archaeological strata can be low in conductivity, they will generally be expected to be high in conductivity because of the greater amount of organic matter which they often contain. The conductivity is a bit of a puzzle here and the susceptibility data appear to be clearer at this particular site. Neither conductivity nor susceptibility indicate any significant anomaly at the test pit. The medieval inhumation graves were not detected either.

In light of the excavation findings, a new map of the geophysical anomalies was produced indicating a line of at least five structures to the east of excavation portion F200 (Plate 9.2). This line is roughly parallel to the terraces in portions F80 and F130 found in earlier excavations. While the anomalies themselves are not of the same size, they do not seem to indicate structures of particularly diverse dimensions. It seems likely, given the stratigraphy and sequence in the excavated portions, that there are many more structures than the anomalies indicate and that their disposition is far more complex than it appears on the map.

The Architecture of the Castelluccian Structures

The Daub Fragments

Nancy E. Peterson

Analysis conducted in June of 1990 at the Museo Civico di Licata of more than 140 daub fragments recovered from the Field excavation zone in 1989 revealed that slightly more than half bore the impressions of straw, reeds, and wooden members which formed the framework of the Castelluccian huts (Plates 9.3, 9.4 and 9.5). These impressions present not only the diameters of the construction materials but also their various arrangements[32].

Daub was recovered from Huts 2, 3 (Upper), and 3 (Lower) by excavation portion. Both the nature of the recovery technique and the condition of the collapsed daub limit the specification of the provenience of each sample simply to one hut or the other. The attribution of samples to structural components within each hut remains a matter of speculation[33].

In Plate 9.1, impressions in the daub have been grouped into three size ranges. Though somewhat arbitrary, the size ranges of the impressions tend to reflect similar materials with similar functions. Impressions of the construction materials range from less than one centime-

[31] Analysis of the survey data in light of the excavation is based largely on B.W. Bevan, personal communication, 1 February 1992.

[32] A similar study is presented in connection with a neolithic structure in Calabria: A.J. Ammerman, G. Shaffer, and N. Hartman, "A Neolithic Household at Piana di Curinga, Italy," Journal of Field Archaeology 15, 1988, p.121–40, esp. figs. 7–8; cf. also A.J. Ammerman, "Recenti contributi sul Neolitico della Calabria," Atti della XXVI Riunione Scientifica dell'Istituto Italiano di Preistoria e Protostoria, Florence, 1985, p.333–49, esp. p.342–44. See now G.D. Shaffer, "An Archaeomagnetic Study of a Wattle and Daub Building Collapse," Journal of Field Archaeology 20, 1993, p.59–75.

[33] The precise location of daub fragments at Piana di Curinga has been used to trace the original position of hut walls to within one meter; cf. Ammerman, Schaffer and Hartman (here n.32) 124–26.

ter to at least seventeen centimeters in diameter. Of these, 61.3 percent are one centimeter or less and constitute Range I. This percentage is approximate and rather conservative because it was impossible to count all the impressions for their small size and sheer number. Range II impressions include diameters of greater than one centimeter to ten centimeters. Diameters of more than ten centimeters are classified as Range III. Impressions in this last range are infrequent and often lack clear distinction from the slight curvature of an irregular daub surface.

From the size distribution and arrangement of the impressions in the daub, one may infer the function of the materials in each range and possible hut construction techniques. The impressions of Range I materials indicate that straw, small reeds and twigs formed a matting. Though daub impressions show that these materials were in parallel alignment as well as criss-crossed (Plate 9.6, a), no clear evidence of a weaving of materials, a true wattling, has been found.

Range II impressions of larger reeds, branches, and lightweight poles, are less common than Range I impressions. Impressions in the daub show parallel alignment and criss-crossing of materials (Plate 9.6, b). Range II materials provided a frame which carried the Range I matting for the wall, the roof, or both. No more than two Range II impressions appear together, although they often cross the numerous Range I impressions of the matting (Plate 9.6, c). Range II materials also would have provided additional lightweight support. A Range II material could have been inserted into the post-hole in Hut 3 (Lower) which measured 8.5–10 cm in diameter, although it seems doubtful that such a relatively slender member could have provided the necessary support for the superstructure.

Material that formed Range III impressions, the least common, provided the primary support for the structure. Posts and beams would have borne the wooden frame with its matting. A Range III post was best able to endure the weight of a roof, and the post-holes of Hut Nos. 2 and 3 (Lower) bear witness to their use. One post-hole in Hut No. 2 was as large as 30 cm in diameter, and thus Range III materials could have been much larger than the available daub impressions indicate.

Daub was applied for strength, weatherproofing, and smooth surfacing. It cannot yet be determined for certain whether the huts at La Muculufa had daub roofs and/or walls or whether daub was used to finish the interior and/

or exterior of the huts. Bits of straw, too numerous and small to document, served as an organic temper in the daub fabric, and the massive voids which they left in the daub are clearly visible in the samples submitted for thin-section analysis (see Chapter XII). Range I materials could have been applied to the damp daub surface and ignited in order to fireharden the daub. Burned daub fragments have been found in substantial amounts, especially on the bench of Hut No. 2. Unfortunately, daub hardened by this method closely resembles the daub of a hut destroyed by fire; therefore, the cause of firing is difficult to determine. Alternatively, had hut construction been seasonal, perhaps during the summer, the sun could have baked the daub.

The distribution of daub may reflect the particular requirements of each structure. Hut No. 3 (Lower) yielded half of the daub recovered; Hut Nos. 2 and 3 (upper) yielded the other half in roughly even amounts. It is possible that the elliptical structure of Hut No. 3 (Lower) required more daub to build the walls and/or roof than did the circular structure of Hut No. 2. In contrast, the excavation of Hut No. 4 yielded no daub. Its structural design seems to have relied on other means of support.

Round impressions predominate among the daub fragments recovered at La Muculufa but there is one example of a split timber impression which is associated with Hut 3. Perhaps its elliptical structure required hewn wood more than a circular structure would require; however, for reasons of preservation, we cannot exclude the possibility that hewn wood was used also in Hut No. 2[34]. The daub fragment bears a right angle impression (Plate 9.5B); neither the final size of the split timber nor the extent of its reduction can be determined. Part of the hut may have required timber fitted to prescribed dimensions. Splitting a timber could create a desired flat surface or an edge, as well as economize on available resources. Timber may have been scarce or of diminutive proportions permitting only minor modifications.

Daub was the versatile medium that allowed the builders to go beyond the limits of available resources, and it seems to have been derived from the specialized skills developed in ceramic production[35]. It is likely that daub

---

[34] Daub fragments at Piana di Curinga presented a substantial number of impressions of split timbers; cf. Ammerman, Schaffer and Hartman (here n.32) 126–27.

was also used for decoration. Although there is no evidence at present that the daub was ever painted, it appears that it was used for such architectural refinements as moulding. Five samples were recovered from Hut No. 3 (lower) which exhibit two flat surfaces with a smooth, curved edge. These could have lined an entryway, a smokehole in the roof, a wall niche, or perhaps a ledge[36].

Reconstructions of Hut No. 2 and Hut No. 3

The drawings of Hut No. 2 and Hut No. 3 (lower) (Plates 10.1 and 10.2), created by Christopher Whittier under the supervision of Jean Blackburn of the Rhode Island School of Design, are based upon information derived from the plans drawn in the field and from the study of daub fragments. Although an effort was made to utilize only attested planimetric and structural elements, attention was given to reconstructions created previously for Middle Bronze Age huts at Thapsos and Madre Chiesa di Gaffe and for Iron Age structures at Montagnoli di Menfi and especially Luni sul Mignone (below)[37].

Principal considerations in the reconstruction of both huts concern the height of the wall-socle and the way in which the roof was set upon it. In Hut No. 2 cross-beams between lateral posts are set equidistantly from the center of the structure, and they cross at a central post beneath a closed apex[38]. For this reason, the beams for the superstructure supporting the roof of Hut No. 2 have been raised at least two meters above the floor in order to permit an adult to move easily within the interior. There is no direct evidence for the existence of a daub-frame wall above the stone socle, as presented in the drawing of Hut No. 3 (lower), although little stone for the wall-socle was noted in comparison to that for Hut No. 2. It would seem necessary, however, for this wall to have been at least one meter high in order to create sufficient interior space and a doorway[39]. In both reconstructions, the doorway has been placed on the southern side of the hut in order to take advantage of the lower slope of the hill and the availability of sunlight from the south[40]. Unfortunately, the lack of preservation on this side prevents us from checking this arrangement against the structural remains.

It is interesting and important to note that the circular Hut No. 2 and the elongated Hut No. 3 (lower) were larger and notably more regular in plan than Hut No. 4. Although many of the details of these more complex structures remain conjectural, it is clear from the reconstructions that the need to support a roof on a frame of beams across a wide area required a significant degree of planning, planning which involved geometrical concepts and tools, such as a string for a radius and perhaps even a rudimentary unit of measurement. This degree of planning marks the builder of the later structures as a proto-architect. As the study of the daub fragments makes clear, the materials and techniques of ceramic production were certainly involved in the construction process, and among

---

[35] In this context the similarity between the fabric of the daub and ceramic samples is especially significant. See the report by Melissa Moore in this volume.

[36] One of these curved edges measured nine centimeters in diameter, and may indicate the thickness of daub at these possible locations in the hut, as well as the proportions of the walls or the roof.

[37] (Thapsos) G. Voza, "L'Attività della Soprintendenza alle Antichità della Sicilia Orientale, Parte II," Kokalos 22–23, 1976–1977, p.563 and pl. 102; (Madre Chiesa di Gaffe) G. Castellana, Un Decennio di Recerche Preistoriche e Protostoriche nel Territorio Agrigentino, show catalog, Agrigento, 16 June–30 September, 1990, fig. 9, (Luni sul Mignone) P. Hellström, Luni sul Mignone II, 2, The zone of the large iron age building, Skifter utgivna av svenska institutet i Rom, 1975, esp. pls. 13–14. O. Nyström (ibid., 103–106) has calculated that the hut at Luni sul Mignone could withstand the force of wind up to 90 m/s or 324 km/hr. The advantage of this design for the overall shape of the structure should be considered, especially in regard to the windy conditions at La Muculufa.

[38] Discussion of Hut No. 2 in this publication does not consider the superstructure with an open apex presented as an alternative design in B.E. McConnell, "The Early Bronze Age Village of La Muculufa and Prehistoric Hut Architecture in Sicily," American Journal of Archaeology 96, 1992, p.34. It does not seem likely now that the crucial element, the terracotta base found at the center of the hut, could have been part of a ceramic vessel set into the floor because it does not have a form attested among Castelluccian ceramics. For this reason it seems better to interpret this element as a setting for a central post [B.E.McC.].

[39] A minimum height of one meter is given by Paolo Orsi in a verbal reconstruction of a hut at Branco Grande (Camarina); cf. "Due villaggi del primo periodo siculo," Bullettino di Paletnologia Italiana 36, 1910, p.168.

[40] A doorway facing South is clearly evident in the plan of Hut 1 at Torricella (Ramacca); cfr. M. Frasca, F. Messina, D. Palermo, and E. Procelli, "Ramacca (Catania) Saggi di scavo nel villaggio preistorico in contrada Torricella," Notizie degli Scavi di Antichità1975, p.563, fig. 8.

the crafts present in Castelluccian society, ceramics seem to have involved to the greatest degree planning and the conception of forms. Perhaps the Castelluccian proto-architect was in fact a potter[41].

The Circular Hut

It is in this context that the discovery at La Muculufa of a distinct architectural type takes on particular significance. Hut No. 2 displays a number of characteristic features, including a circular stone wall-socle, an interior bench or curbing, a beam-frame roof set on an interior support structure, and a feature in the center of the floor which together may be defined as the Sicilian circular hut. Although direct parallels for this form presently are not known at other Castelluccian sites, aside from a partially preserved stone structure with an interior bench which Paolo Orsi found on Monte Racello (Comiso), there are many examples in contexts ranging in date from the Middle Bronze Age to the Eighth century B.C. at sites across Sicily and on neighboring islands[42].

The appearance of the circular hut at La Muculufa underscores the significance of the Early Bronze Age as a period in which the traditions of indigenous culture in Sicily begin to crystalize. Together with the production of distinctive painted ceramics, incipient metallurgy, and creation of rock-cut chamber tombs in necropoleis along cliff faces, developments in domestic architecture characterize the fundamental trends in Sicilian Early Bronze Age culture which were interpreted first by Paolo Orsi in his original chronological term, the First Sikel Period (*primo periodo siculo*)[43]. Although permanent settlements are known both in the preceding Neolithic and Eneolithic periods, the structures which comprise them as a whole do not share a uniform construction technique nor the kind of uniformity in design which characterizes the Bronze Age circular hut as a building type[44]. Only in the Maltese archipelago is architecture developed to any great extent during the centuries prior to and contemporary with the earliest phases of the Castelluccian culture[45]. Models in limestone and terracotta found in association with megalithic temples at Tarxien and Hagar Qim may indicate that architects were planning and building on Malta in the late Third millenium B.C., but there is still insufficient evidence to determine whether the kind of influence which Maltese megalithic building seems to have had upon Castelluccian funerary architecture is present also in Castelluccian domestic architecture[46].

---

[41] The distinction between an architect and a master builder depends upon the amount of theoretical design involved in the planning of a structure, as well as the degree of occupational specialization. Although specialization is difficult to measure in these circumstances, the notable quantity and quality of Castelluccian ceramics at La Muculufa would seem to indicate that pottery production was performed by full-time craft specialists. We should keep in mind, however, the observation made by Paolo Orsi in regard to the economy of the village at Branco Grande ("Due villaggi del primo periodo siculo," Bullettino di Paletnologia Italiana 36, 1910, p.174–75: "Era dunque un villaggetto di pescatori. Ma ciò non esclude che fossero al tempo stesso pastori nomadi e cacciatori: nell'età preistorica la divisione del lavoro non era così netta ed accentuata come oggi è, e forse non esisteva che in parte."

[42] (Monte Racello) P. Orsi, "Miniere di Selce e sepolcri eneolitici a M. Tabuto e a M. Racello presso Comiso," Bulletino di Paletnologia Italiana 24 1898, p.3–5. At Branco Grande, Orsi describes a seat built in ashes (ceneri) with a surface in terracotta set against the wall of Hut No. II; cf. Orsi (here n.10) p.170–171. A similar construction in stones and clay was found in Hut No. 8 at Manfria; cf. P. Orlandini, Il villaggio preistorico di Manfria presso Gela, Palermo, 1962, p.37, pl. 23, 1. For other parallels and examples from the Middle Bronze Age and later periods, see B. E. McConnell, "The Early Bronze Age Village of La Muculufa and Prehistoric Hut Architecture in Sicily," American Journal of Archaeology 96, 1992, p.37–43.

[43] P. Orsi, "La Sicilia preellenica," Atti della Società italiana per il progresso delle scienze, XII Riunione, Catania, 1923, Città di Castello, 1923, p.1–35, esp. p.8–15.

[44] Cf. (Stentinello) S. Tinè, "Notizie preliminari su recenti scavi nel villaggio neolitico di Stentinello," Archivio Storico Siracusano 7, 1961, p.113–117; (Serra del Palco) V. La Rosa, "L'insediamento preistorico di Serra del Palco in territorio di Milena," Kokalos 30–31, 1984–85, p.475–82, idem, "Un nuovo insediamento neolitico a Serra del Palco di Milena (CL)," Atti della XXVI Riunione Scientifica dell'Istituto Italiano di Preistoria e Protostoria, Florence, 1987, p.801–808; (Piano Vento) G. Castellana, "Il villaggio neolitico di Piano Vento nel territorio di Palma di Montechiaro. Rapporto preliminare," Atti Licata II, p.9–67, also Castellana (here n.37), p.12–29, G. Castellana and F. Mallegni, "The Prehistoric Settlement of Piano Vento in the Territory of Palma di Montechiaro (Agrigento, Italy)," Archivio per l'Antropologia e l'Etnologia 116, 1986, p.61–80. For a treatment of the domus as an ideological entity in Neolithic Europe, see I. Hodder, The Domestication of Europe, Oxford, 1990.

Settlement Layout and Architectural Form

Analysis of the spatial arrangement of the prehistoric structures at La Muculufa in comparison with that at other Early Bronze Age sites in Sicily is useful in determining the development of proto-types for the kind of structured settlements which appear at coastal trading emporia such as Thapsos and at urban centers of the interior such as Sabucina[47]. The way in which Hut No.s 2 and 3 (lower) seem to be aligned parallel with each other and with the line of the terrace walls suggests that the village possessed a rational design. Although the location and dimensions of the terraces were determined in part by the disposition of natural rock outcrops, a degree of planning is evident also in the very adaptation to the terrain itself, in the same way that the village, the open-air sanctuary and the necropolis were adapted to the crest in terms of their location and dimensions. Other evidence of planned organization in the settlement may be seen in paths which linked its various elements, including the rising gravel path in portion F102 and cuttings in the rock along a major path to the eastern end of the prehistoric necropolis and three paths to the necropolis along the crest's southern face[48].

The rational arrangement of structures has been noted as a characteristic of other Castelluccian settlements. At Branco Grande, a coastal site near the ancient Greek city of Camarina, seventeen structures enclosed by a fortification wall within an area measuring 120 x 100 m were seen to have been arranged in rows[49]. At Settefarine (Gela), the poorly preserved structures of a Castelluccian settlement seem to have been distributed in groups on hillocks[50]. At Manfria (Gela) in an area measuring 60 x 45 m nine huts were found in two groups enclosed by a series of hearths in what has been described as a farm compound[51]. A series of compounds may be represented by three groups of huts found in contrada Feudo Nobile (Gela)[52].

The structures at La Muculufa themselves are among the larger known in Castelluccian Sicily. A settlement covering an area of about three hectares at S. Croce near Comiso presented at least eleven elliptical huts of which only two were of dimensions similar to those at La Muculufa[53]. Hut No. 9 at Manfria, which measured 9.0 x 3.25 m, is clearly an exception both at its own settlement and

---

[45] While 1500 years of architectural development in the Maltese archipelago yielded by 2500 B.C. the distinct and characteristic form of the megalithic temples, there is almost no evidence for domestic architecture; cf. D. Trump, "Megalithic Architecture in Malta," in C. Renfrew, ed., The Megalithic Monuments of Western Europe, London, 1983, p.64–76. It is interesting to note, however, that an oval hut of the early third millennium excavated recently on the island of Gozo does display a bench and a central feature in mud-brick described by the excavators as a pillar for the roof. The hut is estimated to have an extension of 8.0x5.0 meters; cf. C. Malone, S. Stoddart and D. Trump, "A house for the temple builders: recent investigations on Gozo, Malta," Antiquity 62 (1988) 297–301.

[46] Trump (here n.45) p.68–69. E. Procelli describes the monumentalization of Castelluccian tomb facades in imitation of the facades of Maltese megalithic temples; cf. "Il complesso tombale di contrada Paolina ed il problema dei rapporti tra Sicilia e Malta nella prima età del bronzo," Bollettino d'Arte n.s. 9, 1981, p.83–110, esp. p.104–106. S. Tusa, "The Megalith Builders and Sicily," Journal of Mediterranean Studies 1, 1991, p.267–285, discusses reasons for the restriction of megalithic architecture in Sicily to funerary contexts.

[47] This topic has been addressed by Owen Doonan IV, Domestic Architecture of the Sicilian Bronze: A Study of Architectural Innovation and Social Transformation, diss. (Brown University) 1993.

[48] Similar adaptation of the landscape may be seen in a rock-cut path associated with several Middle Bronze Age tombs near Caltagirone; cf. D. Amoroso, "Una testimonianza di viabilità preistorica: la strada delle tombe nella necropoli della Montagna di Caltagirone," Viabilità Antica in Sicilia, Atti del Terzo Convegno di Studi, Riposto, 1987, p.15–24. The significance of the ledge-like paths along the southern face of the crest, as noted by N. Peterson, is confirmed by the placement of Castelluccian chamber tomb at significant points along them.

[49] P. Orsi, "Due villaggi del primo periodo siculo," Bullettino di Paletnologia Italiana 36, 1910, p.168 and fig. 1. Orsi estimated that originally there had been between 30 and 40 structures at the site.

[50] Orsi (here, n.49), p.178–80, figs. 5–6.

[51] P. Orlandini, Il villaggio preistorico di Manfria presso Gela, Palermo, 1962, fig. 2; cf. R.R. Holloway, "Scavi alla Muculufa e premesse per lo studio della cultura Castellucciana," in Atti Licata II, p.69–90, esp. p.73.

[52] D. Adamesteanu, Notizie degli Scavi di Antichità 1960, 223, fig. 15. Acknowledgement for this reference is owed to Owen Doonan.

[53] At Santa Croce, Hut No. 2 measured 7.5 x 7.0 m and Hut No. 3 7.5 x 6.0 m.; cf. P. Orsi, "Villaggio e sepolcreto siculo alle Sante Croci presso Comiso (Siracusa)," Bullettino di Paletnologia Italiana 46, 1926, p.5–17.

in Castelluccian Sicily as a whole. At Branco Grande, on the other hand, the huts were notably smaller, between 2.0 and 4.2 m in their maximum planimetric dimension, while at a neighboring site, Poggio Biddini (Acate), the diameters of three circular Castelluccian structures were between the more typical dimensions of 3.0 and 3.5 m[54]. A survey of known Castelluccian buildings shows an articulated range of circular and oval forms, as well as a tendency to weld the structure firmly to the land by setting the floor slightly below the ground surface, as noted at Manfria and Santa Croce[55]. Hut No. 9 at Manfria which measured 9.0 x 3.25 m seems exceptional, but it may find an analog at La Muculufa in a structure indicated by a large anomaly of high magnetic susceptibility and electrical conductivity roughly between 149–157 E and 47–57 S. Despite the limitations of interpreting the survey data from La Muculufa outlined above, one may see cautiously a general arrangement of small anomalies of high magnetic susceptibility around this larger anomaly.

Recent studies ascribe an increase in the number, size and type of settlements to social differentiation within Castelluccian communities, increasing economic interdependence among settlements on a regional basis, and to an intellectual advance from the isolated self-sufficiency of a farm-village (masseria) to greater receptivity toward external influence as a result of reciprocal exchange and contact with people in other parts of the island and overseas[56]. In 1985, R. Ross Holloway identified a fundamental social difference between a farm (fattoria) and a village (villaggio)—the farm is a settlement for a single family which works the immediate territory, while a village is a settlement for a number of families each with a distinct identity[57]. The layout of structures at La Muculufa seems to suggest that it was a relatively densely packed village perhaps with a number of family 'compounds' within it, although much more excavation is needed before any clear picture of the settlement as a whole can emerge.

An interesting hypothesis suggested by the data from La Muculufa is that increasing population and settlement density may have led to greater concern for the definition of domestic and personal space both among the living and the dead. The increase in the scale of construction from Hut No. 4 to Huts 2 and 3 (lower) seems to indicate that the creation of larger buildings forced greater care in the use of space and perhaps greater need for its identification. The series of *corni fittili* found around Hut 3 (lower) and perhaps around Hut No. 2 were of different types, and they include one with a greenstone pendant set into the tip and types with arms or wings (*ali*). It is likely that these objects, distinctive already for their form, were also distinguished by color, inasmuch as a red ground was found on *corni fittili* discovered during the 1989 and 1991 excavation campaigns (Cat. Nos. 221 and 234). Another *corno fittile* (Plate 42, A) found on the eastern Terrace was painted with motifs from the Castelluccian ceramic repertoire in the standard black-on-red-ground scheme. Perhaps these objects served as markers to indicate the land and buildings of a clan or nuclear family, if not specific individuals, as private property.

Concurrent with this notion of land-use is the tendency in Castelluccian settlements, including La Muculufa, to mark off larger areas by means of stone fences. By no means is this a phenomenon exclusive to the Early Bronze Age. Areas bounded by ditches or fences are known from the Neolithic period on in the Tyrrhenian region both on a large and on a small scale. Best known are the areas enclosed by ditches of the Neolithic period in peninsular Italy on the Tavoliere plain[58]. In Sicily bounded areas of the Neolithic and the Copper Age have been found at Stentinello, Serra del Palco and Piano Vento di Palma di Montechiaro[59]. Early Bronze Age settlements with long fences have been found in Castelluccian Sicily at Torricella (Ramacca), Valsavoia (Lentini), Baravitalla (Ragusa) and

---

[54] G. Di Stefano, "Saggi a Poggio Biddini sul Dirillo," Kokalos 22–23, 1976–77, p.647–50, idem, Piccola guida delle stazioni preistoriche degli Iblei, Ragusa, 1984, p.147–53.

[55] S. Tusa, La Sicilia nella preistoria, Palermo, 1983, p.352.

[56] Tusa (here n.55) 287, 319, 329–30, and 353, Holloway (here n.51) 76, cf. idem, Italy and the Aegean 3000–700 B.C., Louvain and Providence, 1981.

---

[57] R.R. Holloway in Atti Licata II, 73: "La fattoria è un complesso a contatto colla terra da cui vive. Per lo più, in tempi recenti, essa porta il nome di una famiglia, la sola ivi residente o l'elemento dominante in una piccola società di padroni e familiari. Il villaggio è un complesso distinto dalla terra in quanto ognuna delle famiglie che lo compongono ha un identità propria. Così c'è una distinzione paese-terra, pure nei casi in cui il terreno agricolo è tenuto in parte o totalmente in comune."

[58] Cf. S. Tinè, Passo di Corvo e la Civiltà Neolitica del Tavoliere Genova, 1983.

Monte Grande (Palma di Montechiaro)[60]. E. Procelli has suggested that these fenced areas may be associated with emergent social groups formed especially through contact with the contemporary megalithic temple culture of the Maltese islands[61].

A similar argument for the definition of family property may be made for the over one hundred and fifty tombs which crowd the necropolis above the settlement at La Muculufa[62]. The original number of tombs is likely to have been higher, but it can no longer be determined because of the collapsed state of the crest; neither is it possible to determine, for the same reason, the original configuration of the tombs within the necropolis, nor whether divisions among the chamber tombs in the necropolis correspond in some way to divisions within the settlement. It is well known from other sites, however, that Castelluccian chamber tombs were used for multiple burials and that the use of crevices as well as chamber tombs for burial at La Muculufa suggests that space in the necropolis was at a premium[63].

Economic specialization may have played a role in the definition of space within Castelluccian communities[64]. The precise function of any of the hut structures at La Muculufa has yet to be determined; however, an interesting hypothesis has arisen out of the study by Laura Maniscalco of ceramic materials from Hut No. 2 (in this volume). This structure contained an extraordinary quantity of ceramics—roughly 100 separate vessels. There is little variation in the vessel shapes (they are restricted to the low pedestal vase or *frutteria*, the dipper or *attingitoio*, and *pithoi*) and the vessel decoration also appears in a restricted series of variations. Perhaps this hut served as the workshop and/or display area for the products of one or more potters. Already, the hand of a single artist has been identified in connection with ceramics from the sanctuary, and it may be possible to do the same here[65]. Several personal effects were found within the building, including a shell necklace.

The definition of common or non-private space, on the other hand, may have its roots in Castelluccian religious concepts manifest in the creation of the sanctuary. Evidence for an open-air sanctuary on a natural terrance at the eastern end of the crest is circumstantial but convincing. It is based upon the discovery of a non-domestic assemblage of high-quality Castelluccian ceramics together with bones predominantly of juvenile sheep or goat and carbon much of which had fallen into a deep fill below poorly preserved sections of terrace walling onto what appeared to be a beaten earth surface with traces of a hearth[66]. Although functional aspects of Castelluccian religion are almost as elusive as its spiritual content, the remains at La Muculufa seem to indicate that it involved feasting in a panoramic setting. Holloway, in fact, has de-

[59] (Stentinello) S. Tinè, "Notizie preliminari su recenti scavi nel villaggio neolitico di Stentinello," Archivio Storico Siracusano 7, 1961, p.113–117; (Serra del Palco) V. La Rosa, "L'insediamento preistorico di Serra del Palco presso Milena," Kokalos 30–31, 1984–1985, II, p.475–82; idem, "Un nuovo insediamento neolitico a Serra del Palco di Milena (CL)," Atti della XXVI Riunione Scientifica dell'Istituto Italiano di Preistoria e Protostoria, Florence, 1987, p.801–808; (Piano Vento) G. Castellana, "Il Villaggio Neolitico di Piano Vento nel Territorio di Palma di Montechiaro (Agrigento), Atti della XXVI Riunione Scientifica dell'Istituto Italiano di Preistoria e Protostoria, Florence, 1987, p.793–99.

[60] M. Frasca, F. Messina, D. Palermo and E. Procelli, "Ramacca (Catania). Saggi di scavo nel villaggio preistorico di contrada Torricella," Notizie degli Scavi 1975, p.557–85; G. Di Stefano, "Cava d'Ispica. Recenti scavi e scoperte, Modica, 1983, p.22; U. Spigo, "L'attività della Soprintendenza Archeologica a Lentini negli anni 1977–1985." in Un trentennio di indagini nel territorio di Lentini antica Lentini, 1987, p.34; G. Castellana, Un decennio di ricerche preistoriche e protostoriche nel territorio Agrigentino, show cat, Museo Archeologico Regionale, 16 June–30 September 1990, p.32–38.

[61] E. Procelli, "Aspetti Religiosi e Apporti Trasmarini nella Cultura di Castelluccio," Journal of Mediterranean Studies 1, 1991, p.260.

[62] G. Parker, "The Early Bronze Age Chamber Tombs at La Muculufa," Revue des Archeologues et Historiens d'Art de Louvain 18, 1985, p.9–33.

[63] B.E. McConnell, G. Morico, C. Corrain and M. Capitanio, "La Muculufa (Butera, Caltanissetta), Stazione Siciliana dell'età del Bronzo Antico," Archivio per l'Antropologia e l'Etnologia 120, 1990, p.115–50. It is possible that bones were transferred from the chamber tombs to rock crevice ossuaries such as the one discussed in this publication in order to create space for later burials. Recycling of space in this manner is as much a by-product of crowding as it is a sign of cultural continuity.

[64] Tusa (here n. 55) 307f. and 353.

[65] S.S. Lukesh, Appendix III in this volume.

[66] R.R. Holloway, M.S. Joukowsky and S.S. Lukesh, "Mining La Muculufa," Archaeology 41, 1988, p.40–47; cf. L. Cruz-Uribe in La Muculufa I, p.11–67.

scribed the emergence of this village-center in Early Bronze Age Sicily as the beginning of a long tradition from the Bronze Age into historical times which linked regional political groupings to religious and economic activities at sanctuaries, and parallels can be seen at a number of sites in the lands around the Tyrrhenian sea[67].

The Crevice Burial: Faunal Remains

Alfredo Riedel

During the 1987 excavation campaign a rock-crevice along a level area at the center of the crest of La Muculufa and directly above the village was found to contain human and animal bones and ceramic fragments. Unfortunately, the archaeological deposit had been disturbed by clandestine activity the traces of which (earth heaped around the natural opening in the rock, fragments of ceramics and bones thrown in every direction) were mixed with larger boulders and stones which had fallen by the crevice long beforehand. Excavation in 1987 explored the deposit on the interior of the crevice, while continued exploration

---

[67] R.R. Holloway, Atti Licata II, p.16–18. The question of Tyrrhenian Federal Sanctuaries was addressed by B.E. McConnell in a paper delivered to the Ninety-Fourth Annual Meeting of the Archaeological Institute of America, New Orleans, 1992 (abstract, "Federal Sanctuaries of the Tyrrhenian," American Journal of Archaeology 97, 1993, p.319); sites discussed include La Muculufa, Monte Grande (Palma di Montechiaro), Palikè, Le Maccalube (Aragona), Rossano di Vaglio (Potenza), and Santa Vittoria di Serri (Cagliari). For a general treatment of this phenomenon with reference to sanctuaries in Etruria, see I.E.M. Edlund, The Gods and the Place: location and function of sanctuaries in the countryside of Etruria and Magna Graecia (700–400 B.C.), Skrifter utgivna av Svenska institutet i Rom, 40, 1987, esp. p.85–93. This indigenous phenomenon may well be encountered in Hellenizing structures at the Sanctuary of Hera Lacinia (Croton) and at Morgantina; cf. F. Seiler, "Un complesso di edifici pubblici nel Lacinio a Capo Colonna," AttiMGrecia 23, 1983, p.231–242; C. Antonaccio, "Writing and Naming at Archaic Morgantina," paper presented to the Ninety-Fourth Annual Meeting of the Archaeological Institute of America, New Orleans, 1992 with subsequent discussion. See also D. Adamesteanu, Macchia di Rossano: il Santuario della Mefitis: rapporto preliminare, Quaderni di Archeologia e storia antica 3, 1992.

during the 1989 campaign extended the excavation in front of the crevice. Analysis of the human osteological material was performed by Prof. C. Corrain and Prof.ssa M. Capitanio; cf. B.E. McConnell, G. Morico, C. Corrain and M. Capitanio "La Muculufa (Butera, Caltanissetta), stazione siciliana dell'Età del Bronzo Antico," Archivio per l'Antropologia e la Etnologia, 120, 1990, p.115–150. [B.E.McC.]

The osteological remains include the three principal groups of domestic animals—cattle, caprines (perhaps only sheep), and pig—as well as red deer (see Tables 1 and 2). There are at least 118 large fragments of whole bones. The bovines are more numerous, and the deer are rare. Calculation of the minimum number of individuals (11) gives analogous proportions, to the disadvantage of the pig. The individuals are for the most part adults or adult in appearance with the exception of a calf and a lamb. Both sexes are present. The apparent forms of the cattle metacarpals are of females, bulls and oxen. The pig remains are of animals which are rather large and the sheep are rather small. Only the cattle may be measured more precisely (see Table 3) and are small animals. Three cattle have a Withers' height of x 109 cm.

Inasmuch as the crevice at La Muculufa served as a place of burial, it was desired to examine whether the osteological depositions of animals were different from those typical of the remains of normal meals. Since the remains of all the principal animals of economic significance, as well as deer, are present, there does not seem to be a selection. There are few pigs, however, and adult specimens are, overall, abnormally numerous. The bones belong to various parts of the skeleton, including the vertebrae and the ribs. Certain areas of the body are not represented, such as the teeth and phalanxes of cattle, etc. Given the scarcity of the remains, however, it may be suggested that this situation is the product of chance selection.

The bones, for the most part, do not present visible signs of butchery, except for two sheep atlases and a sheep axis. The remains are fragmentary, and the separation surfaces seem due more to breaking than to cutting. One may, therefore, suppose that the bones were quite whole when they were thrown, perhaps even without scarnification, into the funerary deposits. However, such an hypothesis could be considered a certainty only if the deposit were important, the archaeological study complete and archaeozoological observations performed during the excavation. Given the poor preservation of the remains the traces of scarnification, the separation and cutting of the bones could have been obliterated or extremely hard to identify. Following closely the interpretation of the data presented by the osteological remains, one may hypothesize only a relation to the funerary complex.

	1	2	3	4	Total
Cattle	31	16	–	13	60
Sheep-goat (sheep)[*]	11(2)	19(3)	–	–	30(5)
Pig	1	2	20	–	23
Deer	2	3	–	–	5

Table 1: Large remains and whole bones

[*]. The individuals determined to be 'sheep-goat' are probably all sheep. Note: Samples 1 and 2 from 1989 excavation; Sample 3 from 1987 excavation, area in front of rock crevice (Tomb S1); Sample 4 from 1987 excavation, area lateral to rock crevice (Tomb S1).

1	Cattle metacarpal GL 186.0 Bp 58.5 SD 33.5 Bd 61.0; Withers' height 115 cm (probably ox)
1	Cattle metacarpal GL 169.4 Bp 53.3 SD 31.0 Bd 60.3; Withers' height 105 cm (probably bull); traces of arthritis on the distal diaphysis
1	Cattle metacarpal GL 171.1 Bp 47.2 SD 23.5; Withers' height 106 cm (female)
2	Cattle metacarpal Bd 59.0
4	Cattle humerus Bd 51.5
2	Sheep humerus Bd 28.5
2	Sheep metacarpal Bp 21.5
2	Sheep phalanx 2 GLpe 21.0 Bp 11.1 SD 8.2 Bd 8.9
2	Sheep-goat M^3+ L 19.2; 20.0
3	Pig pelvis LA 39.0

Table 3: Measurements

	1	2	3	4	4 groups
Cattle	5 adults 1 female 1 perhaps bull 1 perhaps ox 1 male 1 young	2 1 adult 1 perhaps adult		1 perhaps adult.	6 4 adults 1 female 1 perhaps bull 1 perhaps ox 1 male 2 non-adults 1 perhaps adult 1 young
Sheep-goat	2 1 sheep 1 adult 1 young	2 1 sheep 2 adults M_3+			3 1 sheep 1 female; 2 adults M_3+ 1 young
Pig	1 probably adult	1 probably adult	1 probably adult		1 probably adult
Red Deer	1 female	1 adult			1 adult, female

Table 2: Minimum number of individuals

Remains From Historical Periods

Although La Muculufa is best-known as a prehistoric site, and its Early Bronze Age remains far outnumber those of later periods, both structures and artifacts of varying historic date (i.e. from the time of the Phoenician and Greek colonization of Sicily on) have been found in every area along the crest. The following paragraphs describe several noteworthy discoveries from 1988 to 1991. A separate study of the Greek finds by A. Rovida appears in this volume. Three separate studies of medieval remains found at the site have appeared already in other publications[68].

During the 1989 campaign the remains of a rectangular structure in dry-stone masonry were discovered in excavation area F150 (Plates 11.1 and 13.5). The wall was set in a double row of field-stones 0.50 m wide on its northern side, 0.65 m on its western side and 0.70 m on its southern side, and it was preserved between 0.45 and 0.70 m high. The building itself enclosed 2.30 m along its western side; the length along its northern side was greater than the 6.75 m of wall brought to light before the excavation was suspended in this area. A doorway 0.95 m wide marked by two stone orthostates (between 0.25 and 0.30 m thick and 0.50 m high) on either side opened on the southern side of the structure, and the floor in beaten earth lay at an elevation of roughly -1,33 meters[69]. Greek tile fragments found beneath the fall of stones indicated that the structure had been roofed. The entire structure was found to rest on soil containing Castelluccian materials, and a test-pit dug on the exterior of the structure's western side measuring 1.20 m along the wall by 2.0 m out from it and dug to a depth of ca. 1.00 m revealed no noticeable wall foundations.

Finds found in association with the structure came from the stratum of overburden, as well as from a deposit sealed on the floor beneath the collapse of stones from the structure's walls. It seems likely that this structure served as a farm-shed on land used primarily for agricultural purposes, and that it was not part of a larger complex.

The most surprising discoveries in the Field zone, however, were made during the 1991 campaign, and they consist of two skeletons set in pit-graves dug into the prehistoric levels (Plate 8.1). Burial No. 1 was found between 136–138E and 56.5–57.8S and 2.80 to 2.49 meters depth in soil clearly darker than that of the prehistoric levels, and it had been covered with thin gypsum slabs set on an incline contrary to the slope of the hillside (Plate 11.2). The body, which measured 1.60 m in length, had been laid in an extended position on its right flank facing south-south-east (or 168 degrees off magnetic north), and its hands were laid across the groin (Plate 14.4). Burial No. 2 was found in portion F182 between 139–140E and 61.5–62.5S between 2.12 and 2.09 meters in a soil similar to that of Burial No. 1 (Plate 11.3). It was not covered with gypsum slabs (although they may have been removed by plowing). The skeleton was extended on its right flank with the face oriented toward the southeast (128 degrees off magnetic north), and it measured 1.70 m in length. An extension was made in the trench between 140–140.6E and 60–62.5S in order to reveal all of the body. Both burials were adult inhumations, and they have been identified as Muslims of medieval date because of the lack of grave goods, the orientation of the body roughly towards the Mecca and comparison with similar burials elsewhere in Sicily[70].

On a rocky ledge overlooking the Field area and in front of a natural grotto (or more likely an overhang of the cliff) which had been walled over in historic times, there was found a tomb cut lengthwise into the rock. It measured 1.55 m in length, 0.50 m in width and it was 0.60 m in depth and set at an angle roughly 75 degrees above the horizontal. Although its orientation was determined par-

---

[68] B.E. McConnell: "La Muculufa after the Bronze Age," in La Muculufa I, 49–56 (a revised version of this contribution due to appear in R.R. Holloway, et al., "La Muculufa, le campagne di scavo 1982–83," Quaderni Archeologici Messinesi); B.E. McConnell, "L'insediamento medievale alla Muculufa (Butera, CL)," Atti del Congresso 'L'Età di Federico II nella Sicilia Centro-Meridionale' (Gela, 8–9 December, 1990, p.229–33.

[69] The reference point for elevation readings in this excavation area was point 60, the elevation of which was 11.01 meters above point 10, or 320 meters above sea-level.

[70] Muslim burials discovered at Montevago (contrada Caliata) and Contessa Entellina (Rocca d'Entella) and other comparanda are discussed in G. Castellana, ed. Dagli scavi di Montevago e di Rocca di Entella, un contributo di conoscenze per la Storia dei Musulmani della Valle del Belice dal X al XIII secolo, Atti del Convegno Nazionale, Montevago 27–28 ottobre 1990.

tially by the strike of the rock and by the available space on the rocky ledge, a body laid out in this tomb would have been facing roughly the east, and therefore it seems likely that this tomb, too, was a Muslim burial of medieval date.

Discovery of such burials at La Muculufa forces the excavator to re-evaluate the extent of the medieval settlement discussed in prior communications[71]. There may, in fact, be a greater, more stable settlement at La Muculufa than the fortified outcrop previously posited, and a document dated between 1154 and 1171 A.C. from the ecclesiastical archives of Agrigento may refer to it as 'Michalchilfe', a *casale* purchased by the bishop of Agrigento from an Arab owner following the expulsion of the Saracens from Sicily[72].

---

[71] McConnell, "L'insediamento medievale ...," here n.68, p.232.

[72] P. Collura, Le più antiche carte dell'Archivio Capitolare di Agrigento (1092–1282), Palermo, 1961, p.61, doc. 25 (emptio, Agrigento, 1154–1171): "Gentilis episcopus emit a gaito Abdisalemo filio Abdiliabar, omne ius sub dominio eius existens in toto casali, quod dicitur Muccarin, et totum casale quod dicitur MICHALCHILFE [my caps]. predictus etiam Gentilis episcopus emit a pluribus et diversis Saracenis, quando fuerunt expulsi de Sicilia, multa alia casalia, ut casale Misecti et casale Ra[hal]. Sulle, qui videntur fuisse inter Agrigentum, Narum et Licatam." The editor (ibid., n. 2) noted that the location of 'Michalchilfe' had not been identified at the time of publication. The historical context of the expulsions related to in the letter are not identified, but a twelfth century date stands well with the chronological context of glazed wares found at the site; cf. B.E. McConnell, "L'insediamento medievale ...," here n. 68. Recent changes in the dating of early Islamic glazed wares in Sicily (cf. A. Molinari, "La ceramica dei secoli X-XIII nella Sicilia occidentale: alcuni problemi di interpretazione storica," Atti delle Giornate Internazionali di Studi sull'area Elima, Gibellina, 19–22 settembre 1991, Pisa-Gibellina, 1992, p.501–522), on the other hand, accords well with the association of the site 'Mocluse' mentioned in the Eleventh century context by Gaufreddo Malaterra (cf. McConnell, here n.68) with those found at La Muculufa. Further study of this material is merited not only in Sicilian contexts but also those of southern Italy: the large basin from La Muculufa presented in S. Scuto, Fornaci, Castelli & Pozzi dell'Età di Mezzo, (show catalog Gela Museo Archeologico di Gela, 9 giugno–31 dicembre 1990, 141, no. 263) is identical in form and decoration to basins found at Salerno (cf. P. Peduto, "Rapporti tra Salerno e la Sicilia alla luce dei recenti rinvenimenti ceramici del secolo XII," to be published in the proceedings of the round table "Ceramica, città e commercio nell'Italia tardo-medievale e nelle aree circonvicine" held on May 3–4, 1993 at the Centro Universitario Europeo per i Beni Culturali, Ravello, Italy.

II – CATALOGUE OF PREHISTORIC FINDS

Introduction

The number of ceramic pieces, tools in bone and in chipped and ground-stone, and other finds recovered from the relatively limited area of the Castelluccian village excavated to date is quite striking. Over 735 separate finds from the area of Hut Nos. 2–4 have been catalogued to date of which 60% are ceramic vessels, 7% objects in terracotta, 3% bone tools, and 18% are tools in chipped- and ground-stone; other materials constitute the remaining 12% of the items catalogued to date from this area. Most of these materials were found in association with the level of Hut Nos. 2 and 3 (lower), but a significant number in the 1988–89 excavation area could be attributed neither to the upper nor to the lower level of Hut No. 3 because of disturbance to the deposit in portion F134. Still other notable finds were recovered from superficial strata in this area. Finds from the trenches excavated in 1991 were also of notable quality and made significant additions to the typologies established from earlier excavated material, although their particular significance and immediate inter-relationships could not be established because of the contextual limitations imposed by the trenches.

The following sections treat the finds from the Castelluccian village at La Muculufa by category of material and function—pottery, terracotta, bone, ground-stone, chipped-stone and pendants. Although a series of bronze bits were recovered from the Early Bronze Age strata during the course of the excavations, none of the find-spots were clearly without the possibility of contamination. In addition to this problem, the objects themselves were not sufficiently preserved to identify their form[73].

The finds are presented as *corpora* in catalog form with a concordance of inventory numbers and find-spots in Appendix II to this volume. Selection was based on the apparent significance of the find to the corpus as a whole (as well as on factors of preservation and presentability), and the typologies can be considered to be representative samples to the extent that it was humanly possible to reconstruct them. Reference to particularly indicative finds from outside of the village is made to the extent that it increases our knowledge of the corpus as a whole. Although these repertories do not include material excavated at La Muculufa from 1982 to 1987, effort has been made where possible to relate them to the studies published in the prior volume on this site[74]. Each catalog entry has been given with a unique catalog sequence number as well as the excavation inventory number preceded by *Muc* which is based on the year of excavation (e.g. 88/94 refers to an object excavated during the campaign of 1988). Official Superintendency inventory numbers (where available) are given separately.

Special attention here should be paid to the technical studies which appear after the section on the Castelluccian ceramics, as well as to the studies of human and animal osteological remains from the rock-crevice burial. Treatment of finds from the historical period appears here separately in the section on Greek remains, as well as in articles published elsewhere[75].

The Castelluccian Ceramics

Laura Maniscalco

Introduction

The following study has been conceived as a typological repertory of ceramic vessels found in the Castelluccian village. It proceeds with a listing of all whole or partially complete vessels, as well as many significant fragments. Given the enormous quantity of material (about 700 box-

---

[73] The metal finds include: 89/356 portion (S110C), two fragments of bronze (or copper), one 2.8x2.5x0.15 cm., the other slightly smaller; 88/16 (F101), fragment of bronze (or copper), half-lunate shape, without decoration, 3.5x1.5x0.1 cm; 89/82 (F151A), eight fragments of bronze or copper of which the largest measures 3.0x1.8x0.1 cm; 89/49 (T130), instrument (needle?) in bronze, length cm. 1.3, diam. 0.25–0.3 cm, center flattened, length 1.5 cm, thickness 0.5x0.25 cm; 89/7 (T130), ring in bronze, missing roughly one quarter, diam. 2.2 cm, thickness (diameter of the metal) 0.5 cm. From the Terrace zone, metal objects, including several nails and a door-hinge, were recovered from the historical strata and most likely can be ascribed to the medieval occupation.

[74] Cf. R.R. Holloway, et al., La Muculufa I.

[75] Cf. B.E. McConnell, "L'insediamento medievale alla Muculufa (Butera, CL)," Atti del Congresso 'L'Età di Federico II nella Sicilia Centro-Meridionale,' Gela, 8–9 December, 1990, p.229–33; idem, "La Muculufa after the Bronze Age," in La Muculufa I, p.49–56.

es from 1988 to 1991) and the fact that many vessels await a more complete restoration, not every fragment studied could be included; rather, although every fragment excavated between 1988 and 1991 was examined the corpus is based on a sample of pieces selected for their representative character[76]. About half of the ceramics recovered were painted with decorative motifs in black on a red ground; the other half is constituted by thick-walled vessels which are not decorated, as well as a very small number of grey, incised fragments and shiny red ceramics.

Painted Vessels

The painted ceramics are for the most part of a fabric which appears to the naked eye to be rather coarse and red-orange in color. The exterior surfaces are painted as a slip (*ingobbo*) in opaque red and sometimes in opaque yellow. Among the pitchers the interior band along the rim is also slipped and sometimes one may see the irregular brush-strokes which applied the slip (Plate 19.1). The decorative motifs are rendered for the most part in summary fashion (e.g., a decorative element was omitted on pitcher no.72), sometimes hurriedly with a large brush. There is also present, in rare instances, a finer variety of ceramic in which the line is rather subtle and accurate (the so-called Naro style, see below). The most common and characteristic forms are the pedestal bowls on a low foot (Lukesh Form F1, often refered to as fruttiere or vaso a calice) with single or double handles and a pitcher with a distinct neck (Lukesh Form C2). Other forms are dippers, hemispherical cups, spouted vases, jars with plastic handles, cups with a tongue, quadrangular vessels and an example of an amphora.

The painted decoration presents a vast repertory of motifs arranged, especially among the pedestal bowls, in complex decorative syntases. The hatched band is the most popular motif; other common patterns are the wolf's-tooth (often at the rim), hatched diamonds, hatched triangles, wavy and zig-zag lines, cross (X) or plus-signs (+) isolated or in series, butterfly-motifs, fringe-patterns, bands which narrow toward the base, bands with re-

served diamonds, and bands with a reserved zig-zag line. More rare are the fish-bone motifs, arrows joined at the apex, diverging bands of parallel lines, and curvilinear motifs. On ribbon handles the most common decorations consist of ladder-motifs or groups of vertical lines.

Pedestal Bowls

Description

The most common pedestal bowls have a short foot with a deep bowl, and they can be single- or double-handled. They are attested in large, medium and miniature sizes, and it may be possible to place these diverse series in relation to a quantity of measurement for liquids[77]. In several pedestal bowls there is an enlarged ring at the point of the juncture between the foot and the bowl and, in the case of single-handled pedestal bowls, sometimes two knobs opposite the handle.

The decoration painted on the exterior of the bowl consists almost always of simple groups of vertical lines, while on the interior there is greater variety. The most common principal element consists of two hatched bands which cross at the center, one upon the other or more rarely leaving a regular empty square. The four sectors thus obtained are decorated at the edge with lines and fringe-motifs, wolf's-tooth motifs, or wavy lines. Bands and hatched triangles often bordered in white are also very common. The white color sometimes alternates with black lines (e.g. Cat. No. 8) or consists only of a decorative motif (e.g. Cat. No. 64). Less common are groups of lines which delimit spaces with wolf's-tooth triangles, X's, butterflies, bands with reserved diamonds or bands with reserved zig-zag motifs. Crossing lines and the butterflies predominate on the pedestal, but bands of reserved diamonds are also present[78].

Occasionally one encounters fragments of pedestal bowls with repair-holes along the rim and the base. Evidently, the creation of this type of vessel called for a great deal of effort in its formation and decoration; therefore, it was not summarily discarded as soon as it was broken[79].

---

[76] Since a statistical study of the material excavated between 1982 and 1987 has already been performed (cf. Lukesh in La Muculufa I, passim), a typological basis seemed best for this study. The author is pleased to acknowledge the generosity with which Prof. Holloway and Dr. Lukesh placed the drawings of material found before 1987 at her disposition.

[77] The diameters of the basins vary from 12 cm. (small) to 30 cm. (medium), to 45 cm. (large).

[78] For similar motifs in chalice vase from the Sanctuary, cf. Muculufa I, p.22–23.

Pedestal Bowls on a Low Foot

1 Muc 89/39
Pedestal bowl on low foot recomposed from various fragments. Two vertical ribbon handles arranged symmetrically in respect to the pedestal from the bowl to the base. Lacking a portion of the bowl.
Single band painted on rim exterior; on interior five groups of three vertical lines descend toward the poorly preserved center.
H. cm. 19.0, diam. rim cm. 32, diam. base cm. 12.5, h. base cm. 6.5, wall thickness cm. 1.15, handle width cm. 2.55 and 2.45, handle thickness cm. 1.7 and 1.5.
Plates 15.1 and 21

2 Muc 89/113
Pedestal bowl on low foot recomposed from various fragments, lacking portion of the bowl and border of the pedestal. Vertical ribbon handle from the pedestal to the exterior of the bowl. Decoration painted on the exterior in groups of five or six horizontal lines on the handle and groups of vertical lines on the pedestal; on interior traces of red color.
H. cm. 15.5–16.5, diam. rim cm. 26, diam. base cm. 8, h. base cm. 4.5 (incomplete), wall thickness cm. 1.2, handle length. cm.10, width cm. 3.65, thickness cm. 1.25.
Plate 21

3 Muc 89/160
Pedestal bowl on low foot with a vertical ribbon handle from the base to the bowl. Recomposed from various fragments heavily burned after breaking, lacking parts of the border. Knob at the joint between the pedestal and the bowl. Surfaces from the poorly preserved color seem to have a purple tone. Traces of painted decoration on the foot in groups of three lines.
H. cm. 17.5, diam. rim cm. 29, diam. base cm. 13.5, wall thickness cm. 1.0, H. pedestal cm. 6.5, handle width cm. 3.5, handle length. cm. 10, handle thickness cm. 1.0.

Bowls with Hatched Cross

4 Muc 89/85
Pedestal bowl on low foot recomposed from various fragments partially burned after breaking, lacking portion of the bowl. Vertical ribbon handle from the

foot to the bowl. Decoration in brown on red ground. On the interior of the vessel hatched cross creates four sectors with fringe along the rim from which line pairs descend to the center. Groups of three vertical lines on exterior of the bowl; series of X's on the foot; groups of 2–3 horizontal lines on the handle.
H. cm. 16–16.5, diam. rim cm. 25.5, diam. base cm. 12, wall thickness of base cm. 0.8–0.95, thickness of bowl wall cm. 1.1, h. base cm. 6.5, handle width cm. 2.6, thickness cm. 1.2.
Plate 22

5 Muc 89/200 b
Bowl of pedestal bowl. Recomposed from various fragments. Interior and base as Cat. No. 4; on exterior groups of four vertical lines and the attachment of a handle.
Diam. rim cm. 26, wall thickness cm. 1.2.

6 Muc 89/161
Bowl of pedestal bowl on low foot with attachments for two vertical handles. Recomposed from various fragments. Decoration of the bowl interior as Cat. No. 4; on bowl exterior vertical lines on the attachments of the handles and a wavy line from the handle to the rim.
Diam. rim cm. 46, wall thickness cm. 1.4.

7 Muc 88/20
Portion of the rim of a pedestal bowl. Interior as Cat. No. 4 with a hatched band bordered in white.
Diam. cm. 18, thickness cm. 0.8.
Plate 23

8 Muc 91/23
Fragment of the bottom of a bowl. Two hatched bands delimited by thick white lines on both sides which meet at an angle at the bottom leaving a white square. Four adjacent lines bordered in white.
Thickness cm.1.0.
Plate 23

9 Muc 88/25
Part of the rim of a pedestal bowl. On bowl interior hatched bands alternate with lines bordered in white.
Diam. cm. 18, thickness cm. 1.0.
Plate 15.2

10 Muc 89/253
Part of the bowl of a pedestal bowl. On interior hatched bands bordered in white alternate with double lines; on exterior groups of four vertical lines bordered in white, horizontal lines on the handle.
H. cm. 6; thickness cm. 0.8.
Plate 15.3

---

[79] At the late Castelluccian necropolis of Santa Febbronia (Palagonia, Catania) restoration holes are exclusively on the pedestal bowls.

11 Muc 91/57
Fragment of the rim of a pedestal bowl. From the rim two oblique hatched bands unite at the ends; an adjacent large oblique hatched band is united with the smaller ones. All elements bordered in white. On exterior groups of three vertical lines.
Diam. cm. 32, thickness cm. 0.8.
Plate 24

12 Muc 88/103–108
Fragment of the rim of a pedestal bowl. From the rim bands (or a diamond) with a hatched pattern bordered in white unite at the ends. On exterior groups of four vertical lines.
Diam. cm. 34, thickness cm. 1.2.

13 Muc 91/123
Fragment of the rim of a pedestal bowl. From the rim a band with a hatched pattern and perhaps a triangle unite at the ends with another band; all elements are bordered in white. On exterior groups of four vertical lines.
Thickness cm. 1.0.

Bowls with a Hatched Cross and Wavy Line Decoration

14 Muc 89/215–322
Portion of the bowl of a pedestal bowl. Beige fabric with a red surface. On the interior of the bowl survive three elements of a cross with hatched pattern which forms four sectors each with a triple zig-zag line along the rim from which a vertical zig-zag line descends to the center; exterior painted in three vertical lines.
Diam. cm. 30, thickness cm. 1.0.
Plate 22

15 Muc 89/188
Fragment of the rim of a pedestal bowl. Interior as Cat. No. 14 but with double wavy lines on the rim and descending to the center; exterior as Cat. No. 14 with the attachment of a handle.
Diam. cm. 20, thickness cm. 0.7.

16 Muc 89/212
Fragments of the rim of a pedestal bowl. Interior painted in a double wavy line beneath the rim and a double vertical wavy line which descends from the rim probably as Cat. No. 15.
Diam. cm. 38, thickness cm. 1.0.

Bowls with Hatched Band, Triangle and Diamond Decoration

17 Muc 88/104–251
Fragments of the rim of a pedestal bowl. At the rim hatched triangle and a hatched band; in the middle hatched diamond and the beginning of another: all motifs are bordered in white. On exterior vertical lines bordered in white.
Diam. cm. 22, thickness cm. 0.9.
Plate 23

18 Muc 88/159
Fragment of the rim of a pedestal bowl. On rim interior hatched triangles united at the apex and a hatched band.
Diam. cm. 32, thickness cm. 1.6.

19 Muc 88/255
Fragment of the rim of a pedestal bowl. On rim interior hatched triangle united at the apex to a diamond, hatched triangle and a hatched band: all motifs are bordered in white.
Diam. cm. 40, thickness cm. 1.4.

20 Muc 91/85
Fragment of the rim of a pedestal bowl. Surfaces shiny red. Interior painted along the rim in a hatched band alternating with two compositions of hatched triangles arranged to form a large triangle with the apex pointed downward; all of the triangles and the band are bordered in white. On exterior a double vertical line.
Diam. cm. 24, thickness cm. 1.4.
Plate 23

21 Muc 91/63
Fragment of the rim of a pedestal bowl. Shiny ground. Interior painted along the rim in compositions of triangles as 91/85 but only with three triangles visible. Adjacent double vertical lines from the rim. On exterior three vertical lines.
Thickness cm. 1.1

22 Muc 88/169
Fragment of the rim of a pedestal bowl. On rim interior hatched triangle united at the apex to a diamond, hatched triangle and a group of seven zig-zag lines: all motifs are bordered in white.
Thickness cm. 0.9
Plate 24

23 Muc 89/171
Fragment of the rim of a pedestal bowl. Surfaces wine red. At the rim triangle or hatched band bordered in

white; on lower part another small part of a hatched band bordered in white.
Diam. cm. 42, thickness cm. 1.0.
Plate 15.3

24 Muc 88/194
Fragment of the body of a pedestal bowl. Fabric and surfaces gray. Vertical hatched band from which extends a horizontal hatched band from which descend in turn hatched diamonds. All elements are bordered in white.
Thickness cm. 1.6.
Plate 23

25 Muc 91/94
Fragment of the rim of a pedestal bowl. Interior painted beneath the rim in a series of three hatched diamonds with another diamond beneath them at the center; to the sides full diamonds and an adjacent vertical line bordered in white. All of the diamonds are bordered in white.
Diam. more than 52 cm., thickness cm. 1.3.
Plate 24

Bowls with Butterfly Pattern Decoration

26 Muc 89/202
Pedestal bowl restored from several fragments; lacking a portion of the bowl and part of the base. Fabric pink, surfaces yellow-pink. Interior painted with butterflies and double vertical hatched bands which arrive at the center of the bowl. At the joint between the pedestal and the bowl an enlarged ring with two knobs painted with black bands with irregular reserved diamonds.
Diam. cm. 29, thickness cm. 1.0.
Plate 25

27 Muc 89/302
Fragment of the rim of a pedestal bowl. Shiny red surface (Munsell 10R 4/6–5/6). Painted decoration on the interior in three butterfly motifs and a hatched band. On the exterior the attachment of a handle. Painted very finely with a thin brush.
Diam. cm. 36, thickness cm. 0.8.
Plate 15.4

28 Muc 88/9
Fragment of the rim of a pedestal bowl. Butterfly bordered with vertical lines of points.
Diam. cm. 30, thickness cm. 1.1.
Plate 25

29 Muc 89/174
Fragments of rim of a pedestal bowl recomposed with several fragments. Interior painted in a wolf's-tooth pattern and butterfly-pattern from which descends a wavy line.
Diam. cm. 38, thickness cm. 1.0.
Plates 15.4 (before restoration) and 25 (after restoration)

30 Muc 89/217
Almost complete bowl of a pedestal bowl. On the interior four wolf's-teeth along the rim interrupted alternately by four vertical lines and butterfly designs; on the exterior the attachment for a knob handle.
Diam. cm. 24, thickness cm. 1.0.
Plate 25

31 Muc 89/226
Fragment of the rim of a pedestal bowl. Interior painted in a wolf's-tooth pattern and a butterfly-pattern.
Thickness cm. 1.2.
Plate 15.4

32 Muc 89/216
Fragment of the rim of a pedestal bowl. Interior surface red, exterior surface yellow. Interior decoration in a triple wavy line along the rim interrupted by a butterfly-pattern connected by a vertical wavy line and a double wavy line to the rim.
Diam. cm. 34, thickness cm. 1.0.
Plate 25

Bowls with Wolf's-Tooth Pattern Decoration

33 Muc 89/163
Bowl of pedestal bowl. Fabric and surfaces yellowish. Decoration on interior of bowl in groups of five or six wolf's-teeth along the rim alternating with groups of four lines which descend and define seven spaces each with an X at the center. On the exterior groups of four descending lines and an attachment of a knob handle.
Diam cm. 30.
Plate 22

34 Muc 89/201
Bowl of pedestal bowl. Decoration on interior of bowl in a wolf's-tooth pattern along the rim and X's below it. On the exterior groups of three descending lines and X's.
Diam cm. 34, thickness cm. 1.2.

Bowls with Reserved Diamond Decoration

35 Muc 91/73
Fragment of the rim of a pedestal bowl. Fabric pink, surfaces red. Painted decoration in a band of reserved

diamonds and a hatched band. All elements bordered
in white; very strong color.
Thickness cm. 1.8.
Plate 24

36 Muc 89/124
Bowl of a pedestal bowl. On the interior a band with
a triple series of reserved diamonds alternating with a
series of crosses and another band with a double series
of reserved diamonds.
Diam. cm. 38, thickness cm. 1.0.
Plate 15.5

37 Muc 89/170
Fragment of the bowl of a pedestal bowl. Beneath the
rim are painted a zig-zag line and a band with a dou-
ble series of reserved diamonds.
Diam. cm. 44, thickness cm. 1.5.
Plate 15.4

38 Muc 89/249
Fragment of the bowl of a pedestal bowl and of the
attachment of the foot with an enlarged ring. On interior double band of reserved diamonds and line of
dots.
Thickness cm. 2.0.
Plate 24

39 Muc 89/238
Fragment of the bowl of a pedestal bowl. Interior
band with series of reserved diamonds and an adja-
cent butterfly-pattern.
Diam. cm. 26, thickness cm. 1.2.
Plates 15.4 and 24

40 Muc 89/250
Fragment of the bowl of a pedestal bowl and of the
attachment of the pedestal. On interior a reserved di-
amond band and a herring-bone pattern.
Thickness cm. 1.3.
Plate 15.6

41 Muc 89/255
Fragment of the bowl of a pedestal bowl and part of
the attachment of the pedestal with a ring. Inside the
bowl a herring-bone pattern and a band perhaps of
reserved diamonds; on the exterior groups of four
lines.
Thickness cm. 2.0.
Plate 15.6

Bowls with Various Pattern Decorations

42 Muc 89/267
Fragment of the bowl of a pedestal bowl. Inside bowl
a hatched band, fringe and perhaps a herring-bone
pattern.
Thickness cm. 1.0.

43 Muc 89/306
Fragment of the rim of a pedestal bowl. Surface dull.
On the interior vertical dashes to the rim and a her-
ring-bone pattern; on the exterior three lines.
Diam. cm. 25, thickness cm. 1.1.
Plate 15.6

44 Muc 89/214
Portion of the bowl of a pedestal bowl. Fabric pink-
violet; exterior surface pink; interior surface violet
with a darker violet band. Painted fringe along the
rim interrupted by a reserved zig-zag band.
Diam. cm. 40, thickness cm. 1.5.

45 Muc 88/121
Portion of the rim of a pedestal bowl. Interior painted
in a triple vertical zig-zag line descending from the
rim with a series of X's and a hatched band to the
sides; exterior painted in three vertical lines.
Diam. cm. 36, thickness cm. 1.8.

46 Muc 88/92
Fragment of the rim of a pedestal bowl. Interior
painted along the rim in a zig-zag line with a triple
vertical wavy line and a hatched band; exterior painted in groups of four vertical lines.
Diam. cm. 42, thickness cm. 1.2.

47 Muc 89/239
Fragment of the bowl of a pedestal bowl. Shiny surfaces. On the interior two hatched bands alternate
with a series of small crosses; on the exterior groups
of three lines.
Thickness cm. 1.2.

48 Muc 89/91
Fragment of the bowl of a pedestal bowl. On interior
two hatched bands alternate with a series of small
crosses and a double vertical wavy line; on exterior
groups of two lines.
Thickness cm. 1.4.

49 Muc 88/96
Fragment of the rim perhaps of a pedestal bowl. Interior painted in a triple vertical zig-zag line descending
from the rim and bordered in white with another
band which is not clear.
Thickness cm. 1.0.

Pedestal Bowls with Plastic Elements

50 Muc 88/226
Fragment of the bowl of a pedestal bowl with a raised rib. Interior surface painted with hatching.
Diam. over cm. 50, thickness cm. 1.8.

51 Muc 88/167
Fragment of the bowl of a pedestal bowl. At the joint between the pedestal and the bowl an enlarged ring and two knobs with a point at the center; on the ring and at the exterior of the bowl bands with reserved diamonds.
Thickness cm. 1.0.
Plate 26

52 Muc 88/4
Fragment of the base and part of the bowl of a pedestal bowl. A ribbon handle from the join of the pedestal and the bowl; on the opposite side two plastic knobs with four painted vertical lines descending along the pedestal; on one side five vertical lines and on the other a butterfly-pattern (perhaps); horizontal line to the attachment between the bowl and foot which rises above the knobs. On the interior of the bowl a band and vertical lines which are not clear.
H. cm. 14, thickness bowl cm. 0.9.
Plate 26

Pedestals

53 Muc 89/236
Pedestal of a pedestal bowl with X's alternating with triple lines; attachment of a knob handle decorated on the underside with horizontal lines crossed by vertical lines.
H. cm. 8.5; diam. cm. 32.

54 Muc 88/24
Pedestal of a tubular pedestal bowl with an enlarged ring at the lower attachment of a handle; on the side opposite the handle the ring is interrupted forming two pointed knobs and a small portion of the bowl. Grey-pink fabric; exterior surface shiny red. Decoration in brown on the foot in groups of three oblique lines which cross one another; on the ring groups of vertical lines and on the lower part of the bowl there begin groups of vertical lines.
Plate 26

55 Muc 88/129
Portion of the pedestal of a pedestal bowl of elongated form. Curving hatched bands separate butterfly motifs in a low horizontal line beneath which there are a vertical hatched band and vertical lines.
H. cm. 10, thickness cm. 1.0.
Plate 26

56 Muc 89/237
Pedestal of a pedestal bowl with six consecutive butterfly motifs.
H. cm. 8; diam. cm. 14.

57 Muc 89/164
Fragments of the pedestal of a pedestal bowl with the attachment of a knob handle and part of the bottom of the bowl. On the base groups of three lines alternate with butterfly motifs.
H. cm. 10, thickness cm. 1.0–1.5.
Plate 26

58 Muc 88/81
Fragment of the pedestal of a pedestal bowl. Vertical hatched band and band of reserved diamonds, low horizontal band. All of these elements are bordered in white.
Thickness cm. 1.0.

59 Muc 91/79
Fragment of the pedestal of a pedestal bowl of elongated form. Curving hatched band bordered in white; to the sides an elongated hatched clepsydra-motif bordered in white.
Diam. cm. 12, h. cm. 12.5, thickness cm. 0.8.
Plate 26

60 Muc 91/97
Fragment of the pedestal of a pedestal bowl of elongated form. Hatched band bordered in white connected at the corner.
Diam. cm.6, h. cm. 9, thickness cm. 1.2.

61 Muc 89/32
Pedestal of a pedestal bowl with an enlarged ring. Tent-motif at the base; attachment of a handle and a series of X's interrupted by a vertical line on the ring.
H. cm. 8.0 (circa); diam. cm. 18, thickness cm. 1.2–1.5.
Plate 26

62 Muc 88/128
Fragment of the pedestal and part of the bowl of a pedestal bowl. At the join of the foot and the bowl an enlarged ring and knobs. On the foot a tent-motif bordered in white. On the interior of the bowl hatched bands.
H. cm. 5.6, bowl thickness cm. 0.7.

63 Muc 89/105

Pedestal of a pedestal bowl and part of the bowl. On the exterior of the bowl a reserved diamond band; at the base a band in a double row of reserved diamonds and a band of arrows.

H. base cm. 6, thickness cm. 0.6.

64 Muc 88/84

Portion of pedestal of a pedestal bowl. On the exterior groups of seven lines bordered in white alternate with X's reserved in white on red.

Diam. cm. 12, thickness cm. 0.7, h. cm. 8.5.

Comparisons

The pedestal bowl on a low foot, a form already known in the Malpasso style of the Sicilian Copper Age, is a form which is very common at sites of the Sicilian Early Bronze Age. It occurs, in fact at S. Ippolito (Caltagirone), at Settefarine (Gela), in the Infame Diavolo cave (Palma di Montechiaro), at Mizzebbi (Milena), at Adrano in the first phase, and at Naro (Agrigento)[80]. Among the decorative motifs the hatched bands which cross each other on the interior of the bowl are found at Naro and at Partanna, the butterfly motifs are present at Mizzebbi and at Adrano, the wolf's-tooth along the rim is found in the Infame Diavolo cave, at Mizzebbi and, in a more complex form, at Castelluccio; the series of 'X's and the bands with reserved diamonds are present at Mizzebi. The series of X's on the leg of the pedestal bowl is common at S. Ippolito[81]. The plastic decorative elements which recur on some pedestal bowls are found also at Naro. Pacci, in reference to the famous sculpted tomb-portals of Castelluccio, suggests that the knobs have apotropaic significance related to the realm of funerary activity[82], but the provenience of these examples from the village of La Muculufa, as well as those at other habitation sites, does not support this association; furthermore, of all the pedestal bowls presented by Pacci as coming from necropoleis, not one bears a knob. A figurative character is evident, however, in the knobs on example Cat. No. 51 which indicate the eyes and on a vessel from the territory of Palma di Montechiaro with a ring which has holes for pupils and even has eyelashes[83]!

Pitchers

Description

The pitchers have a globular or ovoid body and almost always a distinct neck and they are single-handled [84]. In respect to the pedestal bowl, the pitcher has more uniform dimensions (the height is usually cm. 11–14, the rim diameter cm. 7–9). The narrow neck suggests that they served to hold liquids, the raised handle that they served to dip from another, larger vessel, usually a pedestal bowl. Pitcher Cat. No. 68 lacks the handle and has a hole in the

---

[80] R.M. Albanese, "Calascibetta (Enna)—Le necropoli di Malpasso, Calcarella e Valle Coniglio," Notizie degli Scavi di Antichità 42–43,1988–89, I Supplemento, p.161–225, esp. p.198, fig. 7.5; S. Ippolito: L. Bernabò Brea, "La Sicilia prehistórica y sus relaciones con Oriente y con la Península Iberica," Ampurias 15–16, 1953–1954, p.134ff., fig. 13d, n; Settefarine: P. Orsi, "Due villaggi del primo periodo siculo," Bullettino di Paletnologia Italiana 36, 1910, p.158–193, plate XII, 6; Grotta dell'Infame Diavolo: E. De Miro, "Ricerche preistoriche a Nord dell'abitato di Palma di Montechiaro," Rivista di Scienze Preistoriche 16, 1961, p.50–54, fig. 7: 1074 with a very low base; (Mezzebbi) F. Privitera, "La stazione di Mezzebbi nel contesto del Bronzo Antico del territorio di Milena," La Preistoria del basso Belice e della Sicilia meridionale nel quadro della preistoria siciliana e mediterranea (forthcoming); M. Cultraro, La cultura di Castelluccio nel territorio di Adrano, Tesi di laurea, Università di Catania, Facoltà di Lettere, 1987–1988, form L1; S. Tusa and M. Pacci, La collezione dei vasi preistorici di Partanna e Naro, Palermo, 1990, plate XIV, catalog numbers 89–95.

[81] Hatched bands: Tusa-Pacci (here n.80), plate XXIII, F, Plate VIII, g, cf. Cat. Nos. 80, 85, 89, and 103. Butterfly: Cultraro (here n.80) plate 100, Phase I, cf. Cat. No. 28. Wolf's tooth: De Miro (here n.80) fig. 7, 1074; G. Sluga Messina, Analisi dei motivi decorativi della ceramica da Castelluccio di Noto (Siracusa), in Università degli Studi di Trieste Facoltà di Lettere e Filosofia, Istituto di Archeologia, I, Roma, 1983, p.5–177, esp. p.112. Crossed lines on the legs: Bernabò Brea (here n.80) fig. 13 d, n.

[82] Tusa-Pacci (here n.80) 80, cat. 97 (ring) and 76, cat. 93, 94, and 95 (knobs).

[83] G. Castellana, "Nuove ricognizioni nel territorio di Palma di Montechiaro," Sicilia Archeologica 15, 1982, p.81–102, fig. 40; compare also a form at Adrano (Phase I). See also the relief pasticche on vessels of the earliest phase at Capo Graziano; cf. L. Bernabò Brea, Gli Eoli e l'inizio dell'età del bronzo nelle Isole Eolie e nell'Italia meridionale, Archeologia e leggende, Annali dell'Istituto Orientale di Napoli, Memoria 2, Napoli, 1985, p.63 with comparisons in the Tyrrhenian region e nell'Italia meridionale.

[84] Cf. Lukesh in Muculufa I, p.34, table B, shape groups A2, B2, and especially C2 which is more common in the Village than in the Sanctuary.

neck: probably after the handle was broken off a hole was made in order to use the pitcher as a spouted vase. The only certain example of an amphora (Cat. No. 94) is actually only a variation on the pitcher both in terms of its structure and its decoration.

Painted decoration consists of rather repetitive elements. Generally, there are one or more zig-zag or wavy lines on the neck and on the body vertical narrowing bands alternating with lines which delimit sectors indicated on the shoulder by a fringe or wolf's-tooth pattern with an X, butterflies, or a wavy line at the center. These are the same elements which constitute the decoration of the pedestal bowls. In two cases there is also present figural decoration—a jar decorated with a human face (Cat. No. 93) and a small pitcher with an eye with lashes on the neck (Cat. No. 98); see discussion below.

Several pitchers (Cat. Nos. 81–89) with a squat body and sometimes with an angular profile, actual dippers, present decoration which is slightly more complex. On the neck there is always a series of zig-zags, but on the body between the usual vertical bands there are inserted hatched triangles alternating with a series of large and small X's, emphasizing a kind of *horror vacui*. In these vessels the surface is shiny and the decoration rendered with a fine brush. The presence of one of these pitcher-dippers in the assemblage of Hut No. 2 attests the contemporaneity of this type in respect to the globular pitchers.

Pitchers

65 Muc 88/1
Pitcher with separate neck, ovoid body, slightly concave base and perhaps the attachment of a handle. Recomposed from several fragments. Band along the rim, three zig-zag lines on the neck, on the body groups of vertical bands which descend from the base of the neck to the bottom and define spaces decorated with a fringe above and with a series of three superimposed X's at the center.
H. cm. 14, mouth. diam. cm. 9.5, max. diam. cm. 13, wall thickness cm. 0.6–0.7. h. neck cm. 3.5.
Plate 16.1 and 27

66 Muc 89/97
Pitcher with separate neck, globular body, flat base and ribbon handle with vertical ring from the shoulder to the rim. Grey-pink, compact fabric; surfaces slipped in pink and painted in deep, shiny red. Recomposed from several fragments heavily burned after breakage. Exterior painted in brown on red

ground: band along the rim, two zig-zag lines on the neck; horizontal line at the base of the neck from which descends a motif of two vertical bands, pointed at the bottom, with a line in the center defining spaces decorated with a fringe above and at the center with two small superimposed X's.
H. cm. 11.5, mouth diam. cm. 7.2, max. diam. cm. 10.5, wall thickness cm. 0.6, handle length cm. 2.3, handle width cm. 1.1.
Plate 27

67 Muc 88/157
Concave base and portion of the wall of a pitcher. Hard, pink fabric, shiny surface. Decoration as Cat. No. 66: vertical bands alternating with lines delimit spaces with X's rendered with a fine brush (the X serves as a passage between the X and the butterfly).
Diam. base cm. 6, thickness cm. 0.9.
Plate 16.2

68 Muc 89/151
Pitcher with separate neck and globular body. Under the attachment for the missing handle, a circular hole. Recomposed from several fragments which were heavily burned after breakage. Decoration as Cat. No. 66 but with little butterflies instead of X's.
H. cm. 15.5, mouth diam. cm. 7.5, max. diam. cm. 14, wall thickness cm. 0.8, neck h. cm. 35.
Plate 27

69 Muc 89/143
Pitcher including fragments of the rim and of the body almost to the base. Pink-grey fabric; surfaces slipped in orange; exterior painted in dark red. Good quality fabric and elegant surfaces. Band along the rim, one wavy line on the neck, body as Cat. No. 66 but with wavy line instead of X's.
H. cm. 11.0, mouth diam. cm. 7.3, max. diam. cm. 11.5, wall thickness cm. 0.4–0.5.
Plate 27

70 Muc 89/153
Pitcher with separate neck, globular body, flat base and ribbon handle with vertical ring from the shoulder to the rim. Recomposed from several fragments. Decoration as Cat. No. 69. Wavy line on the handle.
H. cm. 14.5, mouth diam. cm. 8, max. diam. cm. 14, wall thickness cm. 0.7, handle length cm. 13, handle width cm. 2, handle thickness cm. 0.8.
Plate 27

71 Muc 89/154
Pitcher with separate neck, globular body, flat base and ribbon handle with vertical ring from the shoulder to the rim. Recomposed from several fragments

which were burned heavily after breakage. Shiny red surface. Decoration as Cat. No. 69. Wavy line on the handle.
H. cm. 12, mouth diam. cm. 7.5, max. diam. cm. 11.7, wall thickness cm. 0.6., base diam. cm. 5, h. neck cm. 3, handle length cm.11, handle width cm. 2.
Plate 28

72 Muc 89/158
Pitcher with separate neck, ovoid body, flat base and ribbon handle with vertical ring from the shoulder to the rim. Recomposed from several fragments which were heavily burned after breakage. Band along the rim, two wavy lines on the neck, body as Cat. No. 69. In one of the spaces the fringe at the shoulder is lacking.
H. cm. 14, mouth diam. cm. 6, wall thickness cm. 0.7, h. neck cm. 3.2.
Plate 28

73 Muc 89/152
Pitcher with separate neck, globular body, flat base and ribbon handle with vertical ring from the shoulder to the rim. Recomposed from several fragments which were burned after breakage. Band along the rim, zig-zag line on the neck; on the body groups of four vertical lines which descend from the shoulder to the base.
H. cm. 14, mouth diam. cm. 8.5, max. diam. cm. 13.5, wall thickness cm. 0.7, handle length cm. 12, handle width cm. 2,5, handle thickness cm. 0.8–1.0.

74 Muc 89/194
Portion of a pitcher including part of the rim and of the body to the flat base. Knob handle from the rim just above the carination. Horizontal band to the rim from which a fringe descends, horizontal line to the shoulder from which descends a motif of two vertical bands with a line in the center. Groups of horizontal lines on the handle.
H. cm. 13.

75 Muc 88/3
Portion of a pitcher, ovoid body preserved on one side and a ribbon handle with a vertical ring from the shoulder to the rim. Hatched pattern on the neck; on the body vertical bands which descend from the shoulder to the base alternate with vertical lines. On the handle a herring-bone motif and beneath the handle a hatched pattern.
Diam. mouth cm. 7, max. diam. cm. 10, wall thickness cm. 0.5–0.6, handle length cm. 10, handle width cm. 1.0.
Plate 28

76 Muc 88/22
Portion of pitcher including part of the rim and shoulder. Hatched pattern on the rim, vertical bands alternating with lines on the body.
Thickness cm. 0.4.

77 Muc 88/53
Portion of a pitcher including rim, shoulder and ribbon handle. Wavy line on the neck, vertical bands alternating with lines on the body. Ladder-pattern on the handle.
Plate 28

78 Muc 89/187
Fragmentary pitcher. Rosy fabric, dull red surface. Zig-zag line on the neck; on the body groups of four vertical lines and in the center a herring-bone pattern.
Thickness cm. 1.3.
Plate 28

79 Muc 88/115
Fragmentary jar with carinated belly lacking the lower portion. Decoration on the neck in a chain motif; on the body two vertical bands with lines at the center.
Diam. cm. 8; thickness cm. 0.7.

80 Muc 89/301
Fragment of the ovoid belly of a pitcher. Orange fabric; surfaces shiny red. Motifs consisting of a vertical band and a group of lines which converge at an angle and cross lines in the intermediate white spaces.
Thickness cm. 0.9.

Carinated Pitchers (Brocca-attingitoio)

81 Muc 88/6
Dipper with separate neck, squashed globular body, and ribbon handle with vertical ring from the shoulder to the rim. Recomposed from several fragments. Band along the rim, three zig-zag lines on the neck; on the body vertical bands which descend from the shoulder to the base alternating with vertical lines. On the handle groups of three horizontal lines.
H. cm. 9, mouth diam. cm. 10, max. diam. cm. 13, wall thickness cm. 0.5–0.6, h. neck cm. 2, handle length cm. 10, handle width cm. 0.7.
Plate 29

82 Muc 88/2
Dipper with separate neck, squashed globular body, slightly carinated concave base and enlarged ribbon handle with vertical ring from the shoulder to the rim. Recomposed from several fragments. Band along the rim, three zig-zag lines on the neck; on the body vertical bands which descend from the shoulder

to the base alternating with vertical lines. On the forward part of the body, in the place of two bands are a triangle and a hatched diamond joined at an angle. On the handle, groups of three horizontal lines, beneath the lower attachment of the handle triangles joined at an angle.
H. cm. 9, mouth diam. cm. 10.5, max. diam. cm. 12, wall thickness cm. 0.5, h. neck cm. 2.5, handle length cm. 13, handle width cm. 2.
Plate 29

83 Muc 88/80
Fragment of a strongly carinated pitcher. Rosy fabric; scaly shiny surface. Double zig-zag on the neck, on the body a vertical band and hatched triangles joined at an angle with crossing lines and X's in the intermediate white space.
Cm. 6x7, thickness cm. 0.6.
Plate 29

84 Muc 91/62
Fragment of carinated pitcher. Shiny surface. Vertical band and lines, two hatched triangles joined at an angle with X's in the intermediate white space.
Thickness cm. 0.65.

85 Muc 89/98–308
Portion of a strongly carinated pitcher. Rosy fabric, scaly shiny surface. Double zig-zag painted on the neck; on the body, two vertical bands with a line at the center; composition of three hatched triangles and crossing lines in the intermediate white space.
Thickness cm. 0.6.
Plate 29

86 Muc 88/89 and 88/90
Fragments of a carinated pitcher. Rosy fabric, scaly shiny surface. Vertical bands alternating with lines, two elements of a triple hatched triangle and crossing lines below.
Thickness cm. 0.6.

87 Muc 91/102
Fragment of a carinated pitcher. Vertical band and line and a composition of four hatched diamonds.
Thickness cm. 0.7.
Plate 33

88 Muc 91/119
Fragment of a carinated pitcher. Vertical band and line; hatched diamond and lines crossed in a star in the intermediate white space.
Thickness cm. 0.6.
Plate 33

89 Muc 88/59
Fragment of a carinated pitcher. Fringe from the shoulder, vertical band and two hatched diamonds.
Thickness cm. 0.6.

Jug (Orcio)

90 Muc 89/90
Portion of a large jug including part of the neck and of the shoulder. Ribbon handle from the neck to the shoulder. Band along the rim, four zig-zag lines on the neck, vertical bands on the body alternating with thin lines; beneath the neck part of a hatched area perhaps a triangle upside down; groups of four horizontal lines on the handle.
Dia. mouth cm. 14.0, wall thickness cm. 0.9, neck thickness cm. 1.1, handle length cm. 4.3, handle width cm. 2.
Plate 30

91 Muc 89/131
Fragment of the neck, vertical ribbon handle and shoulder of a jug. Double zig-zag decoration on the neck; on the shoulder a group of three vertical lines and a series of triangles arranged vertically and joined to the base.
Wall thickness cm. 1.0, neck h. cm. 8, neck width cm. 1.2, handle length cm. 13, handle width cm. 5, handle thickness cm. 1.0.
Plate 30

92 Muc 89/146
Fragment of the neck, vertical ribbon handle and shoulder of a jug. Zig-zag decoration painted on the neck; on the shoulder vertical bands, on the handle a ladder-pattern.
Wall thickness cm. 1.0, h. neck cm. 7, neck width cm. 1.0.

93 Muc 89/144
Portion of a large jug or amphora including fragments of the neck, the shoulder and a vertical ribbon handle. On the neck: horizontal band along the rim, vertical lines next to the handle, two shorter vertical lines in the center, two curving horizontal lines on the lower part and a vertical line which descends from the center of these and presents at the sides two large dots surrounded by smaller dots. The decoration appears to present a stylized face with the schematic indication of eyes, eyebrows and nose; to the side of the face and of the hair a bang defines the brow. On the lower part of the vessel's neck the usual triple zig-zag descending near the hair. On the shoulder vertical bands with a line in the center and groups of four horizontal lines on the handle. Traces of the repeti-

tion of the hair on the opposite side of the neck leads one to infer the presence of a second face.
Dia. mouth cm. 12.0, wall thickness cm. 0.5–0.7, neck h. cm. 7, neck width cm. 0.7.
Plates 16.3 and 30 and volume cover.

Amphorae

94 Muc 89/150
Amphora with separate neck, globular body and two vertical ribbon handles from the rim to the shoulder. Recomposed from various fragments; lacking part of the body and the base. Band along the rim; on the neck a band of reserved diamonds; on the body groups of two vertical bands which descend from the shoulder to the base defining spaces which are decorated in the middle with long double wavy lines which cross the entire body. On the handle a butterfly motif and three horizontal lines.
H. cm. 15.5., mouth diam. cm. 7.5, max. diam. cm. 14, wall thickness cm. 0.8, h. neck cm. 3.5.
Plate 31

95 Muc 88/112
Probable amphora including separate neck, globular body and the attachment of a handle. Recomposed from various fragments; lacking part of the body. Exterior barely legible because of the burning: traces of a triple zig-zag line on the neck; on the body a group of four vertical lines which descend from the shoulder to the base and vertical bands with lines to the side connected by an X; beneath the handle a hatched triangle pattern with the vertex at the base.
H. cm. 25, mouth diam. cm. 14, wall thickness cm. 1.0, h. neck cm. 7.

Pitcher or Amphora Fragments

96 Muc 88/110
Neck fragment with five zig-zag lines.
Diam. cm. 12, thickness cm. 0.8.
Plate 32

97 Muc 88/21
Neck fragment with a horizontal band along the rim and a curl which descends toward the base.
Diam. cm. 16 ca.
Plate 32

98 Muc 91/61
Neck fragment from a jar. Shiny surface. Band on the rim, four zig-zag lines, and beneath them another band; above the zig-zag lines an eye-motif with lashes and a circle in the center as a pupil.
Diam. cm. 10, thickness cm. 0.5.
Plate 32

99 Muc 89/197
Neck fragment from a jar with the attachment for a ribbon handle. Horizontal band on the rim and a chain-motif.
Diam. cm. 8, thickness cm. 0.8.

100 Muc 91/65
Neck fragment. Painted horizontal band along the rim, chain-motif and band beneath it.
Diam. cm. 25, thickness cm. 0.8.

101 Muc 89/441
Portion of a pitcher including part of the rim and of the shoulder. Wolf's-tooth motif at the rim, on the body group of three lines descending from a vertical line. Trace of a brush along the interior of the rim. See below for technical aspects.
Diam. cm. 8, thickness cm. 0.7.
Plate 19.1 (interior)

102 Muc 89/263
Portion of a pitcher. Zig-zag painted on the rim; on the body a band from which descend vertical bands and three wolf's-tooth motifs with a wavy line.
Diam. cm. 10, thickness cm. 0.7.
Plate 16.4

103 Muc 89/203
Shoulder fragment perhaps from a large amphora. Vertical band which seems thin bordered with lines and wolf's-tooth motifs and from which descends a wavy line pair.
Thickness cm. 1.5.
Plate 32

104 Muc 89/195
Shoulder fragment. Two vertical bands with a line in the center and wolf's-tooth motifs which separate these elements.
Thickness cm. 8.
Plate 32

105 Muc 89/259
Belly fragment from an ovoid pitcher. Painted vertical ladder-pattern, double vertical lines, and a band of reserved diamonds.
Thickness cm. 0.7.

106 Muc 89/182
Portion of the neck and shoulder of an ovoid pitcher. Double zig-zag line on the neck; on the body three

wolf's-tooth motifs alternating with three vertical lines.

Thickness cm. 0.6.

Plate 32

107 Muc 89/205

Part of the rim with a separate neck and enlarged shoulder belonging perhaps to a large amphora. Shiny red fabric. Decoration hardly visible: on the neck a double zig-zag line; on the shoulder vertical lines alternating with a fringe.

Cm. 14x17, max. diam. very large, thickness cm. 1.5.

Plate 32

108 Muc 88/192

Part of the rim with a separate neck and enlarged shoulder belonging perhaps to a large amphora. On the neck a band with reserved diamonds; on the shoulder vertical lines alternating with a wavy line and wolf's-tooth pattern.

Diam. cm. 26, thickness cm. 1.4.

Comparisons

The small globular pitcher is a very common form at S. Ippolito, and it is present also at Settefarine, in the Infame Diavolo cave, at Mizzebi, at Adrano in the first phase and, to a lesser extent, at Naro; it is also found in the necropolis at Malpasso (Calascibetta)[85]. The series of zig-zag lines on the neck, sometimes even superimposed one upon another, is found at Manfria (Gela), Mizzebbi, Adrano, and in the Sanctuary at La Muculufa[86]. The vertical bands alternating with lines and the bands narrowing toward the base are encountered at Adrano in Phases I and II and in the Vecchiuzzo Cave (Petralia Sottana)[87]. The decorative motif of bands which descend vertically and which delimit metopal spaces with butterflies is attested at Naro[88]. The

motif of the bands with a vertical central line with the fringe-pattern is seen on a small pitcher from Poggio Biddini[89], while the fringe-pattern on the shoulder alternating with vertical lines appears at Mizzebbi, as well as at Settefarine where there is also the motif of the wolf's-tooth pattern with alternating lines[90]. The motif of X's delimited by bands is found in the Infame Diavolo cave[91].

For the carinated pitcher a comparison can be made with a vessel from Manfria both for its form and especially for its decorative elements: the zig-zag on the neck and the bands which alternate with lines and with a triangle which bears a checker-board motif[92].

Jars with Modeled Handles

Characteristic of the village, even though they are not very common, are the cylindrical jars with two horseshoe-shaped or quadrangular lugs. The fragmentary character of the examples does not permit us to know if the bases of the jars were flat or set on a foot. The decoration consists of vertical hatched bands alternating with spaces decorated with lines or chains. Vessels with a quadrangular lug are found at S. Ippolito, Mezzebbi and in the first phase at Adrano. The modeled horeseshoe lug is another element present also in the Malpasso style[93]. The jar can be interpreted as a drinking vessel.

109 Muc 89/159

Cylindrical jar with two modeled quadrangular handles. Dull surface. Vertical hatched bands alternating

---

[85] Bernabò Brea (here n.80) fig. 12a, 13a, c, f, h; Orsi (here n.80) plate XII, 10, 11; De Miro (here n.80) fig. 10, f; Privitera (here n.80) fig. 10; Cultraro (here n.80) form D1; Tusa-Pacci (here n.80) plate XII, d, cat. 75; Albanese (here n.80) 193, fig. 7.4, variant D.

[86] P. Orlandini, Il villaggio preistorico di Manfria presso Gela, Palermo, 1962, plate 49, fig. 3–4, plate 28, fig. 1; Privitera (here n.80); Cultraro (here n.80) plate 15, 5, 3, phases II, III; at Castelluccio, the zig-zag motif is on the neck of the amphorae; cf. Sluga Messina (here n.81), p.134; Muculufa I, p.23.

[87] Cultraro (here n.80), plate 101, plate 15, 5 (Adrano), plate 101 (Grotta Pellegriti); J. Bovio Marconi, La grotta del Vecchiuzzo, Roma, 1979, p.82.

[88] M. Pacci, "Lo stile "protocastelluciano" di Naro," Rivista di Scienze Preistoriche 37, 1982, p.187ff., fig. 2.1 and fig. 5.1.

[89] G. Di Stefano, Piccola guida delle stazioni preistoriche degli Iblei, Ragusa, 1984, p.153.

[90] Privitera (here n.80) fig. 11; Orsi (here n.80) plate XII, 10 and 11.

[91] De Miro (here n.80) fig. 7: 912.

[92] Orlandini (here n.86) plate 49, fig. 4 (from the Lavore test-pit in association with a bell-beaker fragment) it is very similar to vessel Cat. No. 76. See also Muculufa I, p.23, fig. 34.

[93] Bernabò Brea (here n.80) fig. 13.1; Privitera (here n.80); Cultraro (here n.80) form A1. For a vessel of the Malpasso style, see De Miro (here n.80) fig. 8: 913 and 989 and L. Maniscalco, "L'età del rame nel territorio di Milena," in La Preistoria del basso Belice e della Sicilia meridionale nel quadro della preistoria siciliana e mediterranea (forthcoming).

with a vertical chain; on the handles above there are zig-zag lines and on the sides horizontal dashes.
H. cm. 10, diam. cm. 12, wall thickness cm. 0.8.
Plate 33

110 Muc 89/199
Cylindrical jar, with two quadrangular modeled handles and an irregular, perhaps ovoid, mouth. Dull surface. Vertical hatched bands alternating with full bands.
H. cm. 8, diam. cm.14, wall thickness cm. 0.8.
Plate 16.5

111 Muc 89/175
Fragment of the rim of a cylindrical jar. Lines and a band which descend from the rim; semicircular modeled handles and part of a vertical ribbon handle below.
Diam. cm. 15, thickness cm. 0.8.

112 Muc 91/95
Fragment of the rim of a jar with a modeled handle which is not bordered. Fabric pink-grey and hard. Black line along the rim and a wedge-motif which descends from the rim toward the base.
Diam. cm.8, thickness cm. 0.7.

Quadrangular Vessels

At La Muculufa there are body fragments from quadrangular vessels which stood on supports and fragments of supports which may belong to other quadrangular vessels[94]. The best preserved quadrangular vessel (Cat. No. 114) is decorated with the usual hatched bands alternating with wavy lines and wolf's-tooth patterns. It does not show traces of fire, and perhaps it was a container not for foodstuffs but served as a type of pyxis.

113 Muc 89/173+46
Quadrangular vessel on two lateral supports of which only one is preserved. Cream colored base bordered in red. Painted decoration well preserved on the front including a band along the rim, vertical hatched bands alternating with three wavy lines and at the corner a series of wolf's-tooth motifs; below, a horizontal band. Traces of wolf's-tooth motifs and wavy lines on the side.
H. cm. 28, width cm. 38, depth cm. 26, thickness cm. 1.5–2.0.
Plate 34

114 Muc 89/156
Fragments belonging to a quadrangular vessel. Decoration painted in vertical bands alternating with groups of lines and bands with reserved diamonds on the interior and a reserved zig-zag line.
H. cm. 13, thickness cm. 1.2.
Plate 34

115 Muc 89/312+317
Fragments belonging probably to a single quadrangular vessel. Only parts of the rim, the side and the base are preserved. Ivory fabric, yellowish surface with decorative motif in brown. Along the rim triangles and diamonds bordered in white; on the side below a double wavy line, vertical bands and at the extremities a series of vertical reserved wolf's-tooth motifs in white. Trichromatic decoration in brown, ivory and white. On the base part of a semicircular attachment.
Thickness cm.1.8.

116 Muc 88/120
Fragment of the foot with a triangular base and a portion of the interior trough perhaps of a quadrangular vessel. Yellowish fabric. Surface painted in red; motif in black triangles below to the sides and a reserved zig-zag band at the corner.
H. cm. 14, wall thickness of the trough cm. 1.5.
Plate 34

117 Muc 89/314
Fragment of the foot perhaps of a quadrangular vessel. Surface painted in red and a series of inverted triangles in black with hatched decoration.
H. cm. 4.5, thickness cm. 1.8.

Cups

The cup with the vertical tongue handle (Cat. No. 118) is unusual in the Sicilian repertory. Cups of similar shape are found at S.Ippolito, but for the tongue the only parallel is with the Borg In-Nadur pottery of Malta[95].

---

[94] A many-footed vessel came from Contrada Marcita; see S. Tusa and I. Valente, "Società e culture nel Belice fra la fine del III ed il II millennio a.C.," in La Preistoria del basso Belice e della Sicilia meridionale nel quadro della preistoria siciliana e mediterranea (forthcoming).

[95] Bernabò Brea (here n.80), fig. 13: m; J. Evans, The Prehistoric Antiquities of the Maltese Islands, London, 1971, p.17, fig. 3, 1–2-3; see also the semi-ovoid cup from Malpasso, cf. Albanese (here n.80) p.191, fig. 7.1 and fig. 13.2–3.

descend along the body. Under the surmounted handle there is always an X; on the rims of pedestal bowls there are saw-motifs, on the bowls themselves there are diamond-chains, and on the foot there are panels with series of wavy-lines. Various fragments present checker-board motifs, eye-motifs and, exceptionally, circular motifs.

Dipper-Cup(tazza-attingitoio)

137 Muc 89/118
Rim, shoulder and carinated belly of a dipper-cup. Band beneath the rim, two horizontal bands include long panels with horizontal lines alternating with short spaces and vertical lines; below a horizontal band from which descend a vertical line ending in a drop and a large band, perhaps a wedge.
Diam. cm. 10, thickness cm. 0.6.
Plate 35

138 Muc 91/120
Portion of a dipper-cup. Decoration as Cat. No. 137. On the handle groups of vertical lines, an X at the lower attachment of the handle.
Diam. cm. 10, thickness cm. 0.6.
Plate 35

139 Muc 91/81
Rim fragment, shoulder and carinated belly probably of a dipper-cup. Band beneath the rim, two horizontal bands enclose a long panel with hatching; below a horizontal band from which descends a large wedge.
Diam. cm. 7, thickness cm. 0.6.

140 Muc 91/84
Rim fragment, shoulder and carinated belly probably of a dipper-cup. Band beneath the rim; two horizontal bands enclose a long panel with hatching alternating with short spaces with vertical lines; below a horizontal line from which descend vertical lines, a band and a hatched band.
H cm. 7, diam. cm. 8, thickness cm. 0.6.
Plate 35

141 Muc 91/66
Fragment of the shoulder and belly probably of a dipper-cup. Panel with a checker-board pattern, near vertical lines; below a horizontal line from which descends a large wedge and a vertical line.
Thickness cm. 0.5.
Plate 35

142 Muc 91/40
Rim fragment, shoulder and carinated belly probably of a dipper-cup. Band along the rim; two horizontal bands enclose a panel with zig-zags with dashes alternating with vertical lines; below a horizontal band from which descends a vertical line terminating in a drop.
Diam. cm. 12, thickness cm. 0.6.
Plate 17.2

143 Muc 89/282
Rim fragment, shoulder and carinated belly probably of a dipper-cup. Band along the rim; panel with zig-zag; vertical lines within a double line which continues in the panel; below a horizontal line from which descend a double line and bands.
Diam. cm. 10, thickness cm. 0.4.

144 Muc 89/279
Fragment of the shoulder and carinated belly probably of a dipper-cup. Panel with zig-zag and with dashes; below a horizontal band from which descends a checkerboard panel.
Thickness cm. 0.4.

145 Muc 91/47
Rim fragment, shoulder and carinated belly of a dipper-cup. Band beneath the rim; two horizontal bands enclose a long panel with hatching; below a horizontal band from which descends a vertical line terminating in a drop.
Thickness cm. 0.6.

146 Muc 89/276
Fragment of the shoulder and belly probably of a dipper-cup. Fabric grey, compact and hard; surfaces shiny red (Munsell 10R 5/8). Double vertical lines interrupted by a double horizontal line to the base of the shoulder from which descend vertical lines with an elongated wedge at the center.
Thickness cm. 0.7.
Plate 35

Pedestal Bowls

147 Muc 89/284
Rim fragment of a pedestal bowl. Along the rim a fringe and below the begining of a diamond-chain with dashes.
Diam. cm. 32 ca.; thickness cm. 1.5.
Plate 36

148 Muc 91/106
Fragment of the bowl of a pedestal bowl. Dense fabric. Interior surface painted with a large X, exterior with groups of hatched lines. Hole probably for restoration near the rim.
Thickness cm. 1.5.

149 Muc 89/290 and 288

Fragments belonging to the base and the bottom of the bowl of a pedestal bowl. Shiny red surface (10R 4/8). Horizontal lines with a wavy line in the middle at the attachment of the base and the bowl, groups of vertical lines in the base and on the exterior of the bowl, black painted quadrangular lug handle and above a checkerboard panel.
Thickness cm. 2; h cm.13
Plate 36

150 Muc 91/44

Fragment of a basin with the beginning of the base of a pedestal bowl. Ring at the attachment. On the base a series of butterfly-motifs; on the bowl exterior groups of vertical lines; on the interior a hatched cross with a regular empty square at the center.
Thickness cm. 1.1.
Plate 17.3

151 Muc 91/56

Fragment of a bowl with the beginning of a base of a pedestal bowl. On the exterior groups of vertical lines alternating with double wavy lines with points at both sides.
Thickness cm. 1.0.
Plate 36

152 Muc 91/69

Fragment of the pedestal of a pedestal bowl. Two vertical panels filled with horizontal wavy lines and a diamond-chain in the white spaces in between.
Thickness cm. 1.0.

153 Muc 89/285

Fragment of the pedestal probably of a pedestal bowl. Two vertical panels filled with horizontal wavy lines; leaf-motifs in the white spaces in between.
Thickness cm. 1.0.
Plate 36

Other Fragments

154 Muc 89/291

Fragment of an extroverted rim. Band along the rim, below horizontal hatched band with a reserved zig-zag.
Diam. cm. 14, thickness cm. 7.0.
Plate 35

155 Muc 89/286

Fragment of a rim belonging to a closed form. Band along the rim; below, a horizontal band beneath which oblique spaces filled with parallel lines.
Diam. cm. 26, thickness cm. 1.0.
Plate 35

156 Muc 88/145

Fragment of an extroverted rim. Band along the rim; below four rows of squashed concentric circles. Shiny red surface.
Diam. cm. 18 ca., thickness cm. 0.7.

157 Muc 88/253

Fragment of an extroverted rim. Band along the rim, below irregular diamond chain with lashes and a metopal space with horizontal zig-zag lines. Shiny red surface.
Diam. cm. 10 ca., thickness cm. 1.1.
Plate 37

158 Muc 91/103

Body fragment. Two wavy vertical lines ending with eye-motif.
Thickness cm. 1.0.
Plate 37

159 Muc 91/117

Body fragment. Double wavy vertical lines ending with eye-motifs.
Thickness cm. 1.0.
Plate 37

160 Muc 91/41

Body fragment. Horizontal zig-zag line with dashes ending with eye-motifs.
Thickness cm. 5.0.
Plate 37

161 Muc 91/80

Attachment of a surmounted handle with the beginning of another little handle towards the base. On both sides there is black ground and a reserved space with two diamond chains crossing.
Thickness cm. 1.5.
Plate 37

162 Muc 89/289

Fragment of a ribbon handle with a hole at the center. Shiny red surface, on the sides a saw motif.
Length cm. 14, thickness cm. 2.0.
Plate 37

163 Muc 88/247

Ribbon handle. Surface red, motifs painted in black: two vertical bands including a irregular diamond chain with lashes as Cat. No. 158.
Length cm. 14, thickness cm. 2.0.
Plate 17.5

These ceramics, in particular the dippers, are very similar to those which have been found at La Muculufa in the Sanctuary zone[99]. Dippers which are closely comparable in form and decoration have been found also at Naro (Agrigento), Manfria (Gela), the Ticchiara cave (Favara), the Pietrarossa cave, contrada Passarello (Campobello di Licata), Canicattì, Palmintelli (Caltanissetta), and contrada Ragusetta and other sites in the territory of Palma di Montechiaro[100]. In particular, the metopal space with the hatched pattern is found in the Sanctuary, the checkerboard pattern at Ragusetta and at Canicattì, and the zig-zag line (Cat. No. 143) is found at Palmintelli. The pendular-drop motif and the handle with an 'X' on the lower attachment are found in the Sanctuary at La Muculufa and at Canicattì. The zig-zag with dashes (Cat. Nos. 143 and 144) appears in the Sanctuary at La Muculufa, at Monte S. Giuliano (Caltanissetta), at Manfria, Castelluccio (Noto), Santa Febbronia (Palagonia), Adrano and Biancavilla. In terms of surface, fabric and several decorative patterns (the zig-zag with dashes, the wedge) the dippers resemble ceramics of the Copper Age Serraferlicchio style[101]. The form of the dippers is similar to a type of the initial phase of the Capo Graziano style in the Aeolian islands and to the dipper-cups of the earliest phase at Ciavolaro (Ribera) considered by G. Castellana to be contemporary with the ceramics of La Muculufa[102].

The diamond chain is one of the most interesting motifs in the Castelluccian decorative repetoire which is found on pedestal bowls and one which has been attributed a figurative meaning by Sluga Messina. It is found in the La Muculufa Sanctuary, at Casalicchio, Manfria, Castelluccio, Monte Tabuto, Santa Febbronia and across the region of Mount Etna. The saw-motif of fragment Cat. No. 162 recurs at the Sanctuary, and at Monte San Giuliano (Caltanissetta)[103].

Circular motifs are very rare in the Castelluccian repertory: the unique series of concentric circles on rim fragment Cat. No. 156 is similar to a motif on a rim from the Sanctuary where circular motifs are uncommon[104].

These ceramics evidently constitute a group which is stylistically different from the rest of the ceramics in the village, especially in the decorative motifs which are richer and rendered with greater care, sometimes in such a way as to recall vegetation (e.g., Cat. Nos. 151 and 153). Finding an appropriate label for the ceramic styles present at La Muculufa is problematic in the sense that the ceramics themselves are not mutually exclusive in form, decoration or function and any single term remains inherently rigid both in regard to the present material and in regard to future finds. Since the 1950's the term 'S. Ippolito' and 'Naro' have become a standard part of archaeological literature through the publication of L. Bernabò Brea's insightful book *Sicily before the Greeks*. While 'S. Ippolito' referred to material dated to the Copper Age and found in

---

[99] Muculufa I, p.23, fig. 35, 43, b, d.

[100] Tusa-Pacci (here n.80) entry 55; Orlandini (here n.86) plate 15,2 and plate 47,1; Favara, Pietrarossa, Passarello, Canicattì: M. Pacci, "Nota su alcuni vasi protocastellucciani della Sicilia occidentale conservati all'Ashmolean Museum di Oxford," I Quaderni di Sicilia Archeologica, I, 1987, p.7–38, 23, figs 3–6; Palmintelli : R. Panvini, Da Nissa a Maktorion, Nuovi contributi per l'archeologia della provincia di Caltanissetta, show catalog, Museo Civico, Caltanissetta, 23 June—30 September, 1990, fig. 6; De Miro (here n.80) fig. 17, d.g. and Castellana (here n.83), fig. XLIV.

[101] Muculufa I, motif AA; (Monte S.Giuliano) P. Orlandini, "Statuette preistoriche della prima età del bronzo da Caltanissetta," Bollettino d'Arte n.s. 2–3, 1968, p.55–59, fig.3; Orlandini (here n.86) plate 10, figure 2; Sluga Messina (here n.81) 143 with comparisons which, however, are not convincing; Cultraro (here n.80) plate 102, Phase V; P.E. Arias, "La stazione preistorica di Serraferlicchio presso Agrigento," Monumenti Antichi dei Lincei 36, 1938, col. 816ff., figs. 103, 88. See below n.138.

[102] Capo Graziano: Bernabò Brea (here n.83) fig. 49, g.; Ciavolaro : G. Castellana, "Recenti acquisizioni preistoriche nel versante orientale del basso Belice con riferimento ai nuovi dati delle ricerche nel territorio agrigentino," in La Preistoria del basso Belice e della Sicilia meridionale nel quadro della preistoria siciliana e mediterranea, (forthcoming).

[103] Diamond chain: Muculufa I, "Z" motifs p.24, figs. 23, 24, 30; F. Gnesotto, "Il sito preistorico di Casalicchio-Agnone in territorio di Licata, (Agrigento)," Studi in onore di Ferrante Rittatore Vonwiller, Parte prima Vol.I, 1982, p.195–219, fig.7; Orlandini (here n.86); Castelluccio e Grotta Maniace: Sluga Messina (here n.81) 127; F. Pennavaria, "Grotte sepolcrali sicule a Colle Tabuto nel territorio di Ragusa (prov. di Siracusa)," Bullettino di Paletnologia Italiana 21, 1895, p.160–66, plate VI, 8; Cultraro (here n.80) fase III; Paternò: E. Recami, C. Mignosa, and R. Baldini, "Nuovo contributo sulla preistoria della Sicilia," Sicilia Archeologica 16, 1983, p.45–82; Bronte: A. Consoli, "Bronte- Maletto. Prima esplorazione e saggi di scavo archeologico nelle contrade, Balze soprane, S. Venera, Edera e Tartaraci," Beni Culturali ed Ambientali Sicilia 9–10, 1988–89, p.76, fig.2. Saw-motif Muculufa I, fig.32, Orlandini (here n.101) fig.3.

[104] Muculufa I, fig.22 d; complex circular pattern are also at Monte S.Giuliano, see Orlandini (here n.101) fig.3; Sluga Messina (here n.81) p.157 attributes a ritual meaning to the circular motifs of the bossed-bone plaques.

the region of Caltagirone, 'Naro' was included in the more general framework of a Naro-Partanna style of the Castelluccian culture with a distribution ranging from south-central to western Sicily. S. Tusa and M. Pacci, in a recent study of ceramics from the site of Naro now in Palermo, have demonstrated that the Castelluccian ceramics of Naro and Partanna have clearly different characteristics – these authors define the style of Naro on the basis solely of the ceramics from that site[105].

The typological study of the painted ceramics from the village of La Muculufa demonstrates the existence of two groups with different stylistic characteristics. On the basis of the comparisons illustrated above with the materials already called 'Naro' by Tusa and Pacci, this author chooses to apply the term 'Naro' to the restricted group of finely painted vessels; all of the rest clearly enter into the group defined previously by Bernabò Brea as 'S. Ippolito'.

In both cases a stylistic group of pottery with a homogeneous aspect in terms of technique, shape and decoration distinguishable in the general context of the Castelluccian culture is intended, and neither the style of 'S. Ippolito' nor that of 'Naro' is meant to be a distinct cultural *facies*. The clear difference between the two extremes represented by these groups, evident indeed in the 'Naro' dipper Cat. No. 138 and the 'S. Ippolito' pitcher Cat. No. 70, is not as evident for several ceramics which may be considered to be intermediate types, such as the carinated pitcher. On the other hand, even in their diversity, the ceramics of the 'S. Ippolito' and 'Naro' styles at La Muculufa present a similar decorative scheme: vertical bands which descend to the shoulder from a horizontal band.

The 'Naro' style pottery from Hut No. 3 upper comes from a very limited area in portion F134 in what appeared to be generally a 'S.Ippolito' style context. Is it possible to think of some sort of cache of 'Naro' vessels? Perhaps the 'Naro' vessels were in a basket or in a box kept for special uses or occasions in the manner of a special service (the 'good plates')? The ceramics of the 'Naro' style are distinguished, in fact, by a greater accuracy both in production and in decoration, and it is not by chance that at La Mu-

culufa only the pedestal bowls of this style show holes for restoration in antiquity.

Ceramics with a Red Polished Surface

A small group of fragments is painted with a highly shiny red polished surface which seems similar to that of fine Malpasso ware. The forms attested are the pedestal bowl on a low foot, several hemispherical cups, several triangular tongues and fragments of handles perhaps from part of a type of Malpasso semi-ovoid cup, and a handle in the form of an elephant's head of a type known in the Aeolian Islands during the Copper Age[106].

164 Muc 89/76
Portion of a hemispherical cup. Fabric pink (purified?); interior surface pink, exterior surface shiny coralline red.
Diam. cm. 10, thickness cm. 0.5.
Plates 17.4 and 39

165 Muc 88/178
Portion of a hemispherical cup. Red fabric, exterior surface shiny red badly preserved.
Diam. cm. 14, thickness cm. 0.5.

166 Muc 88/196
Triangular tongue with a rounded point. Broken off at the base. Shiny red surface; rather abraded, grey-red fabric.
H. cm. 2.3, width cm. 3.5, thickness cm. 0.5.

167 Muc 88/61
Portion of the base of a pedestal bowl and part of the bottom of the bowl with the attachment of ribbon handle on the bowl. Dense pink fabric; surface shiny red.
H. cm. 9, diam. cm. 11.5, thickness cm. 1.2.
Plate 39

---

[105] See Tusa-Pacci (here n.80) p.106; for a discussion of the 'Naro' style, especially in regard to the dipper see Pacci (here n.101) p. 23.

[106] For the Malpasso semiovoid cup see Albanese (here n.80) fig. 13.3 and 15.3; for the elephant's head handle see L. Bernabò Brea and M. Cavalier, Meligunis Lipara IV, L'acropoli di Lipari nella preistoria, Palermo, 1980, plate CVII, 2, e; A. Cazzella, "Considerazioni su alcuni aspetti eneolitici dell'Italia Meridionale e della Sicilia," Origini 6, 1972, p.171–298, esp. p.254 with an Aegean parallel—Keos Kephala in a Final Neolithic-Early Bronze Age context.

168 Muc 89/272

Handle in a form resembling an elephant's head on a short body fragment. Dense pink fabric; surface shiny red.

H. cm.3.5, thickness cm. 0.5

Plates 17.4 and 39

In the same polished technique are also three fragments of hemispherical cups painted in a very elegant manner with hatched triangles bordered in white[107].

169 Muc 88/164

Rim fragment pertaining perhaps to a hemispherical cup. Reddish fabric, surface shiny red. Two triangles with vertex below and a hatched pattern below a hatched band. All of the black lines are bordered in white.

Diam. cm. 20, thickness cm. 0.6.

Plate 18.1

170 Muc 88/268

Rim fragment probably of a cup as Cat. No. 171

Diam. cm. 18, thickness cm. 0.6

171 Muc 89/148

Body fragment similar to Cat. No. 171. Reddish fabric, surface shiny red with two oblique bands in brown; a horizontal white line crosses them, and above part of a hatched triangle with the vertex downward. All of the black lines are bordered in white.

Cm. 5.1 x 4.2, thickness cm. 0.6–0.7.

Fragments with Incised Decoration

Very rare, and represented by only small fragments, is a ware with a grey or red surface which is finely incised. The decorative motifs, hatched bands, are similar to those of the painted ceramics. The only recognizable form is a dish on a low base.

172 Muc 88/64

Rim fragment. Fabric grey-pink, surface pink, incised hatched band.

Thickness cm. 0.6.

Plate 18.2

173 Muc 88/65

Fragment. Fabric grey, surface pink-grey, incised hatched band.

Thickness cm. 0.6.

Plate 18.2

174 Muc 88/66

Fragment. Fabric grey, surface pink-grey, oblique band with incised checkerboard design and multiple angles.

Thickness cm. 0.5.

Plate 18.2

175 Muc 88/67

Fragment. Fabric grey, surface pink-grey, incised hatched X-motif.

Thickness cm. 0.6.

Plate 18.2

176 Muc 89/193

Wall fragment and the attachment of a ribbon handle. Fabric and surfaces grey. Incised decoration in a series of horizontal lines.

Thickness cm. 0.8.

Plate 18.2

177 Muc 89/246

Wall fragment. Fabric and surfaces pink-orange. Incised decoration consisting of three vertical hatched bands.

Thickness cm. 0.6.

Plate 18.2

178 Muc 89/283

Wall fragment. Fabric and surfaces brown (Munsell 5YR 5/3). Incised decoration in a hatched band and a series of vertical lines; cf. Cat. No. 179.

Thickness cm. 1.0.

Plate 18.2

179 Muc 89/297

Rim fragment. Fabric and surfaces brown (Munsell 7YR 6/4). Incised decoration consisting of a hatched band and a series of vertical lines.

Thickness cm. 1.1.

Plates 18.2 and 37.

180 Muc 89/298

Wall fragment. Fabric and surfaces pink-white (Munsell 10YR 8/3). Incised decoration consisting of a hatched checkerboard.

Thickness cm. 1.0.

Plate 18.2

181 Muc 89/354

Portion of the base and wall of a plate or pedestal bowl. Fabric pink grey, surfaces pink. Incised decoration consisting of hatched squares, perhaps a checkerboard.

Thickness cm. 1.5.

Plate 38

---

[107] For another example also from the village at La Muculufa, see Muculufa I, fig. 29.

182 Muc 89/353

Wall fragment perhaps belonging to no. 181. Fabric pink grey, surfaces pink. Incised decoration in a hatched checkerboard.

Thickness cm. 1.1.

Plate 38

183 Muc 91/93

Fragment probably of a plate. Fabric and surfaces grey. Two incised bands with a hatched pattern alternating with vertical lines.

Thickness cm. 1.4.

Plate 38

184 Muc 89/316

Fragment of a straight rim. Fabric grey, surfaces shiny grey. Incised decoration in a metopal space filled with a zig-zag and delimited by groups of horizontal and vertical lines.

Diam. cm. 10, thickness cm. 0.7.

Plate 18.3

185 Muc 91/54

Wall fragment. Surface dull black. Double line which crosses itself delimited by a double horizontal line.

Thickness cm. 0.8.

186 Muc 89/299

Group of three wall fragments probably pertaining to the same vessel. Fabric and surfaces black. Incised decoration in thin hatched bands.

Thickness cm. 0.6.

Ceramics with hatched incisions are found at Settefarine, Mezzebbi, Castelluccio, at Monte Tabuto and in the Chiusazza cave (Syracuse)[108]. Incised ceramics of this type have been considered to be of the Tarxien Cemetery type imported from Malta. This is without doubt the case for ceramics from Ognina (Syracuse)[109] and perhaps in the nearby Chiusazza cave. In the other examples, instead, it should be considered a local production stylistically relat-

ed to that of Moarda. Eloquent evidence for this may be seen in the motif and the form of the rim (Cat. No. 184) and of the fragments of a dish (Cat. Nos. 181–182) which recall very closely vessels from Moarda in the bell-beaker tradition[110].

The ceramics with a red polished surface and the incised pottery do not seem belong to a different phase in the life of the Castelluccian village. These ceramics, even though rare in quantity, are associated, sometimes together, in strata with almost all the other forms illustrated in this catalog including the Naro style pottery.

Undecorated Vessels

The undecorated ceramics constitute slightly more than half of the ceramic material found in the village, although the proportion from the huts is more in favor of the painted ceramics. The greater part of these ceramics includes vessels of large dimension, at least to judge from the thickness of the wall inasmuch as they have not been restored, and one may recognize them as being ribbed pithoi with cross motifs[111]. Among the few vessels of smaller dimension are a pitcher, a dipper and a cup with a tongue (Cat. Nos. 187–190). Among the handles there is an example of a bobbin-handle (*ansa a rocchetto*, Cat. No. 212) which is

---

[108] Orsi (here n.80) plate XII, 1; Privitera (here n.80); P. Orsi, "Scarichi del villaggio siculo di Castelluccio," Bullettino di Paletnologia Italiana 19, 1893, p.30–51, plate V, 45/46; Sluga Messina (here n.81) p.92; Pennavaria (here n.103) plate VI, 3; S. Tinè, "Gli scavi nella grotta della Chiusazza," Bullettino di Paletnologia Italiana 74, n.s. 16, 1965, p.123–286, plate XXXI, 3 and fig. 15, plate XXXII, 6. In the Novalucello cave near Catania there is a ceramic with impressed decoration with crosses; cf. S. Tinè, "Giacimenti dell'età del rame in Sicilia e la "cultura tipo Conca d'oro," Bullettino di Paletnologia Italiana 13, 1960, p.113–137, plate V, 8. For the incised pottery from the village of la Muculufa see Holloway 1983, fig.6 and Muculufa I, p.31.

[109] L. Bernabò Brea, "Abitato neolitico e insediamento maltese del bronzo nell'isola di Ognina (Siracusa) e rapporti tra la Sicilia e Malta dal XVI al XIII sec. a.C.," Kokalos 12, 1966, p.40–69, plates XL-XXXIX.

[110] J. Bovio Marconi, "La coltura tipo Conca d'Oro della Sicilia nord-occidentale," Monumenti Antichi dei Lincei 40, 1944, p.1–170, plate XI, 7, 9. The metopal space bordered by a thick zig-zag is also one of the recurring motifs on dippers of the Naro type. For the dish, see both for the form and for the decoration a cup with a checkerboard of dots (*scacchiera a pontillè*) from a tomb in contrada S. Bartolo near Sciacca associated with buttons perforated in a 'V' and three bell-beakers; cf. E. De Miro, "Preistoria nell'agrigentino. Recenti ricerche ed acquisizioni," Atti del XI e XII Riunione Scientifica, Istituto Italiano di Preistoria e Protostoria, Florence 1968, p.117ff., fig. 1, e. The same form, but decorated with incisions of a different type, has been found at Segesta; cf. Bovio Marconi, ibid., n.37, plate XI, 11.

[111] These vessels may have been used for cooking food: the ribs would have served to reinforce the vessel during thermal shock; cf. La ceramica in Archeologia, Roma, 1985, N. Cuomo di Caprio p.116; Bernabò Brea (here n.83) fig. 61, Capo Graziano I phase.

found also in the Aeolian islands and at Settefarine[112], as well as other elongated handles.

There are present also a fragment of a bridge-vessel (Cat. No. 203), a fragment with an internal handle (Cat. No. 204), and one from a vessel with an interior partition (Cat. No. 205). Bridge-vessels (*vasi a ponte*) are well attested in the Castelluccian culture. Vessels with an internal handle have been found at Manfria, Favara, Ramacca, in the Aeolian islands and in the Tyrrhenian region[113]. The bridge-vessel has been interpreted as a system for double boiler cooking, while the latter one has been considered to be an instrument for weaving, or as a cover. The example from La Muculufa (Cat. No. 204) bears traces of burning at the bottom, and probably it was used as a cooking vessel. Cups with an internal partition are found in the Aeolian islands and in the Tyrrhenian region[114].

From the village of La Muculufa there also come several covers with a knob, one of which was decorated on the interior, as well as several fragments of strainers probably used for the preparation of dairy products. Covers are not very common in Castelluccian ceramic typology, but strainers are attested at Settefarine, Castelluccio and in the Chiusazza cave[115].

187 Muc 89/69–264

Portion of a pitcher with a separate long neck, carination and a vertical ribbon handle. Fabric pink and dense with a metallic quality, polished surface with irregular beige and light brown spots.
H. cm. 13, diam. cm. 12, thickness cm. 0.6.
Plate 40

188 Muc 91/113

Portion of a pitcher (*boccale*) with the attachment of a vertical handle. Pink fabric and pink coarse surface with traces of burning.
H. cm.12, diam. cm. 16, thickness cm. 1.1.

189 Muc 89/65

Dipper-cup with hemispherical body recomposed from several fragments. Fabric and surfaces coarse. Vertical ring handle from the rim to the body; heavily burned with cracked surface.
H. cm. 8.0, rim diam. cm. 11.5, wall thickness cm. 0.7, handle width cm. 3.0, handle thickness cm. 1.5.
Plate 39

190 Muc 91/26

Crown-cup (*tazza a calotta*) with slightly enlarged triangular tongue along the rim and traces of the attachments of two other tongues, one opposite the one which is preserved and a third at the center between the two (probably, therefore, there were four tongues). Fabric pink, surface scaly pink.
H. cm. 5.0, Diam. mouth cm. 11.0, Diam. base cm. 5.0, wall thickness cm.0.8.
Plate 40

191 Muc 88/5

Miniature cup, walls slightly concave, separate rim, two holes along the rim. Fabric grey pink, surface pink with traces of burning.
H. cm. 7.5, diam. mouth cm. 5.5; wall thickness cm. 0.6.
Plate 39

192 Muc 89/260

Raised knob handle and portion of the rim and wall with thickening along the interior probably for the placement of a cover.
H. cm 6, thickness cm. 0.6.

193 Muc 89/261

Portion of the rim, wall and vertical knob handle pertaining to a jar (*olla*). Fabric grey, surface pink.
Diam. cm. 24, thickness cm. 0.8.

194 Muc 89/24

Vertical ribbon handle, neck and part of the shoulder of a large jar (*orcio*), rib along the base of the neck. Fabric and surface pink.
Thickness cm. 1.7.
Plate 40

---

[112] Bernabò Brea (here n.83) p.89; Orsi (here n.80) plate XII, 2.

[113] For the bridge-vessel, see L. Bernabò Brea (here n.98) p.33ff.; for the vessel with internal handle at Manfria, cf. Orlandini (here n.86) plate 13, fig. 2; De Miro (here n.110) fig. 1, b from contrada Scintillia; M. Frasca, F. Messina, D. Palermo, and E. Procelli, "Ramacca (Catania) Saggi di scavo nel villaggio preistorico in contrada Torricella," Notizie degli Scavi di Antichità 1975, p.563, fig. 10; Aeolian islands and the Tyrrhenian area: Bernabò Brea (here n.83) fig.s 63–65 with Aegean parallels.

[114] Bernabò Brea (here n.83) p.81.

[115] Privitera (here n.80) fig. 13; Orsi (here n.80), plate XII, 3; Sluga Messina (here n.81) p.91 and in the dumps from the village; Tinè (here n.108) plate XXX, 3.

195 Muc 89/227
Fragments of the wall and a portion of the rim of a large vessel with a horizontal ribbon handle. Fabric and surface pink.
Diam. cm. 40, thickness cm. 1.5.
Plate 40

196 Muc 89/228
Portion of the rim with an elongated grip (*presa*) from a large vessel. Fabric and surface pink.
Diam. cm. 44, thickness cm. 2.2; cf. 88/132.

197 Muc 88/124
Fragment of a rim with four cylindrical knobs. Pink fabric and surface.
Diam. cm. 14, thickness cm. 0.8.

198 Muc 91/76
Fragment of a base perhaps of a bowl with one hole. Pink fabric and pink coarse surface.
H. cm. 10, Diam. cm.20, thickness cm. 1.2.
Plate 18.4

199 Muc 89/248
Fragment of a pithos rim with ribs which cross. Red fabric and pink coarse surface.
Thickness cm. 3.2.

200 Muc 89/303
Rim fragment with cylindrical spout. Fabric grey, surfaces pink and rough.
Wall thickness cm. 0.8.

201 Muc 88/139
Rim fragment of a strainer. Gray fabric and surface. Traces of burning on the rim.
Diam. cm. 20, thickness cm. 1.1.
Plate 18.4

202 Muc 88/160
Rim fragment of a strainer. Pink fabric and surface. Traces of burning on the rim.
Diam. cm. 16, thickness cm. 1.7.
Plate 18.4

203 Muc 91/43
Fragment of the arm with a discoidal apex probably of a bridge-vessel (*vaso a ponte*).
Width cm. 2.5, length cm. 8.0, diam. of discoidal apex cm. 4.5.

204 Muc 89/121
Fragment of a vessel with an internal ribbon handle. Traces of burning on the bottom. Grey-black fabric, surface pink.
Diam. cm. 22, wall thickness cm. 1.3.

205 Muc 89/245
Wall fragment with a portion of the internal partition and two small knobs on the exterior perhaps belonging to a quadrangular vessel. Exterior surface orange, internal surface red.
H. cm. 11, wall thickness cm. 1.4.

206 Muc 88/54
Wall fragment with a horizontal knob handle. Fabric and surface pink with traces of burning.
Wall thickness cm.12; handle thickness cm.15.

Handles

207 Muc 88/166
Elbow handle. Gray fabric and surface. Traces of burning on the surface; irregular fractures.
Thickness cm. 0.2.

208 Muc 89/167
Shackle handle (*ansa a maniglia*). Fabric and surfaces coarse grey. Strong traces of burning.
Length cm. 7.5, thickness cm. 3.0.
Plate 40

209 Muc 88/168
Shackle handle (*ansa a maniglia*) with portion of a rim and body. Gray fabric and pink coarse surfaces. Suited for the right hand.
Thickness cm. 1.5.
Plate 18.5

210 Muc 88/148
Bobbin-handle (*ansa a rocchetto*). Fabric poorly fired, surface pink.
H. cm. 4, length cm. 6.
Plate 18.5

211 Muc 89/240
Double-knobbed handle (*presa a doppio pomello*). Fabric and surface pink, traces of burning.
Cm. 4x3.

212 Muc 91/64
Piaster handle. Fabric and surface red.
Thickness cm. 2.
Plate 18.5

Lids

213 Muc 89/28
Ceramic lid with pointed knob at the center. Damaged along the edge. Interior slightly concave with decoration painted in brown on consistent red ground in a cross-motif.
H. cm. 3.8, diam. cm. 7.6.

214 Muc 89/80
Ceramic lid with handle at the center; bottom slightly concave. Black fabric, surface pink. Recomposed from various fragments; lacks part of the edge.
H. cm. 5.7, diam. cm. 9.2.
Plate 40

215 Muc 88/10
Ceramic lid with cylindrical knob (*presa a pomello*) at the center, convex bottom. Lacks part of the edge. Fabric and surfaces pink with traces of red coloring.
H. cm. 3.0, diam. cm. 8.0.
Plate 40

Discussion

The great quantity of material which has been found in the village of La Muculufa is astonishing. The assemblage within Hut No. 2 is especially rich, including at least 100 vessels: among these there have been identified 38 chalice-vases and 20 pitchers. The vessels, furthermore, were amassed in the hut without any apparent order. It seems improbable that these vessels constitute the typical assemblage of a hut which, for example, in a Middle Bronze Age hut at Gaffe (Licata) consists roughly of 10 vessels [116]. The large quantity of vessels recovered in the structure at La Muculufa, therefore, may reflect its actual use—was the hut a dwelling or a storeroom?

This question brings us to a second one—in the village of La Muculufa was ceramic production a domestic activity or a semi-specialized or fully specialized craft? Despite a general stylistic homogeneity it is possible to distinguish within the range of the S. Ippolito ceramics a rather homogeneous group consisting of the painted vessels of Hut No. 2 [117]. A different character may be seen in several vessels from portions F70 and F102 (1988 excavation) through the miniaturistic character of the decoration and the common use of white color [118].

The great quantity of vessels accumulated in Hut No. 2 and their homogeneity leads one to think of a production which surpasses the immediate needs of a single family or a single hut. In an initial phase of the Early Bronze Age, contemporary to the village of La Muculufa, the professional production of vessels is attested by a cargo of dippers found in a shipwreck at Pignataro di Fuori. The vessels were made on Lipari from imported Sicilian clay, and they were headed probably for the other, smaller islands of the Aeolian archipelago [119]. Vessel standardization and standardized ceramic assemblages of the sort evident at La Muculufa have been interpreted also as a sign of production intensity [120]. On the other hand, the absence of the potter's-wheel, considered one of the characteristics of a fully specialized ceramic craft, leads us to believe that the production at La Muculufa was of a local character which extended beyond the limits of the single family but not beyond the village. From examples of similar cases attested in ages closer to our own, we may imagine that there were women in the village who dedicated themselves to this activity [121]. The very high artistic level of some 'Naro' style pottery leads us to believe that this ware represents another degree of specialization [122], and the restoration-holes present only on 'Naro' pottery indicate perhaps that this pottery was highly prized, perhaps precisely because it had been purchased.

---

[116] G. Castellana, "Madre Chiesa," in Un decennio di ricerche preistoriche e protostoriche nel territorio agrigentino (show catalog, Agrigento—Museo Archeologico Regionale, 16 June–30 September, 1990) p.45.

[117] There are attested exclusively among the pitchers of Hut No. 2 vertical band patterns and lines with butterflies or wavy lines or wolf's-tooth motifs and among the pedestal bowls patterns of hatched crosses and wavy lines.

[118] Pedestal Bowls Cat. Nos. 7, 9, 52, 88/103, 88/105, 62, 64, 88/125 and spouted vase Cat. No. 123.

[119] L. Bernabò Brea, "Considerazioni sull'eneolitico e sulla prima età del bronzo della Sicilia e della Magna Grecia," Kokalos 14–15, 1968–1969, p.20–59; E. Ciabatti, "Relitto dell'età del bronzo rinvenuto nell'isola di Lipari, Relazione sulla prima e la seconda campagna di scavi," Sicilia Archeologica 11, 1978, p.7–35.

[120] P. Arnold III, Domestic ceramic production and spatial organization, Cambridge, 1991, p.95ff.

[121] Q. Milanesi, "Un utile confronto fra ceramiche delle cabili Arabe di montagna dell'entroterra algerino ed alcune ceramiche preistoriche," Atti della XI e XII Riunione Scientifica, Istituto italiano di preistoria e protostoria, Florence, 1968, p.189–197; M. Stark, "Ceramic production and community specialization: a Kalinga ethnoarchaeological study," World Archaeology 23, 1991, p.64–78, see p.66–67 for the forms of semi-specialization; cf. also Arnold (here n.120), p.92ff.

[122] S.S. Lukesh identifies the hand of a master painter whose work may have been known beyond La Muculufa; cf. Appendix III in this volume; Lukesh in Muculufa I, p.17 and p.36; R.R. Holloway, M.S. Joukowsky and S.S. Lukesh, "Mining La Muculufa," Archaeology 41, 1988, p.40–47, esp. p.47.

Form and Repertory

The painted ceramics from the village of La Muculufa present a well-defined repertory of vessel-types: foremost is the very common pedestal bowl, then the pitcher, the cup, the jar with modeled handles and the rectangular vase. The typology of undecorated ceramics is not as well defined.

Few certain conclusions may be reached regarding the use of single vessels. The large, undecorated vessels served presumably to contain foodstuffs, but it is not possible to discern a precise typology for these, as it is for the cooking vessels—e.g., the vessel with internal handle Cat. No. 206 and the jug Cat. No. 190 have traces of burning. Holloway and Lukesh see in the pedestal bowl a container for wine, a sort of krater[123]. In fact, the wide diameter does make the Castelluccian pedestal bowl an excellent container for liquids, while the surmounted handle makes the pitcher suitable for dipping. In the village at La Muculufa the pedestal bowl is often associated with the pitcher and, less often, with other small vessels, such as cups which have the same function as the dipper[124]. Apparently the same combination of 'pedestal bowl + dipper' was discovered in the huts of Manfria, and in Villaggio Garofali at Adrano, and a numerical prevalence of pedestal bowls and pitchers was also noted at Mezzebbi[125]. La Muculufa, therefore, presents the earliest example of a ceramic service (constituted at this time only by these two elements: the bowl on a high pedestal and the pitcher) which would have, in more elaborate versions, an extremely long life in Sicilian prehistory. It is possible, in fact, to follow this service across the ceramic assemblages of the Thapsos and Pantalica cultures through the beginning of the Iron Age[126].

---

[123] R.R. Holloway and S.S. Lukesh, "Un vase castellucien au Museé de Princeton," L'Anthropologie 93, 1989, p.317–320. The wide diameter would serve to facilitate access to liquids; cf. M.F. Smith, Jr., "Toward an Economic Interpretation of Ceramics: relating vessel size and shape to use," in B.A. Nelson, Decoding Prehistoric Pottery, Illinois, 1985, p.254–309, esp. p.305.

[124] In Hut No. 3 pedestal bowl Inv. No. 89/68 was found near dipper Cat. No. 191; in Hut No.2 pedestal bowl Inv. No. 89/94 was found near pitcher Cat. No. 66, pedestal bowl Cat. No. 4 was near cup Cat. No. 118, and pedestal bowl Cat. No. 2 was near carinated pitcher Cat. No. 85.

[125] Orlandini (here n.86) e.g., Hut No. 9, p.43; Cultraro (here n.80); Privitera (here n.80).

Figural Decoration

Both the knobs on the pedestal bowls and the figurative motifs on two pitchers (Cat. Nos. 93 and 98) indicate a tendency toward figural art, particularly emphasizing the human figure through the indication of breasts, eyes, or even the entire human face in accord with a tendency which is rather unusual but not unknown in Sicilian prehistoric ceramic production. It is also possible that the significance of this decoration often was not only ornamental but also magical. As early as the Middle Neolithic, in fact, Stentinello ceramics represent the human face; the eye with lashes is one of the most characteristic aspects[127]. In ceramics of the Copper Age there appear, even if rarely, figural representations of animals on incised ceramics of the San Cono—Piano Notaro—Grotta Zubbia style and on several painted vessels[128]. These representations, however, seem to disappear with the Early Bronze Age. The only figural element known in Castelluccian wares is, in fact, a series of zoomorphic representations on the interior of a bowl from the area of Adrano[129].

---

[126] L. Maniscalco, "The Sicilian Bronze Age Pottery Service," paper presented to the ninety-fourth annual meeting of the Archaeological Institute of America, New Orleans, Louisiana, December 27–30, 1992; forthcoming in J. Morter, J. Robb and R. Tykot, eds., Social Dynamics of the Central Mediterranean. This phenomenon is discussed also in R.R.Holloway, The Archaeology of Ancient Sicily, London, 1991 p.33.

[127] L. Bernabò Brea, La Sicilia prima dei Greci, Milano, 1958, pls. 11–14.

[128] The examples which are known to date include: a vessel with applied plastic decoration along the rim from the Grotta Zubbia (Palma di Montechiaro), cf. Tinè (here n. 108) plate III.4; a vessel from the area of Licata with an incised, stylized quadruped, cf. B.E. McConnell, San Cono-Piano Notaro-Grotta Zubbia Ceramics in Sicilian Prehistory, dissertation, Brown University, 1985, fig. 30; a vessel from the Grotta del Vecchiuzzo with a painted stylized quadruped, cf. Bovio Marconi (here n.87) plate XVI.3. In the area of Milena, furthermore, there have been found a fragment with what seems to be a human protome and a cup from the Fontanazza I cave with an serpent applied to the handle; cf., Maniscalco (here n.93). On Malta an incised human figure appears on a vessel from a Copper Age burial at Zebbug; cf. J.D.G. Baldacchino and J.D. Evans, "Prehistoric Tombs near Zebbug, Malta," Papers of the British School at Rome 22, 1954, p.1ff., fig. 6.4. Although these are not many, they nevertheless are significant examples, especially considering the fact that much material from the Sicilian Copper Age remains to be published.

It is important to underscore the fact that both the vessels from la Muculufa and the example from Adrano belong to the earlier part of the Castelluccian period. The Castelluccian culture seems, in fact, to lose very quickly its figurative character in favor of abstraction. This is predominant in the full Castelluccian period, as it is presented by Bernabò Brea and by Sluga Messina in the many motifs on ceramics from the eponymous site of Castelluccio[130] and in the famous tomb portals where the figural element is only the remote point of departure for an abstract work.

Aegean connections

The Castelluccian culture in many aspects has been considered to be very close to the contemporary cultures of the Aegean; in particular, the style of San Ippolito has been considered to be closely related to ceramic styles of Crete and especially of Cyprus in the Early Bronze Age[131]. The small pitcher (*boccaletto*) recalls forms, in addition to Cypriote ones, from Tigani, Thermi, and Poliochni. The pedestal bowl is present at Troy, while the spouted vessel is common on Crete. The modeled horseshoe lug handle and the *ansa a maniglia* are other elements which are present in Sicily beginning with the Copper Age Malpasso style and which are also common in the Aegean[132].

Sluga Messina, in her corpus of decorative motifs from the eponymous site of Castelluccio, has traced many motifs over a vast area which includes, beyond Greece proper, Anatolia and the Near East as far as Iran[133]. Some of these

motifs are present also at La Muculufa, such as the diamond chain, but the very extent of the area encompassed in the work of Sluga Messina itself does not permit us to draw any useful conclusions of an historical nature. All of these 'connections' involve the Aegean and the Near East in various different phases beginning with the Late Neolithic, and they do not have precise chronological value. Many of the decorative elements are, furthermore, very generic and common everywhere, such as triangles and hatched diamonds, and they may well have an independent origin.

The case of vessel Cat. No. 121 is different, however, inasmuch as its extraneous character in respect to the usual Castelluccian repertory is evident. It is probably an imitation of a shallow bowl of the Early Helladic II period in Greece, and it may represent one of the earliest elements of Aegean derivation in the Castelluccian world[134].

---

[129] From the Petralia cave cf. Cultraro (here n.80) p.660, plate 57. Another parallel, a rather dubious one however, consists of a terracotta piaster from Piano S. Angelo (Cattagirone) on which there is, perhaps, the tentative representation of a human face; cf. D. Amoroso, "Insediamenti castellucciani nel territorio di Caltagirone: indagine topografica," Kokalos 25, 1979, p.25–53, pl. VII, fig. 7.

[130] For an interpretation of the apotropaic significance of several ornamental motifs on Castelluccian ceramics and of other elements (pendants, bossed bone plaques) see Bernabò Brea (here n.98) p.59 and Sluga Messina (here n.81). See Sluga Messina (here n.81) p.110 for the radiate disk motif at Castelluccio which seems to be derived from the sun and from the eye-motif.

[131] Bernabò Brea (here n.80) p.178; Bernabò Brea (here n.98) p.54ff.; Cazzella (here n.106) p.276; Albanese (here n.80) p.218.

[132] For the pitcher see M. Cavalier, "Les cultures prehistorique des Iles Eoliennes et leurs rapport avec le monde egeen," Bullettin du Correspondance Hellenique 84, 1960, p.319–346, fig.9, 1–4; A. Furness, "Some Early Pottery from Samos, Kalimnos and Chios," Proceedings of the Prehistoric Society of London 22, 1956, p.173ff., fig.4: 39–40; W. Lamb, Excavations at Thermi in Lesbos Cambridge, 1936, fig.s 26, 9, 28, 3.; J.R. Stewart, Corpus of Cypriot artefacts of Early Bronze Age, part I, Stockholm, 1988, p.129, group c, type d; at Vounos, Karpas, EC IIB—MC I, pl. XXVIII, 1–3. For comparisons between the pedestal bowl of Malpasso type and Aegean ones, see Cazzella (here n.106) p.253. For the spouted vessel, see Bernabò Brea (here n.98) p.55, and P. Betancourt, A History of Minoan Pottery, Princeton, 1985. For the horseshoe lug handle, see Cazzella (here n.106) p.252.

[133] Sluga Messina (here n.81).

[134] The only imports in the Sicilian Early Bronze Age age are a bone *pomello* from Monte Sallia, beads in glass paste from Valsavoia and a cup in sheet-metal from Adrano, all of which are assignable to the Late Castelluccian period; cf. Bernabò Brea (here n.24) p.24–77, 61; S. Tusa, La Sicilia nella preistoria, Palermo, 1983, p.296, and M. Cultraro, "Il castellucciano etneo nel quadro dei rapporti tra Sicilia, Penisola italiana ed egeo nei secc. XVI e XV a.C.," Sileno 15, 1989, p.259–286. For a probable import in an initial phase of the Early Bronze Age see R.M. Albanese Procelli, "Una cuspide di lancia preistorica del Museo Archeologico di Siracusa," Quaderni dell'Istituto di Archeologia della Facoltàdi Lettere e Filosofia dell'Universitàdi Messina 4, 1989, forthcoming.

Sicilian Context

The study of the painted ceramics of the village of La Muculufa reveals the presence of two well-defined stylistic
groups. One is composed of pedestal bowls, pitchers, rectangular vessels, and jars with a modeled handle, all decorated with very similar motifs based on simple, repetitive
elements—the most common of which are the hatched
bands alternating with lines and wolf's-tooth patterns.
The other group is characterized by dippers (but also there
are pedestal bowls which are not easy to reconstruct) with
a finer fabric, often shiny surfaces, and richer motifs. Typologically the first group rests within the style of 'S. Ippolito', the second in that of 'Naro'.

The 'S. Ippolito' style is attested in the area of Caltagirone and Gela, but it is rather difficult to define as a cultural *facies* by itself. Its affinity with the Copper Age
Malpasso style, and the existence of a Malpasso decorated
pottery production is clear indication of the origin of the
'S. Ippolito' style and the Malpasso and 'S.Ippolito' styles
may even be partially contemporary[135]. Among the
known sites where 'S. Ippolito' pottery has been found the
ceramic group from the Infame Diavolo Cave seems to
present the most archaic characteristics in the presence of
pedestal bowls on a very low foot, few and simple decorative motifs, and the presence also of elements from the
Malpasso tradition[136]. Ceramics from the sites of Settefarine, Mezzebbi and La Muculufa seem to present, instead, more evolved characteristics, closer to those of
'Naro'; the context of recovery at these last three sites includes elements which belong clearly to the Castelluccian
culture, such as bossed bone plaques, 'greenstone' *pseudo-
brassards*, and bridge-vessels (*vasi a ponte*). It is evident,
therefore, that the style of 'S. Ippolito', rather than a cultural *facies* by itself, can be considered an initial ceramic
style within the general framework of the Castelluccian
culture and one which is different from the style of 'Naro'.

The style of 'Naro', attested at La Muculufa especially
in dippers, is perhaps harder to define. Grouped together
with the style of Partanna by Bernabò Brea as an early
phase of the Castelluccian style, it has been shown now by
Pacci to be a separate style[137]. The area of distribution, if
we consider the sites where the unmistakable 'Naro' style
dipper has been found, is the same as that of the style of S.
Ippolito (Manfria, Palma di Montechiaro, Favara, Canicattì, and Caltanissetta; in other words the area covered by
the present provinces of Agrigento and Caltanissetta), but
the sites in which the two styles are attested are always different.

For the present, the only site where both the 'S. Ippolito' style and the 'Naro' style have been found is precisely
the village of La Muculufa. The former is predominantly
in Hut Nos. 2 and 3 (lower); the latter comes from the upper level of Hut No. 3 and from the excavation sector dug
in 1991. It is possible, therefore, to identify a stratigraphic
superposition of the two styles, but we should note that in
the same Hut No. 3 (upper) ceramics in the style of 'S. Ippolito' were also present. It seems most likely, therefore,
that a phase characterized by ceramics only of 'S. Ippolito'
type (e.g., those in Hut No. 2) was followed by one in
which the two styles co-existed. But it is not possible to see
any difference between the 'S. Ippolito' pottery from the
lower level and the 'S.Ippolito' from the upper level. The
chronological separation between the two levels must not
have been great.

It is not possible however to see a stratigraphic association for the presence of trichromic decoration. If in the
typological development the carinated pitcher seems an
intermediary step, in the stratigraphic contest it is not so.
Also the red polished pottery typologically related to Malpasso style is not older in stratigraphic terms. In this respect the petrographic analysis of fragments from the

---

[135] Bernabò Brea (here n.128) p.83–84; idem. (here n.119)
p.34; Cazzella (here n.106) p.230ff.; Albanese (here n.80)
p.213; Maniscalco (here n.93).

[136] Diffusion of 'S.Ippolito' style: S. Ippolito : P. Orsi, "Miscellanea Sicula, Stazione e necropoli al Bersaglio di Caltagirone," Bullettino di Paletnologia Italiana 48, 1928, p.82–88;
Settefarine (territory of Gela): Bernabò Brea (here n.128)
p.84; territory of Licata: unpublished flask in the Museum
of Licata, shown in a museum pamphlet published by Coop.
Alicata, fig. 4; Durrueli (Realmonte): small flask, De Miro
(here n.110) p.120, n.9; Grotta Infame Diavolo (Palma di
Montechiaro): De Miro (here n.80); territory of Palma di
Montechiaro: Castellana (here n.83) fig. XXXIX (small
flask) and perhaps fig. XLI; Grotta Barberia: E. De Miro,
(notiziario) Rivista di Scienze Preistoriche 29, 1974, p.261;
Grotta Fontanazza (Milena): Maniscalco (here n.93), Mez-
zebbi (Milena) Privitera (here n.80); M. Casale: P. Orsi,
"Miscellanea Sicula, M. Casale," Bullettino di Paletnologia
Italiana 48, 1928, p.84, fig. 14; Grotta Palombara: Tinè
(here n.108) p.120–122 and tav.IV, 8; Villafrati, small flask:
Bovio Marconi (here n.110) p.92, plate XII, 7, 9.

[137] Bernabò Brea (here n.98); Tusa-Pacci (here n.80).

village (see below) demonstrates that the sources of clay were the same for both the 'Naro' and 'S. Ippolito' styles.

Clearly, the two styles, although they may be distinguished, have many elements in common both in form and in decoration[138], and they are closely related chronologically insofar as they both belong to the initial part of the Castelluccian period. For its higher quality the 'Naro' style pottery was prefered in the Sanctuary at La Muculufa and in the sacred area at Monte S.Giuliano.

The close relation of the 'S. Ippolito' and 'Naro' styles to the Serraferlicchio style, visible in some of the decorative patterns is not so evident in the shape of the vessel because the Serraferlicchio style is still in the tradition of Copper Age pottery[139]. Some decorative patterns may have been spread by way of other materials such as cloth. In fact Serraferlicchio area is the same as that of 'S.Ippolito' and 'Naro'[140].

Style and Geography

The site of La Muculufa enters into a culturally homogeneous area located between Caltagirone to the North, Gela to the East and Naro to the West. This is precisely the area in which, according to Bernabò Brea, the Castelluccian culture developed. The homogeneity which we are able to discern for the most part by the ceramic styles surely is an index of a more complex cultural affinity. Probably the area in question had a well-defined character of its own, one distinct in other aspects which we are not able to distinguish but which may have included fairs, seasonal festivals and family relations.

The site which presents characteristics most similar to those of La Muculufa is the village at Settefarine near Gela. The village of Mezzebbi near Milena, also considered to belong to an Archaic phase of the Castelluccian culture, presents aspects which are very similar not only for reasons of style but also for the similar prevalence of the two shapes—the pedestal bowl and the pitcher. In the area around Mt. Etna contemporary ceramics of the first phase at Adrano, although they present many elements in common with the pottery of La Muculufa, have a character which is different overall. For the moment, it is not possible to distinguish a *facies* which is both stylistically and chronologically similar to that of La Muculufa in southeastern Sicily.

Typological analysis and comparison leads us, therefore, to date the settlement of La Muculufa to a very archaic phase of the Castelluccian culture which coincides with the appearance of the 'S. Ippolito' style, and then the 'Naro' style. The formal indications of the ceramics seem to agree very well with the indications of radiocarbon dating which place the village between roughly 2300 and 2000 B.C.

Aspects of Ceramic Production

The way in which Castelluccian pottery was produced is illustrated by several fragments recovered at La Muculufa. In this respect there are no noticeable differences between the 'S.Ippolito' and 'Naro' styles. Microscopic examination of the wares' petrography presented below by Melissa Moore demonstrates that the two groups are made of the same types of clays, and macroscopic examination shows clearly that the vessels were prepared in the same manner. The vessels were hand-made with the handles inserted into the body of the vessel as a stopper (*a tappo*) as is illustrated by a pedestal bowl fragment from the Terrace zone (Plate 19.3). The exterior was covered with red or more rarely yellow wash[141] almost as a slip but actually with a brush as one may see in the irregular brush-strokes along

---

[138] Pacci (here n.100) p.31.

[139] Concerning the Serraferlicchio style see L. Maniscalco, Ceramiche dell'eta'del rame dal territorio tra i fiumi Platani e Gallo d'Oro, dissertation of the Scuola di Specializzazione in Archeologia Classica dell'Università degli Studi di Catania, 1988–89, p.171ff. and eadem (here n.93). The hatched pattern and the butterfly are motifs already present in the Serraferlicchio style, the tapering bands seem to be derived from the elongated triangle: Bovio Marconi (here n.87) p.82. The trichromic technique is also present in the style of Serraferlicchio: cf. Pacci (here n.100) p.31. An initial petrographic and physical comparison of Copper Age (San Cono-Piano Notaro-Grotta Zubbia) and Early Bronze Age (Castelluccian, both S. Ippolito and Naro) ceramics has been undertaken (reports by M. Moore and J. Chervinsky appear in this volume), but analysis of Serraferlicchio ware has yet to be attempted.

[140] The Serraferlicchio style is attested at Serraferlicchio (Agrigento, cf. Arias, here n.101), Durrueli (Realmonte), the Colonna cave (Licata), the Montelupo Cave (Eraclea Minoa), at Rocca Aquilia near Milena, and the Vecchiuzzo Cave near Petralia Sottana :Bovio Marconi (here n.87). It is unfortunate that most of these sites are still unpublished.

---

[141] An actual nodule of yellow ochre (Inv. No. 91/16) was found in portion F181 during the 1991 excavation campaign at 139S, 48.5E, 2.68 meters.

the interior rim and base of several fragments (Lukesh inv. 90,043/2 and Cat. No. 65, Plate 19.1)[142]. The vessels were painted before firing as one may see in fragments of an amphora (Superintendency inv. 7824) from the eastern Terrace zone which had been deformed during firing (Plate 19.2).

Some difference between the 'S.Ippolito' and 'Naro' groups may be seen in the surface treatment—the surface of the 'Naro' style is more polished in respect to the matt surface of the 'S. Ippolito' style. In the 'Naro' style the lines seem more subtle and the patterns more accurate. Nevertheless in 'Naro' pottery some mistakes are attested. In the fragment of rim of cup (Cat. No. 157) a herring-bone pattern gone awry was covered with a band (Plate 37). This example also demonstrates that the more complicated patterns, such as the herring-bone, were executed first, and only then were the more simple ones painted. 'Naro' pottery also seems to have been the more highly prized of the two styles, and if broken it was repaired (Plate 19.4). Several fragmentary bases of pedestal bowls with repair-holes are attested at La Muculufa; one example is Superintendency inv. 13948[143].

Petrographic Analysis of Castelluccian Ceramics[144]

Melissa Moore

Petrographic analysis provides valuable information about both the general mineralogical composition of ancient clay fabrics and the possible relationships of these fabrics to the geological environment within which they are found, thereby providing a more complete understanding of the pattern of clay resource exploitation by ancient potters. The technique can also be used to identify specific technological processes (e.g. firing) involved in pottery production at a given site and to supplement traditional classificatory schemes through the identification and comparison of certain diagnostic inclusions (e.g. to distinguish between imports and local wares)[145].

The purpose of the petrographic analysis of the La Muculufa material was twofold. First, a study was made of the range of variation within a small sample of pottery from the site itself in order to begin the identification of a characteristic clay 'signature' for the La Muculufa material. Attention was focused on representative sherds in two established groups: the 'San Ippolito' style group and the 'Naro' style group, both of which belong to an initial stage of the Sicilian Early Bronze Age Castelluccian culture in the second half of the third millennium B.C.[146]. The mineralogical and physical composition of the clay fabrics used in the production of the two types of pottery were compared. Samples of wall daub from the site were also examined.

---

[142] For the precise definition of the term 'slip' (*ingobbo*) and other techniques of application, see Cuomo di Caprio, (here n.111) p.98 and p.113.

[143] Repair holes in Sicily are attested in the Neolithic period, not in the Early Bronze Age. See Bernabò Brea-Cavalier (here n.106), tav.LXIV f, tav.LXXXVI p, tav.LXV n, tav.LXVI,4; C.Cafici, "Stazioni preistoriche di Trefontane e Poggio Rosso in territorio di Paternò Monumenti Antichi dei Lincei 23, 1914, pl.VI, 4; idem., "La stazione neolitica di Fontana di Pepe," Atti della Accademia di Scienze e Lettere di Palermo, 11, 1920, tav.III, 3–5; R.Maggi, "Gli scavi nelle stufe di S.Calogero sul M. Kronio (Sciacca) e i rapporti tra la Sicilia e Malta durante il neolitico," Kokalos, 22–23, 1976–1977, p.510 ff., tav.LXXI, n.

[144] The study of ceramic thin-sections was performed as a project for the course in ceramics offered by the Center for Materials Research in Archaeology and Ethnology of the Massachusetts Institute of Technology, Cambridge, MA, U.S.A. during the academic year 1991–92. The assistance and guidance of both Dr. Ian K. Whitbread and Dr. Michael Geselowitz are gratefully acknowledged.

[145] H. Mynors, "Petrological Analysis of Pottery from Tell Rubeidheh," in R.G. Killick, ed., "Tell Rubeidheh," Iraq Archaeological Reports 2, 1988, p.53–57.

[146] As discussed by Laura Maniscalco in this volume, the 'San Ippolito' style is typologically and geographically distinct from that of 'Naro', and it may even be slightly earlier in date.

Seven local clays from various geological formations sampled by B.E. McConnell were examined as well, in order to explore possible relationships between the clay resources available to the ancient potters and the actual clay fabrics of the ancient pottery. Each of the clays was compared with the pottery samples from La Muculufa. Raw clays with physical and mineralogical properties similar to those of the archaeological ceramics from La Muculufa were identified, and several hypotheses regarding the nature of clay resource exploitation by Castelluccian potters were suggested. Further expansion of the analysis to include a much larger sampling of raw clays and pottery from other nearby sites would allow more detailed testing of these hypotheses.

Methodology

Eighteen samples of pottery from La Muculufa (the samples do not appear in the pottery catalogue of this volume), including nine examples of 'San Ippolito' style pottery (from the area of the Castelluccian village), seven samples of 'Naro' style pottery (six from the terrace and one from the area of the Castelluccian village) and two samples of wall daub (from huts in the area of the Castelluccian village) were thin-sectioned according to the following procedure[147]. All eighteen samples were first impregnated with a consolidant of known optical properties (Epotech epoxy). The samples were then mounted on glass slides and ground to a thickness of approximately thirty microns. Initial grinding was done on the Buehler Petrothin apparatus; the samples were then handlapped to the desired final thickness with successively fine grades of silicon carbide powder. Finally, each sample was sealed with a protective cover slip. A catalogue of the thin-sectioned samples is provided at the end of this report.

The procedure for the sectioning of the raw clay samples was as follows[148]. Each of the seven samples was first levigated in deionized water and then allowed to dry to a 'plastic' state. Each sample was divided and used to make two small tiles. The tiles were allowed to dry completely and were then divided into two sets of seven tiles each. The first set of tiles was fired in an oxidizing atmosphere at a 'low' firing temperature of 650 C and the second set was fired in an oxidizing atmosphere at a 'higher' temperature of 1000 C; the firing of each sample to two different temperatures allowed for observation of the performance of the clays under different firing conditions, providing information that could then be used to develop hypotheses about the firing procedures used on the ancient material should matches be found between the raw clay fabrics and those of the ancient pottery. After the firing, small samples were taken from each tile and were thin-sectioned according to the procedure outlined above. A catalogue of the raw clay samples is provided at the end of this report.

Each sample was then examined under both plane (ppl) and crossed polarized (xpl) light using a petrographic microscope. Qualitative observations of salient characteristics such as color, presence of optical activity, void structure, and distribution of coarse and fine inclusions were made for each sample. Several broad fabric groups were identified based on these observations. Then, the distribution of certain characteristic inclusions was quantified using a 'ribbon-counting' technique, and this quantitative data was examined using multivariate statistical tech-

---

[147] The samples were selected by Laura Maniscalco in the course of a study visit to the archaeological museum of Licata in October of 1991. Special thanks are owed to Dott.ssa G. Fiorentini, Superintendent of the Soprintendenza ai Beni Culturali ed Ambientali di Agrigento e Caltanissetta, for approving the study of these materials and to Dott. G. Castellana for making all necessary inquiries to the Assessorato ai Beni Culturali ed Ambientali of the Regione Siciliana and to the Ministero dei Beni Culturali ed Artistici of the Repubblica Italiana care of the Soprintendenza ai Beni Culturali ed Artistici di Reggio Calabria. Special care was taken to select pieces of size and quality appropriate to classification as 'scientific samples' (*campioni scientifici* as opposed to 'cultural properties', *beni culturali*) in accord with Regional and State laws concerning the removal and export of archaeological materials. All samples were eventually returned to their point of origin (B.E.McC.).

[148] The clay samples were gathered by B.E. McConnell on July 14 and July 23, 1992 from locations identified in the field on the basis of the Carta Geologica d'Italia, Foglio 272, Gela, 2nd edition, 1955. An effort was made to select at least one sample of each clay described on the map, although the clays at times did not seem to fit the map's unambiguous descriptions. The samples were taken from the most accessible clay outcrops which presumably were not radically different from the kind of outcrops utilized in the Early Bronze Age. Each sample weighed roughly four kilograms. A fraction of each sample weighing roughly one kilogram was sent to the U.S.A. for analysis as a 'scientific sample' (*campione scientifico*), while the remaining portion was kept as a reserve. Thanks are owed to Dott. A. Lo Presti and to Dott. F. Nicoletti who accompanied B.E. McConnell on the July 14th excursion (B.E.McC.).

niques such as principal components analysis and cluster analysis in order to test and refine the fabric groupings[149].

Results

Four distinct clay fabric groups were identified within the set of La Muculufa samples. In some respects (such as void structure) the clay fabrics were quite similar to one another; but several differences in color and composition were considered significant enough to warrant division of the clays into four different groups. The clay fabric groups differ most significantly in color, level of optical activity, and relative abundance of three characteristic varieties of inclusions: microfossils, acicular mica fragments, and grog (chamotte). Examination of the patterning of these attributes resulted in the identification of the four groups. These groups do not correspond to the stylistic groupings based on decorative style—examples of both the 'San Ippolito' and the 'Naro' styles are to be found in each group.

One of the most striking characteristics of the clay fabrics is the presence of acicular mica, the quantity of which varies quite dramatically from group to group. An important distinction can, in fact, be drawn between the composition of the first fabric class and the other three—namely, that the first class is highly micaceous and the other three are not.

The first fabric class consists of three samples, including LMN (= La Muculufa Naro) 25, LMN 18, and LMSI (= La Muculufa San Ippolito) 1. Several hundred mica fragments were counted in each of these sections, as compared to counts of fewer than 60 fragments in all other fabrics. Many of the mica fragments are aligned in parallel rows, possibly due to coiling as the vessel shape was first formed. The three samples are similar in color, varying from yellowish brown to brown in ppl, and yellow brown to orange in xpl. The samples also share a similar distribution of both fine and coarse inclusions. Among the fine inclusions mica fragments and quartz (small, moderately well-sorted, sub-rounded to rounded grains) are predominant. Iron oxides are also common. Among the coarse inclusions grog and other clay fragments are most common;

these are only moderately well-sorted, are sub-angular to sub-rounded, and often contain small quartz fragments and iron oxides.

Several different types of grog are present. The clay fabrics in this group contain a large number of gray grog fragments, as well as significant amounts of red and pale green grog fragments. Microfossils (brachiopods and foraminifera), while slightly more common in LMSI 1 and LMN 18 than in LMN 25, are relatively rare. The fabric of LMN 25 is optically active and contains some speckled b-fabric, suggesting that the clay mineral structure of this fabric was only incompletely broken down in the firing process. LMN-18 and LMSI-1 are not optically active, but contain some areas of speckled b-fabric; again, the clay mineral structure in these areas was only incompletely destroyed by the firing process. The clay fabrics in this group share the void structure common to the La Muculufa fabrics—voids account for between seven and ten percent of the fabric texture, and consist primarily of channels and vughs.

The surface decoration of the sherds is clearly visible in thin-section as a sharp, distinct red band along the edge of the sample. This is clearly a wash rather than just a firing effect or a paint; furthermore, it bears a striking resemblance to the bright red fabric of the fourth La Muculufa clay group. On these and other La Muculufa samples, a fine black band lies on the surface of the red wash—this painted decoration is also plainly visible in thin section.

The second La Muculufa clay type is represented by only one pottery sample, LMSI 16, although it appears in the La Muculufa material as a grog in other clay fabric groups, in the form of a slip, and in one of the daub samples. It is characterized by a distinctive, fine, clean clay that is yellowish brown in ppl and pale green in xpl. Mica fragments are extremely rare in this clay fabric. As in the first group, iron oxides are common and quartz appears in the form of small, poorly sorted, sub-angular to sub-rounded grains. Among the coarse inclusions, grog is predominant, and it consists of equal amounts of poorly sorted, sub-angular to angular red, gray and brown fragments which often contain small quartz fragments, iron oxides and even additional grog fragments. This fabric, like group 1, contains a very small percentage of microfossils (brachiopods and foraminifera). LMSI 16 is not optically active and contains no b-fabric. Voids (channels and vughs) account for some ten percent of the fabric texture,

---

[149] I.K. Whitbread, "The Characterisation of Argillaceous Inclusions in Ceramic Thin Sections," *Archaeometry* 28, 1986, p.79–88; A.P. Middleton, I.C. Freestone and M.N. Leese, "Textural Analysis of Ceramic Thin Sections: Evaluation of Grain Sampling Procedures," *Archaeometry* 27, 1985, p.64–74.

and are often lined with crystalline hypocoatings. The fabric of Daub sample 20 (discussed below) is very similar to that of LMSI 16; and this fabric is also found as a wash on sample LMSI 9.

The third La Muculufa clay fabric group, consisting of samples LMSI 6, LMSI 7, LMSI 10, LMSI 13, LMSI 15, LMN 2, and LMN 23, is characterized by a grainy yellow-firing clay fabric that is yellow brown in ppl and yellow orange in xpl. This fabric contains only very small quantities of mica and the void structure is comparable to that of fabric Types 1 and 2. As in the other clay fabric groups, quartz grains and sub-angular to sub-rounded, poorly sorted grog predominate among the fine and coarse inclusions, but very rare pyroxene and plagioclase feldspar are also present. Red, gray, and pale green (i.e. fabric Type 2) grog fragments are most common, and a few brown fragments and fragments of fabric Type 1 appear, as well.

There is considerable variation across this fabric group in the total amount of grog present, with some samples containing more than eighty fragments, and others as few as twenty; moreover, there is considerable variability in the distribution of grog types—some samples contain a much greater proportion of red grog (LMSI 13, LMN 23), others of gray grog (LMSI 7), still others of green grog (LMSI 15). There is also a certain level of variability in the quantity of microfossils (foraminifera and brachiopods). Interestingly, those samples containing the smaller quantities of microfossils (LMN 2, LMSI 7, LMSI 15) also contain only very small quantities of red grog, but an abundance of gray and green grog. Despite these minor variations, however, similarities in color, overall abundance of the microfossils, lack of optical activity (although some samples have areas of speckled b-fabric), and a 'feathery' appearance in crossed polarized light warrant the clustering of these samples into the same broad group. This fabric group does not appear as grog in the other fabric groups, but it is present in Daub sample 8 (discussed below).

The fourth La Muculufa clay group consists of LMSI 9, LMN 17, and LMN 27. This fabric is a characteristic bright red color in both ppl and xpl. It is further distinguished from the other three fabrics by a relatively low quantity of quartz grains and other mineral inclusions, as well as a low quantity of microfossils. The fabric has a void structure comparable to that of the other three fabrics, and it is not optically active. The quantity of grog inclusions is

comparable to that in the other clay fabrics. The grog fragments are gray and pale green (fabric Group 2), are poorly sorted, angular to rounded, and contain quartz grains, iron oxides, and sometimes other grog fragments (red, gray, or pale green). Clay fabric Group 4 is commonly present as a grog in the other three fabrics and as a wash applied as a surface decoration on pottery made of the other three fabric types.

The composition and structure of the two daub samples differed from that of the pottery samples in a few significant ways. Voids are present in the daub samples in a much greater percentage of the total fabric texture, and they are also extremely large—the voids in this material are probably the remnants of decayed or burned out vegetal temper (e.g. straw). Furthermore, the daub samples contain no grog fragments. Nevertheless, the daub samples and the pottery samples can confidently be assigned to the same clay fabric groupings; they simply represent different processing techniques of the clays for different purposes (e.g. grog was not added when the clay was to be used as daub).

Daub sample 8, as noted above, is reminiscent of clay fabric type three and is particularly similar to sample LMSI 10. The fabric of the daub sample is yellow brown in ppl and bright yellow to brown in xpl. Small angular to rounded, poorly sorted quartz grains are predominant. Microfossils are few. The fabric is not micaceous, and no grog fragments are present. There are small patches of speckled b-fabric, and some areas of the clay matrix have a 'feathery' appearance. Daub sample 20, however, bears a stronger resemblance to sample LMSI 16 (fabric Group 2). Like LMSI 16, it is yellowish brown in ppl and a distinctive pale green in xpl. The fabric is not optically active, microfossils are relatively few, and the large voids are often lined with crystalline hypocoatings. Iron oxides and small quartz grains are also present.

It should be noted that two of the La Muculufa samples did not fit well into any of the established groups. LMSI 5, for example, had been burned and was thus problematic because the original fabric color and composition was obscured; even refiring experiments failed to clarify the nature of the clay fabric of this sample. LMN 26 was strikingly different from the other La Muculufa pottery samples, as well. The fabric is yellow brown in ppl, and has a silty yellow brown appearance in xpl. The fabric exhibits some optical activity. The void structure is different from that of the four established clay fabric groups—the channel voids are much shorter, there are fewer vughs, and rounded vesicles are common. The fabric contains few microfossils, and only small quantities of red (fabric Group 4) and pale green (fabric Group 2) grog, in contrast to the other La Muculufa samples which all contain at least a small quantity of gray grog in addition to the red and pale green types.

After examining the sherd samples, it was also possible to identify some of the raw clay samples as possible sources for some of the pottery fabric types. Clay Sample A, when fired at a 'low' temperature, bore a striking resemblance to La Muculufa clay fabric Group 4. The samples were almost identical in color (bright yellow in xpl), lack of optical activity, void structure, and low microfossil and mica content. Clay Samples B and C, when fired at both 'low' and 'high' temperatures, strongly resembled pottery samples LMSI 10 and LMSI 15 in color, level of optical activity, 'feathery' appearance in xpl, distribution of microfossils, and level of mica content. The appearance of the clay when fired at 'high' temperature was not noticeably different from its appearance when fired at a 'low' temperature. Further similarities exist between clay Samples D and G, when fired at a 'high' temperature, and La Muculufa fabric Group 2; and between clay Sample E, when fired at a 'low' temperature, and LMN 26 (again, similarities in the firing color, distribution of microfossils, mica, and void structure). Sample F, regardless of firing temperature, bore little resemblance to the pottery clay fabrics from La Muculufa. No raw clay 'matches' were found for La Muculufa fabric Group 1.

Discussion

The above results suggest several tentative hypotheses about the nature of clay resource exploitation and ceramic production processes during the Castelluccian period at La Muculufa. At least five local clays may have been used by the Early Bronze Age potters to produce both San Ippolito and Naro style ceramics. Both ceramics styles were produced with each of the five clays; no attempt was made by the ancient potters to produce either of these styles using a single, specific clay resource (although it should be repeated that the sample size of this analysis was small; with a larger sample size, a pattern of clay source preference might well emerge).

A consideration of the geology of the lower Salso valley suggests that this lack of a single preferred clay source in the Early Bronze Age is not altogether surprising. The clay samples were taken from argillaceous alluvium in an area composed primarily of Miocene and Pliocene calcareous deposits, and thus they are quite similar in several important respects. Each sample, for instance, contains a significant quantity of microfossils (brachiopods and foraminifera) and small, weathered quartz grains. These samples are all secondary clays[150] and are thus relatively fine-grained, with very few large inclusions; indeed, the raw clays contain very few inclusions at all other than the quartz and microfossils. All of the raw clay samples exhibit similar qualities of plasticity and workability, and they exhibit comparable levels of shrinkage upon drying and firing.

Not much processing of the raw clays seems to have taken place prior to vessel production—the raw clays and the pottery clay fabrics that match them are different only in that the clay samples do not contain grog. In any case, it is possible to state that the ancient potters were simultaneously (insofar as can be detected archaeologically) exploiting several distinct clay sources which nevertheless exhibit broad regional similarities and similar physical properties, and that they were not deliberately exploiting different clay sources for different purposes[151]. Further clay sampling would probably result in the discovery of a source of clay fabric similar to that of clay Samples D and G that lies closer to La Muculufa than Palma di Monte-chiaro or Monte Dessusino. This clay was used to make wall daub as well as pottery, and it seems unlikely that special effort would have been given to obtaining a non-local clay for wall-daub production.

---

[150] Secondary, or sedimentary, clays are those deposited after transport, while primary or residual clays are those deposited on or in the vicinity of their parent rock; cf. P. Rice, Pottery Analysis, A Sourcebook, Chicago, 1987, p.37.

[151] Although the small sample size of the present study is not capable of furnishing such evidence, a larger sample may indicate that different clays were used for different vessel forms in a manner similar to that noted among the ceramics of the Shipibo-Conibo in Peru; cf. W.R. DeBaer and D. Lahlrag, "The making and breaking of Shipibo-Conibo ceramics," in C. Kramer, ed., Ethnoarchaeology: Implications of Ethnography for Archaeology, New York, 1979, p.102–138, esp. p.116–121 and table 4.4.

The presence of large quantities of mica in a few of the La Muculufa pottery samples is strange, given that mica is not native to the area[152]. It is possible, however, that at one time the Salso river carried fragments of mica downstream to the La Muculufa area from sources of mica farther to the north, and thus created an as yet unidentified clay source that was unusually rich in mica. In addition to the unusually high level of mica, a large quantity of grog fragments is found in the La Muculufa fabric Group 1 samples—perhaps because a high percentage of mica, which can act as a flux within the clay body to increase shrinkage during the firing process, may have resulted in a need to 'open up' the clay body with extra grog temper.

The grog temper is itself a striking characteristic of the La Muculufa clay fabrics. As noted above, grog is the primary temper present in the pottery samples. Grog from several different clay fabric groups can be found in each of the pottery samples; often, grog fragments are found that contain other grog fragments. Although some types of grog are present more frequently in some pottery fabric groups (e.g. fabric Group 1 contains large quantities of gray grog) there was apparently no attempt to use specifc grogs for specific purposes—no patterning in terms of findspot of the pottery sample, vessel form, etc., is evident. There are several ethnographic parallels for the curation and 'regeneration' of vessels in the form of grog temper, but such practices and ideologies are difficult to document archaeologically[153]. It is certainly possible that the ancient potters simply used grog made from whichever broken vessels were closest to hand. The presence of second and even third generation grog in several samples indicates that grog tempering was a fairly well-established process, and one that the ancient potters at La Muculufa apparently considered to be indispensable. The practice may have helped to reduce cracking or shrinkage during drying and firing of the pottery.

Some tentative conclusions about the firing techniques apparently used by the potters at La Muculufa can be reached, based on the comparison of the pottery samples and the raw clay samples. It is clear that the ancient potters were capable of firings that reached temperatures at least approximating 1000 C, because in at least two cases the pottery samples most closely match the raw clay samples when fired to these higher temperatures[154]. Some firings may have proceeded at temperatures as low as 650 C, however, as shown by the resemblance of some pottery fabrics to low fired raw clay samples. Both the high and low firing temperatures could be achieved in pit firing or in simple kilns. The presence of a gray core in several pottery samples within fabric Group 3 (LMSI 6, LMSI 10, LMSI 15 and LMN 23) which was matched with clay fabrics G and C, may suggest that the pottery was fired in a reducing atmosphere and then allowed to cool in an oxidizing atmosphere. Clays B and C, when fired at both low and high temperatures in an oxidizing atmosphere, did not exhibit the gray core effect. Further experimentation with a larger set of samples might help to clarify these results.

The technique of surface decoration was, as noted above, apparently the same for both the San Ippolito and

---

[152] Profs. R. Cristofolini and A. Pezzino, Istituto delle Scienze della Terra, Università degli Studi di Catania, personal communication. Mica is found in the Peloritani mountains at Sicily's northeastern tip. See also R. Fabiani, Ciò che da il sottosuolo di Sicilia, catalog of the "Mostra del Minerale Italiano," Rome 18 November 1937–31 January 1938, Palermo, 1938.

[153] The regional procurement of clay and the use of grog apparent at La Muculufa finds an ethnographic parallel, as well as a physio-chemical one, in the Shipibo-Conibo pottery of eastern Peru. Fieldworkers describe the way in which potters of this region procure clay, as well as pigments, from a variety of sources, clean it of impurities and add temper including broken potsherds. In fact, Shipibo-Conibo potters, who are female, prefer to use archaeological potsherds of the sort which typically litter the ground around their settlements as grog for the practical reason that it is softer and easier to pulverize. See W.R. DeBaer and D. Lahlrag (here n.151) p.110–111, p.128–133, fig. 4.2 and table 4.1. We should not exclude, however, the possibility that a greater significance was given to the use of grog in the form of a kind of animism which would give the recycled ceramic a symbolic rebirth in the creation of a new vessel. See Michael B. Stanislawski, "If Pots Were Mortal," in R.A. Gould, ed., Explorations in Ethnoarchaeology, Albuquerque, 1978, p.201–227 who describes the way in which Native American potters in New Mexico collect the whole pots of their deceased colleagues but chip the rim in order to satisfy the spirit of the prior owner and Hopi potters who place ceramic wasters in shrines in order to avoid bad luck.

[154] A temperature between 900 and 1000 C is appropriate to firings using the manganese-black technique; cf. W. Noll, R. Holm and L. Born, "Painting of Ancient Ceramics," Angewandte Chemie, International Edition 14, 1975, p.602–613, esp. p.608. Manganese may be found in the Tortonian clays of Contrada Poggio del Conte Bosco at Ravanusa, not far from La Muculufa.

the Naro style pottery. The applied red wash and applied black paint used to create these decorative styles are both clearly visible in thin section. The red wash itself, as noted above, belongs to the same clay fabric group found in several pottery samples at both La Muculufa (La Muculufa fabric 4 and raw clay Sample A from La Muculufa). Preliminary chemical analysis using the PIXE technique (see following report) confirms this observation.

As noted above, expansion of this small study to include a larger sample of archaeological ceramics from both La Muculufa and other Castelluccian sites in southern Sicily would provide valuable insights into problems such as the presence of mica in certain samples, or the possible use of different clay sources in the production of different vessel forms. This study, however, has resulted already in the tentative identification of a characteristic clay fabric 'signature' for the La Muculufa ceramics, as well as several distinct raw clay sources for this material, and several hypotheses regarding the nature of ceramic production technology at La Muculufa have been presented. Further study of material from other sites in the region would be of value in the identification of La Muculufa's place in the Castelluccian ceramic tradition.

Catalogue of Pottery Samples (selected illustrations Back Cover)

Sample #	Portion	Style	Fabric Munsell Color	Wash Munsell Color
1:	F200	San Ippolito	fabric 5YR 2/6	wash 2.5YR 6/8.
2:	F200	Naro	fabric 5YR 7/4	wash 10R 5/8.
5:	F200	San Ippolito	burned gray core	interior and exterior wash 10YR 8/1.
6:	F200	San Ippolito	gray core fabric 2.5YR 6/8	interior and exterior wash 10R 5/8.
7:	F200	San Ippolito	fabric 5YR 6/6	interior wash 10R 5/8 exterior wash 10YR 8/1.
8:	F200	daub	burned fabric 5YR 6/6.	
9:	F200	San Ippolito	fabric 2.5YR 5/8	wash 5YR 8/4.
10:	F130	San Ippolito	gray core fabric 7.5YR 7/6	wash 10R 5/8.
13:	Hut 2	San Ippolito	fabric 5YR 7/6	wash 5YR 6/8.
15:	F182	San Ippolito	gray core fabric 5YR 7/6	wash 2.5YR 6/8.
16:	F132	San Ippolito	fabric 5YR 8/4	wash 7.5YR 2/0.
17:	T60b	Naro	gray core fabric 2.5YR 6/6	wash 2.5YR 5/8.
18:	T60b	Naro	fabric 7.5YR 7/6	wash 10R 5/8.
20:	Field daub		burned fabric 10YR 8/3	
23:	T60	Naro	gray core fabric 7.5YR 7/6	wash 10R 5/8.
25:	T10	Naro	fabric 7.5YR 7/6	interior wash 10R 5/8 exterior wash 7.5YR 2/0.
26:	T10	Naro style	fabric 2.5Y N/4	wash 10R 4/8.
27:	T10	Naro	fabric 5YR 7/6	interior wash 2.5YR 6/6 exterior wash 7.5YR 2/0

Catalogue of Raw Clay Samples with accompanying description from the Carta Geologica d'Italia, Foglio 272, Gela, II edizione, 1955 (B.E.McC.)

Sample A: La Muculufa, west side of Ravanusa-Riesi road, down-slope from Bruscato farmhouse, lower sample, 23-VII-92; description: "M10a, argille avana o bru-nastre a volte scagliettate, talora con intercalazioni di arenarie e brecciole calcaree, contenenti microfaune dei vari piani dal'Elveziano all'Oligocene inclusi (Mio-Oligocene)." In the field this sample had a clearly reddish tinge.

Sample B: La Muculufa, west side of Ravanusa-Riesi road, down-slope from Bruscato farmhouse, upper sample, 23-VII-92; description: "Mab, collata argillosa in generale, e.g. argille brecciata, intercalata nella formazione sottostante alla Serie Solfifera, sopratutto in quella del Miocene Medio," or M10a (above).

Sample C: Monte dei Drasi, northwest side on west bank of Salso river up gully ca. 10 meters, 23-VII-92; description: as Sample B.

Sample D: Palma di Montechiaro, along old tract of state highway (s.s.) 115 at km. 202, 23-VII-92; description: "P2a, argille e marne grigio-azzurre, più o meno sabbiose con fossili marini banali." .

Sample E: Agrigento, coastline half-way between the mouth of the Naro river and Punta Bianca, same formation as Punta Bianca, 23-VII-92; description: same formation as Sample D.

Sample F: Ravanusa, La Montagnola, along northern side of Bourbon road from Salso river, 14-VII-92; description: "M2a, argille grigiastra più o meno salata, talora rossastra o brunastra con abbondanti Globigerine."

Sample G: Monte Desusino, southeast flank, along west side of Falconara-Riesi road, 23-VII-92; description: "P2a, argille grigio-azzura, sabbiosa fossilifera."

Qualitative Elemental Analysis of Castelluccian Pottery using PIXE

John F. Chervinsky

Castelluccian pottery sherds supplied for proton induced x-ray emmision (PIXE) elemental analysis were run in the presence of M. Moore on October 26, 1992 and in the presence of B.E. McConnell on February 22, 1993 at the Cambridge Accelerator for Materials Science (CAMS) at Harvard University. The sherds had rough surfaces with black, red, and white painted areas that appeared non-uniform in thickness over a given area and from piece to piece. Some of the pieces had been sawed (for petrographic analysis) exposing cross-sectional area.

Experimental Setup

A finely collimated, 2MeV beam of protons, produced by a tandem ion accelerator, is brought out of vacuum into air through a 7.5 micron Kapton window. The sample is held tightly in place at a fixed angle with an indexed sample holder. The proton beam strikes the sample producing x-rays of discrete energies that are characteristic of certain elements within the sample. A Si(Li) x-ray detector is used to determine peak energies and intensities. Beam current normalization is accomplished using the signal produced by the trace amount of Argon in the air, the K alpha x-ray peak of which the integral is proportional to the number of protons striking the sample[155]. Spectral analysis is performed with the aid of GUPIX, an interactive software package written specifically for PIXE analysis[156].

Data

Inasmuch as very little is known of the major elemental composition of the ceramic material or of the applied paints at the time of analysis, the following trace elemental results are to be used for qualitative purposes only (Table 1). For the purpose of correcting for x-ray attenuation through the matrix, we will assume, for the time being, that it is composed predominantly of silica. Errors due to this assumption will be taken to be systematic. Because of the large variation in x-ray absorption coefficients, we are not able to compare elemental ratios within a given sample or run. If, however, we are to assume an order of magnitude consistency as indicated in the various spots run on the cross-sectional and black-painted samples, we can make a valid comparison in the presence or absence of certain elements among these samples or similar samples obtained from different sites[157].

A striking feature of this data is the obvious Manganese peak found in all of the black painted samples compared to that of the cross-sectioned as well as the red-ground samples. The black paint also seems to contain more iron than the ceramic base material. Sample

---

[155] S.A.E. Johansson and J.L. Campbell, PIXE, A Novel Technique for Elemental Analysis, New York, 1988, p.120.

[156] J.A. Maxwell, J.L. Campbell and W.J. Teasdale, "Practical problems with a proton probe," Nuclear Instruments and Methods in Physics Research, B56/57, 1991, p.694–698.

[157] PIXE analysis has been performed on fragments of Kamares Ware from Minoan Crete; cf. P.P. Betancourt and C.P. Swann, "PIXE Analysis of Middle Minoan Pigments from Kommos," in Y. Maniatis, ed., Archaeometry (Proceedings of the 25th International Symposium, Amsterdam, 1989) p.177–181.

Element	Sample	LMN18			LMSI13				LMN27		
		X-Sec.	Red	Black	X-Sec.	Red	Black	White	X-Sec.	Red	Black
Si	1	2391	1210	1447	1967	245	1500	1085	2009	1465	918
	2	2449		716	1964		981		2201		
	3	1929									
Cl	1	5	2	0	28	13	13	14	13	29	29
	2	3		4	35		25		11		
	3	10									
K	1	152	235	155	134	27	221	151	119	186	166
	2	167		136	124		154		139		
	3	173									
Ca	1	429	81	110	640	1328	284	299	370	184	182
	2	400		102	557		225		459		
	3	532									
Ti	1	23	20	16	21	3	23	20.1	21	24.2	24
	2	31		14	19		26		22		
	3	28									
Mn	1	7	2.7	76	5	2	72	298	8	7.4	233
	2	5		114	4		126		6		
	3	5									
Fe	1	220	280	486	189	36	515	995	207	262	180
	2	242		512	185		686		210		
	3	278									

Table 4: Trace Elements in Castelluccian Ceramic Samples from La Muculufa

Normalized Counts – Note: The table lists counts separately for Spots 1, 2, and 3 (indicated in parentheses).

LMSI13 has a small white spot on top of an intersection of two black lines. Because the spot is smaller than the beam spot and it appears translucent to the eye we do not see any dramatic elemental features. The very large manganese signal could be attributed to the double brush stroke of the underlying black paint[158].

The red ground samples did not appear to be much different from the cross-sectional pieces, but the observable trend is the suppression of most of the elemental peaks. This could be due to the presence of lighter elemental constituents in the paint absorbing the x-rays from the base material. It seems to confirm the observations from the petrographic analysis that the red paint is an oxidized form of the base material[159].

[158] Several fragments of painted Castelluccian ceramics from La Muculufa (samples LMN 25, LMSI 6, LMSI 15, and LMSI 16) were analyzed by X-ray fluorescence spectrometry in the laboratories of the Louvre Museum, Paris. This technique indicated that all black painted decoration on all of the samples analyzed was executed with a pigment containing Manganese (personal communication, A. Kaczmarcyk). Thanks are owed to Miriam Evenot who performed the analysis and to Professor Alexander Kaczmarcyk, formerly of the Department of Chemistry at Tufts University, Medford, Massachusetts, U.S.A. who arranged for the analysis as well as for bibliographic references (B.E.McC.).

[159] Cf. report by M. Moore in previous chapter.

Addendum by Brian E. McConnell

Decorative combinations of black and white paint on a red wash or ground are common not only in the Mediterranean but also in other parts of the world (e.g. South America)[160]. The manganese-black technique which can be achieved through a single oxidation firing process together with red firing is less widespread than the iron-reduction technique because it seems to be tied to the more limited distribution of manganese mineral resources. Manganese-black has been discovered in archaeological contexts in the eastern Mediterranean dating prior to the time of Castelluccian pottery (e.g. in the 6th/5th Millennium B.C. contexts in Anatolia and in 4th/3rd Millennium B.C. contexts in Anatolia and the Balkans, which might indicate that it was a specialized techique spread to the West by a process of cultural/technological diffusion[161], however, it also appears in the West as a major pigment in the much earlier Upper Paleolithic context of the caves of the Magdalenian culture in France and Spain. Detailed study of manganese pigments and their procurement has been performed at Lascaux (France)[162].

In Sicily, manganese has been mined at Castelvetrano (Fontanelle mine) and deposits of manganese (more specifically pyrolusite, its most common form)[163] have been searched quite close to La Muculufa in clays of the Tortonian strata of contrada Poggio del Conte Bosco at Ravanusa[164]. It seems likely that manganese could have been obtained in the Early Bronze Age from minerals originating in Eocene or Oligocene strata which then were eroded and deposited as nodules in the Tortonian clays of the succeeding Miocene period in a manner similar to flint or red ochre[165].

A theory for future examination regards the process of development in the technique of painting ceramics from the Copper Age to the Early Bronze Age in regard to the processes of mineral extraction. The development of the Castelluccian technique of manganese-black-on-red-ground, in fact, may be closely related to Copper Age techniques of applying red and yellow ochre on a ceramic surface precisely because manganese and ochre were obtained in the same way. The techniques used in painting

---

[160] W. Noll, R. Holm and L. Born, "Painting of Ancient Ceramics," Angewandte Chemie, International Edition, 14, 1975, p.602–613, esp. p.610–612; R. Treuil, Le neolitique et le Bronze Ancien Egeens, Paris, 1983, p.195; W.R. DeBaer and D.W. Lathrap, "The Making and Breaking of Shipibo-Conibo Ceramics," in C. Kramer, ed., Ethnoarchaeology, Implications of Ethnography for Archaeology, New York, 1979, p.102–138, esp. p.111–115.

[161] Noll, et al. (here n.160) p.609–610 with fig. 12.

[162] C. Couraud and A. Laming-Emperaire, "Le colorants," in A. Leroi-Gourhan and J. Allain, eds., Lascaux Inconnu (XXIIe supplement à "Gallia Prehistorie," Paris, 1979, p.153–170, esp. p.156; English summary in M. Ruspoli, ed. The Cave of Lascaux, The Final Photographs, New York, 1987, p.192–195.

[163] Manganese dioxide is obtained from the following minerals—hausmanite, manganite, braunite, and polianite/pyrolusite, as well as from black ochre, a type of clay rich in the dioxide of manganese and graphite. Regarding pyrolusite, see Enciclopedia Italiana delle Scienze, Scienze Naturali, Minerali e Rocce, 1, Novara, 1968, p.131.

[164] (Castelvetrano) Ministero delle Corporazioni, Direzione Generale delle Miniere della Metallurgia, Corpo Reale delle Miniere, Relazione sul servizio minerario e statistica delle industrie estrattive in Italia nell'anno 1935, anno XLVI, Num. 61, Roma, 1938, p.87; (Ravanusa) Ministero Industria, Commercio e Lavoro, Direzione Generale dell'Industria e delle Miniere, Corpo Reale delle Miniere, Relazione sul servizio minerario e delle industrie estrattive in Italia nell'anno 1939, anno L, Num. 65, Roma, 1945, p.524: "Ricerca di minerali manganese "Poggio del Bosco" territorio di Ravanusa (provincia di Agrigento): Permissionario, Raja Antonio.—Furono fatti assaggi superficiali in alcuni straterelli marnosi manganesiferi, compresi nelle argille del tortoniano, ma i risultati furono praticamente di nessuna importanza." The clay at Ravanusa is included among those sampled for this project (cf. previous chapter in this volume, Sample F).

[165] Special thanks are owed to P.M. Dott. Luigi Infantino, Corpo Regionale delle Miniere, Caltanissetta for this theory on the accessibility of manganese in antiquity. See H. C. Jenkyns, "Fossil manganese nodules from Sicily," Nature 216, 1967, p.673–674; A. Bosellini, E. Mutti, F. Ricci Lucchi, Rocce e Successioni Sedimentarie, Torino, 1989, p.180–82; A. Cavinato, Depositi Minerari con speciale riguardo alle miniere ed ai minerali utili italiani, Torino, 1952, p.757–58; and R. Fabiani, Ciò che da il sottosuolo di Sicilia, catalog of the show "Mostra del Minerale Italiano," Rome, 18 November 1937–31 January 1938, Palermo, 1938, p.20 with p.9, Fig. 1. Study of the deposition of manganese in Israel has shown that lateral transport downslope of manganese-rich nodules can increase concentrations by 50–80%; cf. D.H. Yaalon, C. Jungreis and H. Koyumdjisky, "Distribution and Reorganization of Manganese in Three Catenas of Mediterranean Soils," Geoderma 7, 1972, p.71–78. On the general distribution and concentration of manganese, see K.K. Turekian and K.H. Wedepohl, "Distribution of the elements in some major units of the Earth's crust," The Geological Society of America Bulletin 72, 1961, p.175–92.

Copper Age Serraferlicchio ceramics seem to be a key step in this process of development and one worthy of detailed study.

Objects in Terracotta

Introduction

Objects in terracotta are distinguished here from ceramics in that they do not serve as containers nor are they used directly in connection with containers (e.g. covers). They include the so-called terracotta horns (*corni fittili*), bases (for statuettes?), discs (*oscilla*), and braziers (*alari*). Almost all of the artifacts discussed below appear in a sandy fabric which is far coarser than that used for many Castelluccian ceramics.

La Muculufa is particularly useful in that it offers a wide typology of *corni fittili*. The types include:

A. narrow circular base with tapering body,

B. discoid base with cylindrical body,

C. wide, oval base with tapering body,

D. oval base with a tapering body and two arms or 'wings' (*alette*).

Often, a cavity was created in the base most likely to aid in the drying and firing of the piece. Each object was created by hand, and within each category a certain degree of variation can be noted. One *corno fittile* (Cat. No. 216, plates 20.1, 20.2 and 41) is distinguished by the presence of a smoothed stone similar to those used for pseudo-brassard pendants (cf. Cat. Nos 299–403) which was set horizontally into the tip. Although this object may have been used as a tool, it seems likely that an impact repeated only a few times would have provoked significant damage; therefore, the interpretation of it as a symbolic object seems more likely.

Traces of paint similar to that used for the red ground of Castelluccian ceramics were found also on one *corno* found in the village in the area of Hut No. 3 (Cat. No. 221), while another one found earlier in trench T90 of the Sanctuary bore a series of triangles painted vertically on a red ground (Plate 42, A, from trench portion T90); clearly, these motifs are derived from ceramics. There may, in fact, be some sort of hierarchy in their form and significance in the way in which they are placed at the site, especially given their placement around the structures of Hut No.s 2 and 3.

Corni fittili are known primarily from domestic contexts, although they have been found in tombs. A particularly unusual find of these objects was made on the acropolis at Gela where a bowl filled with seven *corni* was discovered in a Castelluccian domestic context[166]. They are generally regarded as representations of the male phallus, presumably with some sort of symbolism rooted in a desire for apotropaic protection or fertility. As apotropaic objects they could either protect the living or the deceased from malign spirits[167]. As symbols of fertility they could serve to encourage the well-being of wild or domestic plants and animals, or regeneration in the household. In funerary contexts, the *corni fittili* could serve to symbolize continued life through the cycle of birth and the passing of new generations[168]. It seems likely that the meaning of the *corni fittili* is as varied as the types and find-spots. Their generalized form seems to reflect a trend toward abstraction and perhaps some sort of codification which characterizes the decoration of Castelluccian ceramics in comparison to their Copper Age predecessors; they may lie at the end of a Copper Age sculptural tradition yet to be identified[169]. In fact, the *corni fittili* actually may be an aniconical variation on the kind of terracotta statuettes which have been found at other Castelluccian sites[170].

---

[166] Cf. R.R. Holloway, The Archaeology of Ancient Sicily, London, 1991, p.24 and fig.29. In the excavation report by D. Adamesteanu and P. Orlandini, "Gela," Notizie degli Scavi di Antichità 1962, p.360–362 and fig. 22) different forms of the *corni* are noted—one was tall and conical, four had round bases, and two had arms or wings. The same excavators report (ibid., p.399–400 with fig. 78) the discovery of another *corno* in the context of a tomb cut in the local tufo; it was found next to the head of the skeleton.

[167] Cf. L. Bernabò Brea, "Eolie, Sicilia e Malta nell'età del Bronzo," Kokalos 22–23, 1976–1977, p.56–57 and E. Procelli, "Aspetti religiosi e apporti trasmarini nella cultura di Castelluccio," Second International Conference on Archaeology of the Ancient Mediterranean, 'Religion and Society in the Prehistoric Mediterranean', Journal of Mediterranean Studies 1, 1991, p.252–266.

[168] A general relation can be seen with the famous sculpted tomb portals of Castelluccio which show a phalli-form symbol entering female genitalia with stylized breasts above; cf. L. Bernabò Brea, Sicily Before the Greeks, London, 1957, pl. 33. For an apotropaic meaning of the same sculpted portal, see Holloway (here n.166) p.21–22 and fig. 26.

Bases in terracotta were found at La Muculufa both in the village (Cat. Nos. 242, 243) and in the rock-crevice burial (Inv. No. 87/12). These bear traces of two, three or four attachments for vertical members which may have been similar to those found to form a circular terracotta model at Monte Grande di Palma di Montechiaro. A terracotta disc (*oscillum*, Cat. No. 240) with painted decoration similar to that of Castelluccian ceramics was also recovered in the Terrace zone[171]. Perhaps the presence of an *oscillum* in the Terrace zone at La Muculufa presents further confirmation of the zone's sacred character.

Another class of terracotta object which deserves particular attention is the so-called 'brazier' (*alare*). Although their form suggests that they served in some way to propagate heat (presumably, hot coals would be placed in a cavity underneath them), these objects bear little or no traces of actual contact with fire. Similar objects are well-known in Early and Middle Bronze Age domestic contexts[172].

La Muculufa also offers important information regarding spindle whorls and bobbins[173]. There are several types which have been recovered—bi-conical, spherical and amorphic. The bi-conical forms appear with sharp or rounded edges. A rare example of a conical form was found, as well, although it actually may be of historical date. Bobbins appear with a narrow center or with a cylindrical form. Bi-conical spindle-whorls measure roughly 3 cm in length, 4 cm in diameter, and weigh roughly 40 grams; spherical ones measure between 3 and 4 cm in diameter (3.5 cm is a frequent measurement) and weigh between 20 and 65 grams at regular intervals of 5 grams; amorphic spindle-whorls have similar measurements and weight. Bobbins which are narrow in the center measure between roughly 4.5 and 6 cm in length, between 4.5 and 5.5 cm in diameter and between 30 and 225 grams in weight (there may be weight categories between 90 and 135 grams and around 220 grams); cylindrical bobbins tend to be longer (betwen 5.0 and 6.0 cm in length) in respect to their diameter (between 4.5 and 5.0 cm; most were measured at 4.5 cm) and weight between 45 and 140 grams perhaps at intervals of 10 to 20 grams. It should be noted that not all examples of each type were in condition to be measured.

While the diameter of the hole in the spindle-whorl is almost invariably one centimeter, the traces of fibre impressions on the bobbins are significantly more narrow. It is likely that the holes were made slightly wider than the material which would have passed through them in order to facilitate threading and that the bobbins would have held a tightly-spun thread, but nevertheless both objects must have been created for heavy fibres probably from the wool of sheep the bones of which lie in abundance at the site[174]. It is not known how such fibres may have been used—whether for weaving actual textile fabrics or as a

---

[169] A stone object which appears to be a *corno* from a Copper Age tomb discovered recently in the Copper Age necropolis of Piano Notaro on Capo Soprano (Gela), is elongated and enlarged at one end in a manner which recalls the form of Castelluccian terracotta *corni fittili*; cf. here Note 166. The object is on display in the museum of Gela, and it would seem to fill the lacuna noted so far in respect to this class of object in the Copper Age; cf. A. Cazzella, "Considerazioni su alcuni aspetti eneolitici dell'Italia meridionale e della Sicilia," Origini 6 (1972) 171–299, here 242f.

[170] See statuettes from Monte Grande (Palma di Montechiaro) and contrada Ciavolaro (Ribera) in G. Castellana, Un decennio di ricerche preistoriche e protostoriche nel territorio Agrigentino, (show catalog, Museo Archeologico Regionale, 16 June–30 September 1990), p.36, fig. 17 and p.52, fig. 30. Statuettes found at Monte San Giuliano (Caltanissetta) appear in P. Orlandini, "Statuette preistoriche della prima età del bronzo da Caltanissetta," Bullettino d'Arte 52, 1968, pp.55ff.

[171] (La Muculufa, rock-crevice burial) B.E. McConnell et al., "La Muculufa (Butera, Caltanissetta), stazione siciliana dell'Età del Bronzo Antico," Archivio per l'Antropologia e la Etnologia CXX, 1990, p.119 and fig. 5; (Palma di Montechiaro) Castellana (here n.170) p.35, fig. 15. For other examples of *oscilla*, see O. Adamo, "Pendagli e amuleti della facies di Castelluccio in Sicilia," Archivio Storico per la Sicilia Orientale 85, 1989, p.7–69, esp. p.22 and plate II, nos. 5–8.

[172] L. Bernabò Brea, "Eolie, Sicilia e Malta nell'età del Bronzo," Kokalos, 22–23 1976–77, p.33–110, esp. p.56 and p.102 Fig. C, 1–2 ; (Madre Chiesa di Gaffe) Castellana (here n.170) p.43, figure (upper right); idem, "Ricerche nella piana di Gaffe nel territorio di Licata," in I Quaderni di Sicilia Archeologica 1, 1987, p.133 and fig. 9. This object reaches massive proportions in examples from the site of I Faraglioni on the island of Ustica; cf. R.R. Holloway, "Ustica, Report on the Excavations of the Bronze Age Site of Faraglioni 1990," Archaiologischer Anzeiger, 1991, p.359–65.

[173] The assistance of O. Doonan in recording this data is gratefully acknowledged.

[174] Cf. K. Cruz-Uribe, "The Mammalian Fauna" in La Muculufa I, p.57–64.

cord or thread to bind other materials (e.g. leather or wood)[175].

The relatively regular proportions and weights of the spindle-whorls and bobbins undoubtedly reflects the dimensions of the hands that formed them, but also they seem to indicate the kind of notion of standardized weight and measure which one may see in Castelluccian ceramics and architecture. The so-called spindle-whorls were meant to be used in groups inasmuch as many were found together in a deposit of burning in portion F110. Perhaps they served as weights for a loom or other strung device.

Cazzella sees a chronological difference between the bi-conical form and the globular and spherical forms of spindle whorl: the former predominates in Copper Age contexts, while the latter predominates those of the Early Bronze Age[176]. The proportion documented at La Muculufa seems to support this conclusion, as well, although overall there are too few examples from too few sites to reach conclusions with any confidence.

Statistical analysis of spindle whorls is also important to discussions of textile production and exchange. The discovery of so many spindle whorls at La Muculufa in 1988 would seem to place in question the necessity for textile imports from Malta and/or other locations, as proposed by this author; however, we should not exclude the production and exchange of textile goods as items of prestige[177].

Catalogue of Objects in Terracotta

Horns(Corni Fittili)

216 Muc 89/47 *Corno fittile* (or pestle)
coarse fabric, surfaces striated vertically in an irregular manner; on the top is inserted horizontally a
smoothed stone 3.3 cm. long and 0.7 cm. wide; on the bottom an irregular concavity (a mould?);
H. cm. 15.5, diam. base cm. 8.3/9.2, diam. body cm. 5.7(average), diam. tip cm. 3.7/3.0.
Plates 20.1, 20.2 and 41

217 Muc 89/2 *Corno fittile*
cylindrical body and narrow circular base; missing the upper part and part of the base;
H. cm. 11.6; diam. base cm. 11.8 x 10.5.
Plate 42

218 Muc 89/33 *Corno fittile*
cylindrical body and disc base;
H. cm. 12.5, diam. base cm. 11.3 x 11.1, base thickness cm. 2.9–3.35.
Plate 42

219 Muc 89/86 *Corno fittile* with 'wings'
firing hole in the base 4.0 cm. deep; missing the upper portion, wings damaged, signs of heavy burning;
H. cm. 9.0, diam. base cm. 12.3 x 10, thickness cm. 2.9–3.35.
Plate 43

220 Muc 89/89 *Corno fittile* with 'wings'
missing upper portion, signs of heavy burning;
H. cm. 10.3, diam. base cm. 13.6 x 8.8.
Plates 20.3 and 43

221 Muc 89/122 *Corno fittile*
cylindrical body and narrow circular base; missing the upper part and part of the base; traces of red paint.
H. cm. 11.5; diam. base cm. 11.7 x 10.5.

222 Muc 89/132 *Corno fittile*
narrow ovoid base (almost circular), body missing;
H. cm. 5.0, base cm. 11.0 x 10.0.

223 Muc 88/118 *Corno fittile*
wide ovoid base, carination between the body and the base, missing most of the base; painted with a red ground as a ceramic (ground poorly preserved);
H. cm. 10.0, body 4.2 x 6.0 cm.

224 Muc 88/162 *Corno fittile*
narrow circular base in 3 fragments, missing part of the base, cylindrical body, missing the tip;
H. cm. 7.0, body diam. cm. 3.0, base diam. cm. 8.2 x 8.7.

225 Muc 89/63 Tip of a *corno fittile*
cylindrical type, heavily burned;
H. cm. 5.0, diam. 2.5 cm.

---

[175] See E.J.W. Barber, Prehistoric Textiles, (Princeton, 1989).

[176] Cazzella (here, note 169) p. 243, 280.

[177] A range in the form of spindle whorls similar to that at La Muculufa is found in Tarxien Cemetery contexts in the Maltese archipelago; see J.D. Evans, The Prehistoric Antiquities of the Maltese Islands, London, 1971, fig. 55, nos. 1–6. Regarding Siculo-maltese trade in textiles, see B.E. McConnell, San Cono—Piano Notaro—Grotta Zubbia Ceramics in Sicilian Prehistory (diss. Brown University, 1985) p. 51

226 Muc 87/37 *Corno fittile* with 'wings'
recomposed from many fragments, narrow circular
base, missing part of the base and the tip, burned;
H. cm. 8.5, base diam. cm. 10.5.

227 Muc 88/185 Base of a *corno fittile*
narrow circular body, similar to 89/132;
Current h. cm. 7.0, body thickness cm. 2.2, current
base diam. 10.0 x 8.0.

228 Muc 91/28 *Corno fittile*
ovoid base, marked forward curve of body, tip partially broken, missing roughly half of the base, surface
spalled and pitted, coarse fabric with orange color,
traces of burning;
H. cm. 16.3, base width ca. cm 15.0 x 9.7, body
width cm. 11.5 x 4.0.
Plate 43

229 Muc 91/29 Tip of a *corno fittile*
broken, exterior color orange;
L. cm 5.0, max. preserved width cm. 3.3 x 2.7.

230 Muc 91/31 Tip of a *corno fittile*
surface orange;
H. cm 7.3, max. diam. cm. 3.1.

231 Muc 91/33 *Corno fittile* with two 'wings'
tip missing and the left wing;
H. cm 10.5, partially broken base cm. 12.0 x 7.0.

232 Muc 91/35 *Corno fittile*
tip broken, base chipped, coarse fabric;
H. cm 9.0, base cm. 8.7 x 8.0.

233 Muc 88/171 *Corno fittile*
missing the base, tip chipped, orange surface;
H. cm 10.0, max. 5.7 x 4.3.

234 Muc 91/36 Tip of a *corno fittile*
narrow ovoid base (similar to Cat No. 228), surface
possibly slipped; traces of red paint;
H. cm. 7.5, max width cm. 7.8 x 4.0.

Braziers(Alari)

235 Muc 91/20 Corner fragment perhaps of a brazier
surface painted red and smooth;
H. cm. 18.

236 Muc 89/129 Fragment of a brazier
missing the left side, large knob on the side, corners
and knob chipped and burned;
H. cm. 14.2, base cm. 10.0 x 9.0, body thickness cm.
5.7, diam. knob cm. 5.5.
Plate 41

237 Muc 91/104 Corner fragment of a brazier (right leg?)
similar to 89/129;
H. 8.2 cm, width 7.7 cm., thickness 5.0 cm.

238 Muc 91/100 Corner fragment (a brazier?)
interior rounded, exterior angular, hole on one side,
heavily burned; wall thickness 1.7—1.0 cm., hole diam. cm. 1.8.

Discs

239 Muc 88/154 Disc recomposed from two fragments
missing roughly one-eighth; reddish fabric, surface
pink with traces of burning;
Dia. cm. 9, thickness cm. 1.4.

240 Muc 89/140 (from the Terrace zone) Portion of a terracotta disc (*oscillum*)
fabric and surfaces with slight traces of burning; one
of the two sides is painted in brown on red ground:
multiple angles and between two bands a group of
five lines; on one side about 1.8 cm. from the edge a
half-drilled hole; on the other side almost at the same
point 1.6 cm. from the edge another, similar hole—is
this a cover or a fragment of an idol?
Cm. 11.0 x 3.7, thickness cm. 1.05.
Plate 42

Other Objects

241 Muc 88/7 89/247 89/269 88/202 Fragments from a
cylindrical object
exterior surface with irregular black streaks on red
ground, on the interior a series of knobs in relief;
thickness cm. 1.58; other flat fragments have irregular black streaks and finger-marks on the interior
(thickness cm 2.0).

242 Muc 88/150 Portion of a base
traces of attachments for three handles;
H. cm. 17

243 Muc 91/14 Base
traces of two attachments each measuring cm.2.5 x
1.8; surface pink-gray and rough, burned;
Dia. cm. 9, thickness cm. 1.3
Plate 41

Spindle-Whorls

244 Muc 88/113 Spindle whorl
bi-conical, four pairs of incised radial lines on one
side;
Cm. 3.2 x diam.4.5, wgt. 40 g.;
Plate 44

245 Muc 89/147 (from the Terrace zone) Spindle whorl
rounded bi-conical, dark brown, burnt fabric;
Cm. 2.8 x diam. 4.3, wgt. 35 g.

246 Muc 89/220 Spindle whorl
globular (spherical) form; finer ceramic, thin size;
Cm. 2.0 x diam. 2.6, wgt. 14 g.

247 Muc 89/30 Spindle whorl
elongated globular (spherical) form; surface discolored by burning;
Cm. 3.6 x diam. 3.3, wgt. 35 g.;
Plate 44

248 Muc 88/77 Spindle whorl, half preserved
globular (spherical form); coarse light orange fabric;
Cm. 3.5 x diam.3.6, current weight 16g (original ca. 32g).

249 Muc 89/87 Spindle-whorl
found near the position of shell necklace Cat No. 411;
H. cm. 3.0, diam. cm. 3.8, diam. hole cm. 0.75.
Plate 44

250 Muc 89/296 Miniature cup (used as a spindle-whorl or bobbin?)
H. cm. 2.8 cm., diam. 3.8 cm., diam. hole 0.8 cm., internal diam. 2.0 cm., wgt. 23 g.

Bobbins

251 Muc 89/145 Bobbin
cylindrical form with slightly concave sides; whole except for one side (preserved to 3/4)
Dia. edge cm. 6.0, diam. at the center cm. 4.8; length cm.5.3, wgt. 183 g.
Plate 44

252 Muc 88/14 Bobbin
cylindrical form, incised line marks where string was held at an oblique angle;
Cm. 5.5 x diam. 4.3, wgt. 147 g.

253 Muc 88/23 Bobbin preserved to 4/5
cylindrical form, incised line parallel to transverse faces, marks where the string was tied;
Cm. 5.0 x diam. 4.5, wgt. 94 g.
Plate 44

Cat./ Inv.*	Type†	Len.	Dia.	Hole Dia.	Wgt.	Comments	Portion
	?					12 frags.	F110
244#	1						
89/169#	1						
89/231	1						
	2	3.00	4.00	0.09	25	1/2 remains	F110
	2	3.00	4.00	1.00	40		F110
	2	3.00	4.50	1.00	45		F200
245	2						
89/113	2						
88/116#	2						
88/214	2						
91/32	2						
	3	3.00	3.50	1.00	20		F90
	3				20	2 frags.	F110
	3	3.50	3.50	0.70	25		F110
	3				25	1 frag.	F110
	3	3.00	3.50	1.00	25		F110
		2.50	3.50	1.00	30		F110
	3	2.50	3.20-3.50	0.90	30		F110
	3	3.50	3.50	1.00	30		F110
	3				30	1 frag.	F110
	3	3.00	3.20	1.20	30	almost cylindrical	F110
	3	4.00	5.00		35		F110
	3	3.20	3.50	0.60	35		
	3	4.00	4.20	1.00	40		F110
	3	3.30	3.50	0.80	40		
	3	3.50	4.00	0.60	40		
	3	3.50	3.60	0.80	40		F110
	3	4.00	3.80	0.80	40		F182
249#	3	3.50	3.40	1.40	40		
91/39	3	3.50	4.50	1.00	45		F190
	3	.400	4.00	1.00	55		
	3	4.00	4.00	1.00	55		F110
	3	3.50	4.30	1.00	65		F182
	3					5 frags.	F110
	3					1 frag.	F110
	3					1 frag. (squat)	F110
	3					5 frags.	F110
	3	3.00	4.00	1.00			F182
89/221#	3						
246	3						
247#	3						
89/222#	3						
88/114	3						
248	3						
89/87	3						
250	3						
	4	2.50	3.70	0.90	25	discoid	F110

Table 5: Spindle Whorls and Bobbins (measurements in centimeters and grams)

Cat./Inv.*	Type†	Len.	Dia.	Hole Dia.	Wgt.	Comments	Portion
	4	3.50	4.00	0.60	50		F110
	4						F110
	4	3.50	4.00	1.00		5 frags.	F110
	4					5 frags.	F110
	4					1 frag.	F110
	4					4 frags.	F110
	4					4 frags.	F110
89/266	4						
252#	5	3.80	5.00	0.40			
	6				30	1 frag.	F110
	6				50	1 frag.	
	6		4.40		60		
	6	4.30	4.50	0.90	90		F110
	6	4.50	5.60		95		F110
91/30	6	4.50	4.50–5.00		106	sporadic	
	6	4.50	5.50		110		F110
	6	4.40	4.50–5.00		115		F110
	6	4.50	5.50		125		F110
	6		5.00		135		F110
	6	6.00	5.70–6.00		220		F75
	6	6.20	5.50		225		F75
251	7						
89/295	6						
88/164	6						
	7				30	1 frag.	F110
	7				40	2 frags.	F110
	7		4.50		45		F110
	7				45	1 frag.	F110
	7				55	1 frag.	F110
	7	5.00			55		F110
	7		4.50		55		F110
	7		4.50		55		F110
	7	6.00	5.00		75		F110
	7	5.00	4.30		85		
	7	5.00	4.50		115		F90
	7	4.70	4.50		120		F110
	7	5.50	4.30		120		F90
	7	5.50	5.00		140		F110
	7					1 frag.	F110
	7					1 frag.	F110
252#	7						
89/140#	7						
88/51	7						

Table 5: Spindle Whorls and Bobbins (measurements in centimeters and grams)

*: Inventory number noted by # indicates illustration in Plate 44.

†: Types: 1, bi-conical; 2, bi-conical (rounded); 3, spherical; 4, amorphous; 5, conical; 6, bobbin, concave center; 7, bobbin, cylindrical.

Ground-Stone Tools

Throughout the site both in the Field and the Terrace excavation zones there were recovered stones smoothed to forms which could have been used as tools. A thorough study of the range of ground stone types present at the site based on the sample of materials recovered during the campaigns of 1982, 1983 and 1985 has been published by M.S. Joukowsky[178]. Here are discussed only those stones recovered between 1988 and 1991 which themselves present clear traces of modification regardless of the archaeological context. The following catalog is presented by category (axes, hammerstones, manos, whetstones, grinding-platforms, and other smoothed stones), and it shows that ground-stone tools were used for chopping, hammering, and polishing directly and for the preparation of other tools, as well as for grinding grain and/or other foodstuffs. Many other stones bearing little or no alteration may well have been utilized for various purposes.

Special note should be given to the basalt axes which were recovered from the village. They present marvellous craftsmanship and fit into the tradition of basalt axes known at other sites[179]. A particularly important find at La Muculufa may be a rectangular block of basalt (Cat No. 290) which may have served as the basis for an axe which could then have been produced by chipping and grinding in order to create the specific, desired characteristics. Even though the material itself seems to have been imported to the site, the actual final stages of production may well have been done at La Muculufa thus demonstrating that the ground-stone industry was a semi-domestic activity with specialists active only in the procurement, rough preparation and distribution of the raw material[180].

It should be noted that basalt was used not only for axes but also for other forms, including what appears to be

---

[178] M.S. Joukowsky, "L'industrie de la pierre et du materiel de broyage au debut de l'âge du Bronze á la Muculufa, en Sicile," L'Anthropologie (Paris) 91, 1987, p.273–282; cited in reference to corresponding artifact types in the catalog as Joukowsky, 1987.

[179] R. Leighton, "Ground Stone Tools from Serra Orlando (Morgantina) and Stone Axe Studies in Sicily and Southern Italy," PPS 55, 1989, p.135–159 cited in catalog as Leighton, 1989; R. Leighton and J.E. Dixon, "Jade and Greenstone in the Prehistory of Sicily and Southern Italy," OJA 11, 1992, p.179–200.

a grinding and polishing stone (Cat. No. 282, Plate 46). Besides basalt, another type of stone was particularly popular for the production of hammerstones and grinding stones. It is a fine-grain stone with a gray-brown color which appears to turn reddish perhaps through contact with heat either as flames or through actual use. Petrographic study of the ground-stone tools would specify the materials described here in qualitative terms and may some day provide further insight into their procurement and use.

Catalogue of Ground-Stone Tools

Laica NR 701K kitchen balance used for weight measurements

Axes

254 Muc 89/3 Basalt handaxe
cutting end worn smooth and chipped, face chipped, square cutting edge 3.8 cm., rounded butt, surface pitted, oval section, Munsell 5Y 4/1–5/1; cf. Joukowsky, 1987, p.277, no.3, Leighton, 1989, fig. 3, no.41;
L. cm 9.4 x 4.7 x 3.7, wgt 230g;
Plate 45

255 Muc 89/78 Basalt handaxe
broad cutting edge, rounded butt; oval section, Munsell 5Y 6/2 (light olive gray), butt end pointed, sides slightly chipped, cutting edge smoothed but chipped, medium body macrowear;
cf. Joukowsky, 1987, 277, no.3, Leighton, 1989, Fig. 2, no.24;
L. cm. 9.25 x 6.3 x 4.2, wgt. 326g.
Plate 45

256 Muc 89/78B Basalt(?) handaxe
straight cutting edge, flattened section, cutting edge well preserved and smooth, butt chipped, faces also chipped, Munsell 2.5Y 4/2 (dark grayish brown), heavy body macrowear; cf. Joukowksy, p.277, no.3, Leighton, 1989, Fig.3, no.41;
L. cm. 8.0 x 3.7 x 2.0, wgt. 95g.
Plate 45

257 Muc 89/8 Basalt handaxe (re-used as a hammerstone?)
rounded butt, oval cutting section, hand end slightly flattened on one side, hammer end flat with slightly convex shape (3.5 cm long x 1.5 cm wide) and slightly chipped on one side, light chipping and pitting, Munsell 5Y 4/1–5/1; cf. Leighton, 1989, 148;
L. cm. 7.0 x 4.9 x 4.25, wgt. 210g.
Plate 45

258 Muc 89/117 Basalt handaxe
broad cutting edge, rounded butt, Munsell 5Y 4/1–5/1 (dark gray), body macrowear surface pitted, on one side surface smoothed in a concave manner to form a cutting edge; cf. Leighton, 1989, Fig. 5, no.81, Joukowsky, 1987, p.277, no.3;
L. cm. 8.1 x 5.6 x 4.1, wgt. 285g.
Plate 20.5 and 45

259 Muc 88/126 Basalt handaxe,
rounded butt, broad cutting edge, oval section, one face pitted, blade chipped slightly, Munsell 5Y 5/2 (olive gray—actually greenish);
L. cm. 9.4 x 6.9 x 4.6, wgt. 409g.

260 Muc 88/135 Basalt handaxe
heavily worn or used as a hammerstone, rounded butt, broad cutting edge, flattened through use, surface rough but without major pitting, Munsell 5Y 5/2 (olive gray);
L. cm. 8.9 x 6.1 x 4.5, wgt. 333g.

261 Muc 88/197 Basalt handaxe
butt broken off, straight narrow cutting edge, chipped on one face, one face flattened, section almost circular;
L. cm. 8.0 x 4.5 x 4.1, wgt. 217.

262 Muc 88/198 Handaxe in a fine grain stone
heavily weathered, broad cutting edge, rounded butt, oval section, surface smooth except for natural imperfections in the stone (splits), butt and cutting edge pock-marked;
L. cm. 9.4 x 6.6 x 4.5, wgt. 345.

263 Muc 88/207 Fragment of a handaxe in basalt
pointed, angular butt preserved, cutting edge all but ruined, surfaces once very smooth, Munsell 2.5Y 5/0 (gray);
L. cm. 8.5 x 2.6, butt edge cm 2.0 wide, current wgt. 117g.

---

[180] Cf. Leighton (here n.179) 142ff. A similar block was noted by Paolo Orsi in the Basile collection; cf. P. Orsi, "Curiosità della collezione Basile ora nel R. Museo di Siracusa," Bullettino di Paletnologia Italiana 40, 1914, p.43–52.

264 Muc 89/360 (from the zone of the Rock Crevice burial) Basalt handaxe
narrow cutting edge, rounded butt chipped on one side, oval section, one face flattened smooth, other face convex, Munsell 2.5Y 5/2 (grayish brown);
Cm. 8.1 x 5.4 x 3.6, wgt. 221g.

265 Muc 89/343 Fragment (ca. 1/2) of an handaxe in basalt
butt broken, cutting edge wide, one face flattened, the other curved, Munsell 10YR 6/3 (Pale brown);
Current l. cm. 6.5 x 8.0 x 4.0, wgt. 318g.
Plate 45

266 Muc 88/266 Basalt handaxe
broken in half, butt missing, ovoid section, squared cutting edge chipped on the sides;
Current l. cm. 7.0 x 7.5 x 5.5, wgt. 385g.

267 Muc 89/447 (from the zone of the Rock Crevice burial) Basalt handaxe
squared point, concave butt, squashed ovoid section, one face concave, one with a concave depression, burned, Munsell 10YR 6/2 (light brownish grey);
L. cm 4.5 x 4.8 x 2.6, wgt. 97g.
Plate 46

Hammerstones

268 Muc 89/120 (from the zone of the Rock Crevice burial) Hammerstone (basalt?)
elongated form, slightly spherical at the extremities each one of which is flattened in an angle from use, Munsell 2.5Y 6/2 (light brownish gray),
L. cm. 13.5 x 6.5 x 4.5, wgt. 637g.
Plate 46

269 Muc 88/199 Discoid hammerstone in basalt
chipped by percussion almost at the center of one face, Munsell 2.5Y 6/4 (light yellowish brown);
Cm. 8.9 x 9.3 x 4.2, wgt. 490g.

270 Muc 89/357 Discoid hammerstone(?)
base used to smooth other instruments, squashed ovoid section, ovoid form, concave depression on one face, sandy crystalline stone (Munsell 2.5YR 4/4, reddish brown, fired this color?); cf. Joukowsky, 1987, p.277, no.6 (type A);
Cm. 13.5 x 10.6 x 6.2, wgt. greater than 1kg.

271 Muc 89/358 (from the Terrace zone) Discoid hammerstone (Joukowsky 1987 type A); ovoid form, percussion mark at the center of both faces; Munsell 5YR 4/3 (dark reddish gray);
Cm. 13.0 x 11.0 x 4.0, wgt. 890g.

272 Muc 88/204 Discoid hammerstone in a fine grained rock as Cat. No. 270, percussion marks on both faces, Munsell 10R 4/3 (weak red);
Cm. 9.3 x 9.9 x 4.5, wgt. 662g;
Plate 46

273 Muc 88/206 Discoid hammerstone in fine sandy-grained stone, percussion mark off-center on one face;
Cm. 11.1 x 8.7 x 4.0, wgt. 554.

274 Muc 89/364 Fragment (ca. 1/3) of a hammerstone
concave percussion point(?), oval section, smoothed exterior, Munsell 2.5YR 3/0 (very dark gray);
Current l. cm. 5.7, current width 7.5, current thickness cm 9.0, diam. cm. 2.5–3.0, current wgt. 314g.

Mano

275 Muc 88/200 Mano, same material as Cat. No. 269
Munsell 2.5Y 6/4 (light yellowish brown);
Cm. 5.4 x 4.6 x 3.8, wgt. 130g.

276 Muc 88/211 Mano, same material as Cat. No. 273
Munsell 10R 4/3;
Dia. cm 6.5, wgt. 410g.

277 Muc 89/448 (from the zone of the Rock Crevice burial) Mano
percussion mark on one side;
Dia. cm 4.3–4.5, wgt. 97g.
Plate 46

Whetstones

278 Muc 89/16 Whetstone in basalt
triangular section, one side flattened, Munsell 2.5YR 4/2 (weak red);
L. cm. 19.0 x 7.0 x 5.65, wgt. greater than 1kg.
Plate 47

279 Muc 89/358b Whetstone
long rectangular section with rounded butt and point cut at an angle, Munsell 5Y 5/1 (gray);
Cm. 7.8 x 1.5 x 2.15, wgt. 50g.
Plate 47

280 Muc 89/361 (from the zone of the Rock Crevice burial) Whetstone?
oblong form, oval section, one face flattened with ends chipped in a concave form; fine grained stone, Munsell 2.5Y 5/2 (grayish brown);
L. cm 8.1 x 4.3 x 3.4, wgt. 200g.
Plate 46

281 Muc 89/362 (from the zone of the Rock Crevice
burial) Whetstone, same material as Cat. No. 272;
tapers toward one end, both ends chipped (one at a
regular angle); Munsell 5YR 5/2 (reddish gray);
L. cm. 10.8 x 2.0 x 3.0, wgt. 107g.
Plate 46

Grinding Stones

282 Muc 88/205 Discoid grinder(?) in basalt
smoothed on one side (stone rubbed or burned red),
Munsell 5Y 4/1 (dark gray, but greener) and 10R 4/
3 (weak red), carenation along one side gives a slightly bi-conical section;
Dia. cm 7.5–7.7, thickness cm 3.9, wgt. 350g.
Plate 46

283 Muc 88/209 Grinder/hammerstone
smoothed convex plane, opposite face with percussion mark at the center, Munsell 10YR 5/4 (yellowish
brown);
Cm. 9.5 x 12.0 x 4.0, wgt. 776g.

284 Muc 88/210 Fragment of a grinder in basalt (or gran-
ite)
large grains, Munsell 7.5YR 4/0 (dark gray);
Current l. cm 14.3, x 9.5 x 5.5, current wgt. 850g.

285 Muc 88/212 Grinder in basalt
one face flattened, Munsell 10YR 5/4 (yellowish
brown);
L. cm. 11.0 x 9.5 x 5.0, wgt. 820g.

286 Muc 89/359 Fragment of a grinding platform in
black lava;
Section thickness 7.5 cm.

287 Muc 89/363 Grinder, same material as Cat. No. 272
flat on one face, Munsell 2.5Y 5/4 (light olive brown)
and 10R 4.3 (weak red—fired this color?);
L. cm. 14.0 x 6.8 x 3.7, wgt. 517g.
Plate 47

288 Muc 89/365 Grinder
grinding plane slightly convex, stone as Cat. No. 273,
Munsell 11R 4/3 (weak red), fine grain;
L. cm. 16.8 x 21.5 x 5.5, wgt. greater than 1kg.
Plate 47

Other Groundstone

289 Muc 88/201 Smoothed stone
Munsell 5Y 5/2 (olive gray),
L. cm. 6.3 x 2.6 x 1.65, wgt. 50g.

290 Muc 88/203 Basalt block (basis for a handaxe?)
highly crystaline stone, Munsell 10YR 5/1 (gray)
speckled white and black, squared section with bev-
elled edges and rounded ends, one corner
chipped—rough-cut block for a handaxe? (cf. Leighton, 1989, 142ff.);
L. cm. 11.1 x 6.1 x 6.7, wgt. 765g.

Chipped-Stone Tools

Many tools in chipped stone have been found in archaeological contexts both of the village and of the Terrace. A
study of material found during the 1982 and 1983 excavation campaigns has appeared in La Muculufa I[181]. Inasmuch as that study demonstrated that little difference
could be found between the chipped-stone tools in the
Village and the Sanctuary a preliminary selection of these
Early Bronze Age finds from the 1988–1991 campaigns is
presented here without the distinction. As in the case of
the ground-stone tools, only those artifacts which for the
nature of their chipping showed clear signs of treatment to
create a recognizable type are presented. No attempt has
been made to analyze the chipping debris, which was also
recovered in significant quantities from the archaeological
strata, nor have statistical, material, provenience, or use
studies been performed. It is hoped that a specialized
study of these remains will be undertaken in the future.

Among the artifacts selected, several distinct classes of
tool can be identified. They include:

A. blades with a double edge for cutting on the sides,
most likely with a push-pull motion, cf. Leurquin,
1990, p.38; these occur both as long, narrow tools
with either a trapezoidal section (A.1) or a triangular section (A.2), or as shorter, narrow tools with a
triangular section (A.3); a hooked blade (A.4)
which may have been used to cut plants as a scythe
was also noted;

B. blades created from chips for light chopping on the
ends and for cutting on the sides with a chopping
or a push-pull motion, cf. Leurquin, 1990, p.38:
'end-scrapers'; these occur with either a trapezoidal
section (B.1) or a triangular section (B.2); a variation on this type with a smooth surface (B.3) was
also noted; a related light chopping tool with a

---

[181] J.L. Leurquin, "Chipped Stone Industry," in La Muculufa I,
p.37–46 (here cited in the text as Leurquin, 1990).

semicircular blade (B.4) was noted in a fragmentary form;

C. blades with a single edge for chopping created in a gray-green crystalline rock (C.1 and C.2); no prior mention is made of this class of material;

D. awls with a long, rhombic section (D.1) and a short, triangular section (D.2); cf. Leurquin, 1990, p.38: 'piercers';

E. small blades with denticulation (E.1 and E.2); denticulation is considered by Leurquin, 1990, p.38, to be the product either of deliberate retouching or use-wear;

F. points both in silicaceous stone and gray-green crystalline stone for arrows without a tang (F.1 and F.2) and with a tang (F.3 and F.4), as well as a point or sling-pellet with a rhombic section; cf. Leurquin, 1990, p.40 and 44.

The relatively small number of tools in obsidian, noted by Leurquin, 1990, p.40 and 45f., is reflected also in the sample presented here. Several cores in flint were also found in the village thereby supporting the apparent evidence that chipping activity took place primarily in the settlement[182].

Many examples of flint and other worked stone do not fit closely the tool-types established either by Leurquin or the present report, and secondary working (such as that for burins and composite tools; cf. Leurquin, 1990, p.38, 40 and 44) are not discussed here. An especially elegant arrowhead in flint showing considerable working was recovered from the village (Cat. No. 371, Figure 54). Two large examples of so-called 'Campignano-style' axes in chert were recovered from the village (Cat. Nos. 379–380), and they may have been used particularly in the preparation of tree-trunks and branches for hut construction. The recovery of these axes from secure Castelluccian contexts underscores the need to define the relationship between Paleolithic and Early Bronze Age typologies and to explain the significance of apparent similarities[183]. Study is needed also in defining the relationship between Sicilian chipped-stone typologies and those of North Africa, as well as those of Europe[184].

Catalogue of Chipped-Stone Tools

Type A: double-edge blades

291 Muc 89/109 Flint blade, type A.1
curved along the proximal end, monofacial, retouching along the blade, distal end broken; Munsell 2.5Y 4/4;
L. cm.9.5 x 2.5 x 0.4, wgt. 19 g.;
Plate 50

292 Muc 89/230 Flint blade, type A.1
monofacial, triangular section, proximal end trapezoidal, distal end narrow and broken, gentle curve along spine; Munsell 10YR 5/8 (yellowish brown);
Current l. cm. 5.3 x 1.2 x 0.2, wgt. 4 g.
Plate 51

293 Muc 88/17 Flint blade, type A.1,
monofacial, double-edge, trapezoidal section, highly curved, slight retouch along the blades, distal end broken; Munsell 10YR 5/6 (yellowish brown);
L. cm. 5.7 x 1.9 x 0.45, wgt. 7 g.

294 Muc 88/217 Blade fragment in obsidian, type A.1
trapezoidal section, monofacial, double-edge, proximal and distal ends broken; Munsell 2.5Y 3/0 (very dark gray or black);
Current l. cm 2.6 x 1.0 x 0.2.

---

[183] For a discussion of the definition and chronology of the Early Bronze Age 'Campignano' axe, see G. Battaglia and F. Nicoletti, "Ricerche Tipometriche sui Tranchets Campignani di Poggio Biddini-Ragusa," SicArch 24, 1991, p.53–66. An early discussion appears in I. Cafici, "Stazione dell'età della pietra a S. Cono in provincia di Catania," BPI 5, 1879, p.33ff. The problems raised by the so-called Campignano axe underscores Leurquin's comments (1990, p.46) concerning the continuity of technique in burin production from the Upper Paleolithic through the Early Bronze Age. See now F. Nicoletti, "Il campignano di Biddini (RG). Approccio alle industrie bifacciali oloceniche e all'attività mineraria della Sicilia preistorica," Archivio Storico per la Sicilia Orientale, 86, 1990, 7–59.

[184] Regarding relations between Europe and northern Africa from the Neolithic period through the Bronze Age with considerable reference to chipped-stone tool industries, see the many studies by G. Camps: "Notes de Protohistoire Nord-Africaine, III—Industries en obsidienne de l'Afrique du Nord," Libyca 12, 1964, p.293–299; "Les premiers navigateurs mediterraneens," L'Histoire 13, 1979, p.6–13; "Les relations entre l'Europe et l'Afrique du Nord pendant le Neolithique et le Chalcolithique," in Scripta Praehistorica F. Jorda Oblata, Salamanca, 1984, p.187–208; La Prehistoire, 1982, Italian ed. La Preistoria, Milano, 1985, passim.

---

[182] Leurquin (supra n.181, 40) notes that significantly more debris was recovered from the village area than from the Terrace.

295 Muc 88/224 Flint blade type A.1
double-edge, monofacial, trapezoidal section, blade retouched, distal end broken, mottled flint; Munsell 5YR 4/4 (reddish brown), 7.5YR 7/10 (light gray); L. cm 7.2 x 2.5 x 0.5, wgt. 15g.

296 Muc 89/439 Flint blade, type A.1
double-edge, monofacial, distal end broken; Munsell 10YR 6/8 (brownish yellow); L. cm. 5.0 x 1.35 x 0.2.

297 Muc 88/31 Flint blade fragment, type A.1, proximal end broken, point curving to the right, trapezoidal section, double-edge, monofacial, Munsell 10YR 5/4 (yellowish brown); L. cm. 3.0 x 1.3 x 0.4.

298 Muc 89/370 Fragment of a flint blade, type A.2 triangular section, double-edge (one blade larger than the other), distal end broken; Munsell 7.5YR 4/2 (brown/dark brown); Current l. cm. 2.0 x 0.8 x 0.3.

299 Muc 89/376 Flint blade, type A.2
monofacial, single blade, distal end broken, Munsell 10YR 5/6 (yellowish brown); L. cm. 5.6 x 0.9 x 0.2.

300 Muc 89/378 Flint blade, type A.2
triangular section, dorsal ridge off-center, lacking distal and proximal ends, monofacial, double-edge, slight retouch along the edges; Current l. cm. 3.1 x 0.25 x 0.8.

301 Muc 89/389 Flint blade, type A.2
monofacial double-edge, proximal end squared, distal end squared, Munsell 10YR 6/2 (light brownish gray); L. cm. 4.4 x 1.1 x 0.5. Plate 51

302 Muc 89/400 Flint blade, type A.2
triangular section, monofacial, double-edge, long curve, distal end squared, inset on one blade next to proximal end, Munsell 10YR 5/6 (yellowish brown); L. cm. 2.3 x 0.7 x 0.3. Plate 50

303 Muc 89/401 Flint blade, type A.2
distal end broken, flat and wide at the proximal end, triangular section; Munsell 2.5YR 4/6 (red); Current l. cm. 2.7 x 1.8 (proximal end) x 0.25. Plate 50

304 Muc 88/257 Blade in gray-green stone, type A.2 rhomboid form, triangular section, retouch along the edges, double-edge, monofacial, Munsell 5Y 4/1 (dark gray); L. cm.4.8 x 2.8 x 1.0.

305 Muc 88/28 Flint blade, type A.2
slight curve, distal end broken, monofacial, double-edge, proximal end sharpened, triangular section, Munsell 10YR 5/6 (yellowish brown); L. cm. 5.3 x 1.3 x 0.4. Plate 50

306 Muc 89/128 Pair of thin flint blades, type A.3 monofacial, triangular section, gentle curve to body; Munsell 5YR 5/6 (yellowish red), A: L. cm. 3.2 x 0.5 x 0.2, wgt. less than 5 g.; B: proximal end broken, Current l. cm. 2.8 x 0.5 x 0.1. Plate 50

307 Muc 88/218 Fragment of a flint blade, type A.3 half of the proximal end preserved, monofacial, triangular section, lacking retouch, Munsell 2.5YR 3/6, dark red); L. cm. 2.6 x 1.3 x 0.4. Plate 51

308 Muc 89/369 Fragment of a flint blade, type A.3 proximal end and distal end broken, triangular section, Munsell 5YR 4/4 (reddish brown); Current l. cm. 1.4 x 1.0 x 0.2.

309 Muc 88/5 Flint blade, type A.3
triangular section, double-edge, monofacial, distal end broken, Munsell 2.5YR 4/4 (reddish brown); Current l. cm. 4.3 x 1.1 x 0.35, wgt. 3 g.

310 Muc 89/382 Flint blade, type A.3,
double-edge, monofacial, triangular area above percussion bulb, Munsell 10YR 5/6 (yellowish brown); Current l. cm. 2.4 x 1.15 x 0.4.

311 Muc 89/100 Flint blade
monofacial, trapezoidal section, light retouching on both blades; Munsell 10YR 5/8 (yellowish brown), notable arching on blade near percussion bulb; L. cm. 8.0, width cm. 1.5, max. thickness cm. 0.3, wgt. 5 g. Plate 50

312 Muc 88/219 Fragment of flint blade
proximal end a chevron, monofacial, double-edge very irregular, distal end broken; Munsell 2.5YR 3/6, Dark Red); L. cm. 4.0 x 1.65 x 0.35. Plate 50

313 Muc 88/220 Fragment of flint blade
double-edge, monofacial, triangular section, imperfect flint, coarse on one side, fine and slightly retouched on the other;
Current l. cm. 5.3 x 2.9 x 1.0; Munsell 2.5YR 5/0 (gray).

314 Muc 89/367 Fragment of flint blade split halfway along the spine
proximal end only monofacial, double-edge, Munsell 5YR 4/6 (yellowish red);
Current l. cm. 3.7 x 0.4 x current width cm. 0.9.

315 Muc 89/368 Fragment of flint blade
proximal end preserved, rest broken, monofacial, one side of the blade larger, Munsell 10YR 5/6 (yellowish brown);
Current l. cm 2.9 x 2.6 x 0.4.

316 Muc 89/372 Microflint blade
monofacial, double-edge a triangular section, Munsell 5YR 4/4 (reddish brown);
Current l. cm. 2.1 x 0.6 x 0.2.

317 Muc 88/221 Flint blade
distal end broken, triangular section, monofacial, double-edge; Munsell 10YR 4/6 (dark yellowish brown);
Current l. cm. 4.1 x 1.2 x 0.25, wgt. 4 g.

318 Muc 88/222 Blade
monofacial, single blade with rounded distal end, triangular section broken, Munsell 5Y 5/1 (gray);
L. cm. 3.5 x 0.9 x 0.3.
Plate 50

319 Muc 88/223 Blade
monofacial, double-edge, triangular section, distal end broken, blade slightly retouched;
Current l. cm. 5.2 x 2.0 x 0.5, wgt. 8 g.

320 Muc 89/377 Flint blade
proximal end broken, distal end squared, triangular section, Munsell 10YR 4/1 (dark gray);
Current l. cm 5.2 x 2.15 x 0.6.

321 Muc 88/242 Blade fragment in obsidian
trapezoidal section, proximal and distal ends broken;
Current l. cm. 3.1 x 1.3 x 0.35.

322 Muc 89/387 End fragment of blade
proximal end broken, point curved, double-edge, monofacial, triangular section;
L. cm. 2.1 x 1.0 x 0.2.

323 Muc 89/390 Blade fragment in obsidian
fragment of the proximal end, monofacial, triangular section;
Current l. cm. 2.4 x 1.6 x 0.4.
Plate 49

324 Muc 88/245 Proximal end of flint blade
monofacial, double-edge, blade retouched, trapezoidal section, Munsell 2.5YR 3/6 (dark red);
Current l. cm. 2.5 x 2.6 x 0.75.

325 Muc 89/392 Flint blade
proximal end broken, monofacial, double-edge, trapezoidal section, Munsell 5YR 5/2 (reddish gray),
Current l. cm. 2.6 x 1.0 x 0.2.
Plate 50

326 Muc 89/393 Flint blade, proximal end and distal end broken, monofacial, double-edge, trapezoidal section, retouch on blade, burnt to Munsell color 7.5YR 5/0 (gray), light brownish core visible;
Current l. cm. 3.5 x 0.8 x 0.3.

327 Muc 89/394 Flint blade in two fragments, monofacial, double-edge, retouching on underside of the blade, triangular section, burnt, Munsell 10YR 5/1 (gray);
Current l. cm. 5.0 x 2.2 x 0.6.

328 Muc 89/395 Flint blade in two fragments (part of Cat. No. 327)
burnt, Munsell 10YR 5/1 (gray);
Current l. cm 4.5 x 2.0 x 0.5;

329 Muc 89/397 Flint blade
double-edge, monofacial, trapezoidal section, distal end lacking, Munsell 2.5YR 4/8 (red);
Current l. cm. 2.5 x 0.8 x 0.25.

330 Muc 89/417 Flint blade
double-edge, monofacial, slight curve, trapezoidal section at the proximal end, triangular section, at the distal end, Munsell 7.5YR 5/4 (brown);
L. cm. 5.5 x 1.1 x 0.2–0.25.
Plate 51

331 Muc 89/425 Flint blade
proximal end with barbs, distal end rounded, triangular section, Munsell 2.5Y 3/0 (very dark gray);
L. cm. 2.2 x 1.4 x 0.3.
Plate 51

332 Muc 89/428 Flint blade
irregular secton (trapezoidal-triangular), double-edge, distal end slightly broken;
Current l. cm. 6.2 x 1.4 x 0.2.
Plate 50

Type B: 'endscrapers'

333 Muc 88/256 Blade in gray-green stone, type B.1
trapezoidal section, distal end squared, monofacial,
double-edge, Munsell 5Y 4/1 (dark gray);
L. cm. 4.5 x 2.8 x 0.85.
Plate 51

334 Muc 89/366 Fragment of flint blade, type B.2
monofacial, double-edge, triangular section, distal
end broken?, rectangular form, Munsell 7.5YR 5/2
(pinkish gray);
L. cm. 3.8 x 2.0 x 0.5, wgt. 5 g.
Plate 51

335 Muc 89/371 Fragment of flint blade, type B.2
triangular section, monofacial, double-edge, proximal end, distal end broken, Munsell 10YR 4/1 (dark
gray);
Current l. cm. 1.6 x 1.0 x 0.2.

336 Muc 88/225 Flint blade, type B.2
distal end broken, monofacial, double-edge, slight retouch, Munsell 7.5YR 5/6 (strong brown);
Current l. cm. 3.6 x 1.5 x 0.2.

337 Muc 88/258 Flint chip, type B.3
single-edge on the distal end, blade wide, form triangular, with point at the proximal end, Munsell 7.5YR
3/0 (very dark gray);
L. cm. 4.1 x 3.1 x 0.65.
Plate 52

338 Muc 89/438 Flint blade, type B.3
distal end squared in a straight blade, blade retouched
along the sides, lens-like section (bi-facial?);
L. cm. 3.9 x 2.7 x (blade) 0.4/(percussion bulb) 0.9.
Plate 52

339 Muc 88/29 Flint blade, type B.3
double-edge, monofacial, edges chipped from use or
retouched, distal end broken, proximal end widened,
Munsell 10YR 3/1 (very dark gray);
Current l. cm. 3.2 x 1.8 x 0.6.

Type C: single-edge razors in gray-green stone

340 Muc 89/383 Razor in gray-green stone, type C.1,
one side retouched along the edges, upper part of the
chip concave, triangular section, single-edge, curved,
Munsell ca. 5Y 4/1 (dark gray);
L. cm. 6.4 x 4.5 x 1.5.

341 Muc 88/261 Razor in gray-green stone, type C.2
triangular section, retouching along the wide blade;
L. cm. 4.6 x 5.7 x 1.1.

342 Muc 89/384 Razor in gray-green stone
monofacial, left side in an arc, right side straight,
wide blade on distal side, proximal end broken,
Munsell 10YR 5.2 (grayish rown);
L. cm. 7.2 x (blade distale) 5.0 x 1.2, wgt. 55 g.
Plate 52

343 Muc 89/402 Incomplete razor in gray-green stone
monofacial, one face chipped on three sides, Munsell
2.5YR 3/0 (very dark gray);
L. cm. 5.5 x 5.0 x 2.2, weight 72 g.
Plate 52

344 Muc 89/403 Blade in gray-green stone, type A.2 section
distal end broken, double-edge, monofacial, burnt as
Cat No. 327, Munsell 10YR 5/1 (gray);
Current l. cm 14.5 x 1.1 x 0.5.

345 Muc 89/414 Razor in gray-green stone (chip from a
round stone)
monofacial, slight retouching along the edges, slightly concave;
L. cm. 8.1 x 5.6 x 2.0, weight 93 g.

346 Muc 89/435 Razor in gray-green stone
triangular form, triangular section, retouching along
the edges on three sides;
L. cm. 4.8 x 5.2 x 2.1, weight 45 g.
Plate 52

347 Muc 89/429 Flint razor
squared, monofacial, double-edge, retouching on the
lower side, in mottled flint, Munsell 7.5YR 3/0 (very
dark gray);
L. cm. 3.0 x 3.0 x 1.0.
Plate 51

348 Muc 88/265 Flint razor
wide blade, proximal end narrow and raised, retouching along the blade, monofacial, Munsell 5Y 6/1
(gray/light gray);
L. cm. 6.4 x 4.0 x 0.6.
Plate 52

349 Muc 89/444 Point in gray-green stone, type F.4
proximal end narrowed into a tang, monofacial,
Munsell 5Y 3/1 (very dark gray);
L. cm. 6.3 x 4.9 x 1.8.
Plate 52

Type D: awls

350 Muc 89/381 Flint awl, type D.1
rhomboid section, proximal end rounded and flattened, distal end broken, Munsell 10YR 5/6 (yellowish brown);
Current l. cm 4.0 x (prox. end) 1.35 x 0.6.

351 Muc 89/374 Awl(?) in obsidian
L. cm. 2.3 x 1.1 x 0.45, wgt. 3 g.

352 Muc 88/41 Flint awl, type E.1
lower edge not as a saw, Munsell 10YR 3/1 (very dark gray);
L. cm. 3.0 x 0.65 x 0.7.
Plate 48

353 Muc 89/379 Flint awl
rhomboid section, diagonal cutting on the distal side, Munsell 7.5YR 5/4 (brown);
L. cm. 4.2 x 1.3 x 0.3.
Plate 48

Type E: denticulated blades

354 Muc 89/409 Flint awl, type E.1
distal end broken, one side in a smooth curve, the other (lower one) retouched as a saw, Munsell 10YR 6/2 (light brownish gray);
L. cm. 4.2 x (end) 0.7 x 0.8.

355 Muc 89/410 Flint awl, type E.1
created from a blade, trapezoidal section, lower part as a saw, upper part in a smooth curve, mottled color, Munsell 10YR 4/3 (dark brown/brown);
L. cm. 14.1 x 1.7 x 0.8.
Plate 48

356 Muc 89/398 Saw in flint, type E.2
monofacial, one side straight, the other with at least three points of a saw, Munsell 10YR 4/3 (brown/dark brown);
L. cm. 5.0 x 1.5 x 0.6.
Plate 48

Type F: points and arrowheads

357 Muc 88/244 Spearpoint in black flint, similar to type A.3
triangular section, double-edge, monofacial, Munsell 2.5Y 3/0 (very dark gray);
L. cm. 2.3 x 1.0 x 0.2.

358 Muc 89/399 Flint point, similar to type A.3
monofacial, single-edge, flat section, Munsell 10YR 5/6 (yellowish brown);
L. cm. 1.0 x 0.8 x 0.2.

359 Muc 89/445 Flint point, similar to type A.3
double-edge, distal end, curve to the left, monofacial, Munsell 10YR 5/4 (yellowish brown).
Plate 49

360 Muc 89/385 Flint point, type F.1
monofacial, double-edge, right side broken, retouch along the edges, distal end at the point, Munsell 10YR 4/1 (dark gray);
L. cm. 2.7 x 1.6 x 0.35.

361 Muc 89/375 (from the Terrace zone) Flint blade, type F.3
end broken, Munsell 10YR 5/1 (gray);
L. cm. 3.7 x 1.6 x 0.4, tang thick cm 0.8.
Plate 48

362 Muc 89/391 Flint spearpoint, type F.1
monofacial, double-edge, concave at proximal end upper side, half-lunate section, Munsell 10YR 7/3 (very pale brown);
L. cm. 2.5 x 1.7 x 0.3.
Plate 49

363 Muc 89/396 Flint chip, type F.1
retouched in order to create three blade edges, burnt, Munsell 10YR 5/1 (gray);
L. cm. 2.8 x 2.3 x 0.8.
Plate 49

364 Muc 89/406 Flint point, type F.1
bifacial, double-edge, Munsell 10YR 5/6 (yellowish brown);
L. cm. 2.5 x 1.2 x 0.4.
Plate 49

365 Muc 89/408 Flint point, type F.1
monofacial, double-edge, Munsell 10YR 5/6 (yellowish brown);
L. cm. 1.9 x 1.2 x 0.25.
Plate 49

366 Muc 89/433 Flint point, type F.2
triangular section;
L. cm. 4.2 x 3.3 x 1.0.
Plate 49

367 Muc 89/434 Flint point, type F.2
triangular form, monofacial, retouching along the edges, Munsell 2.5Y 2/0 (black);
L. cm. 1.5 x 1.2 x 0.4.
Plate 49

368 Muc 89/407 Flint point, type F.3
long tang, distal end broken, Munsell 10YR 3/2 (very dark grayish/gray);
Current l. cm. 3.1 x 1.0 x 0.35, tang cm. 0.5 x 0.15.
Plate 48

369 Muc 88/39 Flint point, type F.1
Munsell 5Y 2.5/1 (black);
L. cm. 1.3 x 1.0 x 0.2.
Plate 49

370 Muc 89/373 Irregular point in flint
triangular section, without retouch, highly curved, Munsell 7.5YR 4/0 (dark gray);
L. cm. 3.5 x 1.5 x 0.55, wgt. 6 g.

371 Muc 89/72 Arrowhead
bifacial, double-edge, retouching along the blades, two barbs along the side, upper face with a spine, lower face with concave cutting; Munsell 10YR 5/4 (yellowish brown);
L. cm. 4.4, width cm. 2.3, thickness cm. 0.6, tang length cm. 1.1, tang width cm. 1.5, wgt. 7 g.
Plate 48

372 Muc 89/380 Point in black flint
trapezoidal section, monofacial, slightly curved to the right;
L. cm. 1.23 x 1.0 x 0.4.
Plate 49

373 Muc 89/386 Sling-pellet or spearpoint in flint
rounded rhomboid section, one side broken, Munsell 10YR 4/1 (dark gray);
L. cm. 2.7 x 1.5 x 1.35, wgt. 5 g.
Plate 49

374 Muc 89/416 Flint point
monofacial, triangular section, proximal end wide, Munsell 7.5YR 4/0 (dark gray);
L. cm. 4.5 x 2.6 x 0.7.
Plate 48

375 Muc 89/404 Flint point
monofacial, double-edge, slight retouch along the blades
L. cm. 2.2 x 1.3 x 0.25.
Plate 49

376 Muc 89/427 Flint point
triangular section, short tang, slight retouch to the sides, Munsell 10YR 4/1 (dark gray);
L. cm. 2.9 x 2.0 x 0.75.

377 Muc 88/x1 Flint point
monofacial, double-edge (perhaps 3 blades?), Munsell 5YR 3/1 (very dark gray);
L. cm. 2.9 x 2.3 x 0.5.
Plate 49

378 Muc 89/413 Point in gray-green stone
monofacial, percussion bulb present, proximal end, double-edge, distal end in a point, coarse trapezoidal section, no retouching, Munsell 10R 4/2 (weak red);
L. cm. 7.5 x 4.2 x 2.5, weight 67 g.
Plate 52

Axes

379 Muc 88/11 'Campignano-type' axe in flint
diagonally cut along the butt, very rough cutting edge, Munsell 10YR 7/2 (light grey);
L. cm. 8.3 x 6.6 x 2.3. wgt. 178g,.

380 Muc 88/117 'Campignano-type' axe in flint
diagonally cut along the butt, very rough cutting edge, Munsell 10YR 7/2 (light grey);
L. cm. 8.4 x 6.7 x 2.3. wgt. 180g,.
Plate 53

381 Muc 88/263 (sporadic find) Axe in a hard, sandy stone
chipped, monofacial, double-edge, retouch along the edges, Munsell 10YR 4/4 (dark yellowish brown);
L. cm. 12.5 x 8.5 x 3.6, weight 466 g.
Plate 53

Cores

382 Muc 89/415 Core in gray-green stone
base flat and ovoid, various chips along the surface;
L. cm. 5.9 x 4.0 x 5.35, weight 136 g.

383 Muc 88/264 Core in gray-green stone
at least 5 chips, Munsell 7.5YR 4/2 (dark brown/ brown);
H. cm. 6.5 x (base) 6.0 x 6.5, weight 340 g.

384 Muc 88/260 Core in flint
at least 10 chips, Munsell 10YR 7/2;
L. cm. 4.7 x 3.3 x 4.3, weight 35 g.

385 Muc 89/411 Core in flint
at least 12 vertical chips, Munsell 10YR 6/1 (light gray/gray);
H. cm. 3.3 x 2.4 x 3.4, wgt. 29 g.

Other Forms:

386 Muc 89/412 Flint in a quadrangular form
monofacial, four blades, mottled Munsell 10YR 5/8
(yellowish brown);
L. cm. 2.9 x 2.3 x 0.6.
Plate 53

387 Muc 88/262 Hook in coarse flint
distal end in form of hook, triangular section, monofacial double-edge, Munsell 10R 4/1 (dark reddish
gray);
L. cm. 6 x 2.8 x 0.8.
Plate 52

388 Muc 89/418 Flint in semilunate form (pendant?)
Munsell 2.5YR 3/6 (dark red);
Cm 4.0 x 3.2 x 0.75.
Plate 53

Bone Tools

A number of tools in bone were found in both the Field
and the Terrace excavation zones during the course of the
excavations. All of them seem to have been made from the
forelegs of sheep/goat, and this use might have contribut-
ed to the significant absence of forelegs noted among the
many animal bones recovered from the strata of the Terrace excavation zone[185].

Bone was used primarily for creating awls (*punteruoli*),
although one object seems to have been an actual needle[186]. The awls had a standard dimension between 8–10
cm. long with a diameter just over cm. 1.0. Both the form
and the diameter, which is roughly equal to the diameter
of the holes in the spindle-whorls, suggests that the awls
were used to puncture holes in sheep/goat hides perhaps
for the creation of clothes. Furthermore, this observation
may be related to the question raised in the preceding section of whether the terracotta spindle whorls and bobbins
were used to make thread for weaving or for sewing together hides as clothing.

---

[185] K. Cruz-Uribe, "The Mammalian Fauna," in La Muculufa
I, p.57–64, esp. p.59f. and 64.

[186] Cf. R.R. Holloway and M.S. Joukowsky, "Worked Bone
and Amulets," in La Muculufa I, p.48.

Catalogue of Bone Tools

389 Muc 89/115 Awl
point cut on one side, cm. 2.7 long, joint at opposite
end;
L. cm. 8.8, body diameter cm. 1.1 x 0.9.
Plate 54

390 Muc 89/36 Awl
point cut on one side only, cm. 5.0 long, joint at opposite end;
L. cm. 8.5, body diameter cm. 1.3 x 0.015.
Plate 54

391 Muc 89/114 Awl
point cut on one side, cm. 2.2 long, joint at opposite
end;
L. cm. 7.3, body diameter cm. 1.5 x 1.2.
Plate 54

392 Muc 89/111 Awl
point cut on one side, cm. 5.3. long, joint at opposite
end;
L. cm. 10.1, body diameter cm. 1.3 x 1.2.
Plate 54

393 Muc 89/134 Awl
wall opposite point cut at right angle;
L. cm. 8.5, body diameter cm. 1.1 x 0.65.
Plate 54

394 Muc 89/10 (from the Terrace zone) Awl
L. cm. 10, body diameter cm. 1.15 x 0.6.

395 Muc 89/141 (from the Terrace zone) Needle
L. cm. 8.1, width cm. 0.6 x 0.3.
Plate 54

396 Muc 89/4 Needle?
L. cm. 8.0, width cm. 0.85 x 0.5
Plate 54

397 Muc 91/9 Awl
L. cm. 9.3, width cm. 2.2 x 1.1
Plate 54

398 Muc 88/13 (sporadic find) Awl in horn
L. cm. 10.0, width cm. 2.75 x 2.0
Plate 54

Pendants and Amulets

A series of pendants and/or amulets in a variety of materials was found at La Muculufa. A pendant is defined here

as a decorative object with clear evidence for having been worn from a string of some sort; an amulet is any other decorative object which is generally similar but which lacks evidence for how or if it might have been worn. Many of these kinds of object are known from other Castelluccian sites[187]. The most common are *pseudo-brassards* in a metamorphic greenstone with either one or two holes for attachment to a string[188]. Many shells of *glycymeris pilosa* and *cardium edule*, salt-water shellfish well-known at other sites, were recovered in Hut No. 2 at 110E/95S (series Cat. No. 411, plate 20.4) in association with a pedestal bowl (Cat. No. 4, plate 22) and a stone pendant (Cat. No. 403). Is it possible that these shells had been conserved in the pedestal bowl? A series of boar's teeth were also found. It is not clear that these were actually used as pendants because they lack a mounting; however, the fact that they were found separately suggests that they had been kept for their aesthetic value or for some other, not strictly decorative purpose[189]. Also recovered was a lunate object in chipped flint (Cat. No. 388—listed among the chipped-stone tools) which may have served as a pendant rather than as an implement. Perhaps the greatest significance of these discoveries lies in the wider range of decorative or apotropaic pendants which is apparent in domestic contexts than was previously evident[190].

Catalogue of Pendants and Amulets

Stone Pendants

399 Muc 88/19 Pseudo-brassard in three fragments
hole in one extremity, other extremity missing, Munsell 5Y 6/1 (light grey); cf. Adamo, 1989, Plate IV, no.13;
L. att. cm. 7,4 x 1.2 x 0.75, wgt. 12g.
Plate 55

400 Muc 88/173 Pendant in sandstone
ovoid form, hole off-center;
cf. Adamo, 1989, Plate I, no.5;
Cm. 4.0 x 5.0 diam. cm. 0.7.
Plate 56

401 Muc 89/119 Pseudo-brassard
holes in each extremity (one 1 mm., other 2 mm.), Munsell 2.5Y 5/2 (grayish brown) 2.5Y 4/1 (dark gray);
L. cm. 4.4 x 1.1 x 0.6, wgt. 6g.
Plate 55

402 Muc 88/111 Pseudo-brassard
rounded on one face, flattened on the other, two holes (2 mm. each) at each extremity; Munsell 2.5Y 4/0 (dark grey), cf. Adamo, 1989, Plate I, no.20;
L. cm. 4.0 x 1.15 x 0.7, wgt. 5g.
Plate 20.4 and 55

403 Muc 89/355 Pseudo-brassard
rounded on one face, flat on the other, two holes at the extremities (one diam. 2mm., the other 1.5mm.), Munsell 5Y 5/1 (gray), found together with shell necklace Cat. No. 411; cf. Adamo, 1989, Plate I, no.20;
L. cm.. 5.5 x 1.1 x 0.65, wgt. 10g.
Plate 55

Boar's Teeth

404 Muc 88/189 Boar's tooth
cf. Adamo, 1989, Plate III, no.13;
L. cm. 5.0 x 1.25 x 0.75.

---

[187] The most complete study of these materials is O. Adamo, "Pendagli e amuleti della facies di Castelluccio in Sicilia," Archivio Storico per la Sicilia Orientale 85, 1989, p.7–69 (here Adamo, 1989). Pendants recovered at La Muculufa in 1982 and 1983 are presented by R.R. Holloway and M.S. Joukowsky in "Worked Bone and Amulets," in La Muculufa I, p.48. Special thanks are owed to O. Adamo for her comments on these materials.

[188] Regarding this type of stone, see Adamo, 1989, p.14–15 with n.30 and D. Evett, "A Preliminary Note on the Typology, Functional Variability and Trade of Italian Neolithic Ground Stone Axes," Origini 7, 1972, p.35–54; R. Leighton, "Ground Stone Tools from Serra Orlando (Morgantina) and Stone Axe Studies in Sicily and Southern Italy," PPS 55, 1989, p.135–159; R. Leighton and J.E. Dixon, "Jade and Greenstone in the Prehistory of Sicily and Southern Italy," OJA 11, 1992, p.179–200. Adamo, 1989, p.41 suggests that the dark green color of this type of metamorphic stone may have had an apotropaic significance.

[189] Adamo, 1989, p.42 notes that in funerary contexts boars' teeth and greenstone pendants (*pseudo-brassards*) are mutually exclusive. Perhaps the boars' teeth were carried in some kind of container (a small sack?) and not worn. It has also been suggested (J. Bruhn) that greenstone pendants and shells would not appear on the same necklace for reasons of weight and a general incompatibility of design concept.

[190] Adamo, 1989, p.38 states that only bossed-bone plaques (*ossa a globuli*) and terracotta discs can be attributed to domestic contexts. It is somewhat surprising that only a single fragment of a bossed-bone plaque has been recovered at La Muculufa to date; cf. Holloway and Joukowsky (here n.187).

405 Muc 89/300 (sporadic find) Boar's tooth
Cm. 5.6 x 1.3 x 0.75.
Plate 56

406 Muc 88/224 (from the Terrace zone) Boar's tooth
point of tooth broken;
Cm. 6.0 x 2.6 x 2.0.

407 Muc 88/193 Boar's tooth
broken at the extremities;
Cm. 3.5 x 1.0 x 0.6.

Beads and Shells

408 Muc 88/241 Shell, glycymeris pilosa (cf. Adamo, 1989, Plate IV, no.2)
edge worn smooth, incisions along the edge;
Cm. 1.8 x 2.0 x 0.5.

409 Muc 89/23 Bead in shell (dentalium)
white;
Cm.. 1.2 x diam. 0.8–1.0 x 1.5.
Plate 20.4 and 56

410 Muc 89/64 (from the zone of the Rock Crevice burial) Biconical bead in stone
hole in center cm. 0.35;
H. cm. 0.8 x width cm. 1.0 x 1.2.
Plate 20.4 and 56

411 Muc 89/83 Necklace of shells, glycymeris pilosa and cardium edule
some with smooth surface, others with radial and circumferential lines, varying in size: 29 shells (14 whole, 15 reconstructed almost whole) ranging in dimension between cm. 1.8 x 1.5 x 0.6 and 5.1 x 3.9 x 1.7; 16 fragments (perhaps of 10 different shells), shells bear 0.2 cm. perforations either at the center or to the left or right of the center according to the placement of the shell on the necklace (P. Farrugia: the hole is always towards the center of the necklace); 319 large and small fragments representing ca. 98 shells (number of shells highly approximate).
Plate 20.4 (selection)

412 Muc 91/37 Shell, glycymeris pilosa
perforation (cm. 0.5 x 0.3) at the center;
Cm. 4.0 x 4.5 x 1.8.

413 Muc 91/38 Shell, glycymeris pilosa
perforation at the center;
Cm. 2.5 x 3.2 x 1.2.

414 Muc 89/453 (sporadic find) Shell, cardium edule
circular, perforation at the center;
cm. 1.8 x 2.0 x 0.6
Plate 56

Some Greek Materials Found at La Muculufa

The site of La Muculufa witnessed the floruit of Greek settlement in Sicily, even though its principal occupation dates to Castelluccian times. This study is limited to evidence for a Greek presence and its historical context[191]. Many artifacts recovered in the village and on the Terrace, despite the fact that they do not come from a single level, but rather from superficial deposits, can delimit the chronological range of the Greek occupation.

A *terminus ante quem* for the earliest group of materials may be identified in the first quarter of the sixth century B.C. Finds dating to the Archaic period include:

415 Muc 89/319 Body fragment of an amphoriskos
yellow-pink fabric, dark purple paint; H. 5.9 cm., width 5.6 cm., thickness 0.5 cm; a zoomorphic frieze delimited by three horizontal bands shows the almost completely preserved body of a panther; rosettes of various dimensions with engraved petals and outlines in the field; late Middle Corinthian[192]
Plate 57

416 Muc 89/348 Fragment of a kothon
chamois-coloured fabric, dark brown and black decoration, height 2.8 cm., width 2.9 cm., thickness 0.4 cm., decorated with a double line of dots delimited by lines. attributable to the White-style of Late Corinthian II[193]

417 Muc 91/1 Fragment of a kotyle
pink-beige fabric, painted in brown and black on the rear, with the exception of the reserved rim, height 3.0 cm., width 1.7 cm., thickness 0.3 cm., zig-zag

---

[191] The author wishes to thank Prof. Brian E. McConnell for having given her the opportunity to study this material and for his assistance, as well as to Dr. Laura Maniscalco for her helpful advice.

[192] J. Boardman and J. Hayes, Tocra: the archaic deposits I, London 1966, pl.VI, 13–14.

[193] H. Payne, Necrocorinthia, Oxford, 1931, p.355.

decoration delimited by bands below and along the rim; late Corinthian II[194]

418 Muc 89/333 Rim and shoulder fragment of an Ionian kylix
pink fabric, painted red and black on the rear, height 3.5 cm., width 2.5 cm., thickness 0.4 cm., second half of the sixth century B.C.

To a second phase it is possible to attribuite an artifact dating from the beginning of the fifth century B.C.:

419 Muc 89/342 Fragment of a lamp
pink fabric, painted decoration in red, height 3.1 cm., width 3.0 cm., thickness 0.5 cm., interior painted solid, on the exterior two concentric circles[195].

Furthermore, to this phase it is possible to attribute several unpainted ceramics, including part of a large bowl with a handle and several hydriae decorated with horizontal bands.

To the middle of the fifth century B.C. it is possible to ascribe:

420 Muc 89/1 Female head in terracotta
red-orange fabric; no traces of paint, height 6.4 cm., the figure wears a polos; the face, not perfectly preserved, is framed by hair which spreads in front toward the shoulders; along the brow the hair is rendered in wavy furrows. In the rear it is possible to notice an attempt to model the polos
Plate 57, illustrated also in La Muculufa I, p.64, fig. 87

It is difficult to determine the typology of the head, which may represent an offerant—Demeter with a little pig, a seated woman with a decoration on her breast, or more generally, a seated woman. Although these kinds of figures are found often in sacred areas, they have been found also in other contexts and used for a variety of purposes[196]. For example, a doll displayed in the Archeological Museum at Gravina di Puglia has a face which presents the stereotypical features of the above-mentioned female figures, while the characteristics of the body make it clear that it was used as a toy[197]. Inasmuch as the head from La Mu-

culufa was not found together with other evidence for a sacred area, we may suggest that it served a similar, simple purpose.

Although materials from the latter part of the fifth century B.C. have yet to be found at the site, during the 1989 excavation campaign a structure datable to the fourth century B.C. was discovered in Field excavation portion F150 (Plates 11.1 and 13.5). The western side of this structure measures 4.25 m, while the length remains to be determined[198]. The excavation of the structure permitted the recovery not only of materials dating from earlier periods (they were recovered from relatively superficial strata or inconsistent contexts) but also of a consistent deposit preserved beneath the collapse of the structure on its floor. The more notable pieces include:

421 Muc 89/329 Fragment of a patera
reddish fabric, irridescent black paint, height 2.04 cm., width 5.6 cm., thickness 0.6 cm., interior also painted, late fifth–early fourth century B.C.[199]

422 Muc 89/6 and 89/81 Mortar
fabric with a red core, yellow exterior, diameter 34.3 cm., rim flattened and furnished with two modeled handles, the bowl is wide and shallow, and a long spout (7.5cm) extends out from it, beginning of the fourth century B.C.[200]
Plate 57

---

[196] M. Bell, Morgantina Studies I, The terracottas, Princeton, 1981, pl.7, 28; R. Higgins, Catalogue of the terracottas in the Department of Greek and Roman Antiquities of the British Museum, London, 1975, nos. 1139–1140; Greci e Indigeni... (here n.194) p.118, 152. According to Bell, the female figures discovered in Sicily (they have been found at Gela, Camarina, Grammichele, Akragas, Siracusa, Megara Hyblea and most of all at Selinus) whether formed locally or imported, reflect the influence of several East Greek cities as well as Gela.

[197] See L. Patruno, "Gioiello nascosto," Bell'Italia 68, December, 1991, p.128.

[198] See B.E. McConnell, "La Muculufa after the Bronze Age," in La Muculufa I, p.49–56.

[199] See B.A. Sparkes and L. Talcott, The Athenian Agora, XII, Black and plain pottery, Part II, Princeton, 1970, pl. 33; Greci e Indigeni... (here n.194) p.92, 79.

[200] See The Athenian Agora, XII (here n.199) pl. 92, nos. 1914–1848. This is a typical round-top mortar which appears at Corinth between the end of the fifth and the beginning of the fourth century B.C.; its use continues through the end of the fourth century B.C.

---

[194] Payne (here n.193) p.344, fig. 180; Greci e indigeni nella Valle dell'Himera. Scavi a Monte Saraceno di Ravanusa, show cat., Università di Messina, Italy, 14 April–9 May 1985, p.57 and 21.

[195] See the type 19B described in R. Hubbard Howland, The Athenian Agora, IV: Greek Lamps and their survivals, Princeton, 1958, p.40–41.

423 Muc 89/326 Amphora handle

pink fabric, yellow slip, height 4.0 cm., width 3.4 cm., thickness 2.5 cm., twisted handle of which only part of the attachment is preserved, last decades of the fourth century B.C.[201]

424 Muc 89/344 Fragment of a black-figure vessel

pink fabric, glossy black and red paint, height 4.0 cm., width 2.2 cm., thickness 0.4 cm., rear not painted, ivy decoration painted in red with white margins and incised veins on the leaves, last decades of the fourth century B.C.[202]

425 Muc 89/325 Terracotta hut model

yellow-pink fabric, height 4.01 cm., base diameter 4.0 cm., fixed on an almost circular base, the hut has a tronco-conic shape; a trapezoidal opening on the side represents a door[203]
Plates 19.5 and 57

Two finds on the interior of the structure are of special interest: a *corno fittile* (Cat. No. 217, Plate 42) and a basalt axe (Cat. No. 254, Plate 45). The presence of prehistoric materials in an historic context is not so unusual in Sicily, and it may be explained by antiquarian curiosity in a chance discovery from the field; the axe may even have been re-utilized[204].

There is also a terracotta *oscillum* found in the Terrace zone.

426 Muc 87/10a

pink clay, diameter 8,5 cm., gorgoneion represented on it in relief, traces of a yellowish paint can be noticed all over it, the lower lip is stiff, the eyes are represented by two round hollows, the nose is of trapezoidal shape, there are two suspension holes, last decades of fourth century B.C.[205]
Plate 57, also illustrated in La Muculufa I, 59, fig. 82.

Among the materials found at the site, we may cite two stamped amphora handles found in the Terrace excavation zone (Cat. No. 427, Muc 89/9, Plate 57, and Cat. No. 428, Muc 89/11, Plate 57). It is probable that the two handles were part of Rhodian wine amphoras of a type which traveled widely during the first half of the third century B.C.[206]. Thirteen circular terracotta loom-weights were also found, each with two round holes placed at a distance of about 2 cm. (diam. 7.4 cm., illustrated in La Muculufa I, p.63, fig. 84). The loom-weights vary in weight (100, 145, 150, and 155 grams) in a way which describes a scale of measurement.

Another area providing us with Greek materials is the area of the saddle on the crest above the Castelluccian village where the rock crevice burial had been explored in 1987 and 1989[207]. Along with the Bronze Age bones and ceramics, there were recovered a few historical artifacts. The latter are mostly unpainted ceramics, including fragments of hydriae, amphorae, oinochoai and olpai. From the disturbed deposit of the crevice interior there comes the base of a kotyle (Cat. No. 429, Muc 87/104, pink fabric, height 3.5 cm., thickness 0.3 cm., diameter 5 cm.). In front of the crevice there were found fragments of black painted cups dating from the late fifth century B.C.

The data presented here confirm the historical picture which has emerged from recent archaeological discoveries: the Geloans, while extending their control along the coast and founding Akragas were interested in gaining control of the semi-circle of ridges and hills surrounding the fertile alluvial plain to the east and west of the river Salso. In order to do this they did not hesitate to destroy or to absorb several indigenous centers, including Monte Desusino, Monte Agribona, and Butera, which were inhabited according to tradition by the Sicans[208].

The discovery of fragments dating from the Middle and Late Corinthian periods confirms a secondary coloni-

---

[201] For this type of amphora, see H.A. Thompson and D.B. Thompson, Hellenistic Pottery and Terracottas (reprinted from Hesperia with a preface by S.I. Rotroff, Princeton, 1987, p.334–35, 15–16 B3 (P1106).

[202] This type of decoration, typical of Italiot ceramics, belongs usually to oinochoai, acrocups, and lekanai.

[203] Two terracotta hut models found in different contexts on Monte Saraceno at Ravanusa (the sacred area and the habitat) are similar to the one described here. See Greci e Indigeni… (here n.194) p.61 no. 33, p.123 no. 161.

[204] Cf. R. Leighton, "Ground stone tools from Serra Orlando (Morgantina) and Stone Age Studies in Sicily and Southern Italy," PPS 55, 1989, p.135–59.

[205] Cf. P. Orlandini, "Materiali Archeologico Gelese del IV sec. a.C.," ArchCl 12, 1960, p.61–62, pl. XV.

[206] For a thorough study of this subject see V. R. Grace, "Notes on the Amphoras from Koroni peninsula," Hesperia 32, 1963, p.319–334; idem, "Revisions of Early Hellenistic Chronology," AM 89, 1974, p.193–200; idem, Anatolian Collection of Charles University, Kyme I Prague, 1974, p.89–98; idem, Amphoras and ancient wine trade, Athenian Agora Picture Book Series, Princeton, 1961, p.115–126; L. Criscuolo, Bolli d'anfora greci e romani, Bologna, 1982.

[207] See B. E. McConnell e G. Morico, "La Muculufa: un anfratto per sepoltura del Bronzo Antico," Archivio per l'Antropologia e la Etnologia 120, 1990, p.115–126.

zation on the crest of La Muculufa which stands in a key position for controlling the Salso river valley. The absence of structures datable to the archaic period makes one suppose that there was not an actual settlement but instead some sort of simple watchpost. Such a location is typical of sixth century B.C. Greek colonization in which the western Greeks would encircle and strengthen pre-existing towns through new foundations[209]; the second wave of colonization served the urgent need to cover southern Sicily with new centers in the face of the advancing Carthaginians[210].

From the second quarter of the sixth century B.C. the Greek presence at La Muculufa may be connected with the political expansion of Phalaris which touched several centers to the west and east of the river Salso [211]. La Muculufa was occupied throughout the sixth century B.C., while, as it has already been pointed out, during the second half of the fifth century B.C. there is no evidence for a human presence. Although we should not exclude the possibility that the lack of later fifth century B.C. remains is due to chance, it may also be explained by the tumultuous events which occurred between 406 and 345 B.C.[212].

Only under Timoleon (345–317 B.C.) did the situation become stable[213]. Undoubtedly, the historical sources which discuss Timoleon are excessive in describing the ruinous state in which he found Sicily, but it may well be the case that with his arrival the towns and smaller centers indeed were repopulated by a new wave of settlers who were attracted by the newly established stability[214].

It is probable that the building found in Field excavation portion F150 can be placed in reference to such repopulation. Archaeological investigation elsewhere has confirmed the rebirth during the period of Timoleon of many urban centers and of smaller rural agglomerations or individual farm-steads[215]. The latter often appear in easily defensible places which were previously frequented, some even from prehistoric times. The re-use of agricultural areas in many parts of Sicily, and especially in the south-central region, leads us to suppose that the new agricultural settlement was favored by the creation of small parcels of land. This accords well with the theory by which, already at the end of the fourth century B.C., the agricultural landscape was characterized predominantly by small properties, the continuity of which would reach at least into Roman times[216].

---

[208] Pausanias, VIII, 49, 2. The possession of the plain was important to the Geloans for its obvious agricultural use and moreover for raising horses, as reflected in the iconography of the earliest Geloan coinage which shows a nude rider; cf. R.R. Holloway, The Archaeology of Ancient Sicily, London, 1991, p.125–126 and fig. 157.

[209] By contrast, the first wave of colonization aimed mainly at creating settlements on sites of great geographical importance.

[210] F. Cordano, Antiche fondazioni greche, Palermo, 1986, p.86–94; G. Maddoli, "Il VI e V sec. a.C.," in La Sicilia Antica, Naples, 1980, 2, p.3–102.

[211] The tyrant organized his campaigns in order to hellenize the Sicans, who were not subject to his power, as well as to hinder Punic advances. Indeed, by this time the Carthaginians had placed Selinus under their influence and aimed at weakening the Greek sea power which represented a menace to their trade; cf. E. De Miro, "La fondazione di Agrigento e l'ellenizzazione del territorio fra il Salso e il Platani," Kokalos 8, 1962, p,122–152; S. Bianchetti, Falaride e Pseudo Falaride, Storia e leggenda, Roma, 1987, p.1–98; O. Murray, "Falaride tra mito e storia," in Agrigento e la Sicilia Greca, Atti della settimana di studio, Agrigento, 2–8 May, 1988, p.47–61.

[212] In 406 B.C. the Carthaginians sacked Akragas, while in 405 B.C. they destroyed the vast territory between Gela and Camarina, starting with military maneuvers and then outright war.

[213] In 339/8 B.C. a treaty was signed with the Carthaginians (Diodorus Siculus, XVI, 82, 3). It stated that the Carthaginians would settle to the west of the river Lykos or Alykos, identified as the present Platani; therefore the towns which lay to the east of the Lykos were in some way subject to Syracuse. All of this precedes the war between Syracuse and Akragas which broke out between the time of Timoleon's death and 376 B.C..

[214] See M.J. Fontana, "Fortuna di Timoleonte—Rassegna delle fonti letterarie," Kokalos 4, 1958, p.3–23; and R.J.A. Talbert, Timoleon and the Revival of Greek Sicily, Cambridge, 1974.

[215] D. Adamesteanu, "L'opera di Timoleonte nella Sicilia centro-meridionale vista attraverso gli scavi e le ricerche archeologiche," Kokalos 4, 1958, p.31–68.

[216] See G. Manganaro, "La provincia romana: la struttura agraria," in La Sicilia Antica, Naples, 1980, 2, p.428–435; R.J.A. Wilson, "Changes in the pattern of urban settlement in Roman, Byzantine and Arab Sicily," Papers in Italian Archaelogy IV, British Archaeological Reports, International Series, 243, Oxford, 1985, p.313–344. See also G. Manganaro "Tavolette di piombo inscritte della Sicilia Greca," AnnPisa, Series 3, Vol. 7, 1977, p.1329–1349. In this last article there is cited a lead tablet found at Camarina and dated to the end of the second or the beginning of the first century B.C. in which there is registered a sales agreement stipulated according to local norms and without evidence for Roman influence for a parcel of land which is 66 meters wide.

Appendix I

RADIOCARBON DATES FROM THE VILLAGE

Excavation Campaign 1982

laboratory data from J. Buckley, Radiocarbon Laboratory, Teledyne Isotopes, 50 Van Buren Avenue, Westwood, NJ, 07675, communication: 12 January 1983.

1. F25L60, A1+A2, Teledyne Isotopes No. I-12, 819; conventional date 3590±210 bp, -deltaC14 360±16; calibrated ages 1920, 1896, 1893 BC;

   one sigma 2268–2255 BC (2% probability)
   2226–2222 BC (1% probability)
   2204–1684 BC (92% probability)
   1671–1657 BC (1% probability)
   1652–1627 BC (3% probability)

   two sigma 2564–2516 BC (1% probability)
   2490–1427 BC (99% probability)

2. F25L60, B1+B2, Teledyne Isotopes No. I-12, 820; conventional date 3630±210 bp, -delta 364±16; calibrated ages 2008, 1995, 1952 BC;

   one sigma 2285–2241 BC (5% probability)
   2238–1690 BC (95% probability)

   two sigma 2573–2507 BC (2% probability)
   2498–1441 BC (98% probability)

Excavation Campaign 1988

laboratory data from Austin Long, Professor of Geosciences, Laboratory of Isotope Geochemistry—Environmental Isotope Research, Department of Geosciences, The University of Arizona, Tucson, AZ 85721, communication: 28 April 1989

3. F84, 107.3–109.95E, 90.79–92S, bd. 1.82 to 1.58, north of Hut No. 2 wall, 1988–4, University of Arizona No. A-5283; conventional date 3790 ±60 BC, delta13Cpdb(ppt)-24.1; calibrated ages 2200 BC;

   one sigma 2397–2389 BC (3% probability)
   2311–2298 BC (5% probability)
   2292–2129 BC (80% probability)
   2081–2068 BC (6% probability)
   2060–2042 BC (6% probability)

two sigma 2450–2439 BC (1% probability)
2433–2419 BC (1% probability)
2407–2367 BC (6% probability)
2363–2026 BC (90% probability)
2023–2014 BC (1% probability)
1990–1980 BC (1% probability)

4. F102, 97–102E, 108.5–111S, bd. -1.38 to -1.52, 1988–6, University of Arizona No. A-5284; conventional date 3680±100, delta13Cpdb(ppt) -25.2; calibrated ages 2031, 1987, 1982 BC;

   one sigma 2199–1916 BC (96% probability)
   1902–1885 BC (4% probability)

   two sigma 2401–2382 BC (1% probability)
   2338–1767 BC (98% probability)
   1762–1741 BC (1% probability)

Excavation Campaign 1989

laboratory data from Austin Long, Professor of Geosciences,
Laboratory of Isotope Geochemistry—Environmental Isotope Research, Department of Geosciences, The University of Arizona, Tucson, AZ 85721, communication: 3 January 1992

5. F130, Hut 3 (lower), 115–120E, 85–90S, from posthole (A) for hut superstructure in terracotta pavement at 1.20, 8-VIII-89-B, University of Arizona No. A-6547; conventional date 3990±60, delta13Cpdb(ppt) -23.4; calibrated age 2471 BC;

   one sigma 2616–2614 BC (1% probability)
   2574–2508 BC (42% probability)
   2499–2427 BC (38% probability)
   2424–2404 BC (9% probability)
   2376–2352 BC (10% probability)

   two sigma 2834–2815 BC (2% probability)
   2674–2650 BC (2% probability)
   2637–2280 BC (95% probability)
   2246–2232 BC (1% probability)

6. F130, Hut 3 (upper), by wall, 1.80. from carbonized branch, 21-VIII-89-C, University of Arizona No. A-6546; conventional date 3960±70, delta13Cpdb(ppt) -23.5; calibrated age 2467 BC;

one sigma   2568–2513 BC (25% probability)
2493–2398 BC (47% probability)
2387–2329 BC (25% probability)
2320–2313 BC (3% probability)

two sigma   2830–2819 BC (1% probability)
2667–2652 BC (1% probability)
2630–2607 BC (2% probability)
2603–2225 BC (94% probability)
2225–2202 BC (2% probability)

Note: Date Nos. 1 and 2 have been published previously; cf. Muculufa I, p.64–65 (where the series of 17 radiocarbon dates from the Sanctuary is also published); calibration derived from the University of Washington Quaternary Isotope Lab Radiocarbon Calibration Program Rev. 3.0.3 (decadal tree-ring dataset to 6000 cal B.C.) with laboratory error multiplier k = 1.05; see M. Stuiver and P.J. Reimer, "Extended 14-C Data Base and Revised Calib 3.0 14-C Age Calibration Program," Radiocarbon 35 (1993) 215–230 and based on datasets in M. Stuiver and B. Becker, Radiocarbon, 35 (1993) 35–65.

Appendix II

CATALOGUE AND CONCORDANCE OF FINDS

Finds – listed by location

Portion	East	South	Depth	Comment	Material	Description	Inv.	Cat.
F 10/60	102–107	106–111	-1.83 meters		pottery	cup	88/5	191
F 100	97–102	106–111	1.82-(-)0.72		pottery	handle	88/247	163
F 100	97–102	106–111	1.82-(-)0.72		pottery	rim	88/253	157
F 100	97–102	101–106	to 0.35		pottery	spouted vase	88/78	122
F 100	97–102	101–106	to 0.35		stone	flint	88/17	293
F 100	97–102	101–106	to 0.35		terracotta	spindle whorl	88/113	244
F 101	97–102	104–106	-0.45–0.60		stone	flint blade	88/221	317
F 101	97–102	104–106	-0.45–0.60		terracotta	*corno*	88/185	227
F 102	98.5–100.20	106–107.86	-0.77–1.10	joins 88/108	pottery	pedestal bowl	88/103	12
F 102	98.5–100.20	106–107.86	-0.77–1.10		pottery	pedestal bowl	88/104	17
F 102	97–102	106–108	-1.44		pottery	pedestal bowl	88/169	22
F 102	97.6	103.55	-0.47		pottery	pedestal bowl	88/4	52
F 102	97–102	108.5–111	-1.38–1.52		pottery	pedestal bowl	88/128	62
F 102	97.6	103.55	-0.47		pottery	pitcher	88/1	65
F 102	98.5–100.20	106–107.86	-0.77–1.10		pottery	rim	88/110	96
F 102	97–102	108–111	-1.33–1.59		stone	flint axe	88/117	380
F 102	97–102	108.5–115	-1.33–1.59		stone	flint axe	88/11	379
F 102	97.2–98.7	106.5–108.5	-0.95–1.21		stone	flint blade	89/389	301
F 102	97.2–98.7	106.5–108.5	-0.95–1.21		stone	obsidian blade	89/390	323
F 102	97–102	108.5–111	-1.69		terracotta	bobbin	88/14	252
F 102/120	97–99.2	108.5–115	-0.80–1.07		pottery	bobbin-handle	88/148	210
F 102/120	97–100	108.5–115	-1.30–1.43	cf. 88/88	pottery	carinated pitcher	88/80	83
F 102/120	97–100	108.5–115	-1.30–1.43		pottery	cup	88/79	120
F 102/120	97–102	108.5–116	-1.49–1.62		pottery	horned handle	88/166	207
F 102/120	97–100.4	108.5–115	-1.30–1.43		pottery	incised fragm.	88/66	174
F 102/120	97–100.4	108.5–115	-1.30–1.43		pottery	incised fragm.	88/67	175
F 102/120	97–100.4	108.5–115	-1.43–1.58		pottery	pedestal bowl	88/194	24
F 102/120	97–100	108.5–115	-1.30–1.43		pottery	pedestal bowl	88/81	58
F 102/120	97–100	108.5–115	-1.30–1.43		pottery	pedestal bowl	88/84	64
F 102/120	97–99.2	108.5–115	-0.80–1.07		pottery	rim	88/145	156
F 102/120	108.5–116	97–102	-1.49–1.62		stone	pendant	88/173	400
F 102/120	95–100.4	108.5–115	-1.30–1.43		stone	pseudo-brassard	88/111	402
F 103	97–99	105–106	-0.53–0.64		pottery	fragments	88/196	166
F 103	97–99	104–106	-0.61–0.77		stone	blade	88/256	333
F 103	97–99	104–106	-0.40–0.77		terracotta	spindle whorl	88/77	248
F 110	107–112	106–111	-2.20–2.35		pottery	carinated pitcher	88/59	89
F 110	107.5–112	106–108	-1.43	on burned floor	pottery	fragment	88/54	206
F 110	107–112	108.5–111	-2.00	depth below surface	pottery	handle	88/127	129

@: Depth measurement given with respect to local datum point.

N: Horizontal measurements in the Sanctuary (Terrace Excavation Zone) given in meters East and North.

Finds – listed by location

Portion	East	South	Depth	Comment	Material	Description	Inv.	Cat.
F 110	107–112	106–111	-2.35–		pottery	pedestal bowl	88/96	49
F 110	107–112	106–111	-2.20–2.35		pottery	pitcher	88/53	77
F 110	107–112	106–111	-2.35–2.47		pottery	red cup	88/178	165
F 110	107–102	106–111	-2.35–2.47		stone	axe	88/126	259
F 110	107–112	106–108	-1.43–1.68		stone	flint awl	88/41	352
F 110	107–112	106–108	-1.43–1.68		stone	flint blade	88/31	297
F 110	107–112	106–108	-1.43–1.68	floor-level	stone	flint blade	88/28	305
F 110	107–112	106–108	-1.43–1.68	floor-level	stone	flint blade	88/29	339
F 110	107–112	106–108	-1.43–1.68		stone	flint point	88/39	369
F 110	107–112	106–111	-2.35–2.42		stone	hammerstone	88/206	273
F 110	107–112	106–108	-1.43–1.68		stone	pseudo-brassard	88/19	399
F 120	92–102	111–116	-1.69	group 6	pottery	pitcher	88/115	79
F 120	97–102	111–116	-1.34–1.49		terracotta	fragment	88/202	241
F 130	110–115	80–85	2.74–		pottery	foot	89/314	117
F 130	110–122	85–91.5	surface		pottery	incised fragm.	89/246	177
F 130	110–115	88.9–90.9	to 1.70		pottery	incised rim	89/316	184
F 130	118–120	89–91.5	0.66–0.45		pottery	jar	91/95	112
F 130	110–112	90–95	1.65–1.35		pottery	pedestal bowl	89/253	10
F 130	110–115	80–85	2.95–		pottery	pedestal bowl	89/255	41
F 130	110–115	85–88.5	1.85–2.19		pottery	pedestal bowl	89/267	42
F 130	110–115	85–90	1.91–		pottery	pitcher	89/263	102
F 130	110–115	80–85	2.95		pottery	pitcher?	89/259	105
F 130	110–122	85–91.4	surface		pottery	quadrangular vessel	89/245	205
F 130	115–120	90–91.5	3.38		stone	axe	89/8	257
F 130	110–115	80–85		humus	stone	flint blade	89/439	296
F 130	115–122	82.5–85		humus	stone	flint blade	88/218	307
F 130	115–122	82.5–85		humus	stone	flint blade	88/219	312
F 130	110–115	80–85	2.95–		stone	flint blade	89/428	332
F 130	110–115	80–85	2.84–2.74	N of wall 2	stone	flint blade	89/438	338
F 130	110–112	90–95	1.65–1.35		stone	flint point	89/427	376
F 130	110–115	80–85	2.95–		stone	flint razor	89/429	347
F 130			below 1.20	beneath Hut 3 (lower)	stone	grinder	89/363	287
F 130	110–115	85–90	1.91–		terracotta	cylinder	89/247	241
F 131	115–117	82.5–85	1.70–1.47		pottery	incised rim	89/297	179
F 131	115–117.5	82.5–85	1.90–1.70		pottery	pedestal bowl	89/251	17
F 131	115–117.5	82.5–85	1.90–1.70		pottery	pedestal bowl	89/249	38
F 131	115–117.5	82.5–85	1.90–1.70		pottery	pedestal bowl	89/250	40
F 131	115–117	84–85	1.70–		pottery	pitcher	89/441	101
F 131	111–113	85–86	1.77–1.52	cf. 89/312	pottery	quadrangular vessel	89/317	115
F 131	112–115	85–88	2.03–1.84		pottery	rim with handle	89/260	192
F 131	112–115	85–88	2.03–1.84		pottery	rim with handle	89/261	193

Finds – listed by location

Portion	East	South	Depth	Comment	Material	Description	Inv.	Cat.
F 131			1.50–	with daub S of wall	stone	flint awl	89/410	355
F 131	112–115	85–88	2.03–1.84		stone	flint blade	89/400	302
F 131	112–115	85–88	2.03–1.84		stone	flint blade	89/401	303
F 131			1.50–	with daub S of wall	stone	flint core	89/411	385
F 131	112–115	85–88	2.03–1.84		stone	flint point	89/399	358
F 131	112–115	85–88	2.03–1.84		stone	flint saw	89/398	356
F 131	115–117	83.4–85	1.70–		stone	grinder	89/365	288
F 131	112.5–115	85–88	1.84–1.74		stone	obsidian awl?	89/374	351
F 131	115–117	82.5–85	1.90–1.70	out of the wall	terracotta	*corno*	89/86	219
F 131	115–117	82.5–85	1.90–1.70	out of the wall	terracotta	*corno*	89/89	220
F 131	115–117	82.5–85	1.70–1.47		terracotta	spindle whorl	89/296	250
F 131	112.5–115	85–88	1.84–1.74		pottery	incised fragm.	89/193	176
F 132	116–117.2	85–87	1.75–1.37	with Hut 3 (upper) wall	pottery	fragment	89/284a	134
F 132	116–117.2	85–87	1.75–1.37	with Hut 3 (upper) wall	pottery	incised fragm.	89/283	178
F 132	115–116	85–86	1.80–1.58		pottery	incised fragm.	89/354	181
F 132	115–116	85–86	1.80–1.58		pottery	incised fragm.	89/353	182
F 132	116.3–120	87–90	humus		pottery	pedestal bowl	89/306	43
F 132	115–120	83–87	2.01–1.73		pottery	quadrangular vessel	89/173	113
F 132	117.5–118	82.5–85	1.80–1.61		pottery	quadrangular vessel	89/312	115
F 132	117.2–118.2	87.5–90	0.85–0.65		stone	axe	89/117	258
F 132	115–120	85–90	1.77–1.52		terracotta	spindle whorl	89/30	247
F 133	115–120	87.2–89	1.54–1.20		pottery	incised fragment	89/298	180
F 133	110–115	90–95	1.77	beneath 89/17	pottery	pedestal bowl	89/32	61
F 133	113–115	87–90	1.58–1.28	cf. 89/69	pottery	pitcher	89/264	187
F 133	110–115	85–90	1.75–1.64		stone	flint awl	89/381	350
F 133	110–115	85–90	1.75–1.64		stone	flint blade	89/382	310
F 133	111–112	85–87	1.62–1.49	in front of wall 1–2	stone	flint blades	89/128	306
F 133	110–115	85–90	1.75–1.64		stone	flint point	89/380	372
F 133	110–115	85–90	1.75–1.64		stone	razor	89/383	340
F 134	113–115	89–91.5	1.55–1.25		bone	awl	89/36	390
F 134	111–112	87.5–89	1.50		pottery	dipper	89/118	137
F 134	111–113	87–90	1.54–1.49	Hut 3	pottery	dipper	89/282	143
F 134	111–112	87–90	1.62–1.54		pottery	dipper	89/279	144
F 134	111–112	87–90	1.62–1.54		pottery	dipper	89/276	146
F 134	113	89.9	1.26	near 89/68	pottery	dipper-cup	89/65	189

Finds – listed by location

Portion	East	South	Depth	Comment	Material	Description	Inv.	Cat.
F 134	111–114	89–94.5	1.30–		pottery	fragment	89/166	132
F 134	111.5–113	89–91	1.53–1.24		pottery	handle	89/172	125
F 134	111–113	88.9–89.9	1.50-floor	in daub fall	pottery	handle	89/289	162
F 134	115–120	85–90	1.77–1.52	N of Hut 3 (upper) wall	pottery	incised fragment	89/299	186
F 134	111–112	87–90	1.54–1.27	with daub	pottery	internal handle vessel	89/121	204
F 134	122	90.5	1.62		pottery	lid	89/28	213
F 134	111.6	89.9	1.40		pottery	lid	89/80	214
F 134	114	89.8	1.43	near 89/35	pottery	pedestal bowl	89/39	1
F 134	111.5–113	89–91	1.53–1.24		pottery	pedestal bowl	89/171	23
F 134	110–115	85–90	1.77–1.62		pottery	pedestal bowl	89/302	27
F 134	111–113	88.9–89.9	1.50-floor	in daub fall	pottery	pedestal bowl	89/284	147
F 134	111–113	87–90	1.54–1.49	Hut 3	pottery	pedestal bowl	89/290	149
F 134	111–113	88.9–89.9	1.50-floor	in daub fall	pottery	pedestal bowl	89/288	149
F 134	111–113	88.9–89.9	1.50-floor	in daub cf. 89/311	pottery	pedestal bowl	89/285	??
F 134	113.3	89	1.40		pottery	pitcher	89/69	187
F 134	112	91.2	1.32		pottery	red cup	89/76	164
F 134	111–113	87–90	1.54–1.49	Hut 3	pottery	rim	89/291	154
F 134	111–113	88.9–89.9	1.50-floor	in daub fall	pottery	rim	89/286	155
F 134	110–115	85–90	1.91–1.62		pottery	spout	89/303	200
F 134	110–115	88.9–90	1.90		shell	necklace bead	89/23	409
F 134	110–115	85–90	1.91–1.62	South of Structure 3	stone	blade	89/403	344
F 134	110–115	85–90	2.08–1.91	SE of wall	stone	core	89/415	382
F 134	115–120	85–90	1.77–1.52		stone	flint awl	89/379	353
F 134	110–115	85–90	1.54–1.19		stone	flint awl	89/409	354
F 134	115–120	85–90	1.77–1.52		stone	flint point	89/385	360
F 134	110–115	85–90	1.54–1.19		stone	flint point	89/406	364
F 134	110–115	85–90	1.54–1.19		stone	flint point	89/408	365
F 134	110–115	85–90	1.54–1.19		stone	flint point	89/407	368
F 134	115–120	85–90	1.77–1.52		stone	flint point	89/386	373
F 134	111–114	89–91	1.64		stone	razor	89/384	342
F 134	110–115	85–90	1.91–1.62		stone	razor	89/402	343
F 134	110–115	85–90	2.08–1.91	SE of wall	stone	razor	89/414	345
F 134	115	91	1.30		stone	whetstone	89/16	278
F 134	112	86.3	1.62–1.49		terracotta	brazier	89/129	236
F 134	112.2	89.9	1.49	with stone insert	terracotta	*corno*	89/47	216
F 140	115–120	82.5–85.5	2.22–2.10		pottery	'elephant's-head' handle	89/272	168
F 140	115–120	82.5–85.5	2.02–1.80		pottery	fragment	89/189	133
F 140	115–120	82.5–85.5	2.02–1.80		pottery	handle	89/190	126

Finds – listed by location

Portion	East	South	Depth	Comment	Material	Description	Inv.	Cat.
F 140	115–120	82.5–85.5	2.22–2.10	joins with 89/173	pottery	quadrangular vessel	89/46	113
F 140	115–120	80–85	2.65–2.52		stone	flint blade	89/109	291
F 140	115–120	82.5–85.5	2.02–1.80		stone	flint blade	89/230	292
F 140	115–120	82.5–85.5	2.02–1.80		stone	flint blade	89/376	299
F 140	115–120	82.5–85.5	2.02–1.80		stone	flint blade	89/377	320
F 140	110–115	80–85	2.75–2.65		stone	flint blade	89/392	325
F 140	115–120	82.5–85.5	2.22–2.02		stone	flint blade	89/417	330
F 140	110–115	80–85	2.75–2.65		stone	flint point	89/391	362
F 140	115–120	85–87	1.83–1.01	NE stone alignment	stone	obsidian point	89/434	367
F 140	115–120	82.5–87	2.01–1.73	SW side of stone alignment	stone	point	89/413	378
F 140	115–120	85–87	1.83–1.01		stone	razor	89/435	346
F 150	87.4	66.5		humus	terracotta	head	89/1	420
F 151	91.7	64.7	-1.15@		bone	needle	89/4	396
F 151			-1.28/-1.20@		pottery	black-figure fragment	89/344	424
F 151			-1.11@		pottery	kothon	89/348	416
F 151	92.5	63.9	-1.28@		pottery	mortar	89/6	422
F 151	90.3	64.1	-1.11@		stone	axe	89/3	254
F 151	90.5	64.3	-0.91@		terracotta	*corno*	89/2	217
F 151				W of structure	terracotta	lamp	89/342	419
F 151A			-1.48@	in collapse	pottery	kylix	89/333	418
F 151A	94.35	63.6	-1.20@		pottery	mortar	89/81	422
F 151A			-1.39@	in collapse	pottery	patera	89/329	421
F 151A			-1.13–1.20@	in wall collapse	stone	flint point	89/404	375
F 151B			-1.45@	in collapse	pottery	amphora handle	89/326	423
F 151B			-1.56@	at floor level	terracotta	hut model	89/325	425
F 152			humus	S of structure	pottery	amphoriskos	89/319	415
F 152			0.50@	near wall	stone	hammerstone	89/357	270
F 160	100–105	85–97.5	humus	fallen from necropolis?	pottery	miniature vase	89/60	123
F 160	100–105	85–97.5		humus	stone	flint point	89/445	359
F 160	100–105	90–95	2.40–		stone	grinder	89/359	286
F 161	103–105	96–98	1.44–1.12		pottery	pedestal bowl	89/164	57
F 161	103–105	96–98	1.44–1.12		pottery	shackle handle	89/167	208
F 161			1.53		stone	arrowhead	89/72	371
F 161	105–107	92.8–93.4	1.53–1.41		stone	flint blade	89/100	311
F 161	103–107	91–95	1.76–1.61		terracotta	bobbin	89/145	251
F 171	120–125	40–43	5.21–3.96		pottery	dipper	91/120	138
F 171	120–123	40–43	5.21–		pottery	fragment	91/103	158

Finds – listed by location

Portion	East	South	Depth	Comment	Material	Description	Inv.	Cat.
F 171	120–125	44.5–45	3.60		pottery	fragment	91/117	159
F 171	120–125	40–43	5.21–3.96		pottery	pedestal bowl	91/56	151
F 172	120–125	43–50	to 5.21		pottery	incised fragment	91/93	183
F 172	120–125	40–43	5.21–3.96		pottery	incised fragment	91/54	185
F 172	120–125	45–47			terracotta	brazier	91/104	237
F 180	137–138	48–50	surface		pottery	kotyle	91/1	417
F 181	137	51	2.83		bone	awl	91/9	397
F 181	137.5–140	52–55	2.68–2.49		pottery	carinated pitcher	91/119	88
F 181	138–140	55–60	2.83–2.68		pottery	pedestal bowl	91/97	60
F 181	137.5–140	50–55	2.83–2.68		terracotta	brazier?	91/100	238
F 182	135–140	50–55	3.24–2.94		pottery	carinated pitcher	91/102	87
F 182	140–140.6	60	2.09		pottery	crown-cup	91/26	190
F 182	130–135	55–60	3.37–3.15		pottery	dipper	91/40	142
F 182	130–135	55–60	3.37–3.15		pottery	fragment	91/41	160
F 182	134–136.5	60–62.5	2.94–2.64		pottery	fragments	91/105	136
F 182	137	57.5	2.42		pottery	pedestal bowl	91/23	8
F 182	134–136	56–57	2.94		pottery	pedestal bowl	91/57	11
F 182	137	57.5	2.42		pottery	pedestal bowl	91/123	13
F 182	135–137.7	60–62.5	2.64–2.46		pottery	pedestal bowl	91/85	20
F 182	135–137.5	53–55	2.62–2.42		pottery	pedestal bowl	91/94	25
F 182	135–136	60–60.5	2.28–2.02		pottery	pedestal bowl	91/106	148
F 182	137	57.5	2.42		pottery	pitcher	91/61	98
F 182	134–140	55–60	3.24–2.94		pottery	pitcher	91/113	188
F 182	135–136.5	60–61.5	2.28–2.02		shell		91/37	412
F 182	136	57	2.42		terracotta	brazier	91/20	235
F 182	137.4	58.4	2.94		terracotta	*corno*	91/28	228
F 182	139	60.5			terracotta	*corno*	91/33	231
F 182	135.5	57.5	3.24		terracotta	*corno*	91/36	234
F 183	131	59	3.00		terracotta	*corno*	91/35	232
F 190	132.5–135	50–52.5	4.20–3.94		pottery	dipper	91/47	145
F 200	120–125	37.5–40	5.43–4.40		pottery	bridge-vessel	91/43	203
F 200	130–132.5	37.5–40	6.28–6.16	test pit	pottery	carinated pitcher	91/62	84
F 200	130–135	35–40	7.21–6.94		pottery	cup	91/70	121
F 200	130–132.5	37.5–40	6.49–6.44	test pit	pottery	dipper	91/81	139
F 200	130–135	35–37.5	6.75–6.64		pottery	dipper	91/84	140
F 200	130–135	35–40	7.21–6.94		pottery	dipper	91/66	141
F 200	124–126	37.5–40	5.50–5.43		pottery	fragment	91/74	135
F 200	130–135	35–40	7.44–7.21		pottery	fragment	91/80	161
F 200	124–126	37.5–40	5.50–5.43		pottery	fragment with hole	91/76	198
F 200	130–135	35–37.5	6.86–6.75		pottery	handle	91/64	212
F 200	130–132.5	37.5–40	6.28–6.16	test pit	pottery	pedestal bowl	91/63	21
F 200	124–126	37.5–40	5.50–5.43		pottery	pedestal bowl	91/73	35

Finds – listed by location

Portion	East	South	Depth	Comment	Material	Description	Inv.	Cat.
F 200	125–130	37.5–40	5.50–5.43		pottery	pedestal bowl	91/79	59
F 200	120–125	37.5–40	5.43–4.40		pottery	pedestal bowl	91/44	150
F 200	130–135	35–40	7.21–6.94		pottery	pedestal bowl	91/69	152
F 200	130–135	35–37.5	6.86–6.75		pottery	rim	91/65	100
F 200	128.5–131	39–41.5		humus	terracotta	*corno*	91/29	229
F 200	130–132.5	37.5–40	6.28–6.16	test pit	terracotta	*corno*	91/31	230
F 70	112–118.5	91–96	0.88–0.84		pottery	pedestal bowl	88/20	7
F 70	112–117	91–96	1.43–1.03		pottery	pedestal bowl	88/25	9
F 70	112	91–96	1.43–1.03		pottery	pedestal bowl	88/226	50
F 70	117–122	96–101	-0.34–0.67		pottery	pedestal bowl	88/167	51
F 70	112–117	91–96	1.43–1.03		pottery	pedestal bowl	88/24	54
F 70	112–117	91–96	1.43–1.03		pottery	pedestal bowl	88/129	55
F 70	112–118.5	91–96	0.88–0.84		pottery	pitcher	88/22	76
F 70	112–118.5	91–96	0.88–0.84		pottery	rim	88/21	97
F 70	112–117	91–96	1.43–1.03		pottery	rim	88/27	131
F 70	120–122	97–99	-0.95–1.27		pottery	rim	88/164	169
F 70	115–120	85–90	0.38–0.69		shell		91/38	413
F 70	112–117	91–96	1.07–0.62	floor level	stone	axe	88/135	260
F 70	112–117	91–96	1.07–0.62		stone	axe	88/207	263
F 70			-0.30–0.40@	test pit	stone	flint blade	88/224	295
F 70	112–117	91–96	1.07–0.62		stone	flint blade	88/5	309
F 70	112–117	91–96	0.88		terracotta	base	88/150	242
F 70	112–118.5	91–96	0.88–0.84		terracotta	bobbin	88/23	253
F 70	112–117	91–96	1.03–0.88		terracotta	disc	88/154	239
F 71	91–93	112			pottery	pitcher	88/3	75
F 71	112–117	91–93	0.93		stone	flint blade	88/220	313
F 71	112–117	91–93.5	0.93		stone	flint blade	88/225	336
F 71	114–117	91–92	to 0.66		stone	flint razor	88/265	348
F 72	112–117	96–101	0.34-(-)0.06		stone	axe	88/266	266
F 74	119.5–121	96–97.2	-0.94–0.99		bone	boar's tusk	88/193	407
F 74	117–118	96–98	0.22–0.53		pottery	handle	88/187	124
F 74	117–122	91–101	-0.34–0.67		pottery	pitcher	88/157	67
F 74	117–121	96–101	-1.00		pottery	pitcher	89/144	93
F 74	112–124	96–101	to -1.00		pottery	strainer	88/139	201
F 74	119.5–121	96–97.2	-0.94–0.99		stone	flint blade	88/223	319
F 74	117–122	96–101	0.82–0.46		terracotta	*corno*	88/162	224
F 75	110–112	92–97	1.35–1.25		pottery	double-knobbed handle	89/240	211
F 75	111.5	94	1.39		pottery	handle	89/24	194
F 75	110–112	92–97	1.35–1.25		pottery	pedestal bowl	89/238	39
F 75	110–112	92–97	1.35–1.25		pottery	pedestal bowl	89/239	47
F 75	11.5	94	1.10	cf. 89/27	pottery	pitcher	89/90	90
F 75	110–112	92–97	1.35–1.25		pottery	pithos with ribs	89/248	199

Finds – listed by location

Portion	East	South	Depth	Comment	Material	Description	Inv.	Cat.
F 75	105–106.7	91.4–95.8	1.53–1.41		pottery	quadrangular vessel	89/156	114
F 75	110–112	92–97	1.35		stone	axe	89/78	255
F 75	103.7–107	91.6–93.1	1.70–1.53		stone	flint blade	89/378	300
F 75	102.5–105	91.4–95.8	1.47–1.42	W of Hut 2	stone	flint blade	89/372	316
F 75	area E of Hut 2		1.25–1.05		stone	flint blade	89/387	322
F 75	102.5–105	91.4–95.8	1.47–1.42	W of Hut 2	stone	flint blade	89/373	370
F 75	105–107	92.8–93.4	1.53–1.41		stone	obsidian blade	88/242	321
F 75	105–106.7	91.4–95.8	1.53–1.41		stone	pendant?	89/418	388
F 75/82	111–111.8	93–95	1.07–0.78		pottery	pitcher	89/301	80
F 80	105–107	86–91	0.50–0.83		bone	boar's tusk	88/189	404
F 80	105–107	94–96	1.70–1.59		pottery	amphora?	88/112	95
F 80				in deposit of ceramics	pottery	carinated pitcher	88/6	81
F 80	105–107	93–96	1.59		pottery	carinated pitcher	88/2	82
F 80	107–115	91–93	1.47–1.44		pottery	fragment	88/44	119
F 80	105–107	93–94.5	1.70		pottery	handle	88/163	127
F 80	105–110	93–96	1.78–1.59	Hut 2	pottery	pedestal bowl	88/159	18
F 80	105–107	86–91	0.83–		pottery	pedestal bowl	88/61	167
F 80	105–107	86–91	0.50–0.83		pottery	rim	88/192	108
F 80			1.49–1.74@	test pit cf. 88/164	pottery	rim	88/268	170
F 80	105–108	86–88	2.22–2.06		pottery	shackle handle	88/168	209
F 80	105–110	93–96	1.78–1.59	Hut 2	pottery	strainer	88/160	202
F 80			to -0.40@	test pit	shell		88/241	408
F 80	107–112	86–91	0.50@	depth from surface	stone	axe	88/197	261
F 80	105–110	90–96	0.50@	depth from surface	stone	axe	88/198	262
F 80	107.5–110	91–96	2.04–1.79		stone	blade	88/257	304
F 80	105–107.5	93–94	2.11		stone	core	88/264	383
F 80	105–110	90–96	1.88–1.78		stone	flint chip	88/258	337
F 80	105–110	90–96	2.22–2.06		stone	flint hook	88/262	387
F 80	105–110	80–86.7	to 3.48		stone	flint point	89/433	366
F 80			humus		terracotta	*corno*	88/119	223
F 81	105–108	86–90	3.41–3.15		stone	flint blade	88/245	324
F 81	105–107.3	88–89.5	to 2.23		stone	flint core	88/260	384
F 81	108.5–110	86–90	0.50		stone	flint point	89/416	374
F 81	105–107.3	88–89.5	to 2.23		stone	razor	88/261	341
F 81	105–110	86–90	2.39–2.32		stone	spearpoint	88/244	357
F 82	107.7–111.3	98–96	humus		pottery	carinated pitcher	89/308	85
F 82	107–110	92–96		group 3	pottery	foot	88/120	116
F 82	107–110	93–96	to 2.43		pottery	incised fragm.	88/65	173
F 82	107–110	93–96	to 2.43		pottery	incised rim	88/64	172

Finds – listed by location

Portion	East	South	Depth	Comment	Material	Description	Inv.	Cat.
F 82	105–107.55	91–93	2.02–1.82		pottery	pedestal bowl	88/255	19
F 82	107–110	93–96	1.85–1.34		terracotta	*corno*	88/171	233
F 82/75	111–111.8	93–95	1.07–0.78		stone	flint	89/412	386
F 83	104–197	94–96	to 1.64	joins 88/90	pottery	carinated pitcher	88/89	86
F 83	103–105	94–97	2.76		pottery	lid	88/10	215
F 83	103–105	94–96	1.59		pottery	pedestal bowl	88/121	45
F 83	104–197	94–96	to 1.64		pottery	pedestal bowl	88/92	46
F 83	103–105	94–96	1.59		pottery	rim with knobs	88/124	197
F 83	104–107	94–96	to 2.73		stone	grinder	88/210	284
F 83	104–107	94–96	to 2.73		stone	grinder	88/212	285
F 83	104–107	94–96	to 2.73		stone	grinder-hammer-stone	88/209	283
F 83	104–107	94–96	to 1.64		stone	grinder?	88/205	282
F 83	104–107	94–96	to 1.64		stone	hammerstone	88/204	272
F 83	104–107	94–96	to 2.73		stone	mano	88/211	276
F 83	104.6	94.6	1.42		terracotta	*corno*	89/33	218
F 84	107.3–109.95	90.79–92	1.82–1.58		pottery	handle	88/152	128
F 84	107.30–109.95	90.79–80	1.86–1.82		pottery	pedestal bowl	88/9	28
F 84	105–110	91.3–93.4	1.84–1.72		pottery	pedestal bowl	89/170	37
F 84			1.97–1.90		stone	block	88/203	290
F 84	107.3–109.95	90.79–92	1.82–1.58		stone	flint blade	88/222	318
F 84	107.3–109.95	90.79–92	1.82–1.58	N of Hut 2	stone	hammerstone	88/199	269
F 84	107.3–109.95	90.79–92	1.82–1.58	N of Hut 2	stone	mano	88/200	275
F 84	107.3–109.95	90.79–92	1.97–1.90		stone	obsidian blade	88/217	294
F 84	107.3–109.95	90.79–92	1.82–1.58	N of Hut 2	stone	smoothed stone	88/201	289
F 84	107.30–109.95	90.79–80	2.02–1.90	Hut 2	terracotta	cylinder	88/7	241
Hut 2	107.5–110	95–96.5	1.15–1.04		bone	awl	89/115	389
Hut 2	106.5–110	91–97	1.15–1.04		bone	awl	89/114	391
Hut 2	106.80	97	1.21		bone	awl	89/134	393
Hut 2	107.50–110	95–96.5	1.15–1.04		pottery	amphora	89/150	94
Hut 2	107	96.5	1.17		pottery	carinated pitcher	89/98	85
Hut 2	110	95.1	1.15		pottery	cup	89/84	118
Hut 2	107–111	93–95.5	1.50–1.04	with daub	pottery	fragment	89/148	171
Hut 2	107.50–110	95–96.5	1.15–1.04		pottery	jar	89/159	109
Hut 2	107.50–110	95–96.5	1.15–1.04		pottery	jar	89/199	110
Hut 2	107.50–110	95–96.5	1.15–1.04		pottery	jar	89/175	111
Hut 2	107	96.5	1.17		pottery	pedestal bowl	89/113	2
Hut 2	107.50–110	95–96.5	1.15–1.04		pottery	pedestal bowl	89/160	3
Hut 2	110	95	1.15		pottery	pedestal bowl	89/85	4
Hut 2	107.50–110	95–96.5	1.15–1.04		pottery	pedestal bowl	89/200b	5
Hut 2	107.50–110	95–96.5	1.15–1.04		pottery	pedestal bowl	89/161	6
Hut 2	107.50–110	95–96.5	1.15–1.04	joins 89/322	pottery	pedestal bowl	89/215	14
Hut 2	107–111	93–95.5	1.50–1.04	with daub	pottery	pedestal bowl	89/188	15

Finds – listed by location

Portion	East	South	Depth	Comment	Material	Description	Inv.	Cat.
Hut 2	107.50–110	95–96.5	1.15–1.04		pottery	pedestal bowl	89/212	16
Hut 2	107.50–110	95–96.5	1.15–1.04		pottery	pedestal bowl	89/202	26
Hut 2	107.50–110	95–96.5	1.15–1.04		pottery	pedestal bowl	89/174	29
Hut 2	107.50–110	95–96.5	1.15–1.04		pottery	pedestal bowl	89/217	30
Hut 2	107.50–110	95–96.5	1.15–1.04		pottery	pedestal bowl	89/226	31
Hut 2	107.50–110	95–96.5	1.15–1.04		pottery	pedestal bowl	89/216	32
Hut 2	107.50–110	95–96.5	1.15–1.04		pottery	pedestal bowl	89/163	33
Hut 2	107.50–110	95–96.5	1.15–1.04		pottery	pedestal bowl	89/201	34
Hut 2	109	94.50	1.50–1.04	with daub	pottery	pedestal bowl	89/124	36
Hut 2	107.50–110	95–96.5	1.15–1.04		pottery	pedestal bowl	89/214	44
Hut 2	107.50–110	95–96.5	1.15–1.04		pottery	pedestal bowl	89/236	53
Hut 2	107.50–110	95–96.5	1.15–1.04		pottery	pedestal bowl	89/237	56
Hut 2	109.4	95.2	1.17?		pottery	pedestal bowl	89/105	63
Hut 2	109.9	96	1.15		pottery	pitcher	89/97	66
Hut 2	107.50–110	95–96.5	1.15–1.04		pottery	pitcher	89/151	68
Hut 2	107–111	93–95.5	1.50–1.04	with daub	pottery	pitcher	89/143	69
Hut 2	107.50–110	95–96.5	1.15–1.04		pottery	pitcher	89/153	70
Hut 2	107.50–110	95–96.5	1.15–1.04		pottery	pitcher	89/154	71
Hut 2	107.50–110	95–96.5	1.15–1.04		pottery	pitcher	89/158	72
Hut 2	107.50–110	95–96.5	1.15–1.04		pottery	pitcher	89/152	73
Hut 2	107.50–110	95–96.5	1.15–1.04		pottery	pitcher	89/194	74
Hut 2	107.50–110	95–96.5	1.15–1.04		pottery	pitcher	89/146	92
Hut 2	107.50–110	95–96.5	1.15–1.04		pottery	pitcher	89/203	103
Hut 2	107.50–110	95–96.5	1.15–1.04		pottery	pitcher	89/195	104
Hut 2	107–111	93–95.5	1.50–1.04	with daub	pottery	pitcher	89/182	106
Hut 2	107–111	93–95.5	1.50–1.04	with daub	pottery	pitcher?	89/187	78
Hut 2	107.50–110	95–96.5	1.15–1.04		pottery	pithos	89/227	195
Hut 2	107.50–110	95–96.5	1.15–1.04		pottery	pithos	89/228	196
Hut 2	107.50–110	95–96.5	1.15–1.04		pottery	rim	89/197	99
Hut 2	107.50–110	95–96.5	1.15–1.04		pottery	rim	89/205	107
Hut 2	110	93	1.15–1.04	on bench	pottery	pedestal bowl	89/91	48
Hut 2	110	95	1.15	fallen from 89/85?	shell	necklace	89/83	411
Hut 2	107-wall		to 1.15	F75	stone	flint blade	89/370	298
Hut 2	107-wall		to 1.15	F75	stone	flint blade	89/369	308
Hut 2	107-wall		to 1.15	F75	stone	flint blade	89/367	314
Hut 2	107-wall		to 1.15	F75	stone	flint blade	89/368	315
Hut 2	107.50–110	95–96.5	1.15–1.04		stone	flint blade	89/393	326
Hut 2	107.50–110	95–96.5	1.15–1.04		stone	flint blade	89/394	327
Hut 2	107.50–110	95–96.5	1.15–1.04	part of 89/394?	stone	flint blade	89/395	328
Hut 2	107.50–110	95–96.5	1.15–1.04		stone	flint blade	89/397	329
Hut 2	107-wall		to 1.15	F75	stone	flint blade	89/366	334

Finds – listed by location

Portion	East	South	Depth	Comment	Material	Description	Inv.	Cat.
Hut 2	107-wall		to 1.15	F75	stone	flint blade	89/371	335
Hut 2	107.50–110	95–96.5	1.15–1.04		stone	flint chip	89/396	363
Hut 2	107.50–110	95–96.5	1.15–1.04		stone	hammerstone	89/364	274
Hut 2	109.5	94	1.28–1.15		stone	pseudo-brassard	89/119	401
Hut 2	110	95	1.15		stone	pseudo-brassard	89/355	403
Hut 2	107–111	93–95.5	1.50–1.04	with daub	terracotta	spindle whorl	89/220	246
Hut 2	110	95	1.15		terracotta	spindle whorl	89/87	249
Hut 3	117	84.5	1.55		pottery	pitcher	89/131	91
Hut 3	110–115	90	1.49	on pavement	terracotta	*corno*	89/122	221
Hut 3	119.8	87	1.35		terracotta	*corno*	89/132	222
Hut 4				along wall, N side	bone	awl	89/111	392

Finds—listed by catalog number

Portion	East	South	Depth	Comment	Material	Description	Inv.	Cat.
F 134	114	89.8	1.43	near 89/35	pottery	pedestal bowl	89/39	1
Hut 2	107	96.5	1.17		pottery	pedestal bowl	89/113	2
Hut 2	107.50–110	95–96.5	1.15–1.04		pottery	pedestal bowl	89/160	3
Hut 2	110	95	1.15		pottery	pedestal bowl	89/85	4
Hut 2	107.50–110	95–96.5	1.15–1.04		pottery	pedestal bowl	89/200b	5
Hut 2	107.50–110	95–96.5	1.15–1.04		pottery	pedestal bowl	89/161	6
F 70	112–118.5	91–96	0.88–0.84		pottery	pedestal bowl	88/20	7
F 182	137	57.5	2.42		pottery	pedestal bowl	91/23	8
F 70	112–117	91–96	1.43–1.03		pottery	pedestal bowl	88/25	9
F 130	110–112	90–95	1.65–1.35		pottery	pedestal bowl	89/253	10
F 182	134–136	56–57	2.94		pottery	pedestal bowl	91/57	11
F 102	98.5–100.20	106–107.86	-0.77–1.10	joins 88/108	pottery	pedestal bowl	88/103	12
F 182	137	57.5	2.42		pottery	pedestal bowl	91/123	13
Hut 2	107.50–110	95–96.5	1.15–1.04	joins 89/322	pottery	pedestal bowl	89/215	14
Hut 2	107–111	93–95.5	1.50–1.04	with daub	pottery	pedestal bowl	89/188	15
Hut 2	107.50–110	95–96.5	1.15–1.04		pottery	pedestal bowl	89/212	16
F 102	98.5–100.20	106–107.86	-0.77–1.10	joins 89/251	pottery	pedestal bowl	88/104	17
F 131	115–117.5	82.5–85	1.90–1.70	joins 88/104	pottery	pedestal bowl	89/251	17
F 80	105–110	93–96	1.78–1.59	Hut 2	pottery	pedestal bowl	88/159	18
F 82	105–107.55	91–93	2.02–1.82		pottery	pedestal bowl	88/255	19
F 182	135–137.7	60–62.5	2.64–2.46		pottery	pedestal bowl	91/85	20
F 200	130–132.5	37.5–40	6.28–6.16	test pit	pottery	pedestal bowl	91/63	21
F 102	97–102	106–108	-1.44		pottery	pedestal bowl	88/169	22
F 134	111.5–113	89–91	1.53–1.24		pottery	pedestal bowl	89/171	23
F 102/120	97–100.4	108.5–115	-1.43–1.58		pottery	pedestal bowl	88/194	24
F 182	135–137.5	53–55	2.62–2.42		pottery	pedestal bowl	91/94	25
Hut 2	107.50–110	95–96.5	1.15–1.04		pottery	pedestal bowl	89/202	26
F 134	110–115	85–90	1.77–1.62		pottery	pedestal bowl	89/302	27
F 84	107.30–109.95	90.79–80	1.86–1.82		pottery	pedestal bowl	88/9	28
Hut 2	107.50–110	95–96.5	1.15–1.04		pottery	pedestal bowl	89/174	29
Hut 2	107.50–110	95–96.5	1.15–1.04		pottery	pedestal bowl	89/217	30
Hut 2	107.50–110	95–96.5	1.15–1.04		pottery	pedestal bowl	89/226	31
Hut 2	107.50–110	95–96.5	1.15–1.04		pottery	pedestal bowl	89/216	32
Hut 2	107.50–110	95–96.5	1.15–1.04		pottery	pedestal bowl	89/163	33
Hut 2	107.50–110	95–96.5	1.15–1.04		pottery	pedestal bowl	89/201	34
F 200	124–126	37.5–40	5.50–5.43		pottery	pedestal bowl	91/73	35
Hut 2	109	94.50	1.50–1.04	with daub	pottery	pedestal bowl	89/124	36
F 84	105–110	91.3–93.4	1.84–1.72		pottery	pedestal bowl	89/170	37
F 131	115–117.5	82.5–85	1.90–1.70		pottery	pedestal bowl	89/249	38
F 75	110–112	92–97	1.35–1.25		pottery	pedestal bowl	89/238	39

@: Depth measurement given with respect to local datum point.

N: Horizontal measurements in the Sanctuary (Terrace Excavation Zone) given in meters East and North.

Finds—listed by catalog number

Portion	East	South	Depth	Comment	Material	Description	Inv.	Cat.
F 131	115–117.5	82.5–85	1.90–1.70		pottery	pedestal bowl	89/250	40
F 130	110–115	80–85	2.95–		pottery	pedestal bowl	89/255	41
F 130	110–115	85–88.5	1.85–2.19		pottery	pedestal bowl	89/267	42
F 132	116.3–120	87–90		humus	pottery	pedestal bowl	89/306	43
Hut 2	107.50–110	95–96.5	1.15–1.04		pottery	pedestal bowl	89/214	44
F 83	103–105	94–96	1.59		pottery	pedestal bowl	88/121	45
F 83	104–197	94–96	to 1.64		pottery	pedestal bowl	88/92	46
F 75	110–112	92–97	1.35–1.25		pottery	pedestal bowl	89/239	47
Hut 2	110	93	1.15–1.04	on the bench	pottery	pedestal bowl	89/91	48
F 110	107–112	106–111	-2.35–		pottery	pedestal bowl	88/96	49
F 70	112	91–96	1.43–1.03		pottery	pedestal bowl	88/226	50
F 70	117–122	96–101	-0.34–0.67		pottery	pedestal bowl	88/167	51
F 102	97.6	103.55	-0.47		pottery	pedestal bowl	88/4	52
Hut 2	107.50–110	95–96.5	1.15–1.04		pottery	pedestal bowl	89/236	53
F 70	112–117	91–96	1.43–1.03		pottery	pedestal bowl	88/24	54
F 70	112–117	91–96	1.43–1.03		pottery	pedestal bowl	88/129	55
Hut 2	107.50–110	95–96.5	1.15–1.04		pottery	pedestal bowl	89/237	56
F 161	103–105	96–98	1.44–1.12		pottery	pedestal bowl	89/164	57
F 102/120	97–100	108.5–115	-1.30–1.43		pottery	pedestal bowl	88/81	58
F 200	125–130	37.5–40	5.50–5.43		pottery	pedestal bowl	91/79	59
F 181	138–140	55–60	2.83–2.68		pottery	pedestal bowl	91/97	60
F 133	110–115	90–95	1.77	beneath 89/17	pottery	pedestal bowl	89/32	61
F 102	97–102	108.5–111	-1.38–1.52		pottery	pedestal bowl	88/128	62
Hut 2	109.4	95.2	1.17		pottery	pedestal bowl	89/105	63
F 102/120	97–100	108.5–115	-1.30–1.43		pottery	pedestal bowl	88/84	64
F 102	97.6	103.55	-0.47		pottery	pitcher	88/1	65
Hut 2	109.9	96	1.15		pottery	pitcher	89/97	66
F 74	117–122	91–101	-0.34–0.67		pottery	pitcher	88/157	67
Hut 2	107.50–110	95–96.5	1.15–1.04		pottery	pitcher	89/151	68
Hut 2	107–111	93–95.5	1.50–1.04	with daub	pottery	pitcher	89/143	69
Hut 2	107.50–110	95–96.5	1.15–1.04		pottery	pitcher	89/153	70
Hut 2	107.50–110	95–96.5	1.15–1.04		pottery	pitcher	89/154	71
Hut 2	107.50–110	95–96.5	1.15–1.04		pottery	pitcher	89/158	72
Hut 2	107.50–110	95–96.5	1.15–1.04		pottery	pitcher	89/152	73
Hut 2	107.50–110	95–96.5	1.15–1.04		pottery	pitcher	89/194	74
F 71	91–93	112			pottery	pitcher	88/3	75
F 70	112–118.5	91–96	0.88–0.84		pottery	pitcher	88/22	76
F 110	107–112	106–111	-2.20–2.35		pottery	pitcher	88/53	77
Hut 2	107–111	93–95.5	1.50–1.04	with daub	pottery	pitcher?	89/187	78
F 120	92–102	111–116	-1.69	group 6	pottery	pitcher	88/115	79
F 75/82	111–111.8	93–95	1.07–0.78		pottery	pitcher	89/301	80
F 80				in deposit of ceramics	pottery	carinated pitcher	88/6	81

Finds—listed by catalog number

Portion	East	South	Depth	Comment	Material	Description	Inv.	Cat.
F 80	105–107	93–96	1.59		pottery	carinated pitcher	88/2	82
F 102/120	97–100	108.5–115	-1.30–1.43	cf. 88/88	pottery	carinated pitcher	88/80	83
F 200	130–132.5	37.5–40	6.28–6.16	test pit	pottery	carinated pitcher	91/62	84
F 82	107.7–111.3	98–96	1.17	humus	pottery	carinated pitcher	89/308	85
Hut 2	107	96.5	1.17	joins 89/308	pottery	carinated pitcher	89/98	85
F 83	104–197	94–96	to 1.64	joins. 88/90	pottery	carinated pitcher	88/89	86
F 182	135–140	50–55	3.24–2.94		pottery	carinated pitcher	91/102	87
F 181	137.5–140	52–55	2.68–2.49		pottery	carinated pitcher	91/119	88
F 110	107–112	106–111	-2.20–2.35		pottery	carinated pitcher	88/59	89
F 75	11.5	94	1.10	cf. 89/27	pottery	pitcher	89/90	90
Hut 3	117	84.5	1.55		pottery	pitcher	89/131	91
Hut 2	107.50–110	95–96.5	1.15–1.04		pottery	pitcher	89/146	92
F 74	117–121	96–101	-1.00		pottery	pitcher	89/144	93
Hut 2	107.50–110	95–96.5	1.15–1.04		pottery	amphora	89/150	94
F 80	105–107	94–96	1.70–1.59		pottery	amphora?	88/112	95
F 102	98.5–100.20	106–107.86	-0.77–1.10		pottery	rim	88/110	96
F 70	112–118.5	91–96	0.88–0.84		pottery	rim	88/21	97
F 182	137	57.5	2.42		pottery	pitcher	91/61	98
Hut 2	107.50–110	95–96.5	1.15–1.04		pottery	rim	89/197	99
F 200	130–135	35–37.5	6.86–6.75		pottery	rim	91/65	100
F 131	115–117	84–85	1.70–		pottery	pitcher	89/441	101
F 130	110–115	85–90	1.91–		pottery	pitcher	89/263	102
Hut 2	107.50–110	95–96.5	1.15–1.04		pottery	pitcher	89/203	103
Hut 2	107.50–110	95–96.5	1.15–1.04		pottery	pitcher	89/195	104
F 130	110–115	80–85	2.95		pottery	pitcher?	89/259	105
Hut 2	107–111	93–95.5	1.50–1.04	with daub	pottery	pitcher	89/182	106
Hut 2	107.50–110	95–96.5	1.15–1.04		pottery	rim	89/205	107
F 80	105–107	86–91	0.50–0.83		pottery	rim	88/192	108
Hut 2	107.50–110	95–96.5	1.15–1.04		pottery	jar	89/159	109
Hut 2	107.50–110	95–96.5	1.15–1.04		pottery	jar	89/199	110
Hut 2	107.50–110	95–96.5	1.15–1.04		pottery	jar	89/175	111
F 130	118–120	89–91.5	0.66–0.45		pottery	jar	91/95	112
F 132	115–120	83–87	2.01–1.73	joins 89/46	pottery	quadrangular vessel	89/173	113
F 140	115–120	82.5–85.5	2.22–2.10	joins with 89/173	pottery	quadrangular vessel	89/46	113
F 75	105–106.7	91.4–95.8	1.53–1.41		pottery	quadrangular vessel	89/156	114
F 131	111–113	85–86	1.77–1.52	joins 89/312	pottery	quadrangular vessel	89/317	115
F 132	117.5–118	82.5–85	1.80–1.61	joins 89/317	pottery	quadrangular vessel	89/312	115
F 82	107–110	92–96		gr. 3	pottery	foot	88/120	116
F 130	110–115	80–85	2.74–		pottery	foot	89/314	117

Finds—listed by catalog number

Portion	East	South	Depth	Comment	Material	Description	Inv.	Cat.
Hut 2	110	95.1	1.15		pottery	cup	89/84	118
F 80	107–115	91–93	1.47–1.44		pottery	fragment	88/44	119
F 102/120	97–100	108.5–115	-1.30–1.43		pottery	cup	88/79	120
F 200	130–135	35–40	7.21–6.94		pottery	cup	91/70	121
F 100	97–102	101–106	to 0.35		pottery	spouted vase	88/78	122
F 160	100–105	85–97.5	humus	fallen from necropolis?	pottery	miniature vase	89/60	123
F 74	117–118	96–98	0.22–0.53		pottery	handle	88/187	124
F 134	111.5–113	89–91	1.53–1.24		pottery	handle	89/172	125
F 140	115–120	82.5–85.5	2.02–1.80		pottery	handle	89/190	126
F 80	105–107	93–94.5	1.70		pottery	handle	88/163	127
F 84	107.3–109.95	90.79–92	1.82–1.58		pottery	handle	88/152	128
F 110	107–112	108.5–111	-2.00	depth below surface	pottery	handle	88/127	129
F 70			humus	N of portion	pottery	handle	88/275	130
F 70	112–117	91–96	1.43–1.03		pottery	rim	88/27	131
F 134	111–114	89–94.5	1.30–		pottery	fragment	89/166	132
F 140	115–120	82.5–85.5	2.02–1.80		pottery	fragment	89/189	133
F 132	116–117.2	85–87	1.75–1.37	with Hut 3 (upper) wall	pottery	fragment	89/284a	134
F 200	124–126	37.5–40	5.50–5.43		pottery	fragment	91/74	135
F 182	134–136.5	60–62.5	2.94–2.64		pottery	fragments	91/105	136
F 134	111–112	87.5–89	1.50		pottery	dipper	89/118	137
F 171	120–125	40–43	5.21–3.96		pottery	dipper	91/120	138
F 200	130–132.5	37.5–40	6.49–6.44	test pit	pottery	dipper	91/81	139
F 200	130–135	35–37.5	6.75–6.64		pottery	dipper	91/84	140
F 200	130–135	35–40	7.21–6.94		pottery	dipper	91/66	141
F 182	130–135	55–60	3.37–3.15		pottery	dipper	91/40	142
F 134	111–113	87–90	1.54–1.49	Hut 3	pottery	dipper	89/282	143
F 134	111–112	87–90	1.62–1.54		pottery	dipper	89/279	144
F 190	132.5–135	50–52.5	4.20–3.94		pottery	dipper	91/47	145
F 134	111–112	87–90	1.62–1.54		pottery	dipper	89/276	146
F 134	111–113	88.9–89.9	1.50-floor	in daub fall	pottery	pedestal bowl	89/284	147
F 182	135–136	60–60.5	2.28–2.02		pottery	pedestal bowl	91/106	148
F 134	111–113	87–90	1.54–1.49	Hut 3	pottery	pedestal bowl	89/290	149
F 134	111–113	88.9–89.9	1.50-floor	in daub fall	pottery	pedestal bowl	89/288	149
F 200	120–125	37.5–40	5.43–4.40		pottery	pedestal bowl	91/44	150
F 171	120–125	40–43	5.21–3.96		pottery	pedestal bowl	91/56	151
F 200	130–135	35–40	7.21–6.94		pottery	pedestal bowl	91/69	152
F 134	111–113	88.9–89.9	1.50-floor	in daub cf. 89/311	pottery	pedestal bowl	89/285	153
F 134	111–113	87–90	1.54–1.49	Hut 3	pottery	rim	89/291	154
F 134	111–113	88.9–89.9	1.50-floor	in daub fall	pottery	rim	89/286	155
F 102/120	97–99.2	108.5–115	-0.80–1.07		pottery	rim	88/145	156

Finds—listed by catalog number

Portion	East	South	Depth	Comment	Material	Description	Inv.	Cat.
F 100	97–102	106–111	1.82-(-)0.72		pottery	rim	88/253	157
F 171	120–123	40–43	5.21–		pottery	fragment	91/103	158
F 171	120–125	44.5–45	3.60		pottery	fragment	91/117	159
F 182	130–135	55–60	3.37–3.15		pottery	fragment	91/41	160
F 200	130–135	35–40	7.44–7.21		pottery	fragment	91/80	161
F 134	111–113	88.9–89.9	1.50-floor	in daub fall	pottery	handle	89/289	162
F 100	97–102	106–111	1.82-(-)0.72		pottery	handle	88/247	163
F 134	112	91.2	1.32		pottery	red cup	89/76	164
F 110	107–112	106–111	-2.35–2.47		pottery	red cup	88/178	165
F 103	97–99	105–106	-0.53–0.64		pottery	fragments	88/196	166
F 80	105–107	86–91	0.83–		pottery	pedestal bowl	88/61	167
F 140	115–120	82.5–85.5	2.22–2.10		pottery	'elephant's-head handle	89/272	168
F 70	120–122	97–99	-0.95–1.27		pottery	rim	88/164	169
F 80			1.49–1.74@	test pit cf. 88/164	pottery	rim	88/268	170
Hut 2	107–111	93–95.5	1.50–1.04	with daub	pottery	fragment	89/148	171
F 82	107–110	93–96	to 2.43		pottery	incised rim	88/64	172
F 82	107–110	93–96	to 2.43		pottery	incised fragm.	88/65	173
F 102/120	97–100.4	108.5–115	-1.30–1.43		pottery	incised fragm.	88/66	174
F 102/120	97–100.4	108.5–115	-1.30–1.43		pottery	incised fragm.	88/67	175
F 131	112.5–115	85–88	1.84–1.74		pottery	incised fragm.	89/193	176
F 130	110–122	85–91.5	surface		pottery	incised fragm.	89/246	177
F 132	116–117.2	85–87	1.75–1.37	with Hut 3 (upper) wall	pottery	incised fragm.	89/283	178
F 131	115–117	82.5–85	1.70–1.47		pottery	incised rim	89/297	179
F 133	115–120	87.2–89	1.54–1.20		pottery	incised fragment	89/298	180
F 132	115–116	85–86	1.80–1.58		pottery	incised fragm.	89/354	181
F 132	115–116	85–86	1.80–1.58		pottery	incised fragm.	89/353	182
F 172	120–125	43–50	to 5.21		pottery	incised fragment	91/93	183
F 130	110–115	88.9–90.9	to 1.70		pottery	incised rim	89/316	184
F 172	120–125	40–43	5.21–3.96		pottery	incised fragment	91/54	185
F 134	115–120	85–90	1.77–1.52	N of Hut 3 (upper) wall	pottery	incised fragment	89/299	186
F 133	113–115	87–90	1.58–1.28	joins 89/69	pottery	pitcher	89/264	187
F 134	113.3	89	1.40	joins 89/264	pottery	pitcher	89/69	187
F 182	134–140	55–60	3.24–2.94		pottery	pitcher	91/113	188
F 134	113	89.9	1.26	near 89/68	pottery	dipper-cup	89/65	189
F 182	140–140.6	60	2.09		pottery	crown-cup	91/26	190
F 10/60	102–107	106–111	-1.83		pottery	cup	88/5	191
F 131	112–115	85–88	2.03–1.84		pottery	rim with handle	89/260	192
F 131	112–115	85–88	2.03–1.84		pottery	rim with handle	89/261	193
F 75	111.5	94	1.39		pottery	handle	89/24	194
Hut 2	107.50–110	95–96.5	1.15–1.04		pottery	pithos	89/227	195

Finds—listed by catalog number

Portion	East	South	Depth	Comment	Material	Description	Inv.	Cat.
Hut 2	107.50–110	95–96.5	1.15–1.04		pottery	pithos	89/228	196
F 83	103–105	94–96	1.59		pottery	rim with knobs	88/124	197
F 200	124–126	37.5–40	5.50–5.43		pottery	fragment with hole	91/76	198
F 75	110–112	92–97	1.35–1.25		pottery	pithos with ribs	89/248	199
F 134	110–115	85–90	1.91–1.62		pottery	spout	89/303	200
F 74	112–124	96–101	to -1.00		pottery	strainer	88/139	201
F 80	105–110	93–96	1.78–1.59	Hut 2	pottery	strainer	88/160	202
F 200	120–125	37.5–40	5.43–4.40		pottery	bridge-vessel	91/43	203
F 134	111–112	87–90	1.54–1.27	with daub	pottery	internal handle vessel	89/121	204
F 130	110–122	85–91.4	surface		pottery	quadrangular vessel	89/245	205
F 110	107.5–112	106–108	-1.43	on burned floor	pottery	fragment	88/54	206
F 102/120	97–102	108.5–116	-1.49–1.62		pottery	horned handle	88/166	207
F 161	103–105	96–98	1.44–1.12		pottery	shackle handle	89/167	208
F 80	105–108	86–88	2.22–2.06		pottery	shackle handle	88/168	209
F 102/120	97–99.2	108.5–115	-0.80–1.07		pottery	bobbin-handle	88/148	210
F 75	110–112	92–97	1.35–1.25		pottery	double-knobbed handle	89/240	211
F 200	130–135	35–37.5	6.86–6.75		pottery	handle	91/64	212
F 134	122	90.5	1.62		pottery	lid	89/28	213
F 134	111.6	89.9	1.40		pottery	lid	89/80	214
F 83	103–105	94–97	2.76		pottery	lid	88/10	215
F 134	112.2	89.9	1.49	with stone inset	terracotta	*corno*	89/47	216
F 151	90.5	64.3	-0.91		terracotta	*corno*	89/2	217
F 83	104.6	94.6	1.42		terracotta	*corno*	89/33	218
F 131	115–117	82.5–85	1.90–1.70	out of the wall	terracotta	*corno*	89/86	219
F 131	115–117	82.5–85	1.90–1.70	out of the wall	terracotta	*corno*	89/89	220
Hut 3	110–115	90	1.49	on pavement	terracotta	*corno*	89/122	221
Hut 3	119.8	87	1.35		terracotta	*corno*	89/132	222
F 80				humus	terracotta	*corno*	88/118	223
F 74	117–122	96–101	0.82–0.46		terracotta	*corno*	88/162	224
S 110				humus	terracotta	*corno*	89/63	225
					terracotta	*corno*	87/37	226
F 101	97–102	104–106	-0.45–0.60		terracotta	*corno*	88/185	227
F 182	137.4	58.4	2.94		terracotta	*corno*	91/28	228
F 200	128.5–131	39–41.5		humus	terracotta	*corno*	91/29	229
F 200	130–132.5	37.5–40	6.28–6.16	test pit	terracotta	*corno*	91/31	230
F 182	139	60.5			terracotta	*corno*	91/33	231
F 183	131	59	3.00		terracotta	*corno*	91/35	232
F 82	107–110	93–96	1.85–1.34		terracotta	*corno*	88/171	233
F 182	135.5	57.5	3.24		terracotta	*corno*	91/36	234

Finds—listed by catalog number

Portion	East	South	Depth	Comment	Material	Description	Inv.	Cat.
F 182	136	57	2.42		terracotta	brazier	91/20	235
F 134	112	86.3	1.62–1.49		terracotta	brazier	89/129	236
F 172	120–125	45–47			terracotta	brazier	91/104	237
F 181	137.5–140	50–55	2.83–2.68		terracotta	brazier?	91/100	238
F 70	112–117	91–96	1.03–0.88		terracotta	disc	88/154	239
T 60				from trench balk	terracotta	disc	89/140	240
F 120	97–102	111–116	-1.34–1.49		terracotta	fragment	88/202	241
F 130	110–115	85–90	1.91–	joins 89/269	terracotta	cylinder	89/247	241
F 84	107.30–109.95	90.79–80	2.02–1.90	Hut 2	terracotta	cylinder	88/7	241
F 70	112–117	91–96	0.88		terracotta	base	88/150	242
	124	37	+6.83		terracotta	base	91/14b	243
F 100	97–102	101–106	to 0.35		terracotta	spindle whorl	88/113	244
T 60			1.69		terracotta	spindle whorl	89/147	245
Hut 2	107–111	93–95.5	1.50–1.04	with daub	terracotta	spindle whorl	89/220	246
F 132	115–120	85–90	1.77–1.52		terracotta	spindle whorl	89/30	247
F 103	97–99	104–106	-0.40–0.77		terracotta	spindle whorl	88/77	248
Hut 2	110	95	1.15		terracotta	spindle whorl	89/87	249
F 131	115–117	82.5–85	1.70–1.47		terracotta	spindle whorl	89/296	250
F 161	103–107	91–95	1.76–1.61		terracotta	bobbin	89/145	251
F 102	97–102	108.5–111	-1.69		terracotta	bobbin	88/14	252
F 70	112–118.5	91–96	0.88–0.84		terracotta	bobbin	88/23	253
F 151	90.3	64.1	-1.11		stone	axe	89/3	254
F 75	110–112	92–97	1.35		stone	axe	89/78	255
					stone	axe	89/78b	256
F 130	115–120	90–91.5	3.38		stone	axe	89/8	257
F 132	117.2–118.2	87.5–90	0.85–0.65		stone	axe	89/117	258
F 110	107–102	106–111	-2.35–2.47		stone	axe	88/126	259
F 70	112–117	91–96	1.07–0.62	floor level	stone	axe	88/135	260
F 80	107–112	86–91	0.50	depth from surface	stone	axe	88/197	261
F 80	105–110	90–96	0.50	depth from surface	stone	axe	88/198	262
F 70	112–117	91–96	1.07–0.62		stone	axe	88/207	263
S 110C			-0.49–0.80		stone	axe	89/360	264
Sporadic					stone	axe	89/343	265
F 72	112–117	96–101	0.34-(-)0.06		stone	axe	88/266	266
S 110A			0.44–0.56	humus and fall	stone	axe	89/447	267
S 110A					stone	hammerstone	89/120	268
F 84	107.3–109.95	90.79–92	1.82–1.58	N of Hut 2	stone	hammerstone	88/199	269
F 152			0.50	near wall	stone	hammerstone	89/357	270
Terrace			from 0.9	south area	stone	hammerstone	89/358	271
F 83	104–107	94–96	to 1.64		stone	hammerstone	88/204	272
F 110	107–112	106–111	-2.35–2.42		stone	hammerstone	88/206	273

Finds—listed by catalog number

Portion	East	South	Depth	Comment	Material	Description	Inv.	Cat.
Hut 2	107.50–110	95–96.5	1.15–1.04		stone	hammerstone	89/364	274
F 84	107.3–109.95	90.79–92	1.82–1.58	N of Hut 2	stone	mano	88/200	275
F 83	104–107	94–96	to 2.73		stone	mano	88/211	276
S 110A			0.44–0.56	humus and fall	stone	mano	89/448	277
F 134	115	91	1.30		stone	whetstone	89/16	278
					stone	whetstone	89/358b	279
S 110B				humus and fall	stone	whetstone	89/361	280
T 138			-11.53–11.83		stone	whetstone	89/362	281
F 83	104–107	94–96	to 1.64		stone	grinder?	88/205	282
F 83	104–107	94–96	to 2.73		stone	grinder-hammer-stone	88/209	283
F 83	104–107	94–96	to 2.73		stone	grinder	88/210	284
F 83	104–107	94–96	to 2.73		stone	grinder	88/212	285
F 160	100–105	90–95	2.40–		stone	grinder	89/359	286
F 130			below 1.20	beneath Hut 3 (lower)	stone	grinder	89/363	287
F 131	115–117	83.4–85	1.70–		stone	grinder	89/365	288
F 84	107.3–109.95	90.79–92	1.82–1.58	N of Hut 2	stone	smoothed stone	88/201	289
F 84			1.97–1.90		stone	block	88/203	290
F 140	115–120	80–85	2.65–2.52		stone	flint blade	89/109	291
F 140	115–120	82.5–85.5	2.02–1.80		stone	flint blade	89/230	292
F 100	97–102	101–106	to 0.35		stone	flint	88/17	293
F 84	107.3–109.95	90.79–92	1.97–1.90		stone	obsidian blade	88/217	294
F 70			-0.30–0.40 depth fm. surface	test pit	stone	flint blade	88/224	295
F 130	110–115	80–85		humus	stone	flint blade	89/439	296
F 110	107–112	106–108	-1.43–1.68		stone	flint blade	88/31	297
Hut 2	107-wall		to 1.15	F75	stone	flint blade	89/370	298
F 140	115–120	82.5–85.5	2.02–1.80		stone	flint blade	89/376	299
F 75	103.7–107	91.6–93.1	1.70–1.53		stone	flint blade	89/378	300
F 102	97.2–98.7	106.5–108.5	-0.95–1.21		stone	flint blade	89/389	301
F 131	112–115	85–88	2.03–1.84		stone	flint blade	89/400	302
F 131	112–115	85–88	2.03–1.84		stone	flint blade	89/401	303
F 80	107.5–110	91–96	2.04–1.79		stone	blade	88/257	304
F 110	107–112	106–108	-1.43–1.68	floor-level	stone	flint blade	88/28	305
F 133	111–112	85–87	1.62–1.49	in front of wall 1–2	stone	flint blades	89/128	306
F 130	115–122	82.5–85		humus	stone	flint blade	88/218	307
Hut 2	107-wall		to 1.15	F75	stone	flint blade	89/369	308
F 70	112–117	91–96	1.07–0.62		stone	flint blade	88/5	309
F 133	110–115	85–90	1.75–1.64		stone	flint blade	89/382	310
F 161	105–107	92.8–93.4	1.53–1.41		stone	flint blade	89/100	311
F 130	115–122	82.5–85		humus	stone	flint blade	88/219	312

Finds—listed by catalog number

Portion	East	South	Depth	Comment	Material	Description	Inv.	Cat.
F 71	112–117	91–93	0.93		stone	flint blade	88/220	313
Hut 2	107-wall		to 1.15	F75	stone	flint blade	89/367	314
Hut 2	107-wall		to 1.15	F75	stone	flint blade	89/368	315
F 75	102.5–105	91.4–95.8	1.47–1.42	W of Hut 2	stone	flint blade	89/372	316
F 101	97–102	104–106	-0.45–0.60		stone	flint blade	88/221	317
F 84	107.3–109.95	90.79–92	1.82–1.58		stone	flint blade	88/222	318
F 74	119.5–121	96–97.2	-0.94–0.99		stone	flint blade	88/223	319
F 140	115–120	82.5–85.5	2.02–1.80		stone	flint blade	89/377	320
F 75	105–107	92.8–93.4	1.53–1.41		stone	obsidian blade	88/242	321
F 75	area E of Hut 2		1.25–1.05		stone	flint blade	89/387	322
F 102	97.2–98.7	106.5-108.5	-0.95–1.21		stone	obsidian blade	89/390	323
F 81	105–108	86–90	3.41–3.15		stone	flint blade	88/245	324
F 140	110–115	80–85	2.75–2.65		stone	flint blade	89/392	325
Hut 2	107.50–110	95–96.5	1.15–1.04		stone	flint blade	89/393	326
Hut 2	107.50–110	95–96.5	1.15–1.04		stone	flint blade	89/394	327
Hut 2	107.50–110	95–96.5	1.15–1.04	part of 89/394?	stone	flint blade	89/395	328
Hut 2	107.50–110	95–96.5	1.15–1.04		stone	flint blade	89/397	329
F 140	115–120	82.5–85.5	2.22–2.02		stone	flint blade	89/417	330
					stone	flint blade	89/425	331
F 130	110–115	80–85	2.95–		stone	flint blade	89/428	332
F 103	97–99	104–106	-0.61–0.77		stone	blade	88/256	333
Hut 2	107-wall		to 1.15	F75	stone	flint blade	89/366	334
Hut 2	107-wall		to 1.15	F75	stone	flint blade	89/371	335
F 71	112–117	91–93.5	0.93		stone	flint blade	88/225	336
F 80	105–110	90–96	1.88–1.78		stone	flint chip	88/258	337
F 130	110–115	80–85	2.84–2.74	N of wall 2	stone	flint blade	89/438	338
F 110	107–112	106–108	-1.43–1.68	floor-level	stone	flint blade	88/29	339
F 133	110–115	85–90	1.75–1.64		stone	razor	89/383	340
F 81	105–107.3	88–89.5	to 2.23		stone	razor	88/261	341
F 134	111–114	89–91	1.64		stone	razor	89/384	342
F 134	110–115	85–90	1.91–1.62	`	stone	razor	89/402	343
F 134	110–115	85–90	1.91–1.62	South of Structure 3	stone	blade	89/403	344
F 134	110–115	85–90	2.08–1.91	SE of wall	stone	razor	89/414	345
F 140	115–120	85–87	1.83–1.01		stone	razor	89/435	346
F 130	110–115	80–85	2.95–		stone	flint razor	89/429	347
F 71	114–117	91–92	to 0.66		stone	flint razor	88/265	348
					stone	point	89/444b	349
F 133	110–115	85–90	1.75–1.64		stone	flint awl	89/381	350
F 131	112.5–115	85–88	1.84–1.74		stone	obsidian awl?	89/374	351
F 110	107–112	106–108	-1.43–1.68		stone	flint awl	88/41	352
F 134	115–120	85–90	1.77–1.52		stone	flint awl	89/379	353
F 134	110–115	85–90	1.54–1.19		stone	flint awl	89/409	354

Finds—listed by catalog number

Portion	East	South	Depth	Comment	Material	Description	Inv.	Cat.
F 131			1.50–	with daub S of wall	stone	flint awl	89/410	355
F 131	112–115	85–88	2.03–1.84		stone	flint saw	89/398	356
F 81	105–110	86–90	2.39–2.32		stone	spearpoint	88/244	357
F 131	112–115	85–88	2.03–1.84		stone	flint point	89/399	358
F 160	100–105	85–97.5		humus	stone	flint point	89/445	359
F 134	115–120	85–90	1.77–1.52		stone	flint point	89/385	360
T 60			-13.41–14.56	balk Stratum 5	stone	arrowhead	89/375	361
F 140	110–115	80–85	2.75–2.65		stone	flint point	89/391	362
Hut 2	107.50–110	95–96.5	1.15–1.04		stone	flint chip	89/396	363
F 134	110–115	85–90	1.54–1.19		stone	flint point	89/406	364
F 134	110–115	85–90	1.54–1.19		stone	flint point	89/408	365
F 80	105–110	80–86.7	to 3.48		stone	flint point	89/433	366
F 140	115–120	85–87	1.83–1.01	NE stone alignment	stone	obsidian point	89/434	367
F 134	110–115	85–90	1.54–1.19		stone	flint point	89/407	368
F 110	107–112	106–108	-1.43–1.68		stone	flint point	88/39	369
F 75	102.5–105	91.4–95.8	1.47–1.42	W of Hut 2	stone	flint blade	89/373	370
F 161			1.53		stone	arrowhead	89/72	371
F 133	110–115	85–90	1.75–1.64		stone	flint point	89/380	372
F 134	115–120	85–90	1.77–1.52		stone	flint point	89/386	373
F 81	108.5–110	86–90	0.50		stone	flint point	89/416	374
F 151A			-1.13–1.20@	in wall collapse	stone	flint point	89/404	375
F 130	110–112	90–95	1.65–1.35		stone	flint point	89/427	376
					stone	point	88/x1	377
F 140	115–120	82.5–87	2.01–1.73	SW side of stone align ment	stone	point	89/413	378
F 102	97–102	108.5–115	-1.33–1.59		stone	flint axe	88/11	379
F 102	97–102	108–111	-1.33–1.59		stone	flint axe	88/117	380
sporadic					stone	axe	88/263	381
F 134	110–115	85–90	2.08–1.91	SE of wall	stone	core	89/415	382
F 80	105–107.5	93–94	2.11		stone	core	88/264	383
F 81	105–107.3	88–89.5	to 2.23		stone	flint core	88/260	384
F 131			1.50–	with daub S of wall	stone	flint core	89/411	385
F 82/75	111–111.8	93–95	1.07–0.78		stone	flint	89/412	386
F 80	105–110	90–96	2.22–2.06		stone	flint hook	88/262	387
F 75	105–106.7	91.4–95.8	1.53–1.41		stone	pendant?	89/418	388
Hut 2	107.5–110	95–96.5	1.15–1.04		bone	awl	89/115	389
F 134	113–115	89–91.5	1.55–1.25		bone	awl	89/36	390
Hut 2	106.5–110	91–97	1.15–1.04		bone	awl	89/114	391
Hut 4				along wall, N side	bone	awl	89/111	392
Hut 2	106.80	97	1.21		bone	awl	89/134	393

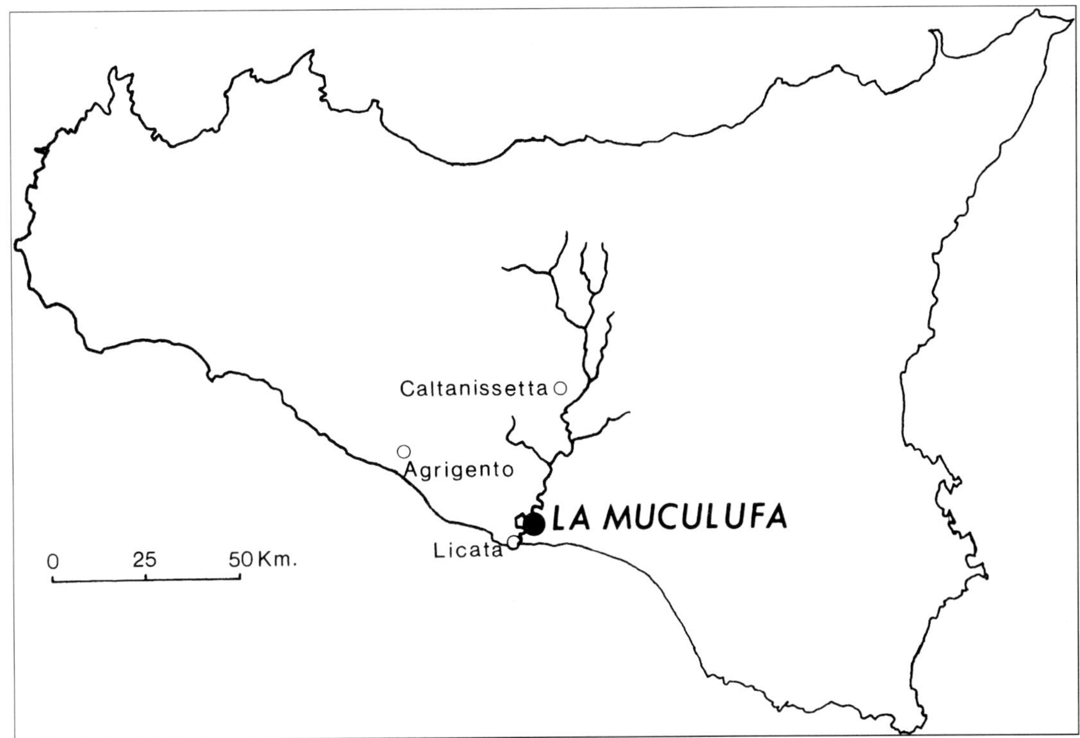

1.1 Map of Sicily

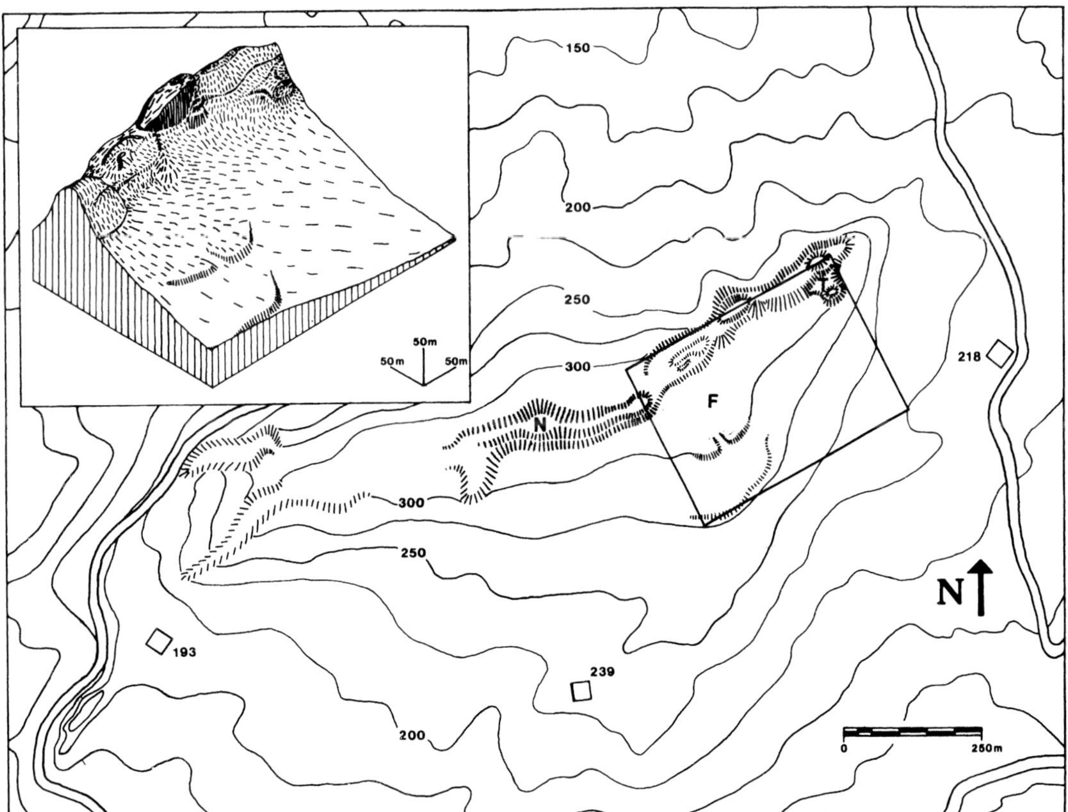

1.2 Map of the La Muculufa crest with excavation zones F (village area) and T (sanctuary area); elevation in meters above sea level.

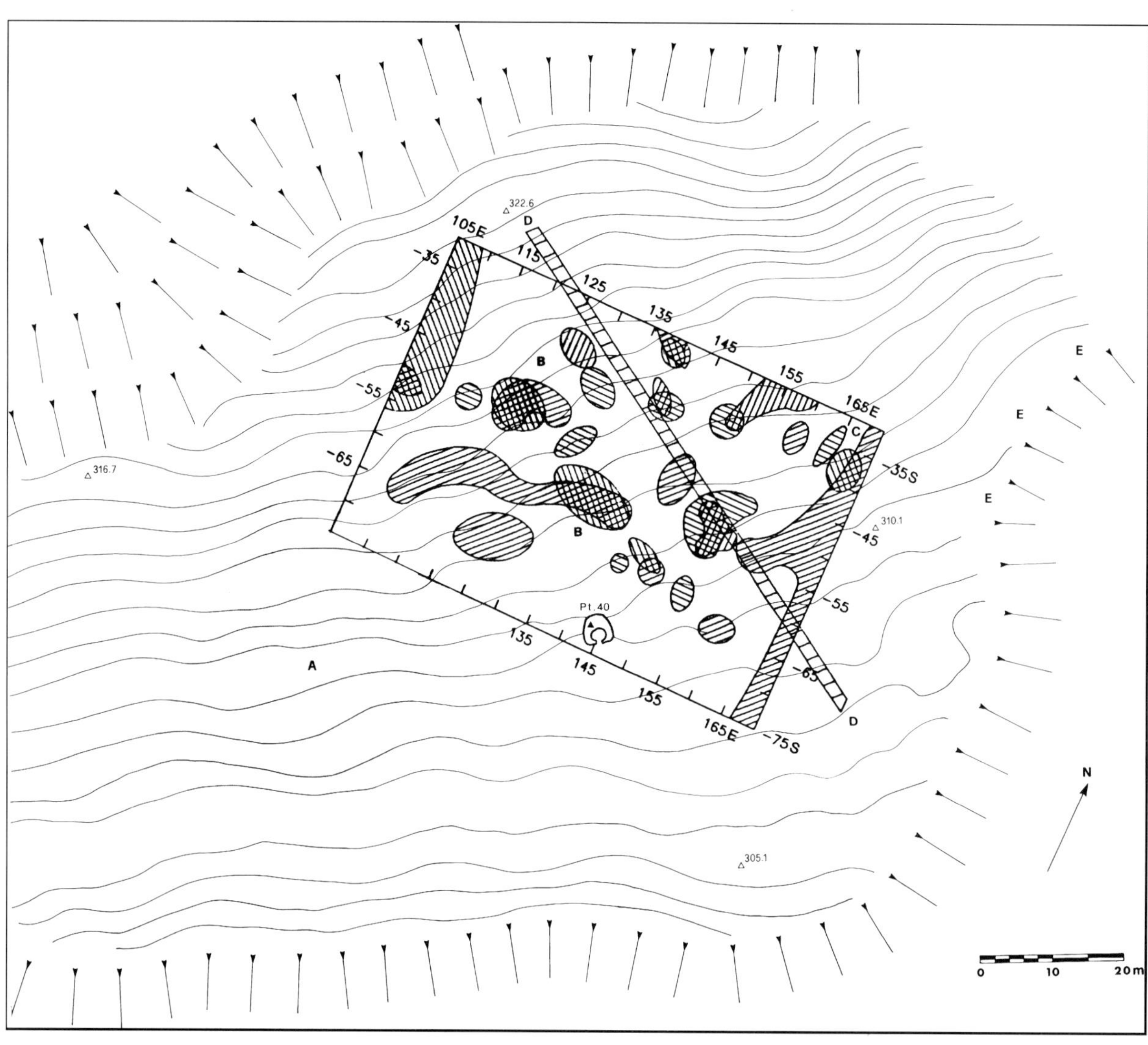

2 Zone F (village area): preliminary map of geophysical survey anomalies (lines vertical and horizontal to the horizontal indicate areas of significantly high conductivity and susceptibility possibly due to presence of hut floors; lines diagonal to the horizontal indicate areas of significantly low conductivity and susceptibility due to natural or man-made stone structures) around 1982–89. (A) and 1991 (B) excavation zones , modern property-division wall (D), and structural remains visible in the Sillitti property (C: hut, E: possible ancient wall alignment).

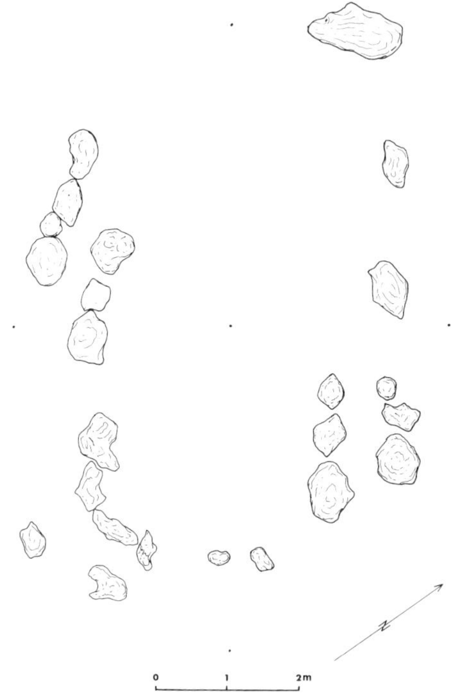

3.1 Plan of hut-structure visible in Sillitti property (C in plate 2).

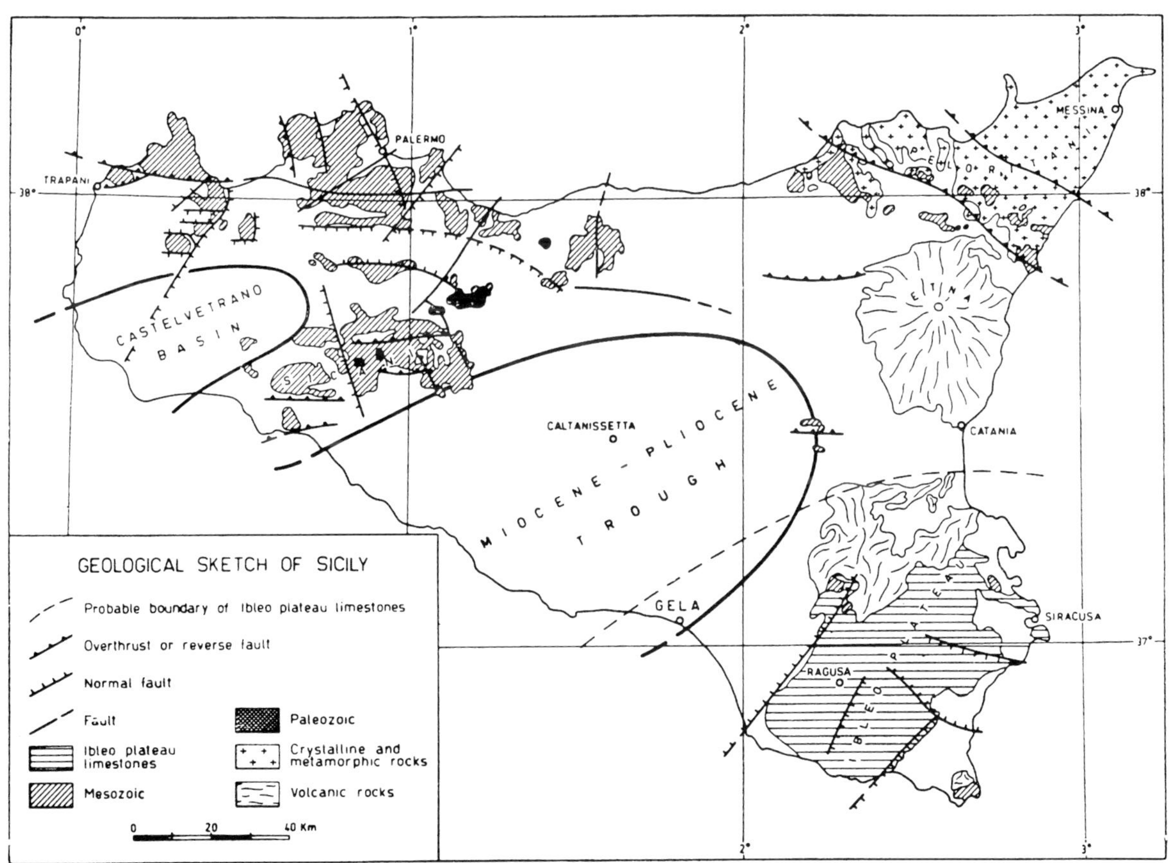

3.2 Geological map of Sicily (from T. Rocco, "Gela in Sicilia, Un singolare campo petrolifero," *Rivista Minevaria Sicili-ana* 10, 1959).

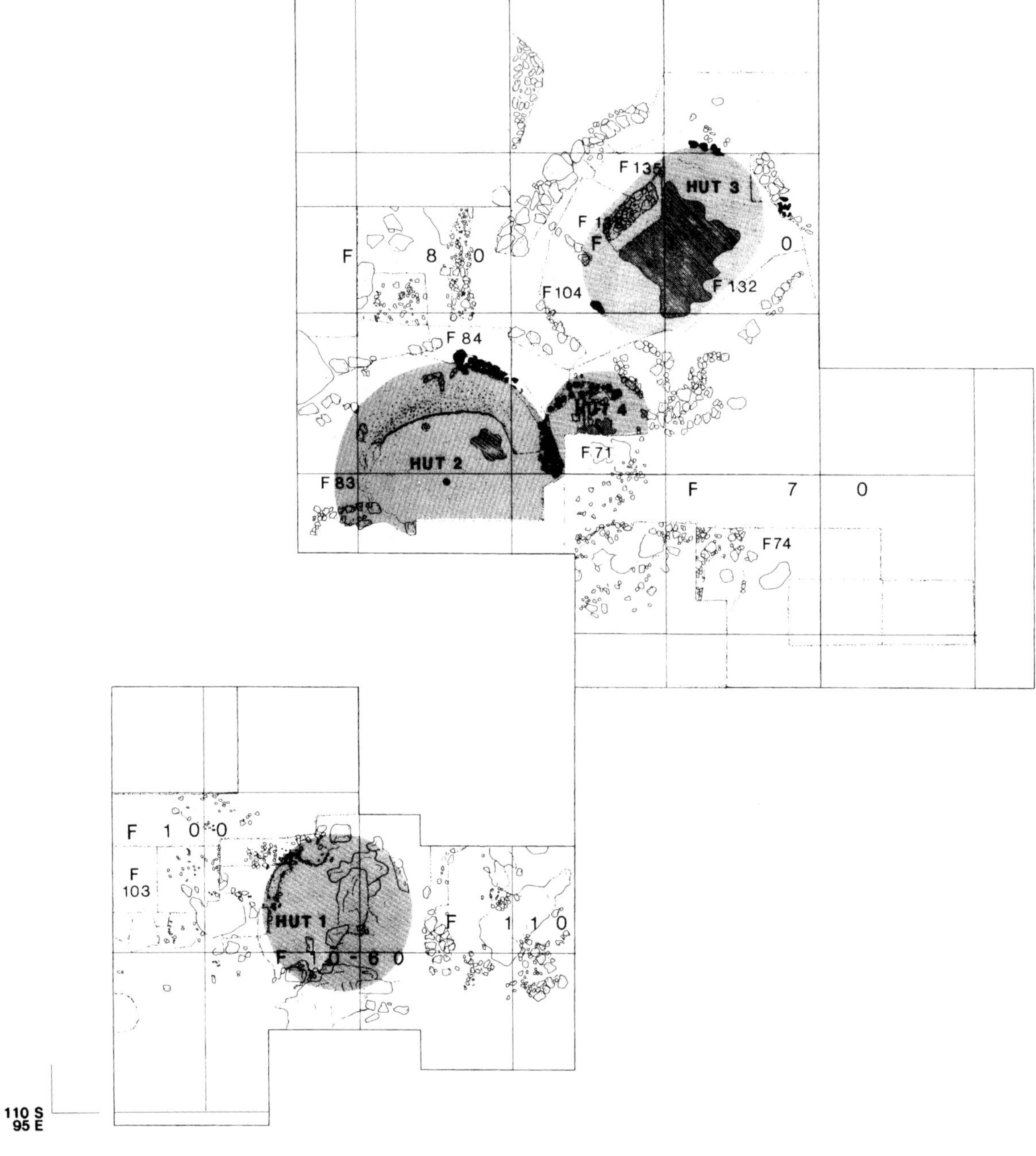

4 Plan of 1988–89 Excavation zone F (Village area) with excavation portions and prehistoric structures.

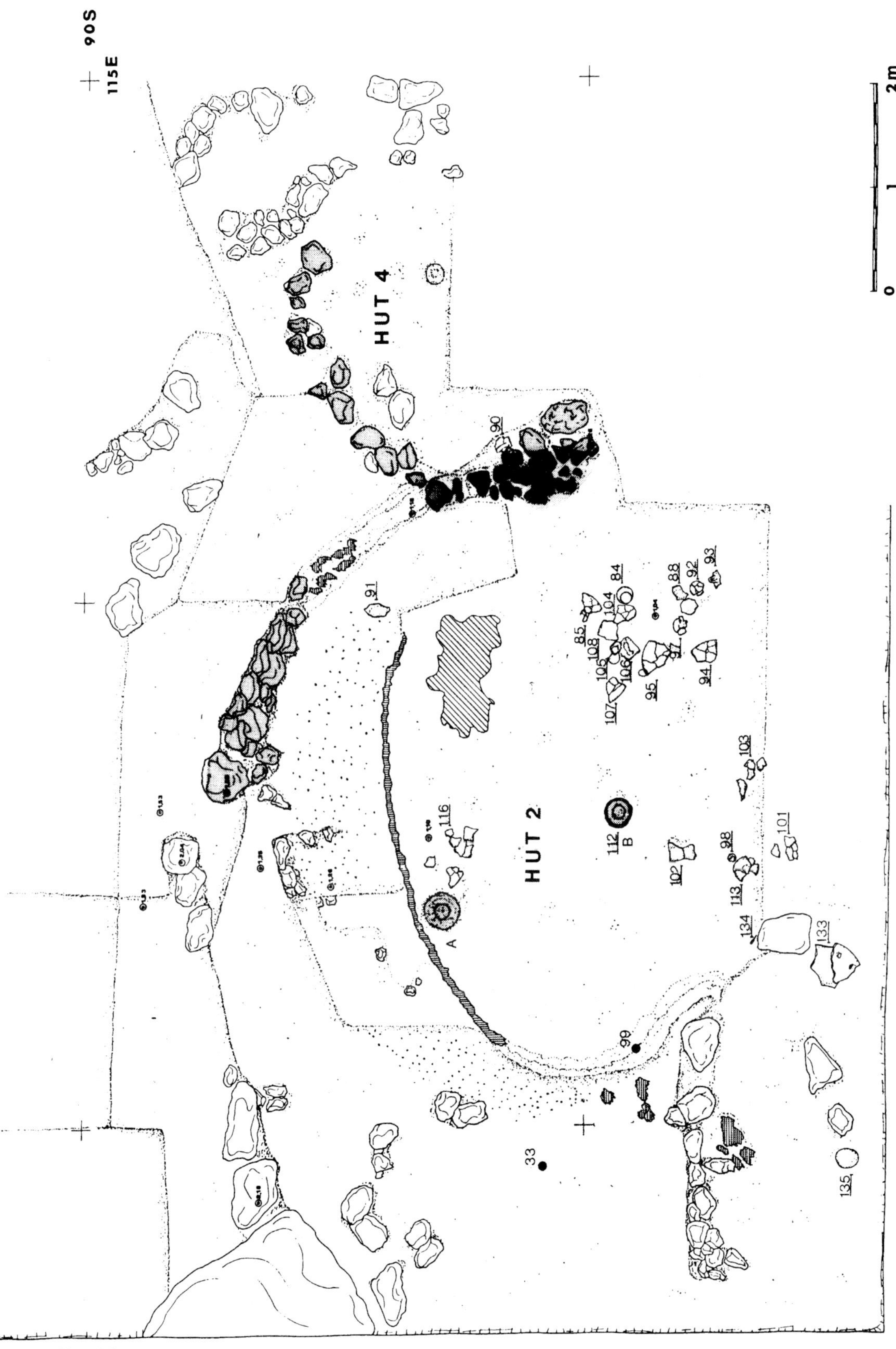

5 Plan of hut No. 2

6 Plan of trench portion F80 (Village area, 1988 excavation) with sections along Hut No. 2 wall in F84.

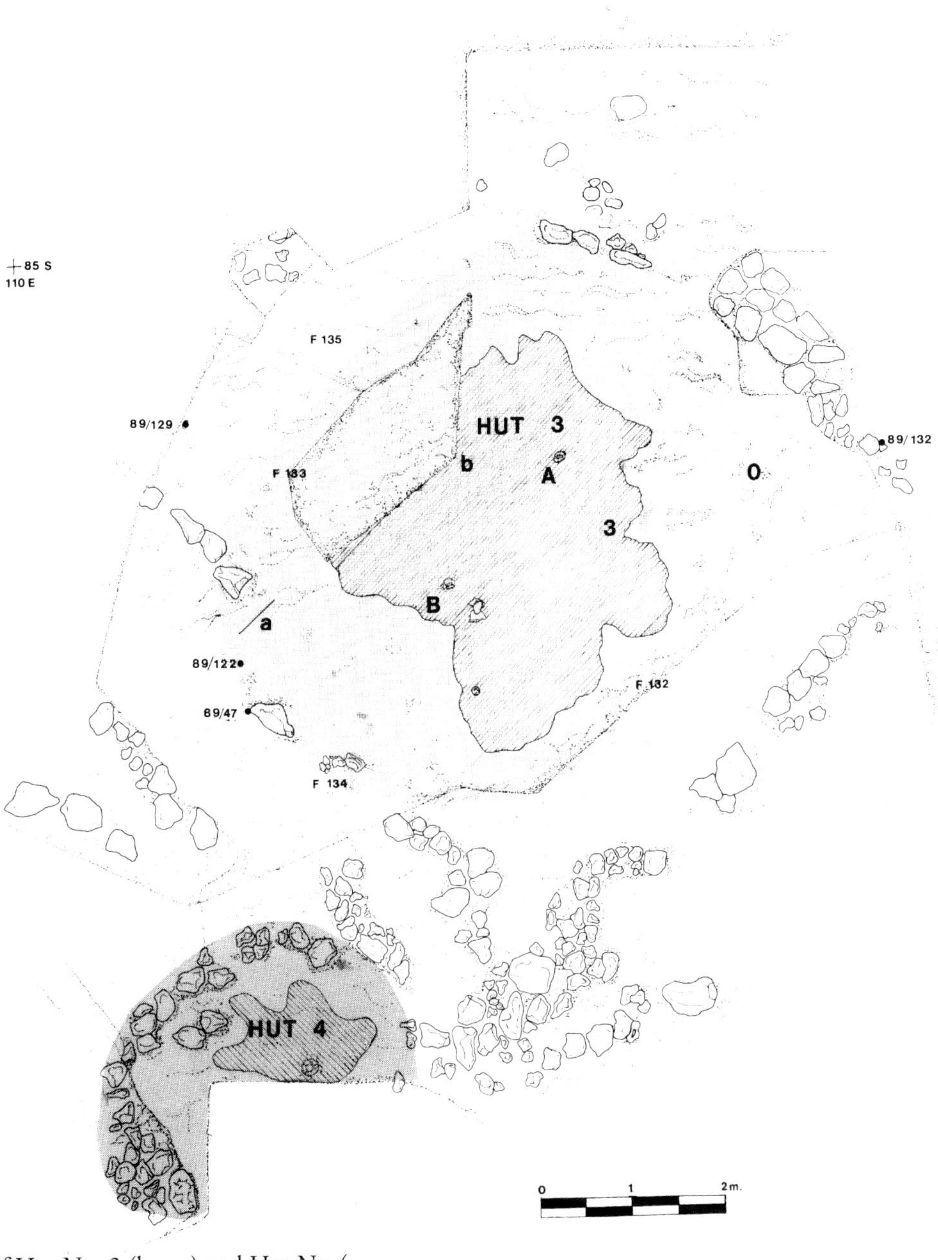

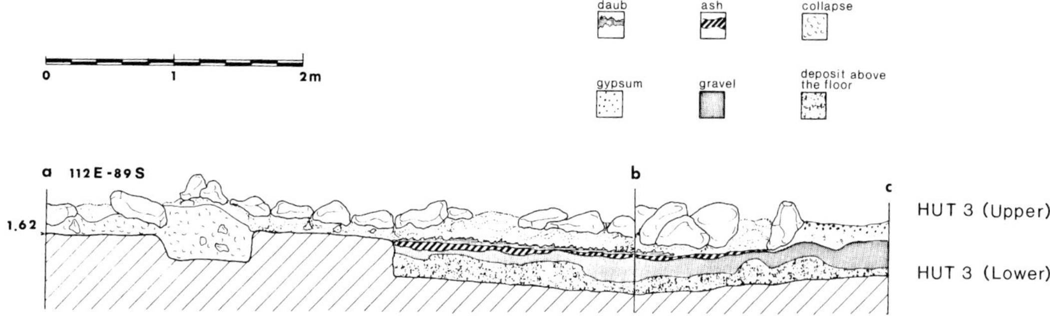

7.1 Plan of Hut No. 3 (lower) and Hut No.4.

7.2 Stratigraphic section of Hut No. 3 (upper and lower).

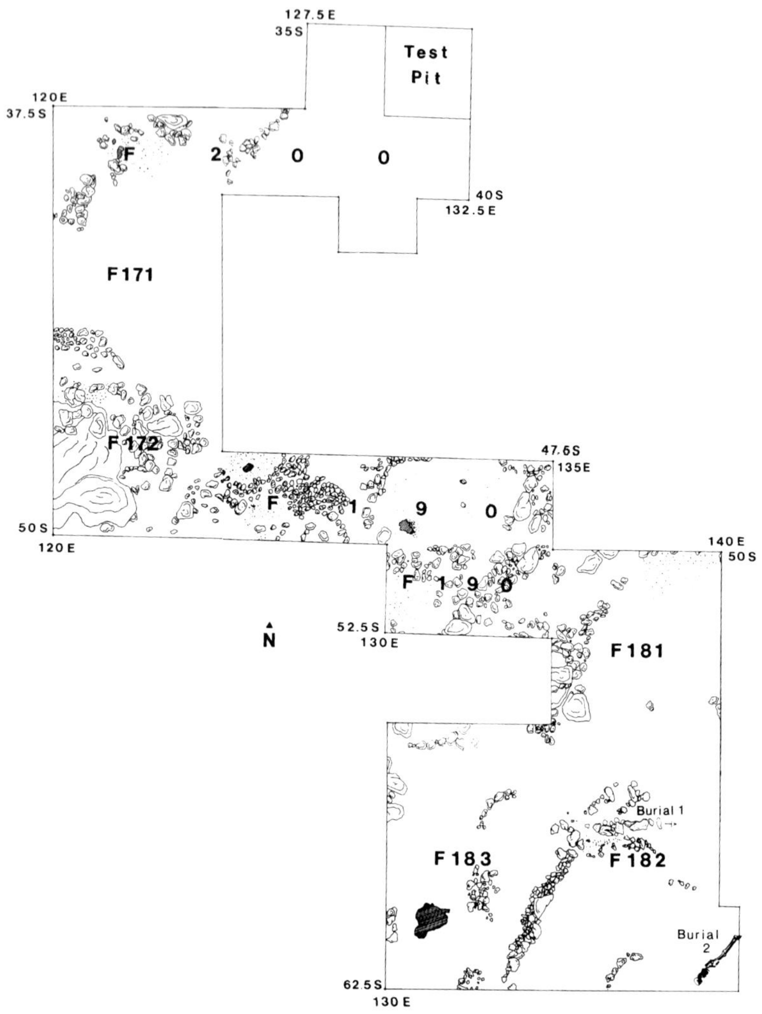

8.1 Plan of 1991 excavation trenches.

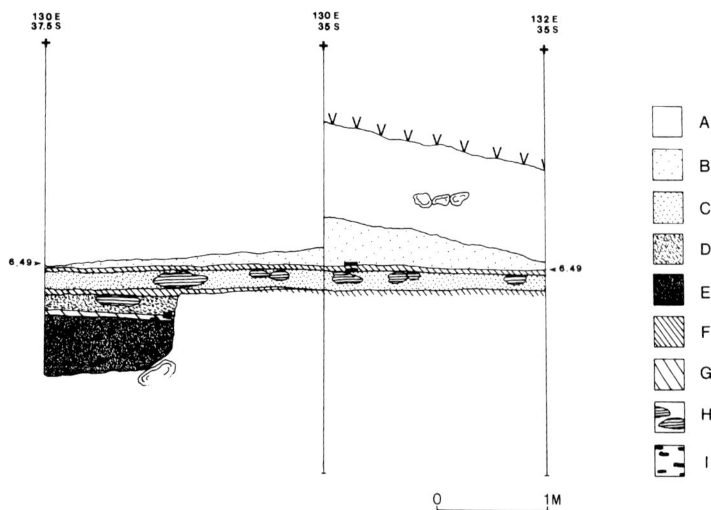

8.2 Stratigraphic section of test-pit in F200: A – humus, B – brown soil, C – ashy soil with ceramics, D – light brown soil, E – dark brown soil with gypsum bits, F – compact gypsum bits, G – brown soil with gypsum bits and carbon, H – ash, I – ceramic fragments.

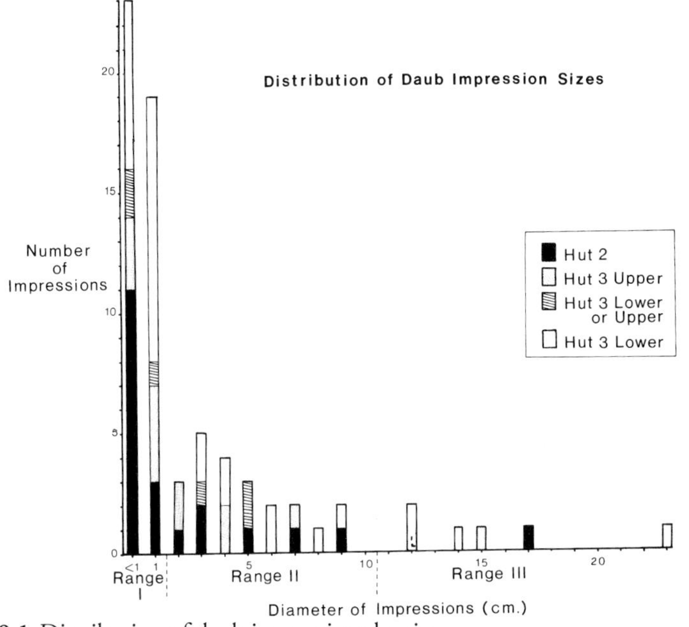

9.1 Distribution of daub impressions by size.

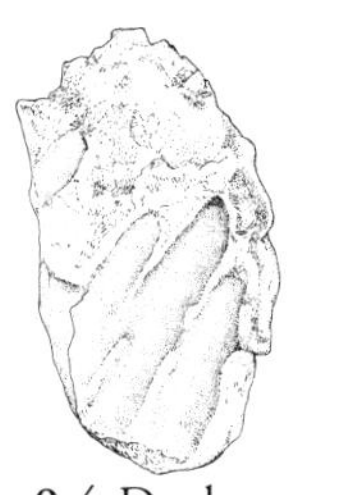

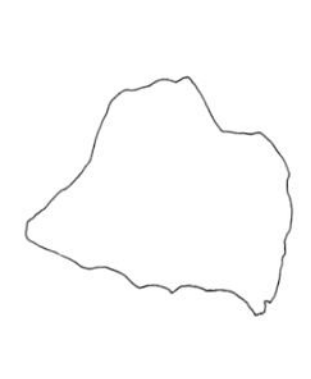

9.3 Daub sample from hut No. 2, at 1.40–1.30 meters

9.4 Daub sample from 112.5–115E, 85–88S, at 1.84–1.74 meters

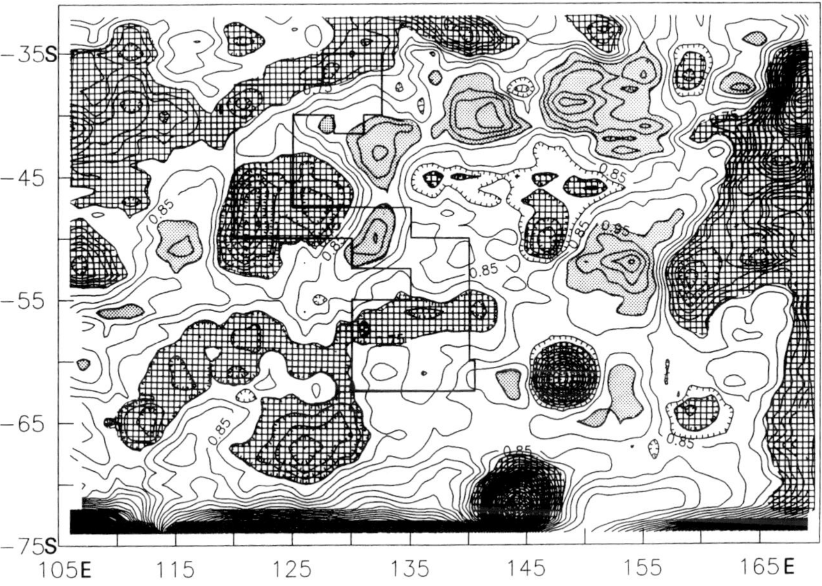

9.2 Field excavation zones (Village area, A: 1982–89, B: 1991) with revised map of geophysical survey anomalies (shading indicates areas of significantly high conductivity and susceptibility possibly due to presence of hut floors; dots indicate areas of significantly low conductivity and susceptibility possibly due to natural or man-made stone structures.

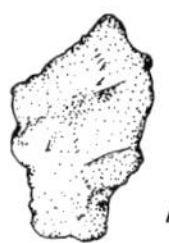

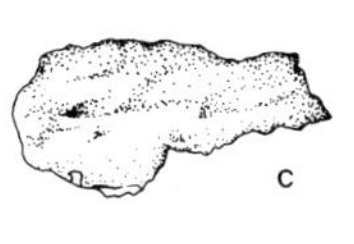

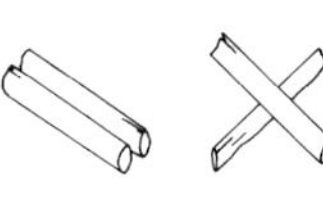

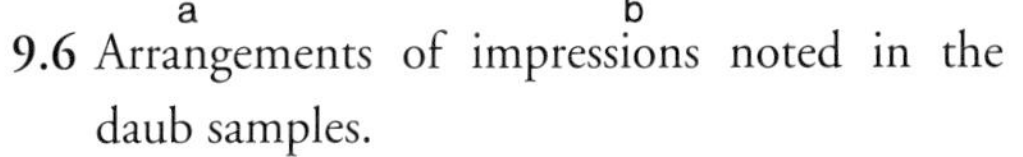

9.5 Daub samples (B: hewn timber impression in daub sample: F 133, 113–115E, 87–90S, 1.58–1.28 meters.).

9.6 Arrangements of impressions noted in the daub samples.

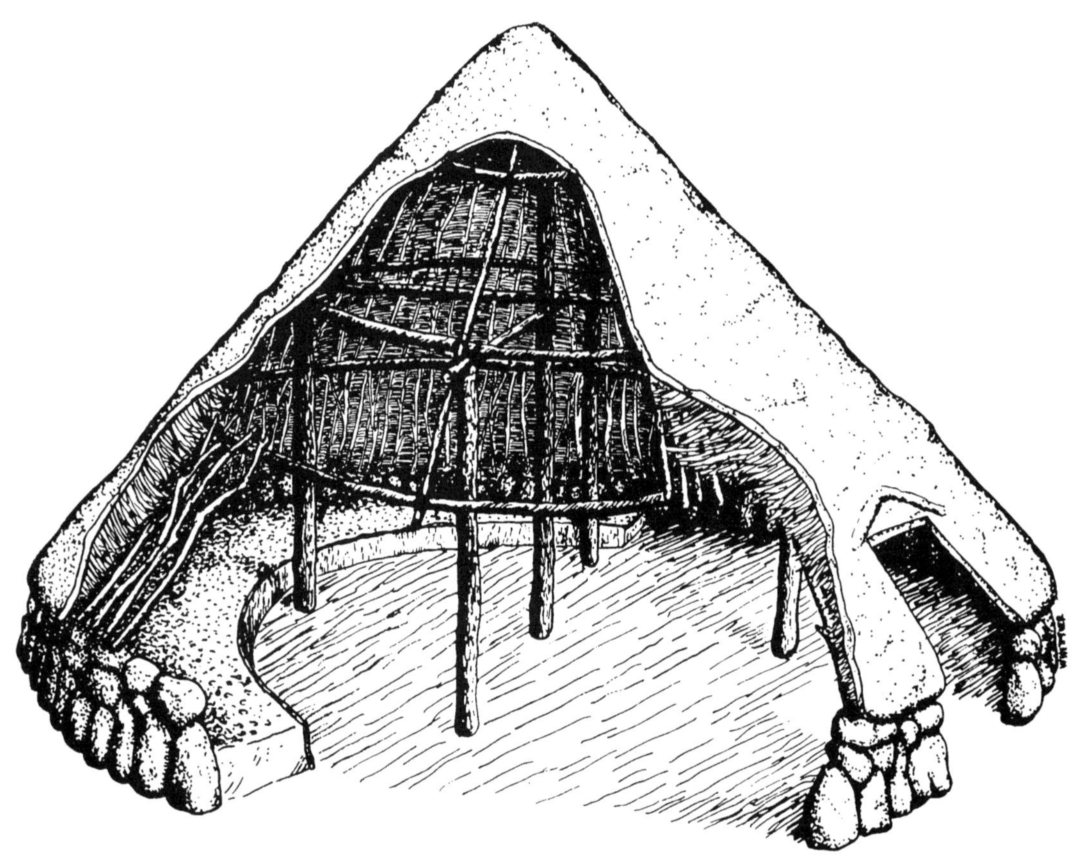

10.1 Reconstruction of hut No. 2 (closed apex) by Christopher Whittier

10.2 Reconstruction of hut No. 3 (lower) by Christopher Whittier

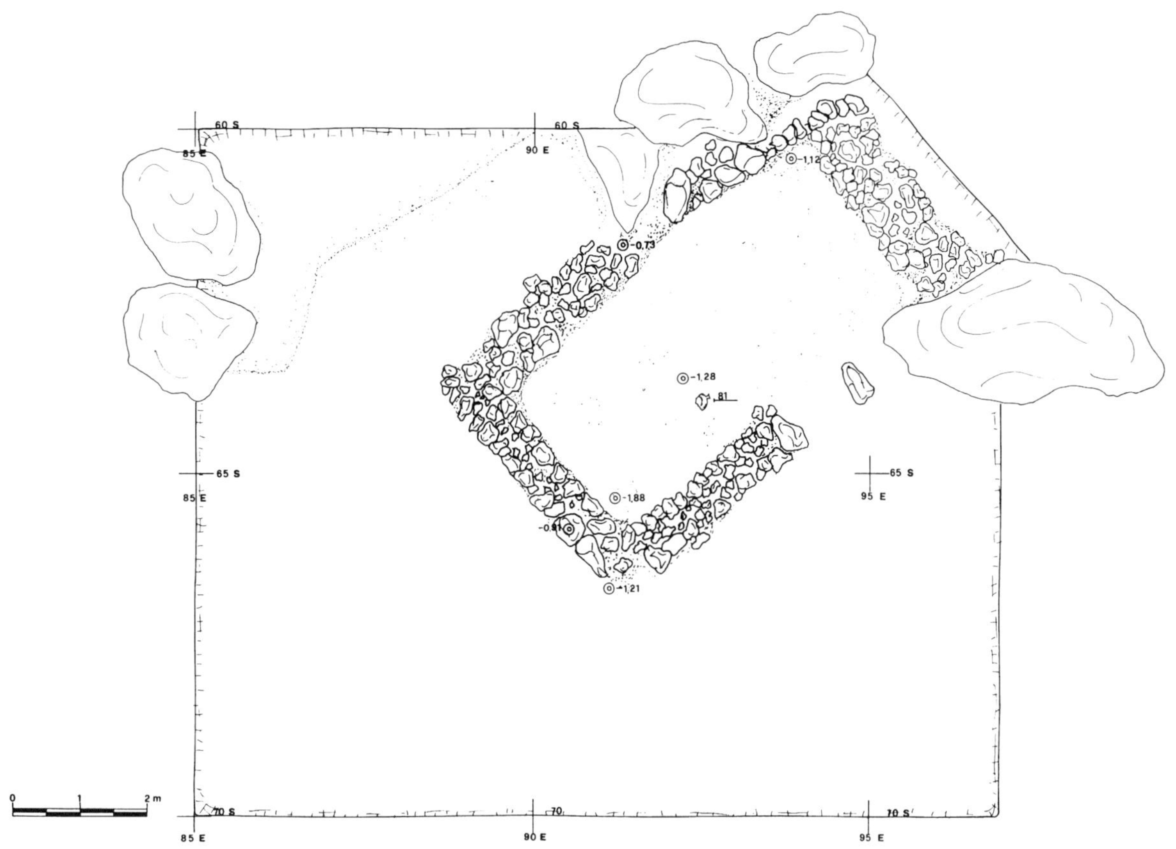

11.1 Plan of F150 (Village area) and Hellenistic structure.

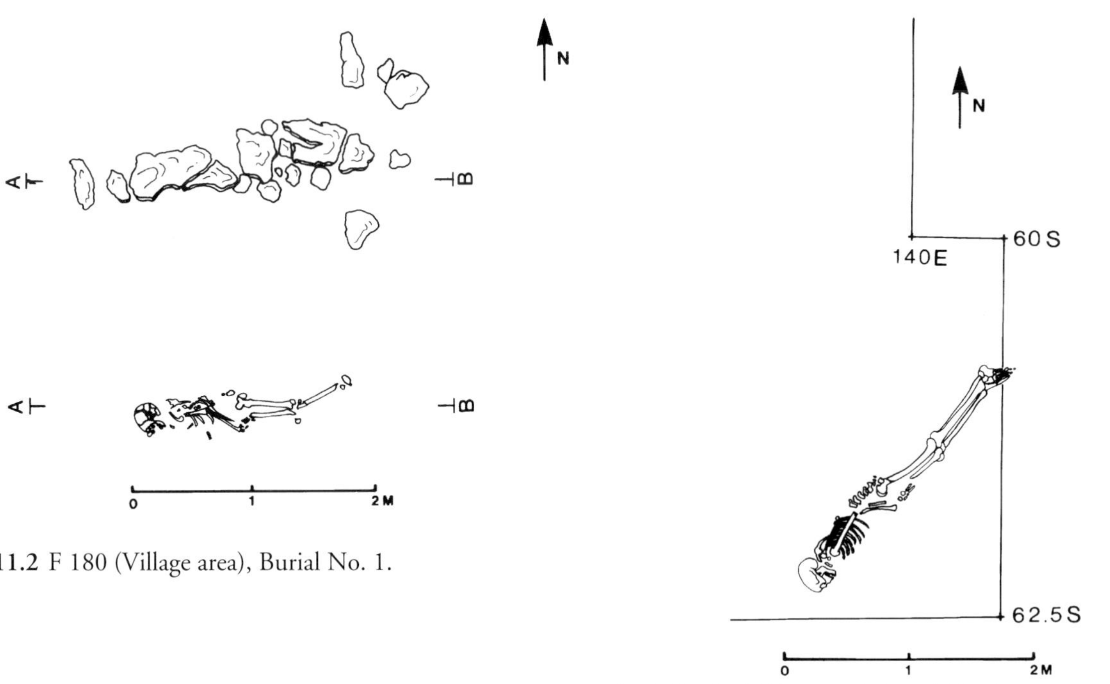

11.2 F 180 (Village area), Burial No. 1.

11.3 F 180 (Village area), Burial No. 2.

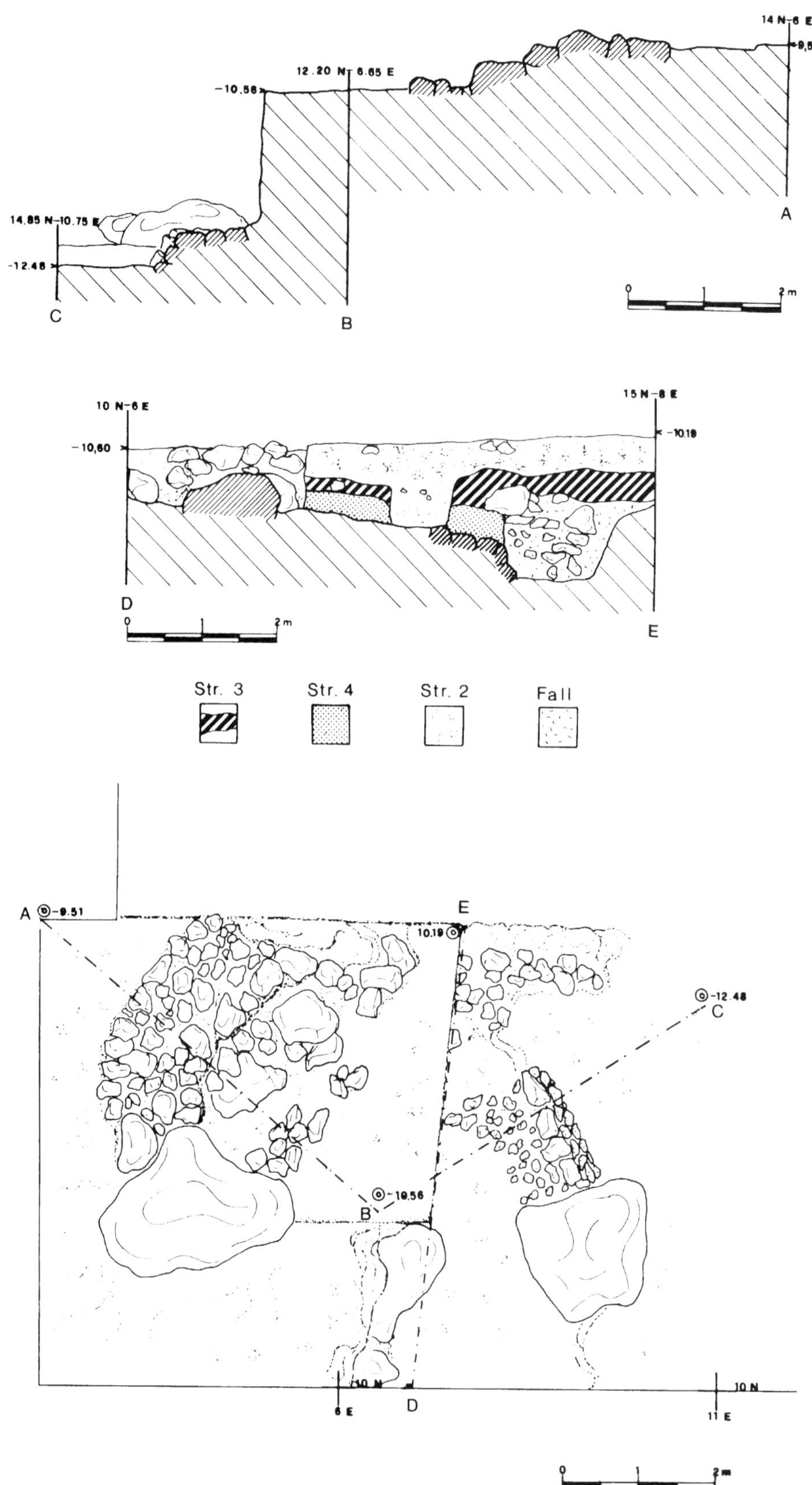

12 Zone T (Sanctuary area), portions excavated in 1989.

13.1 Hut Nos. 2, 3 (upper and lower) and 4 from the crest.

13.4 Hut No. 2 during excavation with fallen wall daub and ceramics.

13.2 Hut Nos. 2, 3 (upper and lower) and 4 towards the east.

13.5 Structure in excavation portion F 150 (Village area).

13.3 Hut No. 2 after excavation

13.6 Field excavation zone (Village area) during the geophysical survey with survey grid lines visible.

14.1 Excavation portion F 134 (Village area) with Hut No. 3 (upper) wall.

14.2 Wall segments of hut No. 3 (upper) and (lower) in superposition.

14.3 Excavation portion S 110B (on the crest) with crevice-burial (right) and Castellucian tomb (left).

14.4 Excavation portion F180 (Village area), burial No. 1.

15.1 Cat. No. 1

15.4 Cat. Nos. 29 (top, l.), 39 (top., r), 37 (bottom, l.), 27 (bottom, c.), and 31 (bottom, r.).

15.2 Cat. Nos. 9 (top, l.), 131 (top, r.), and 88/26.

15.5 Cat. No. 36.

15.3 Cat. Nos. 23 (top, l.) and 10 (bottom, r.).

15.6 Cat. Nos. 43 (top, l.), 132 (top, r.), 40 (bottom, l.), and 41 (bottom, r.).

16.1 Cat. No. 65.

16.4 Cat. No. 102.

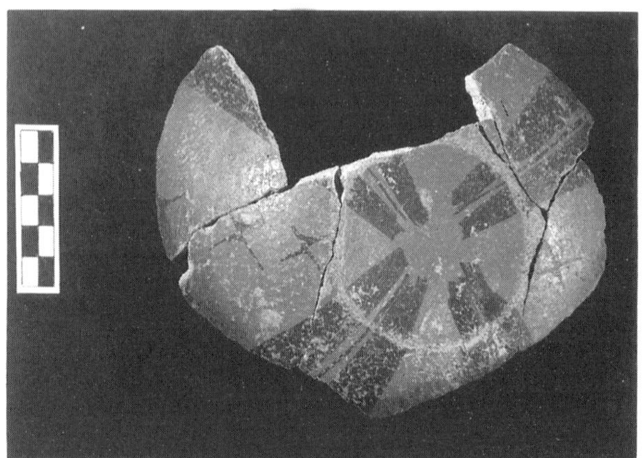

16.2 Cat. No. 67.

16.5 Cat. No. 110.

16.3 Cat. No. 93.

16.6 Cat. No. 121

17.1 Cat. No. 124.

17.4 Cat. No. 164 (top, l.), 89/368 (top, r.), and Cat. No. 168 (bottom).

17.2 Cat. No. 142.

17.3 Cat. No. 150.

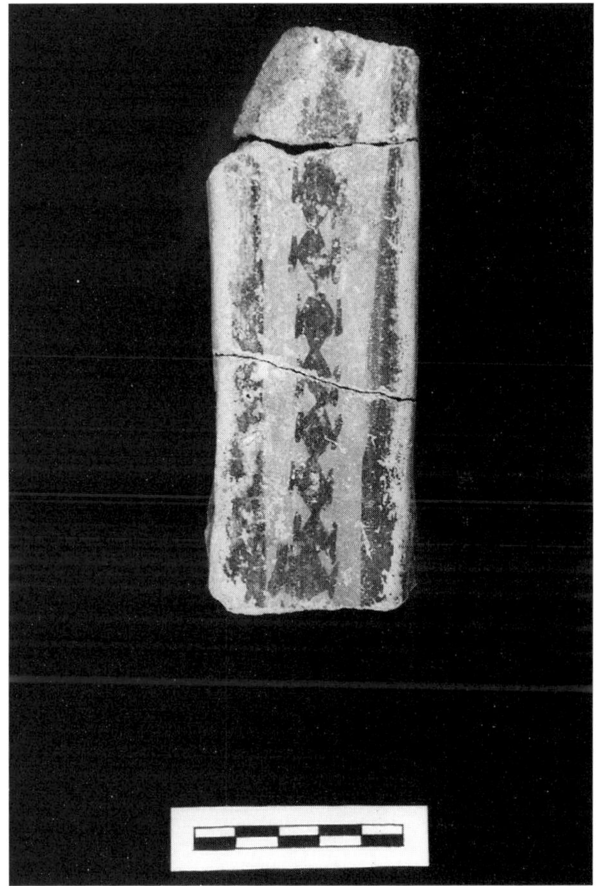

17.5 Cat. No. 163.

18.1 Cat. No. 169.

18.2 Cat. Nos. (top, l. to r.) 179, 177, 173, 180, (center, l. to r.) 89/315, Cat. Nos. 174, 172, 175, and (bottom, l. to r.) Cat. Nos. 176, 178, and s.n.

18.3 Cat. No. 184

18.4 Cat. Nos. (top, l.) 201, (bottom, l.) 202, and (right) 198.

18.5 Cat. Nos. (top, r.) 209, (bottom l.) 212, and (bottom, r.) 210, .

19.1 Cat. No. 65 with paint stroke (left) and inv. 90,043/2 (right)

19.2 Vessel warped in firing from excavation zone T (Sanctuary area).

19.3 Pedestal bowl pedestal with handle insert.

19.4 Pedestal bowl base with repair holes.

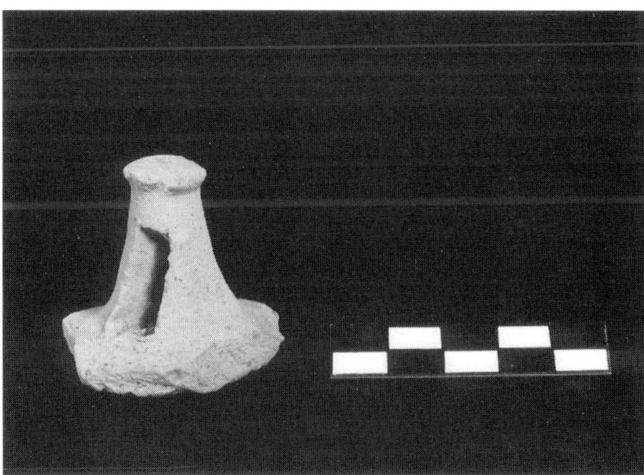

19.5 Cat. No. 425.

20.1 Cat. No. 216.

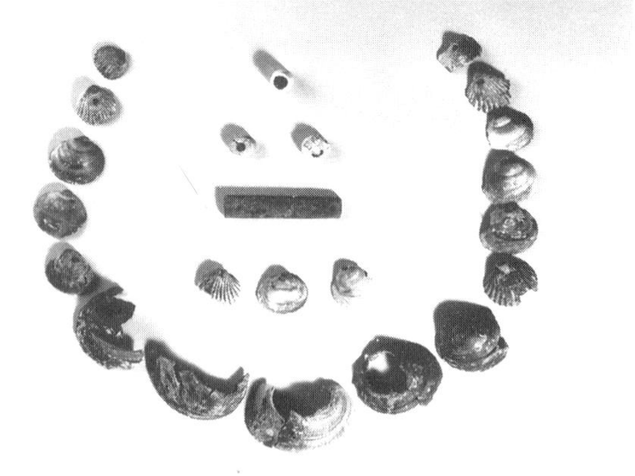

20.4 Cat. Nos. (shells) 411, (pseudo-brassard) 402, (top, c.) 409, (bead, l.) 410, and s.n.

20.2 Cat. No. 216 with stone inserted in tip.

20.5 Cat. No. 258.

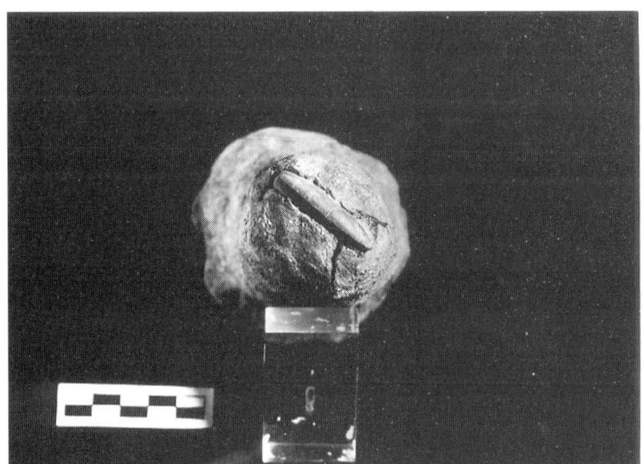

20.3 Cat. No. 220.

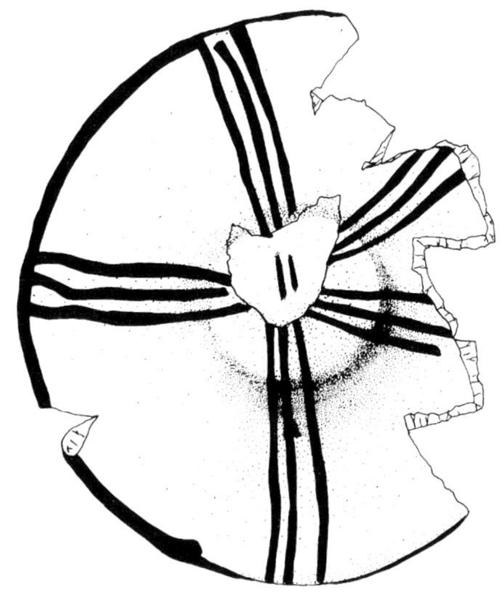

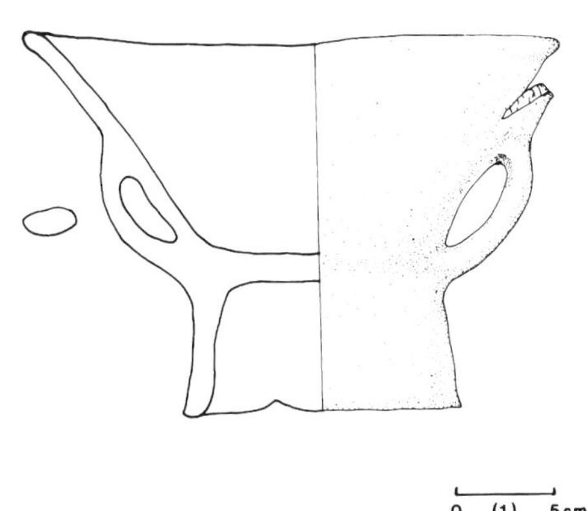

1

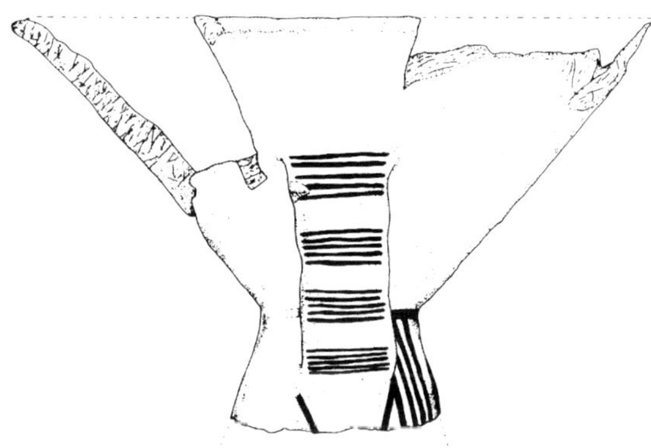

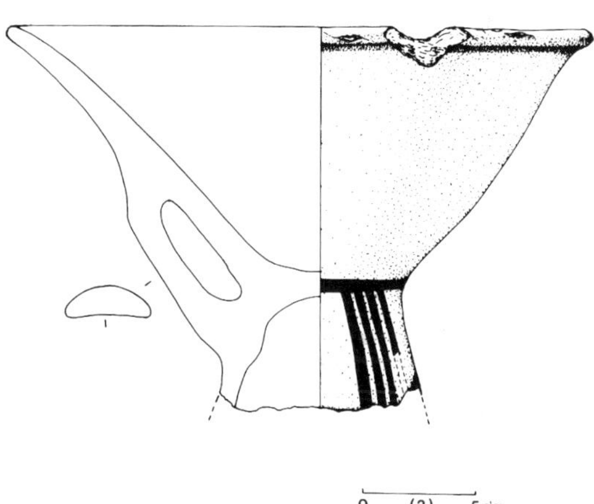

2

21 Pedestal bowls: cat. nos. 1, 2.

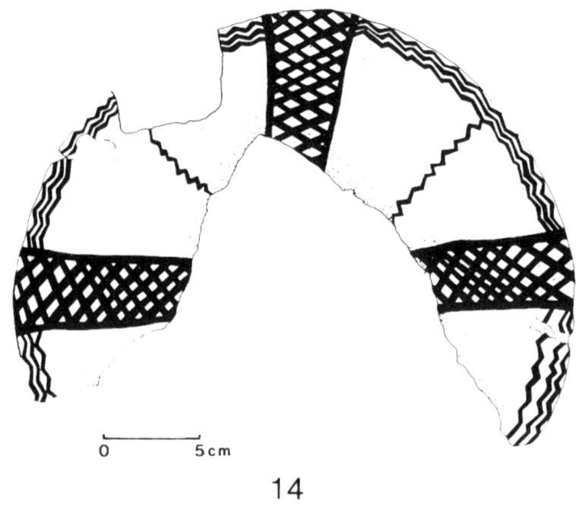

14

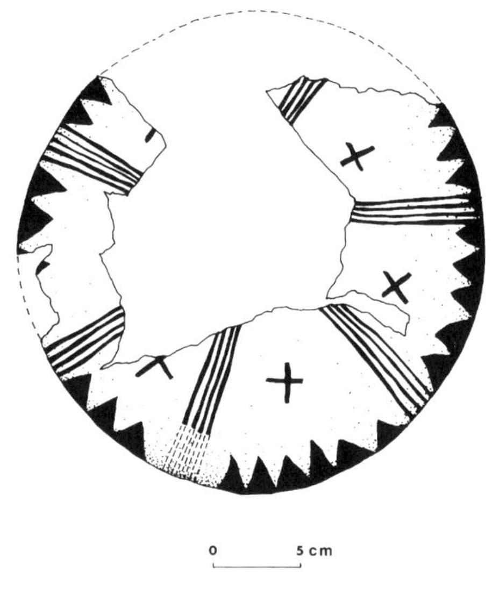

33

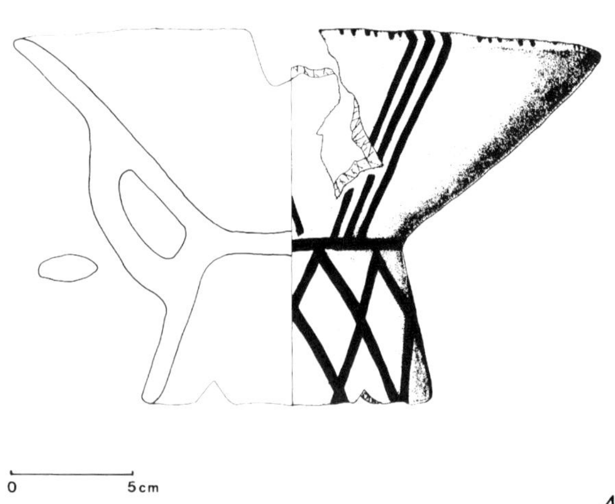

4

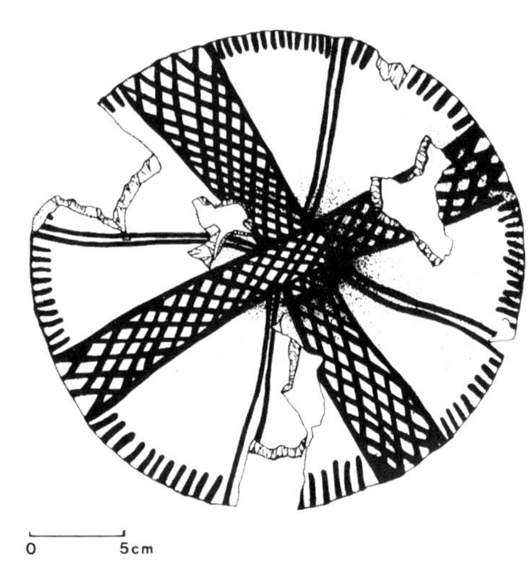

22 Pedestal bowls: cat. nos. 4, 14, 33.

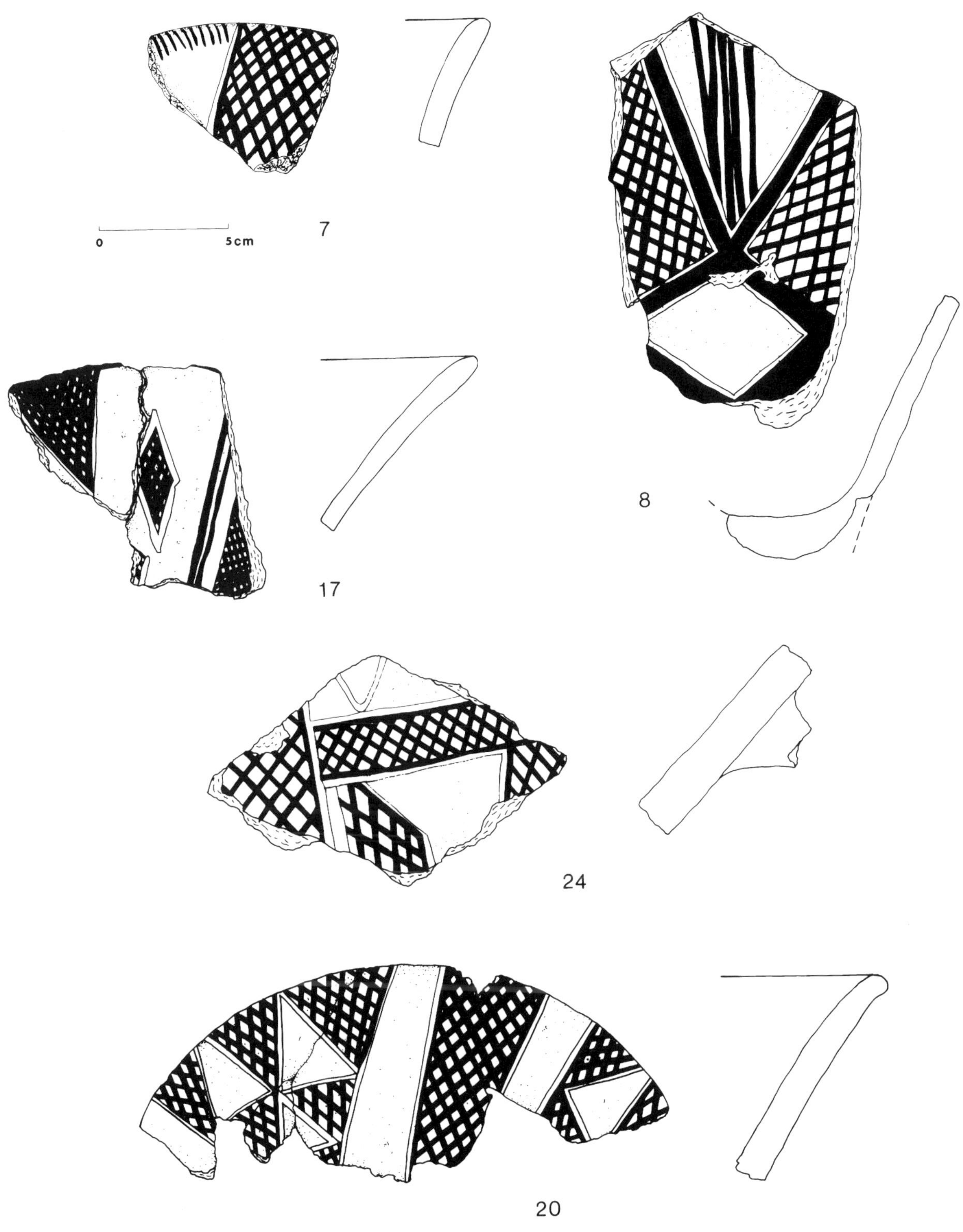

23 Pedestal bowls: cat. nos. 7, 8, 17, 20, 24.

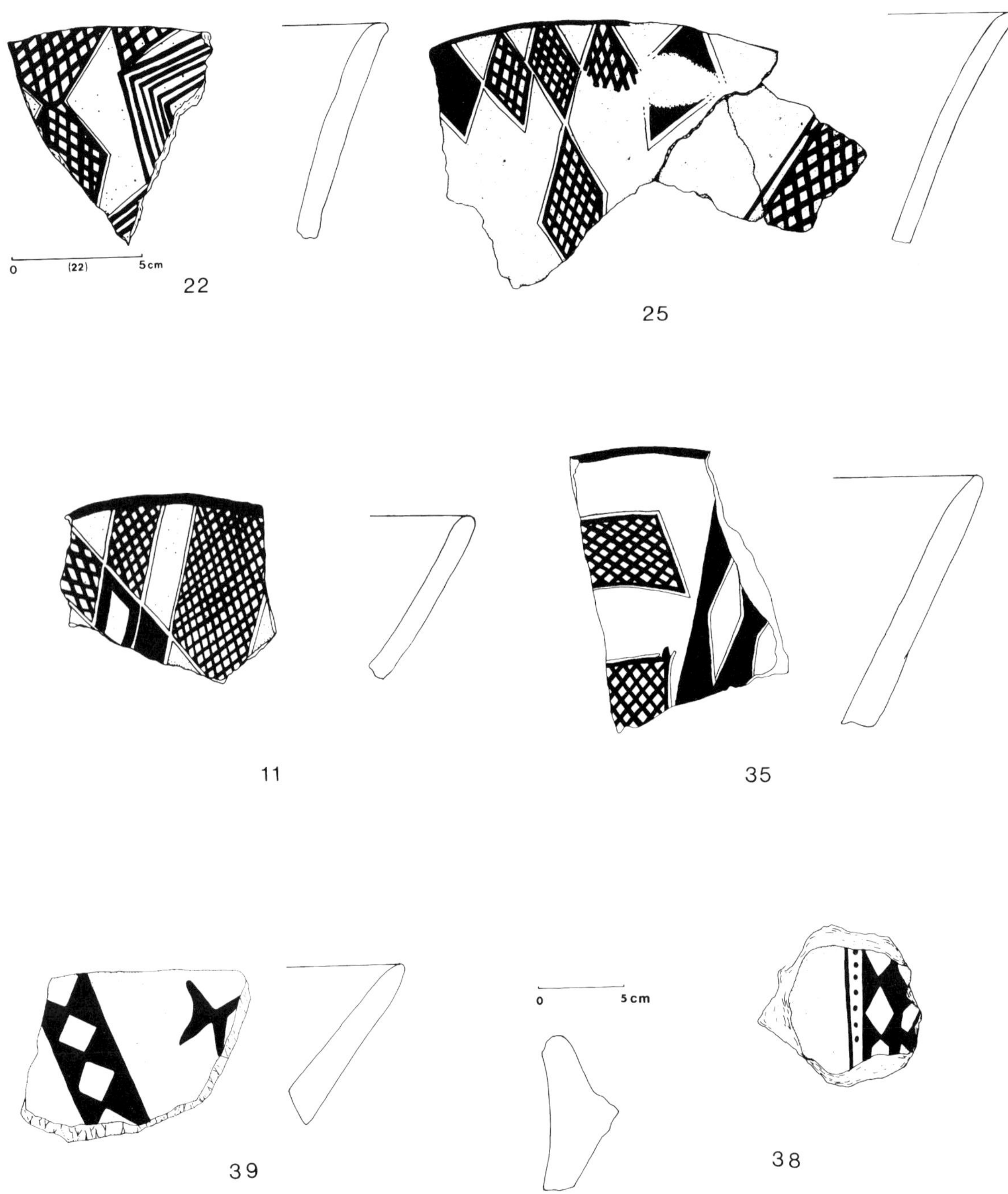

24 Pedestal bowls: cat. nos. 11, 22, 25, 35, 39, 38

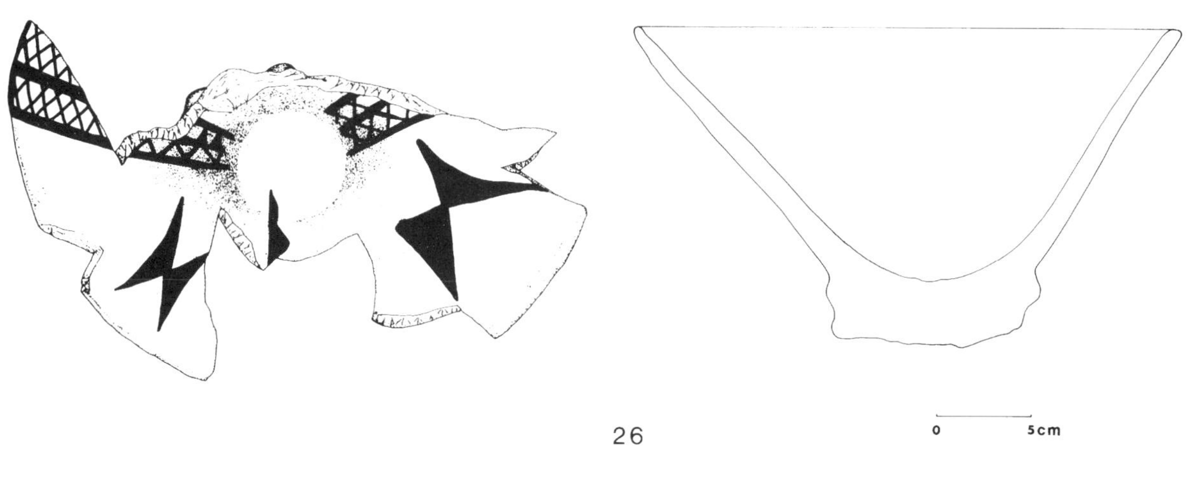

26

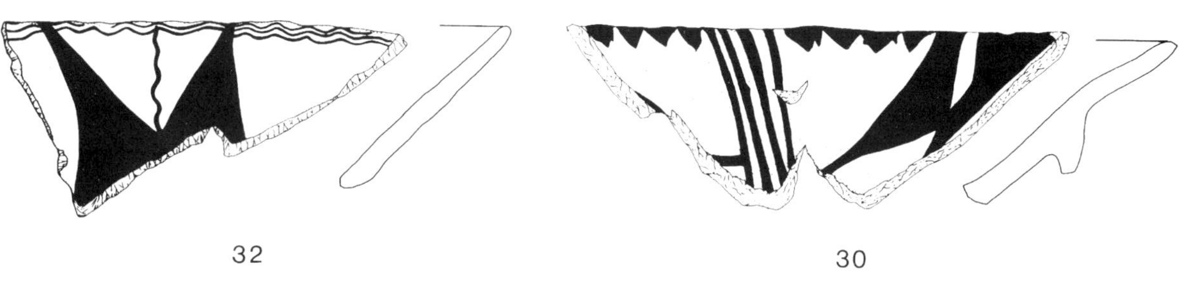

32

30

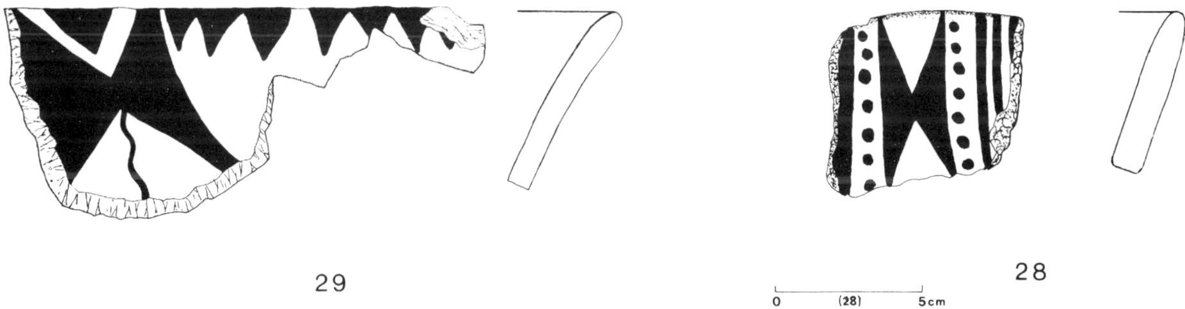

29

28

25 Pedestal bowls: cat. nos. 26, 28, 29, 30, 32

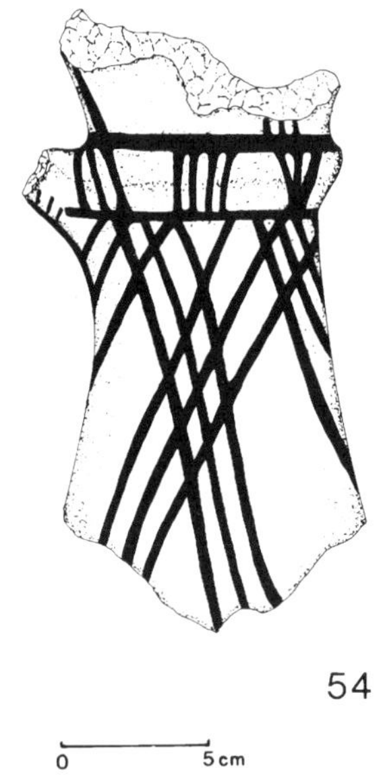

54

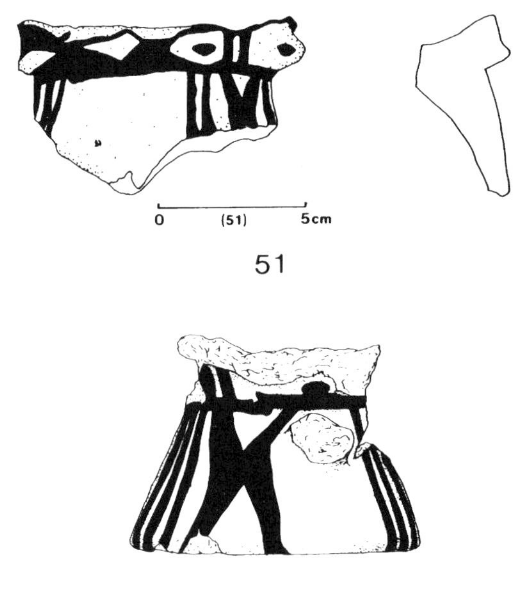

51

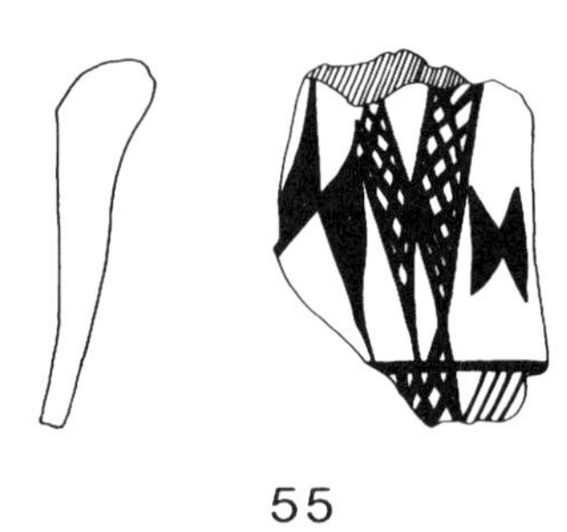

57

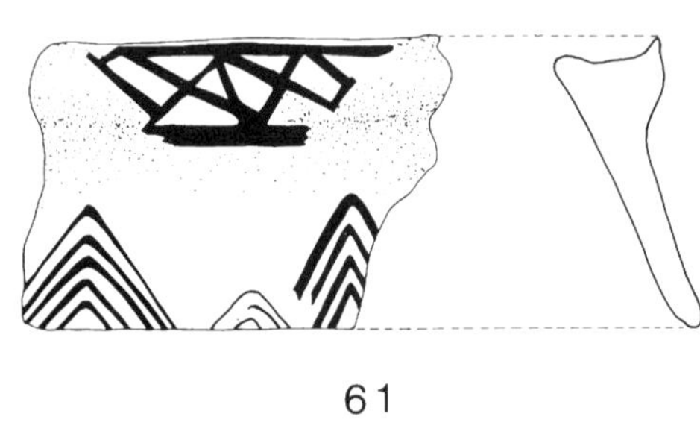

61

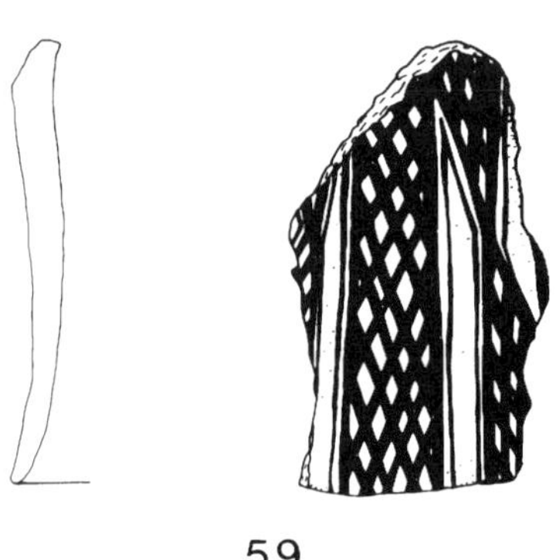

55

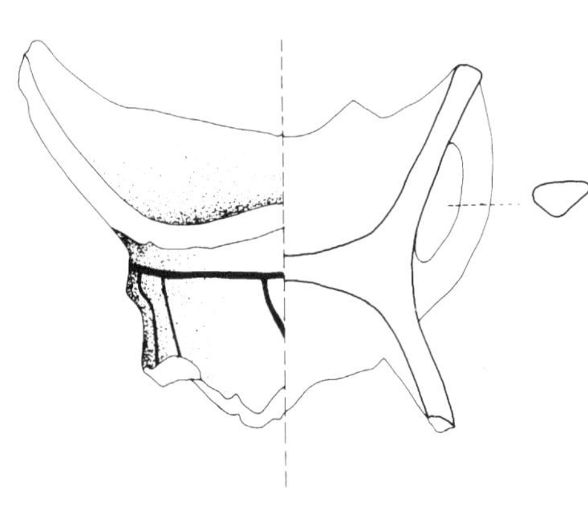

52

26 Pedestal bowls: cat. nos. 51, 52, 54, 55, 57, 59, 61

59

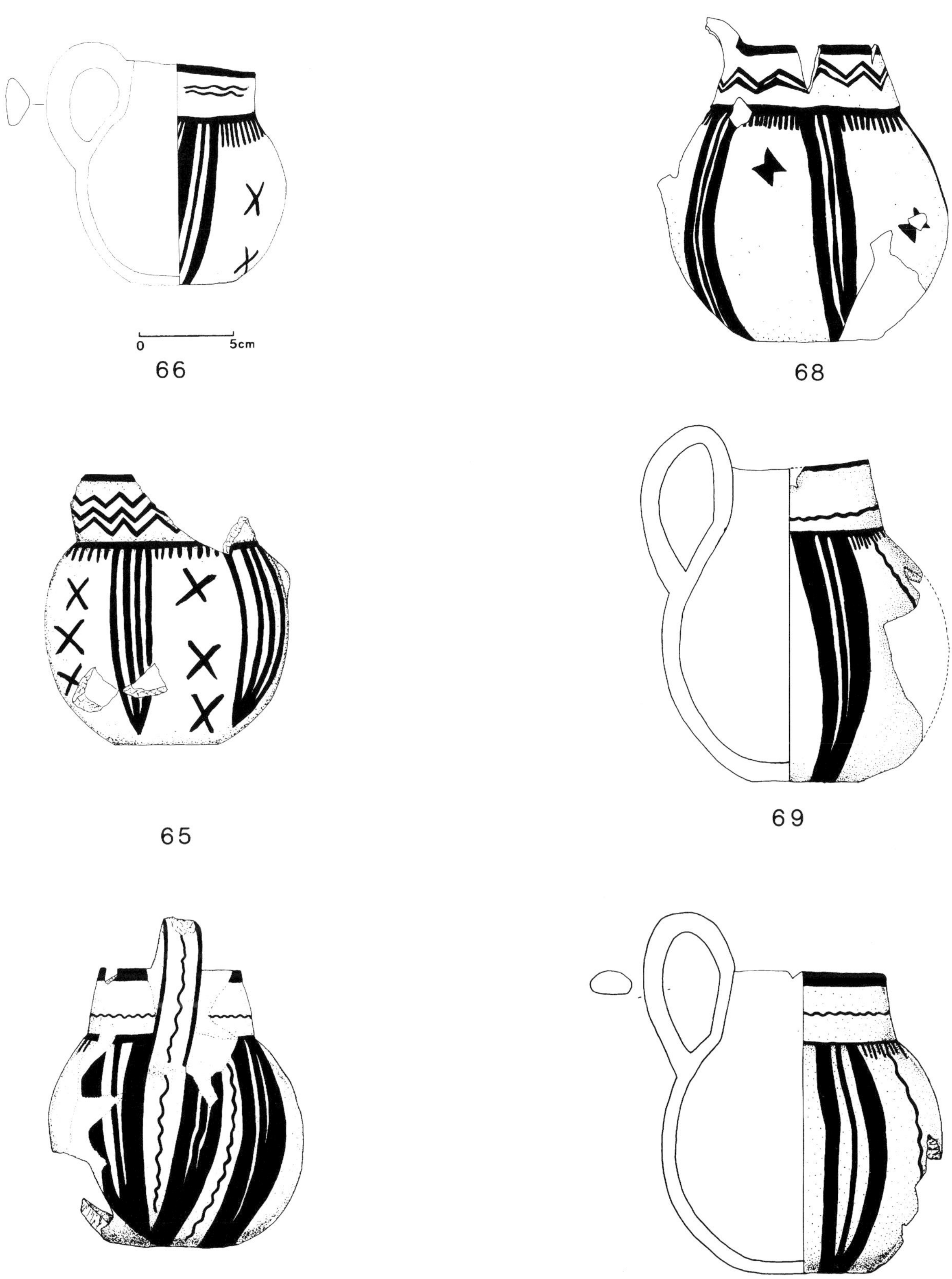

27 Pitchers: cat. nos. 65, 66, 68, 69, 70

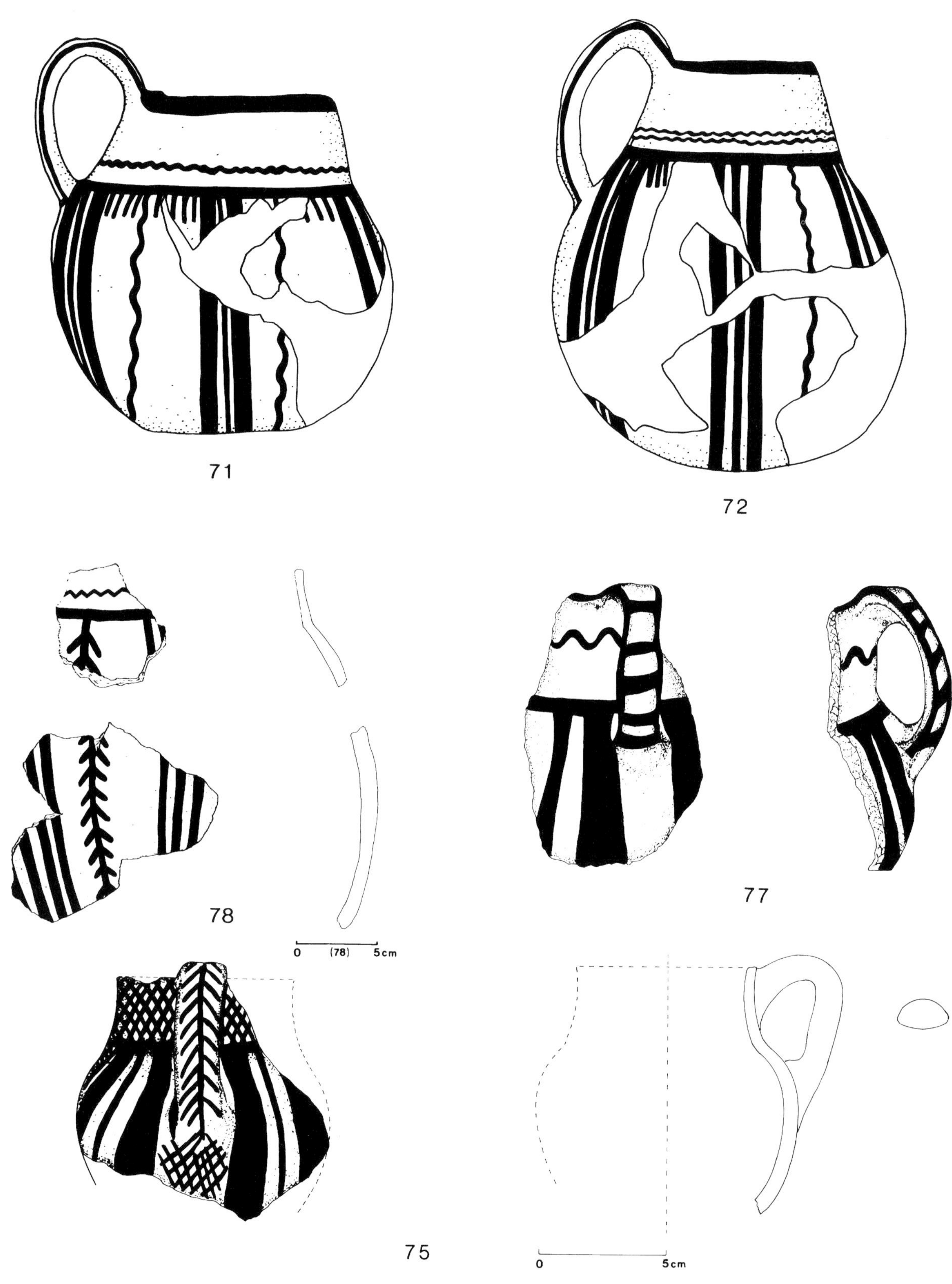

28 Pitchers: cat. nos. 71, 72, 75, 77, 78

82

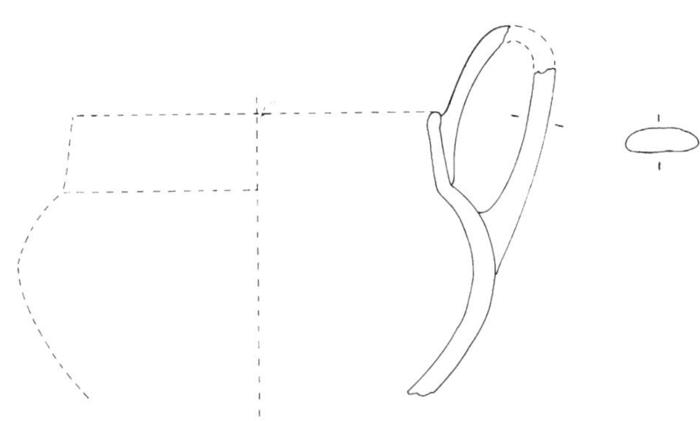

81

85

83

29 Carinated pitchers: cat. nos. 81, 82, 83, 85

91

90

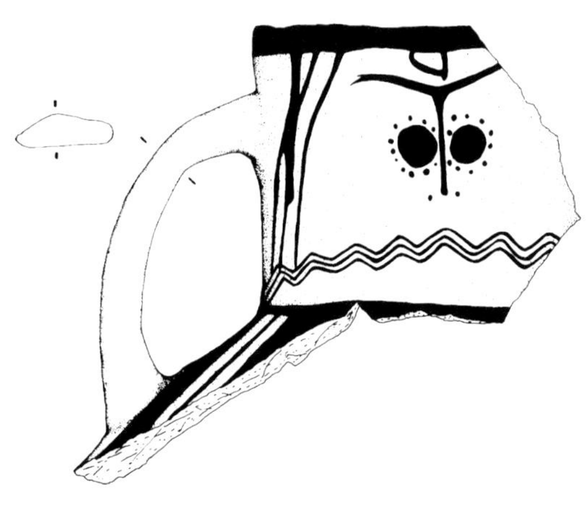

93

30 Pitchers: cat. nos. 90, 91, 93

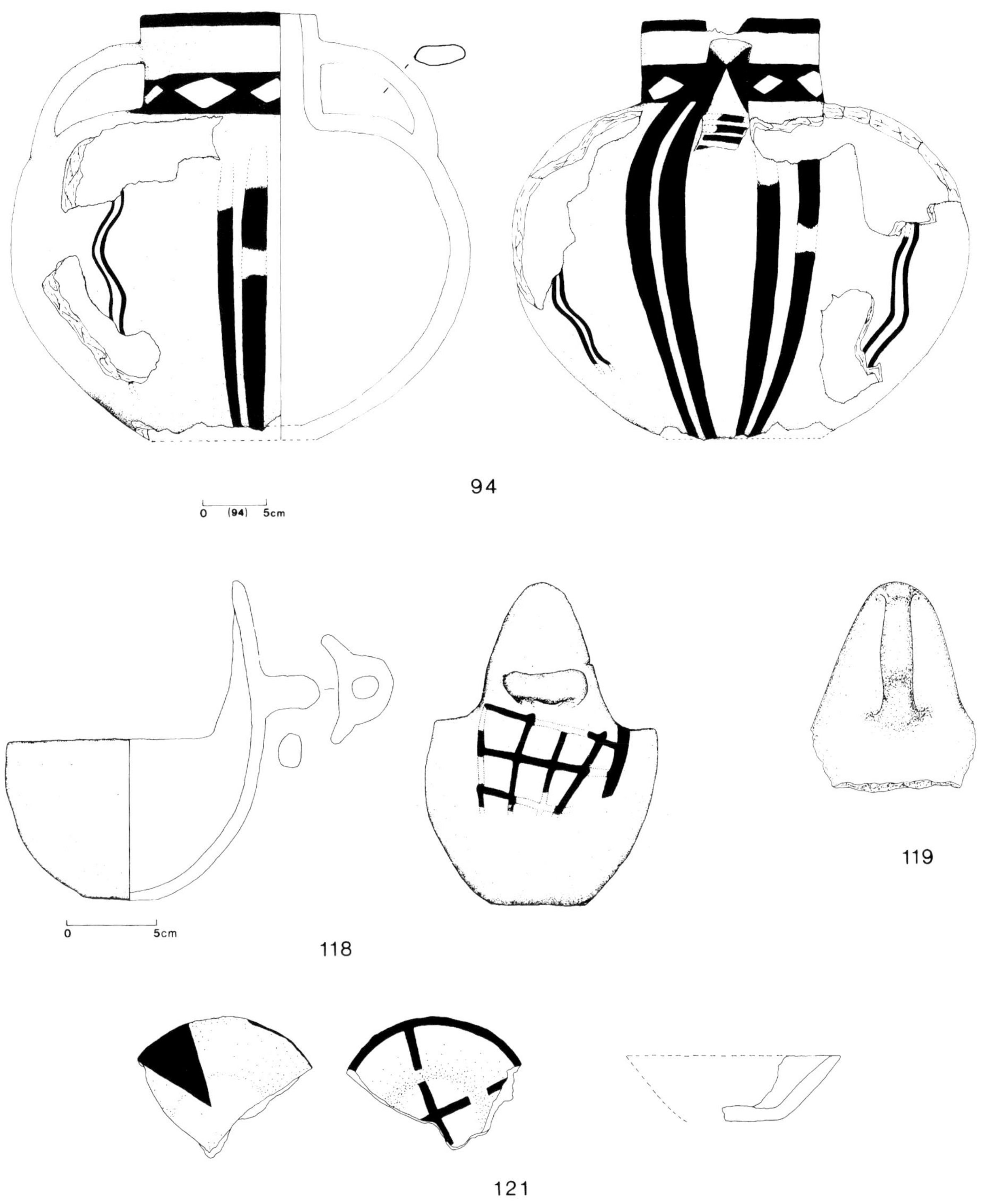

31 Various forms: cat. nos. 94, 118, 119, 121

97

98

96

104

103

107

106

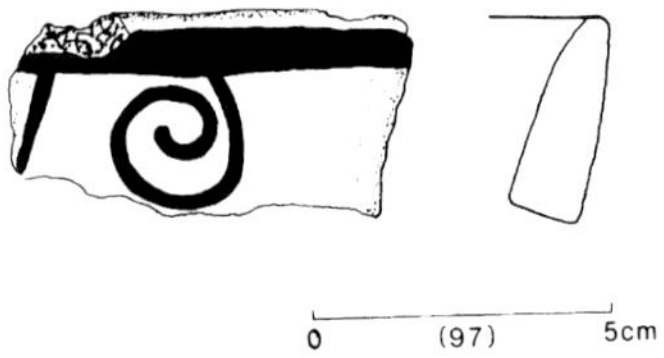

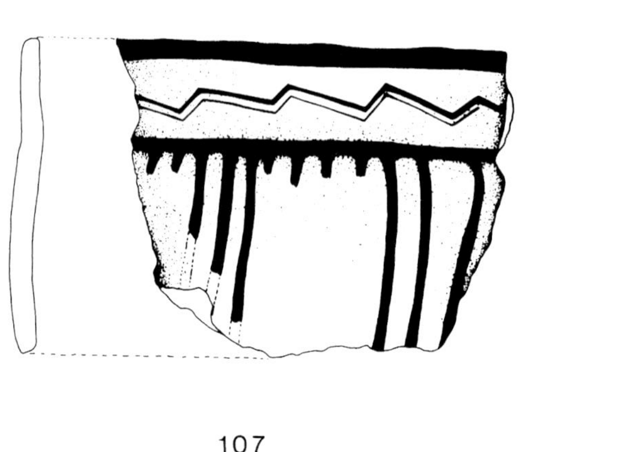

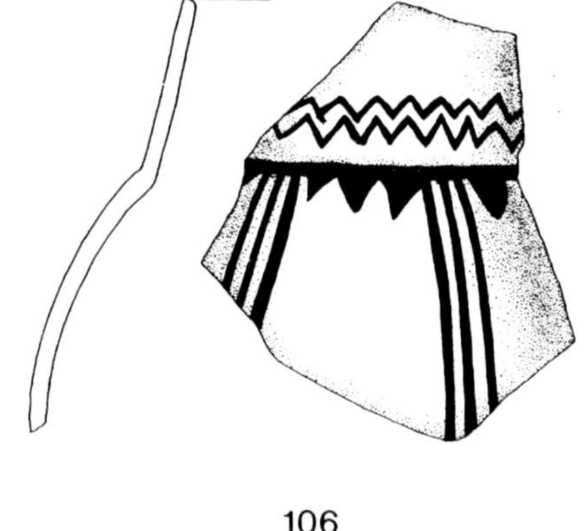

32 Pitchers: cat. nos. 96, 97, 98, 103, 104, 106, 107

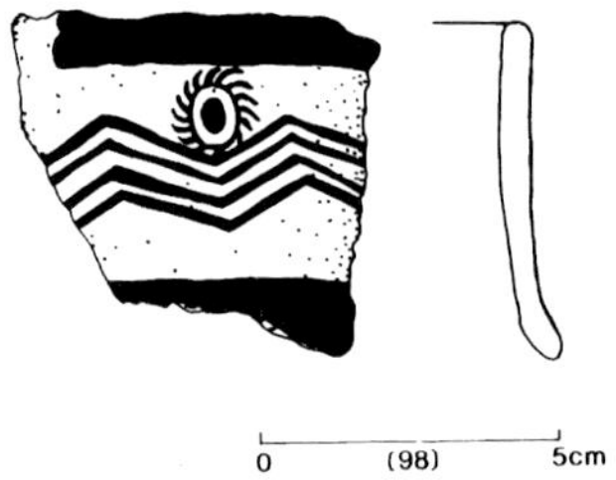

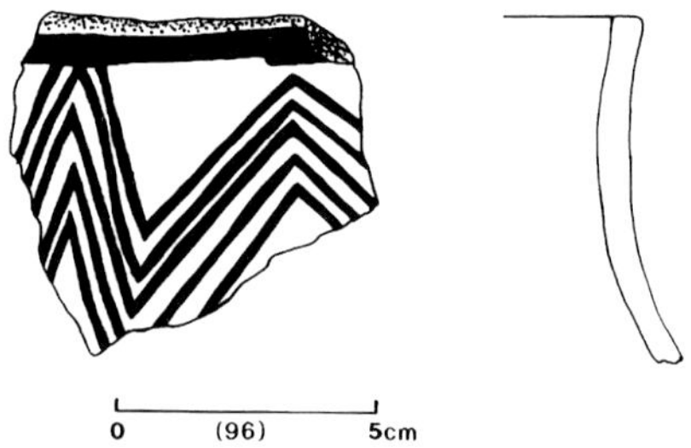

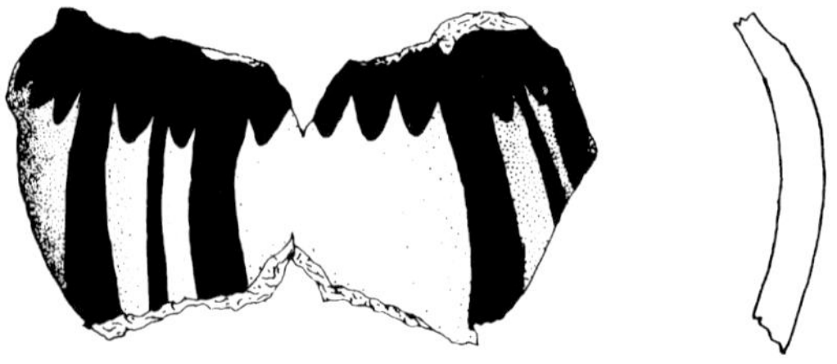

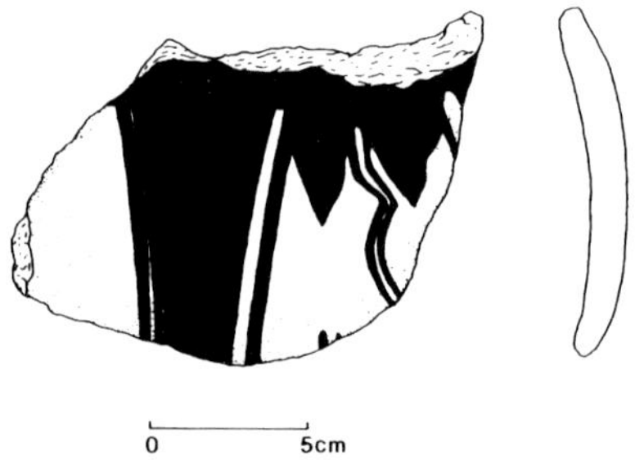

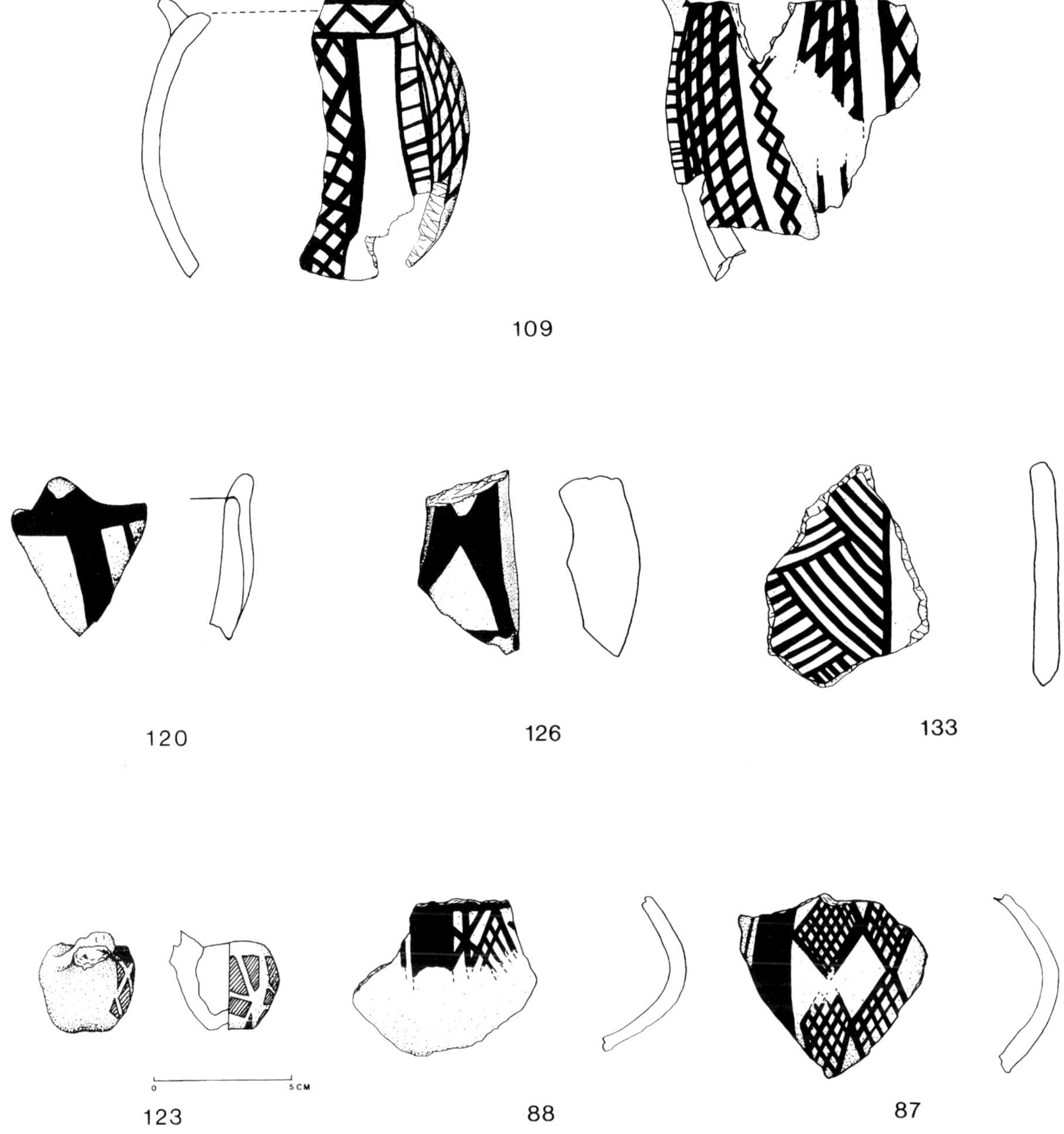

33 Various forms: cat. nos. 87, 88, 109, 120, 123, 126, 133.

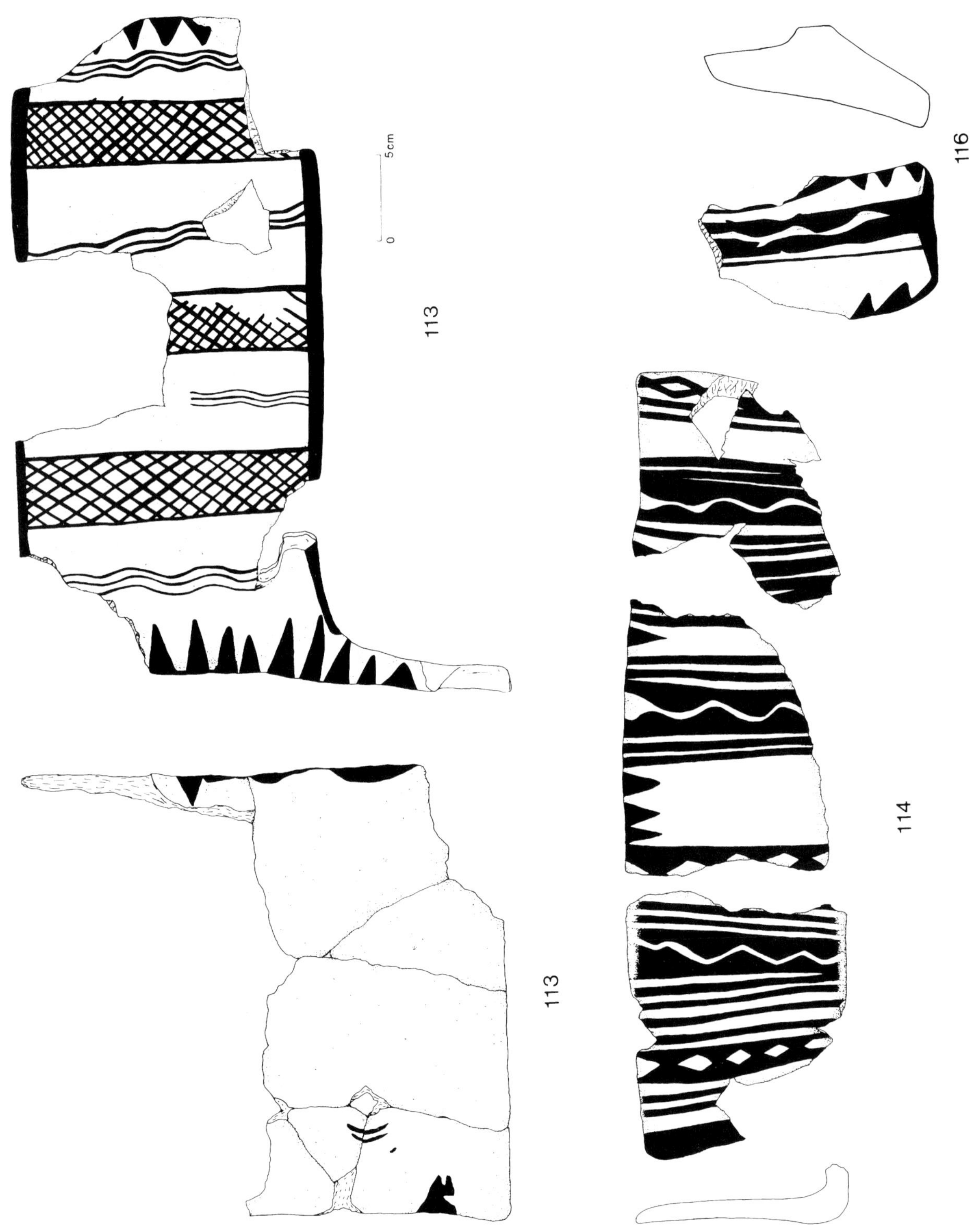

34 Quadrangular vessels: cat. nos. 113 (left-side, right-front), 114, 116.

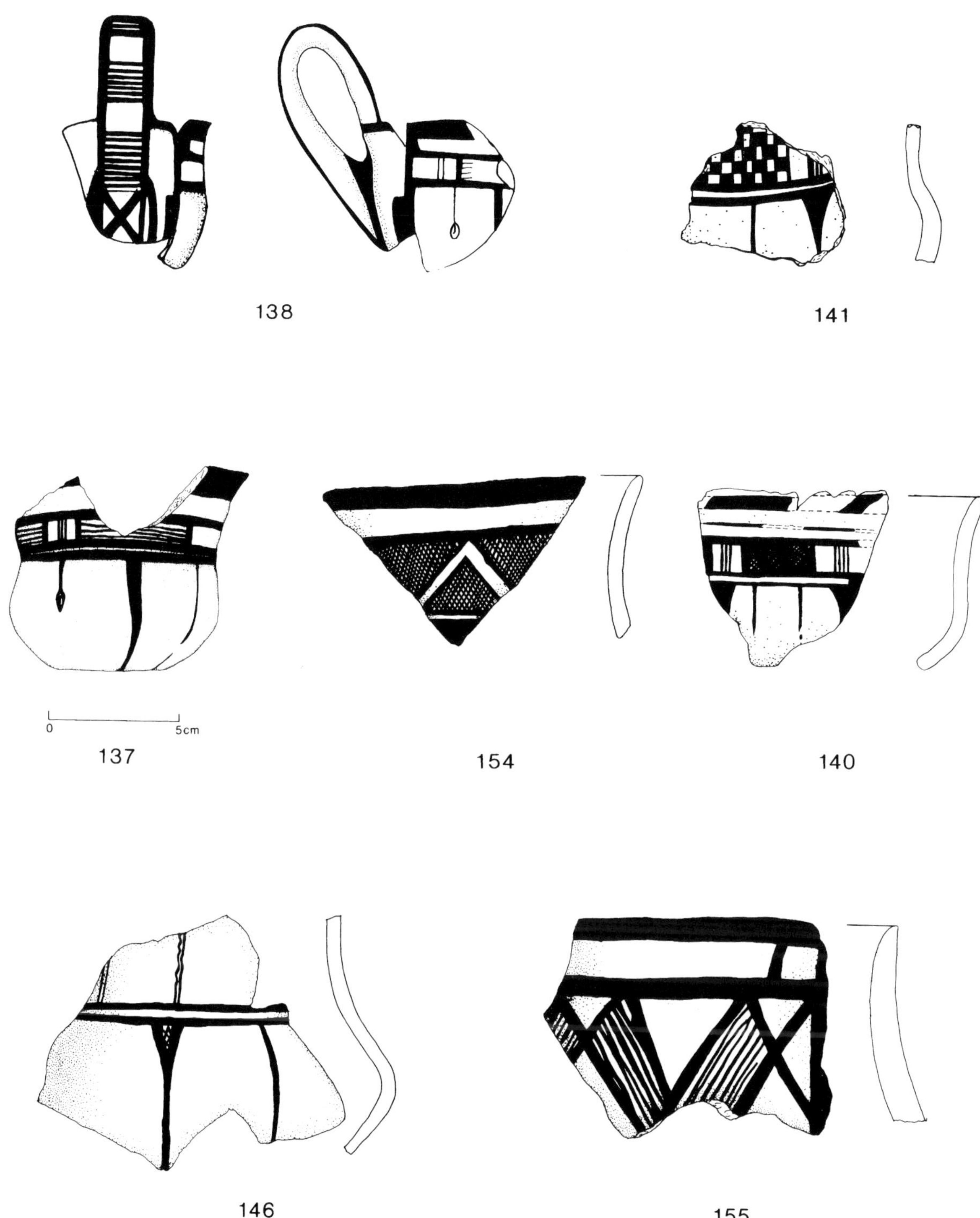

35 Various forms: cat. nos. 137, 138, 140, 141, 146, 154, 155.

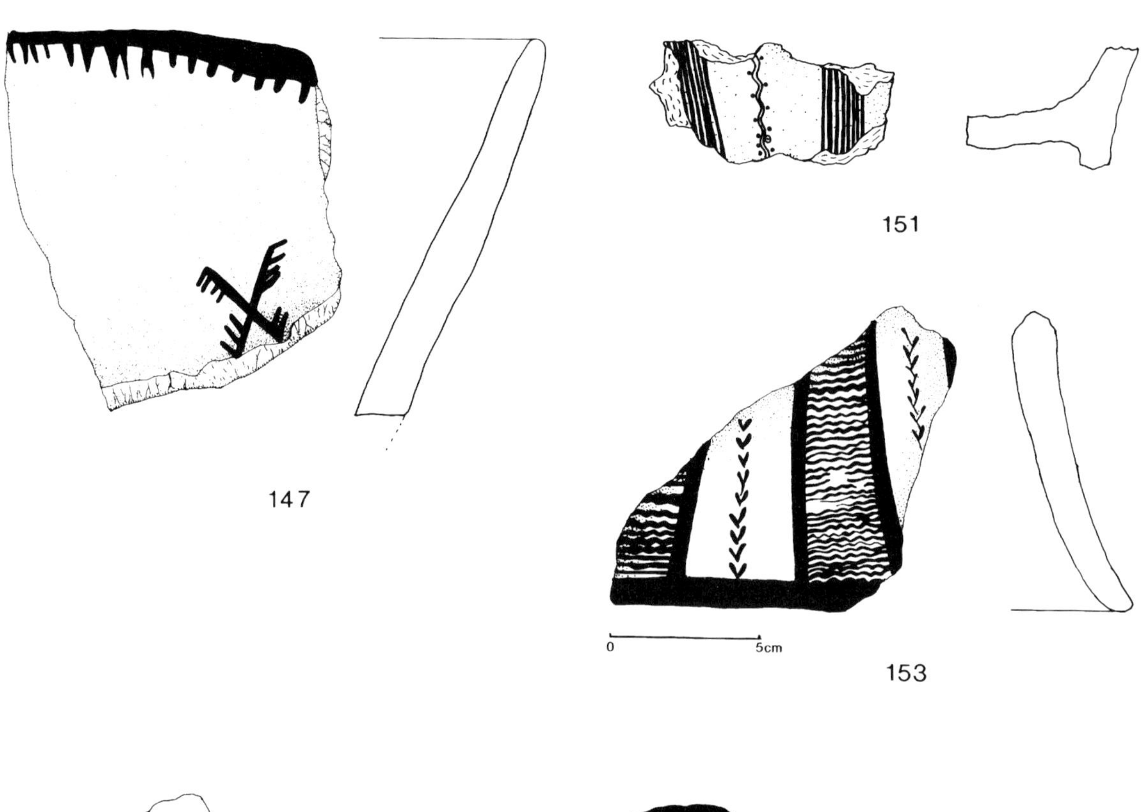

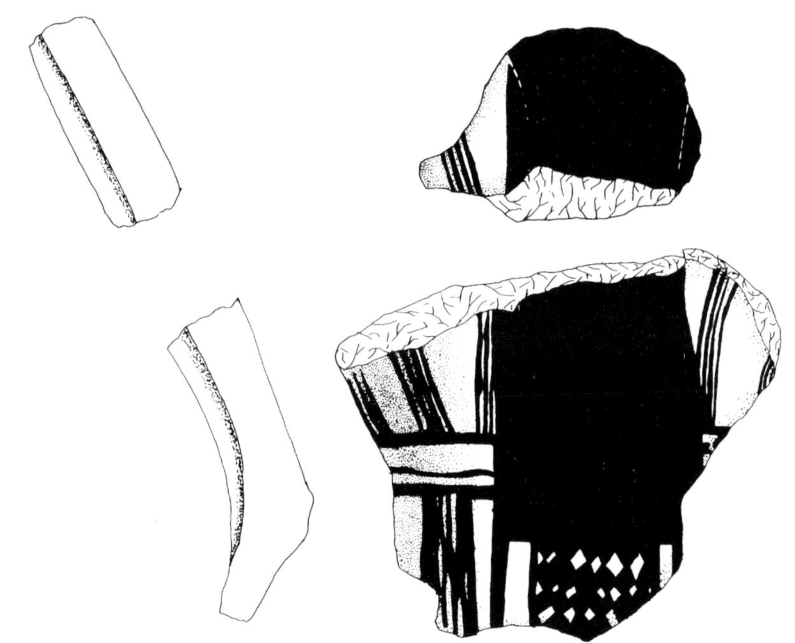

36 Pedestal bowls: cat. nos. 147, 149, 151, 153.

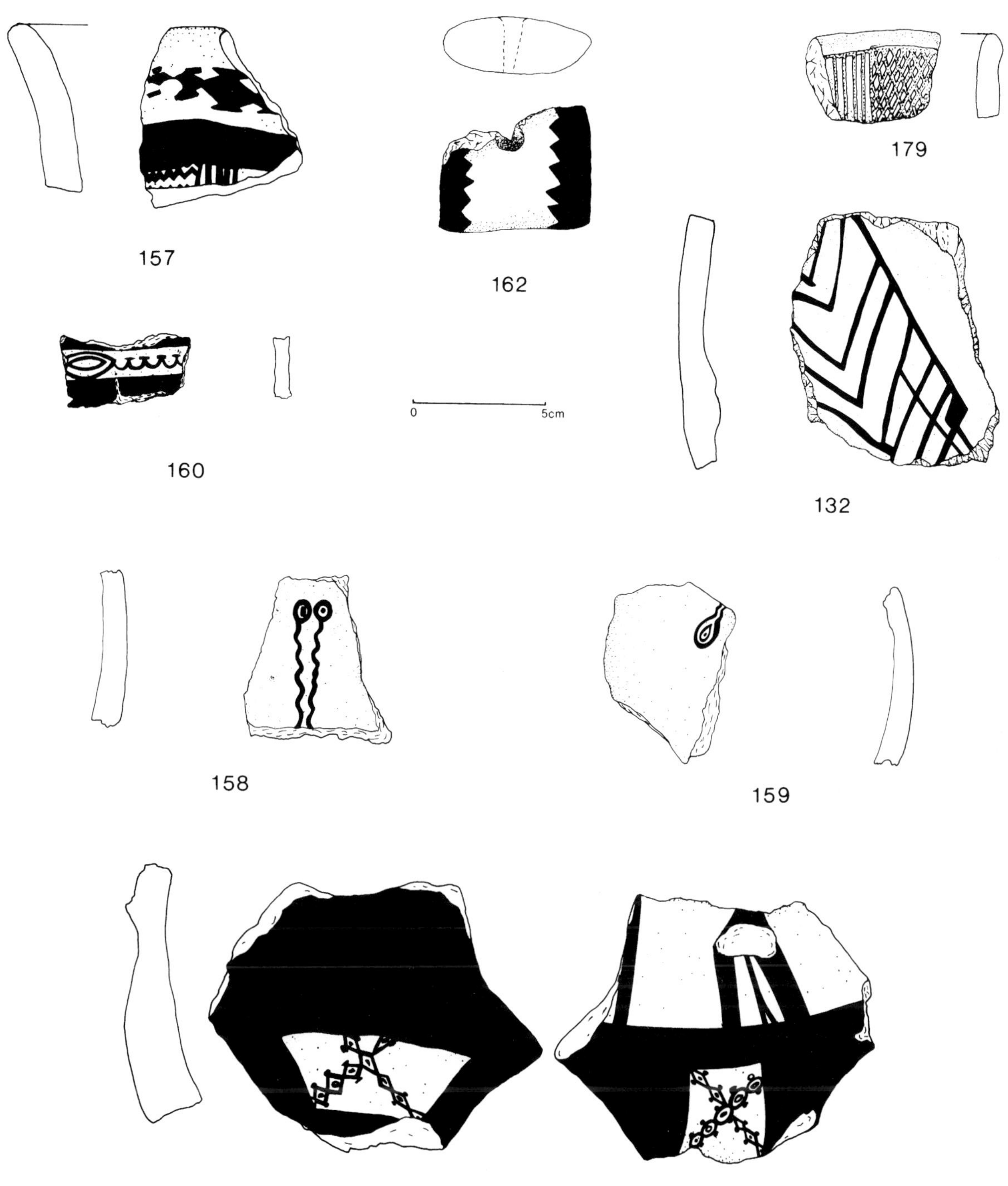

37 Various forms: cat. nos. 132, 157, 158, 159, 160, 161, 162, 179.

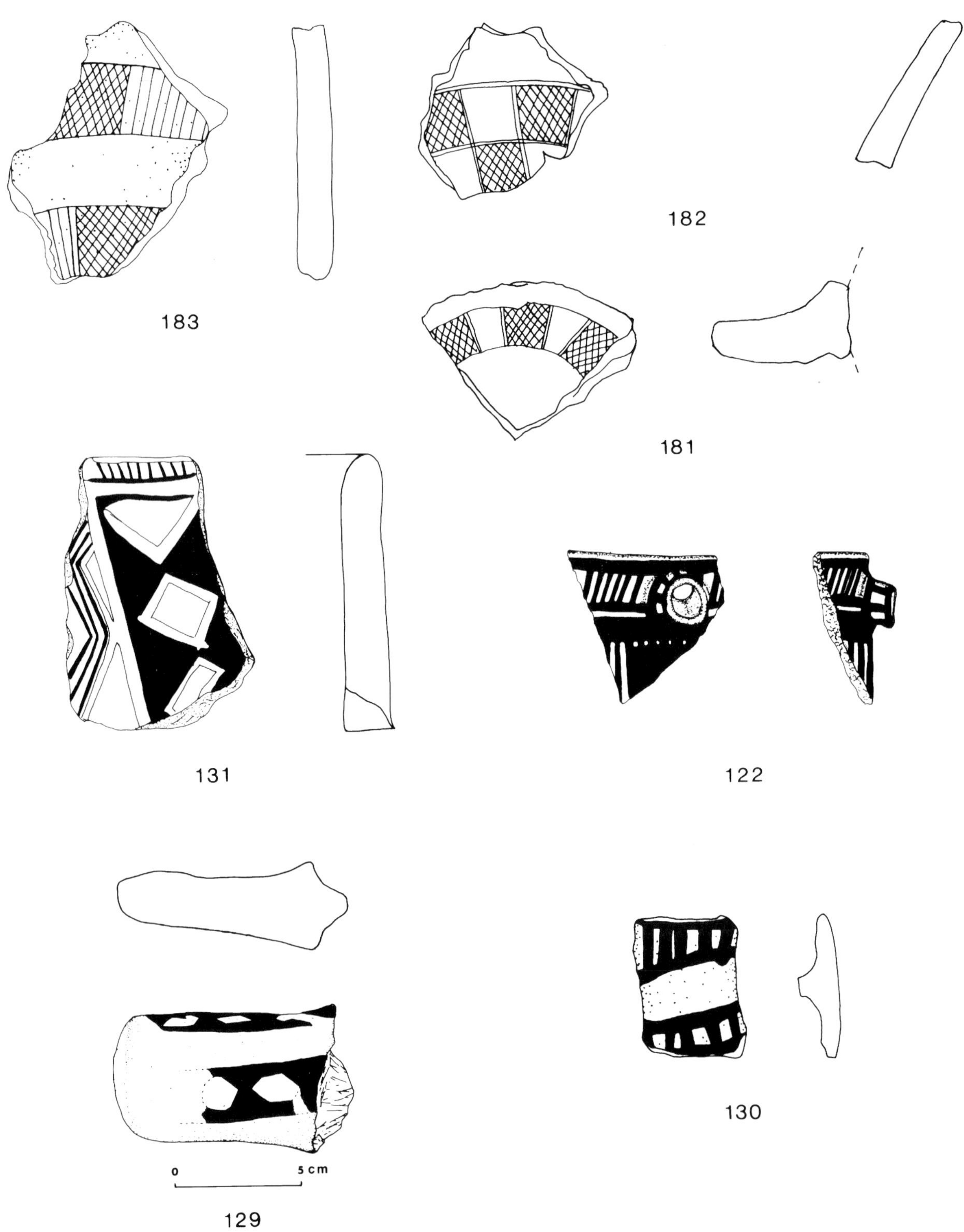

38 Various forms: cat. nos. 122, 129, 130, 131, 181, 182, 183.

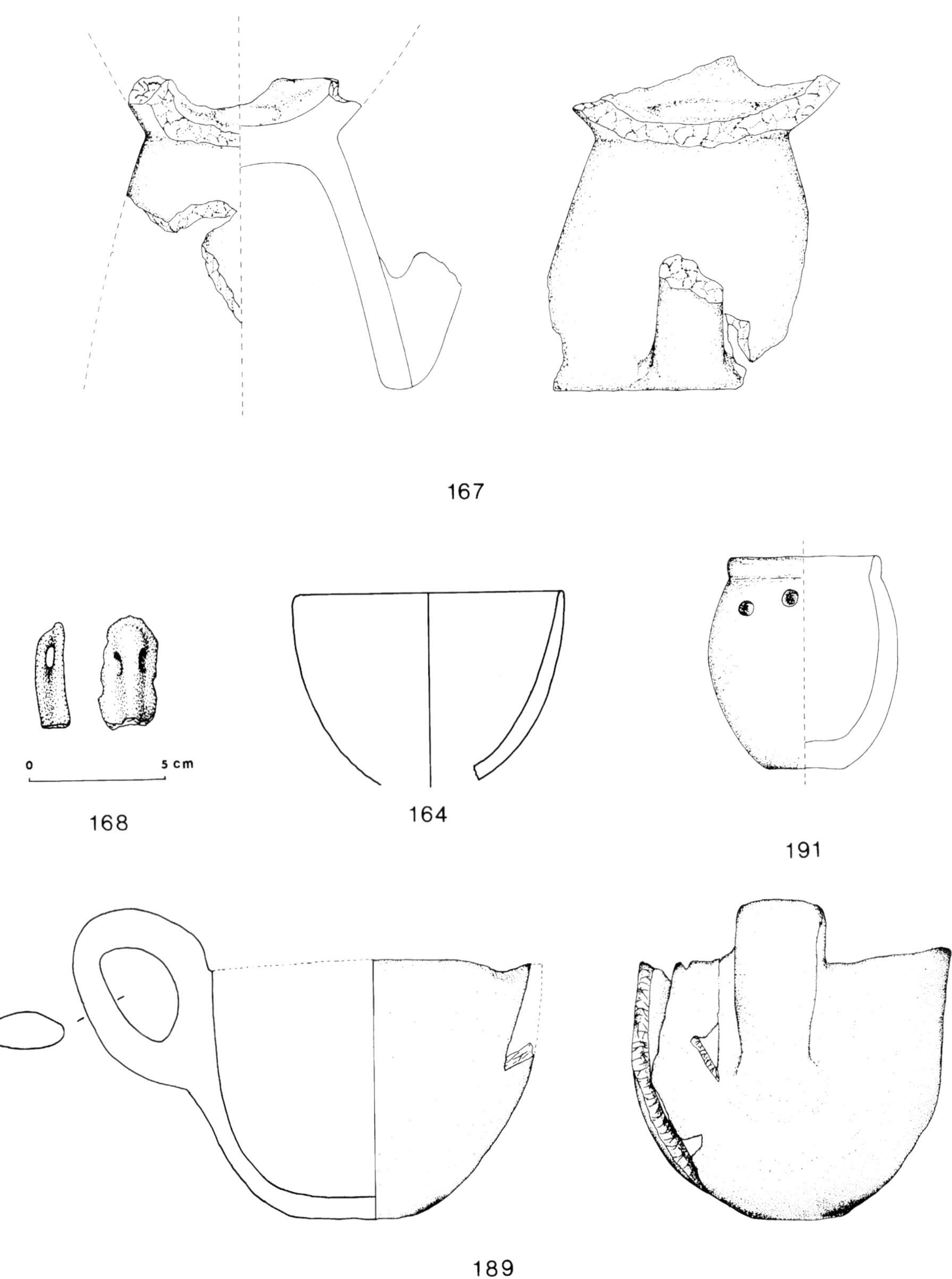

39 Various forms: cat. nos. 164, 167, 168, 189, 191.

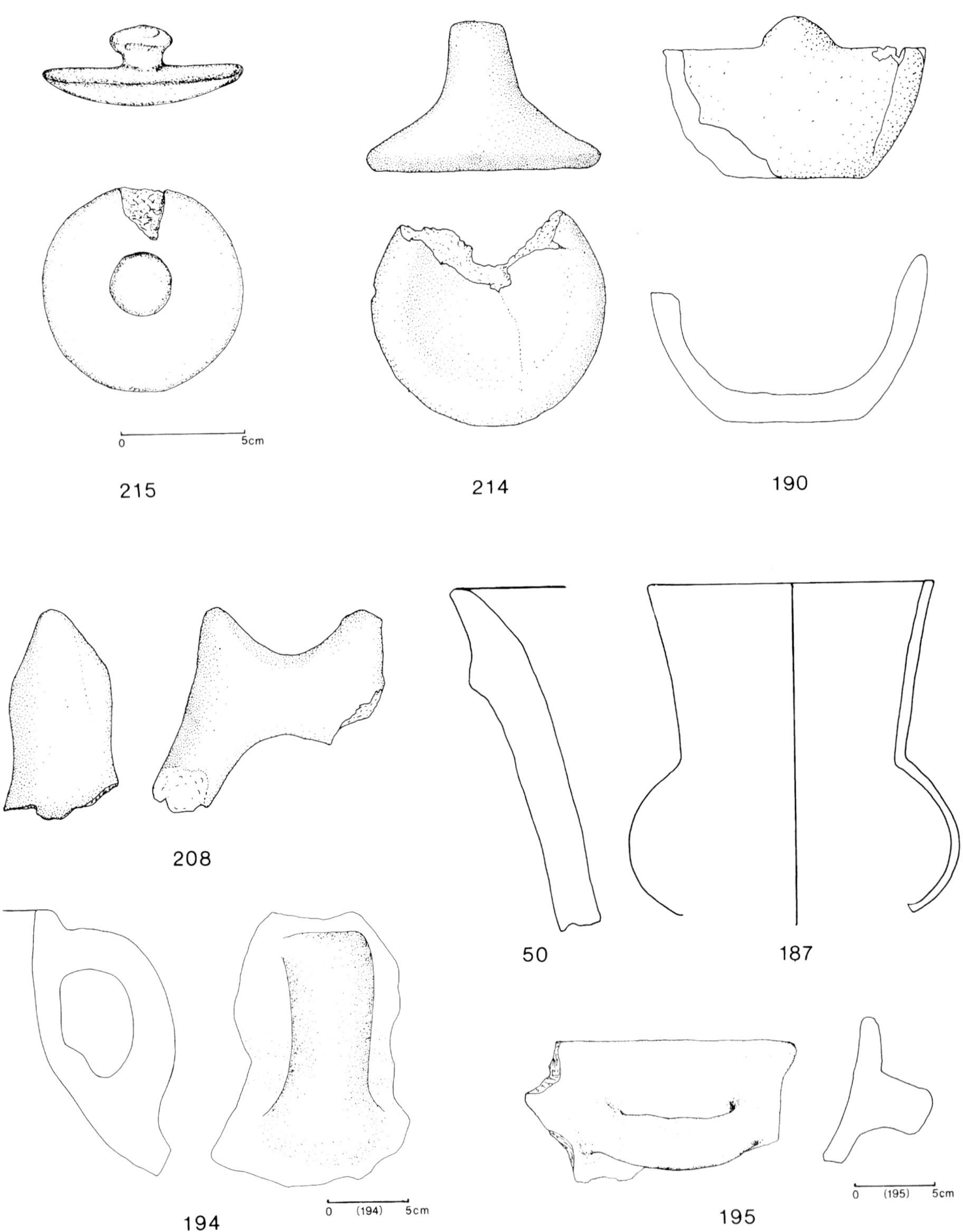

40 Various forms: cat. nos. 50, 187, 190, 194, 195, 208, 214, 215

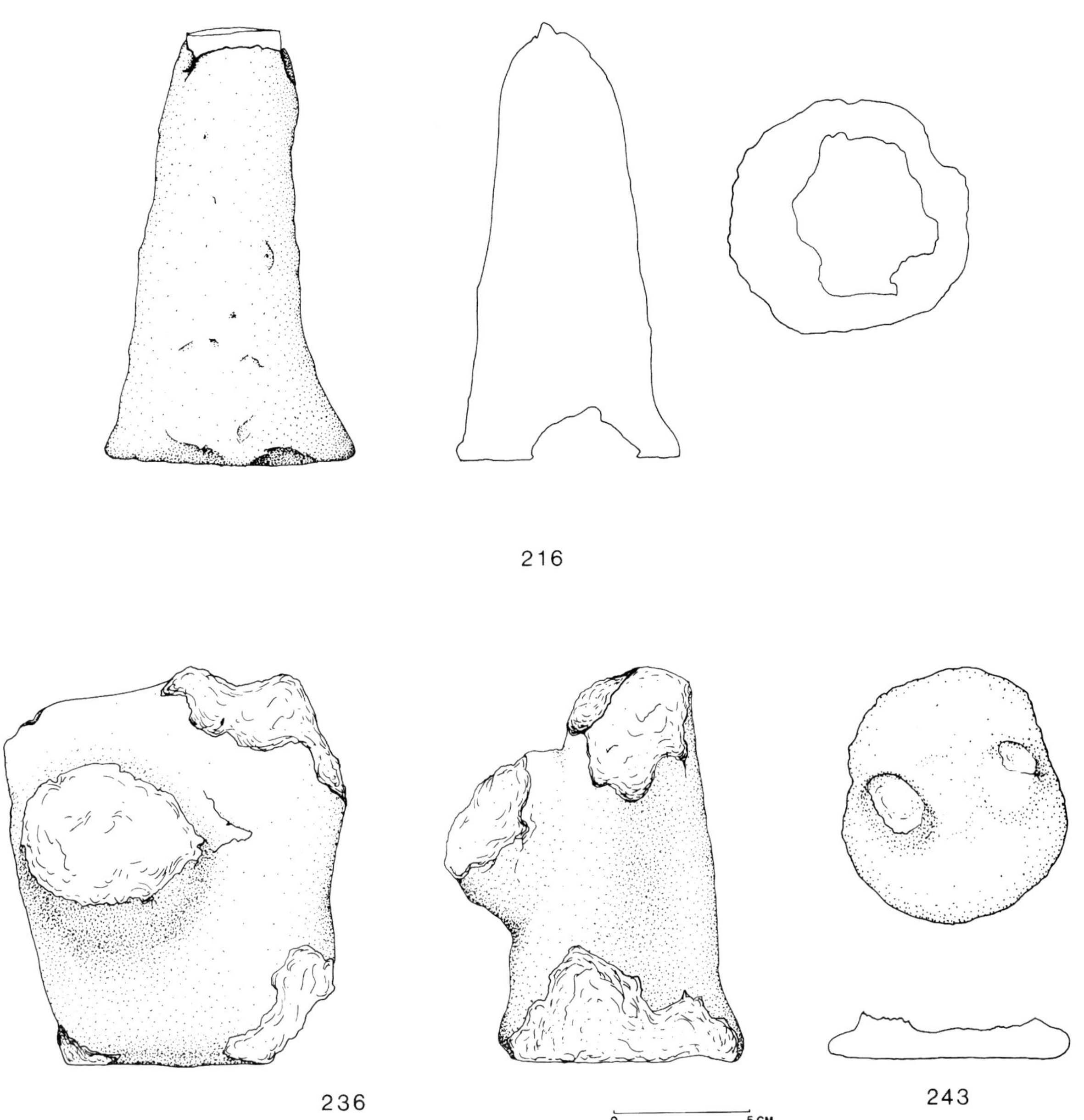

41 Cat. nos. 216, 236, 243.

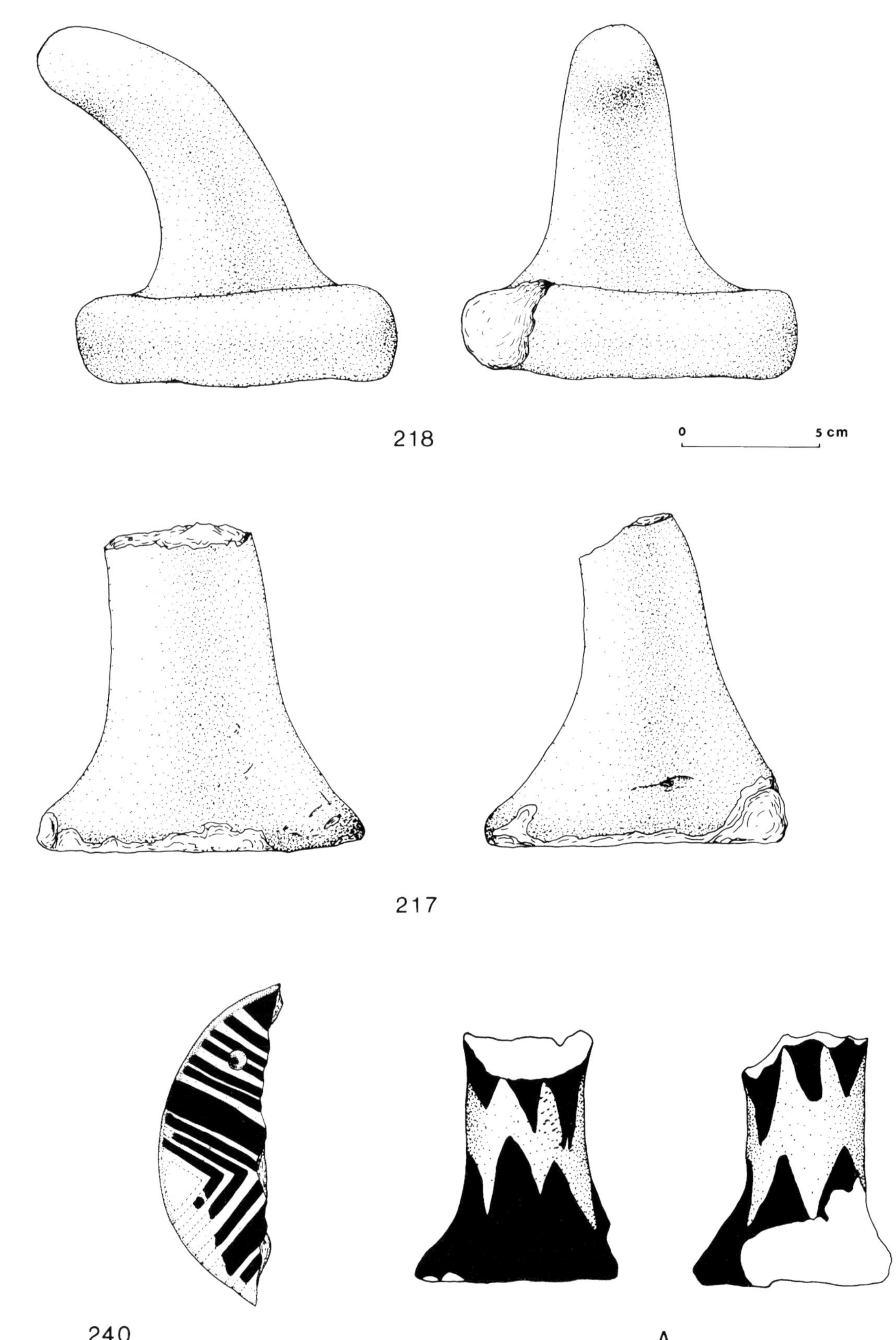

42 Cat. nos. 217, 218, 240; A: *corno fittile* from zone T (T 90).

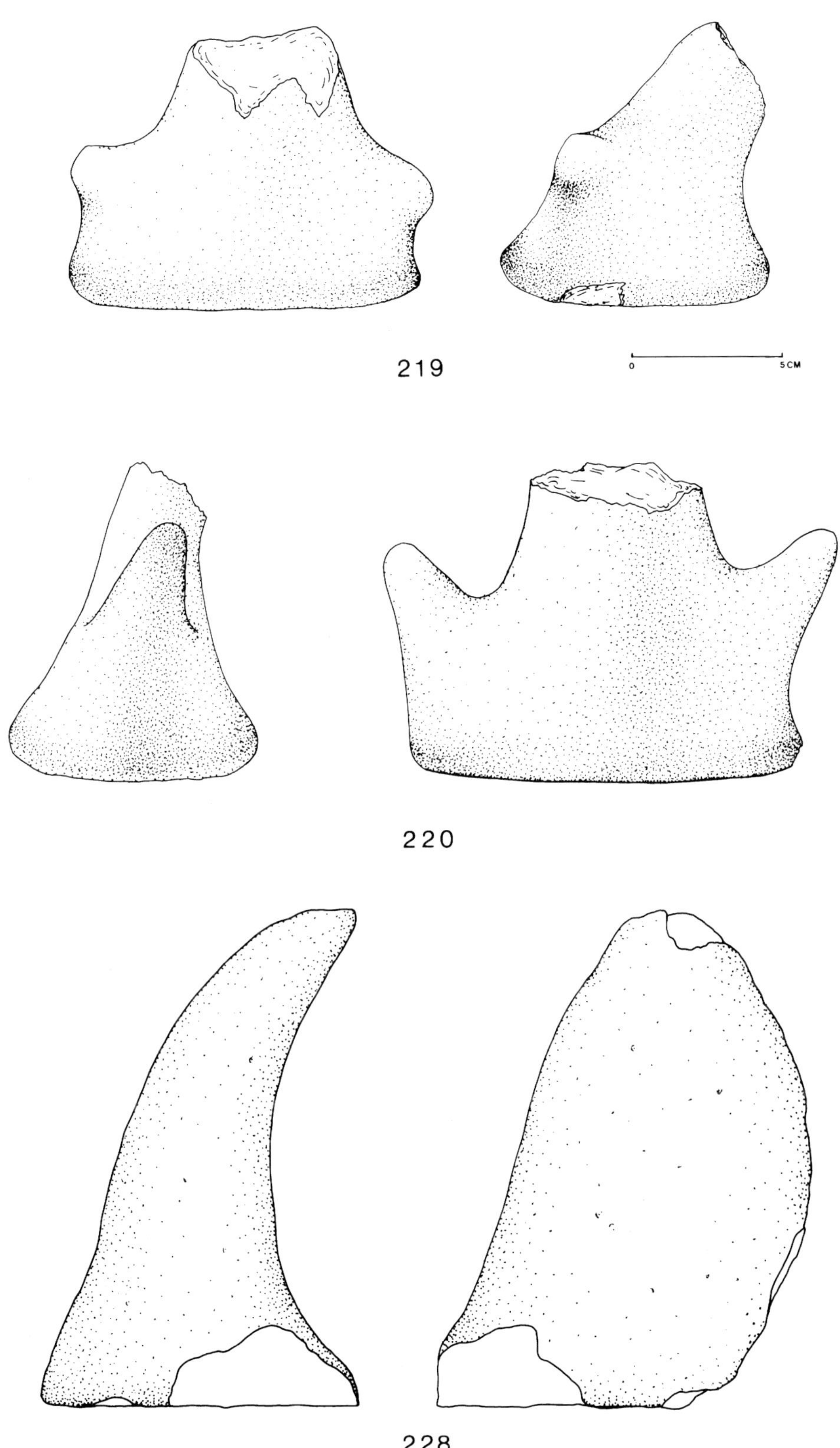

43 Cat. nos. 219, 220, 228.

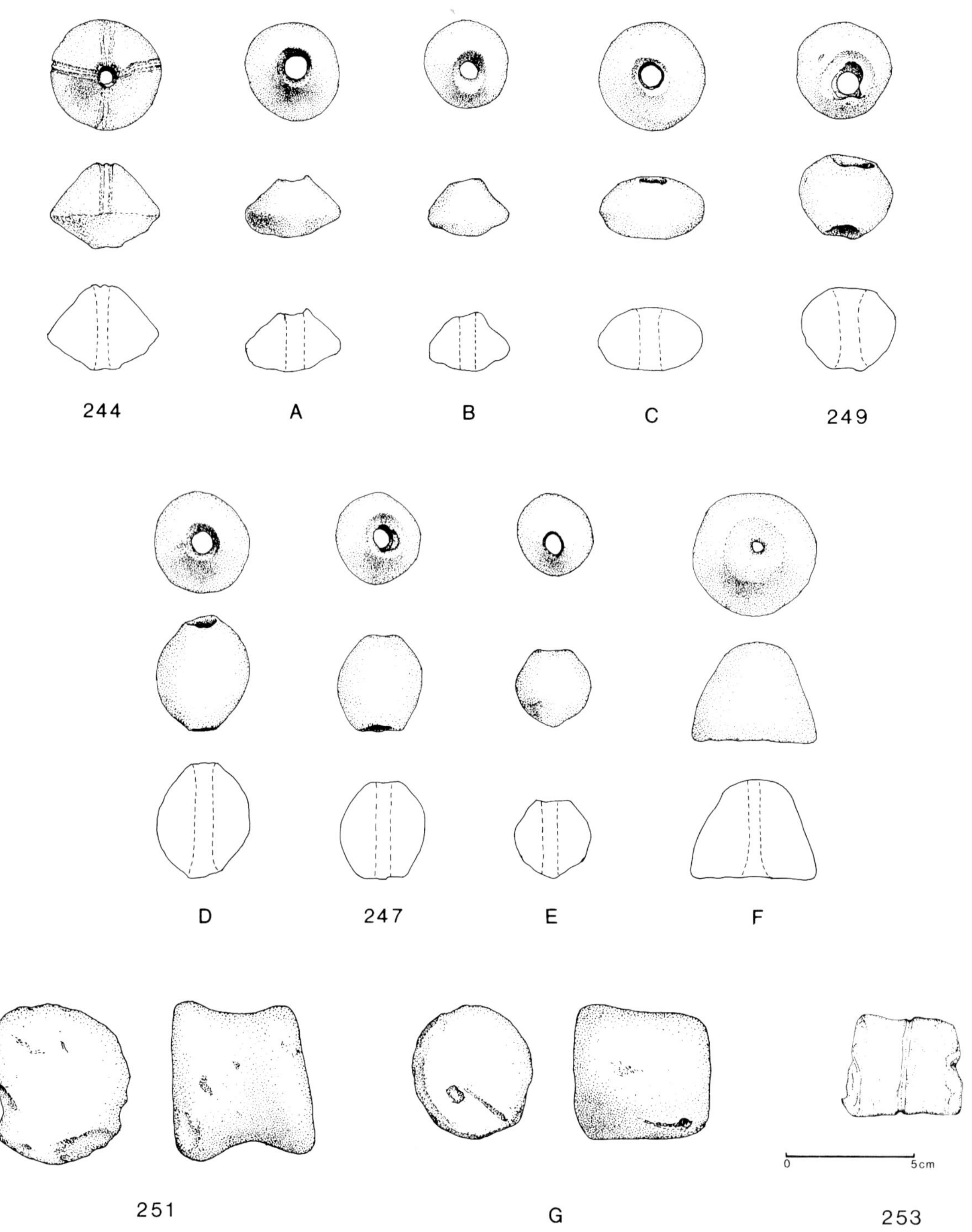

44 Cat. nos. 244, 249, 247, 251, 253; A-E: spindle whorls, F: loom weight, G: bobbin.

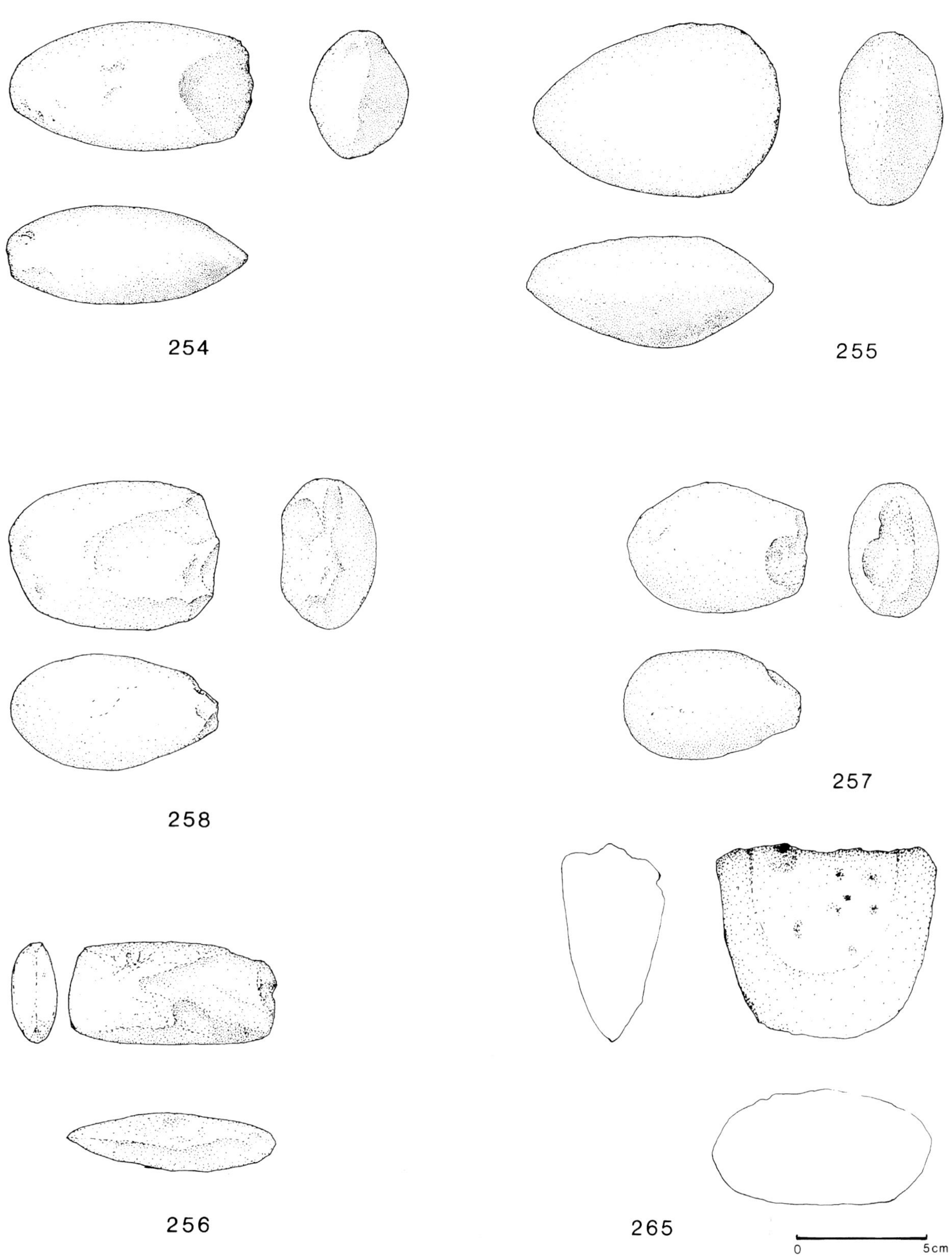

45 Cat. nos. 254, 255, 256, 257, 258, 265.

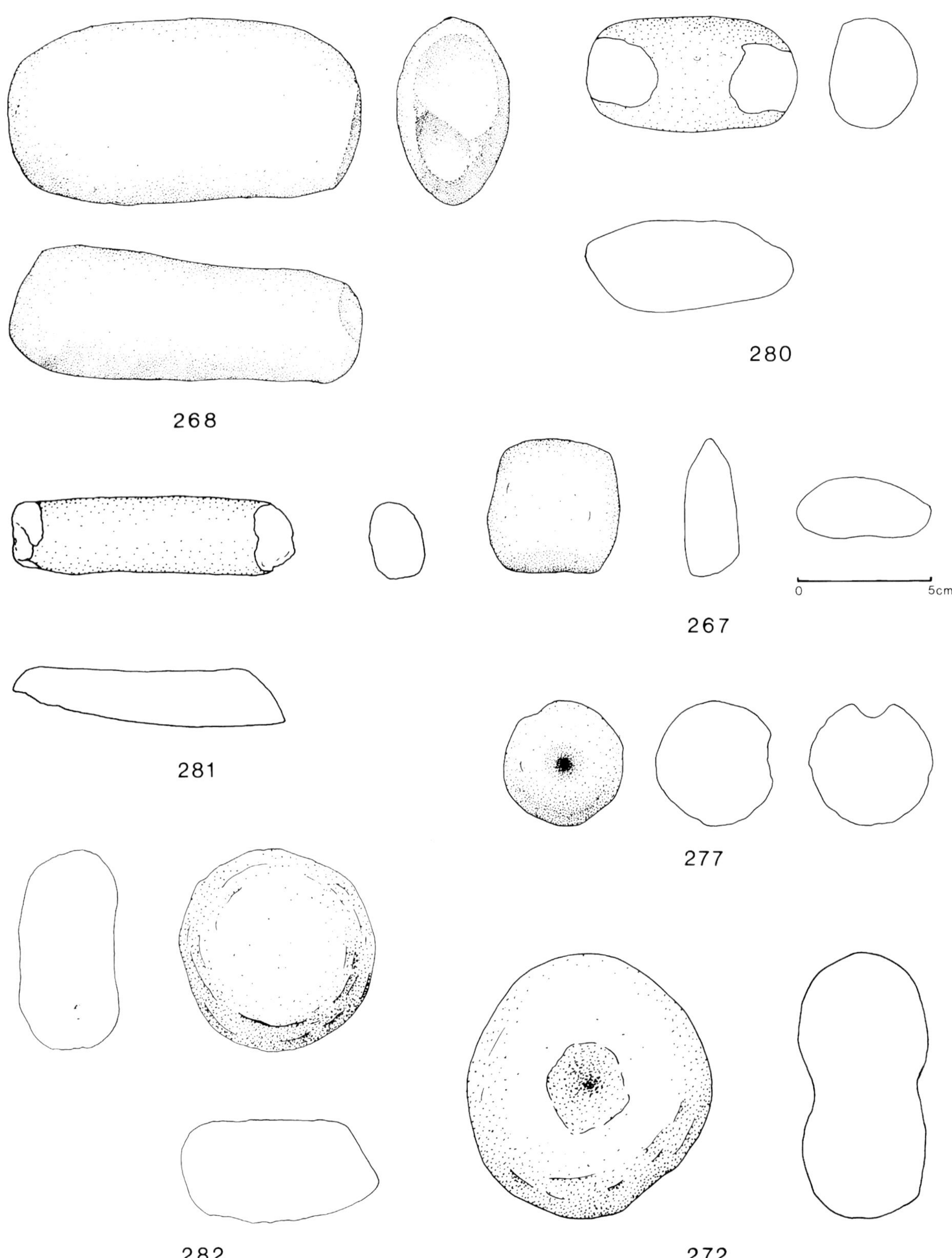

46 Cat. nos. 267, 268, 272, 277, 280, 281, 282.

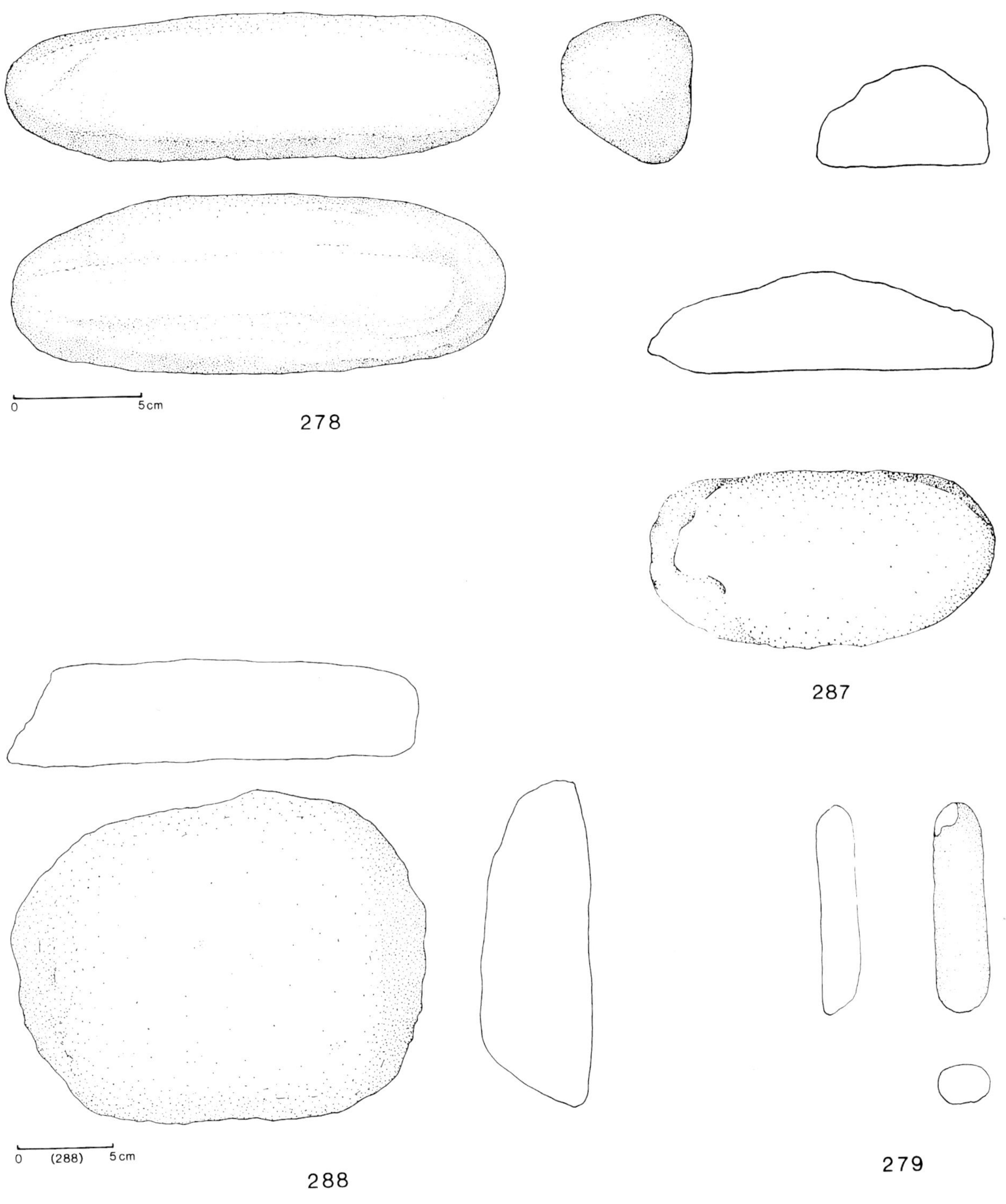

278

287

288

279

47 Cat. nos. 278, 279, 287, 288.

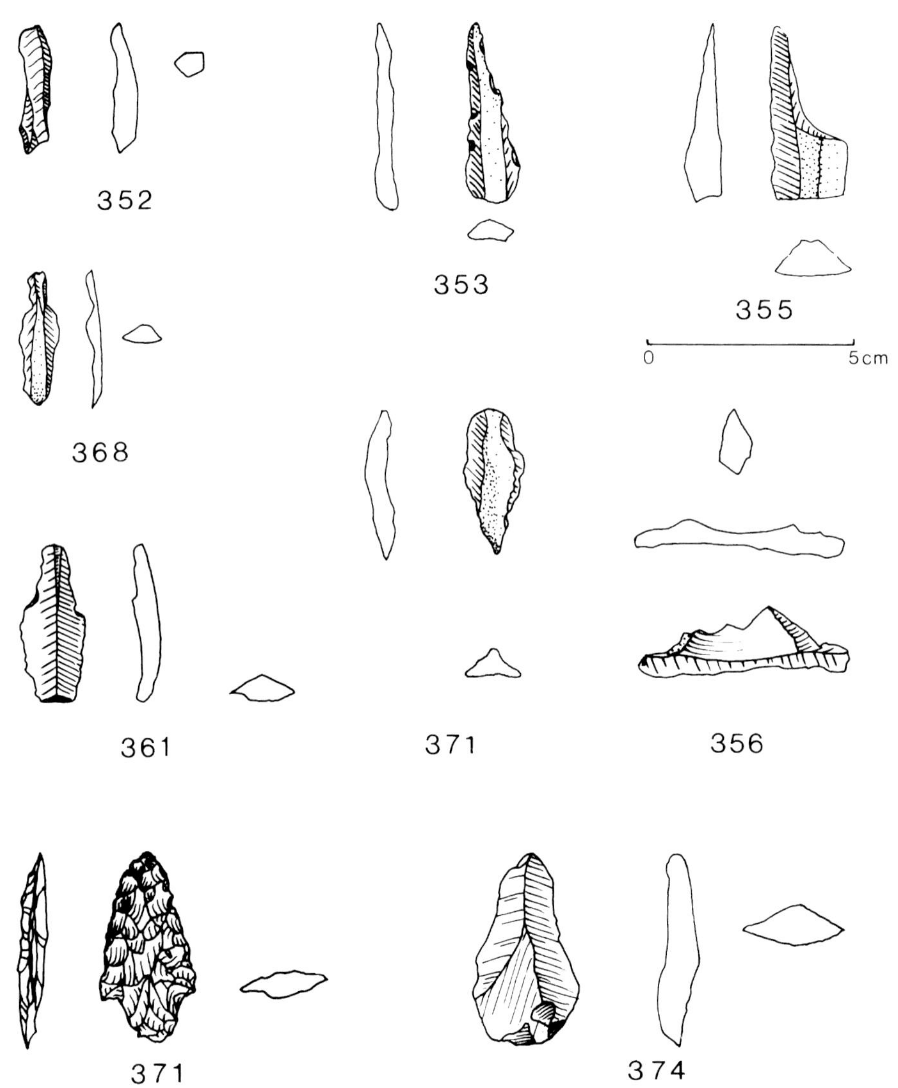

48 Cat. nos. 352, 353, 355, 368, 371, 356, 361, 371, 374.

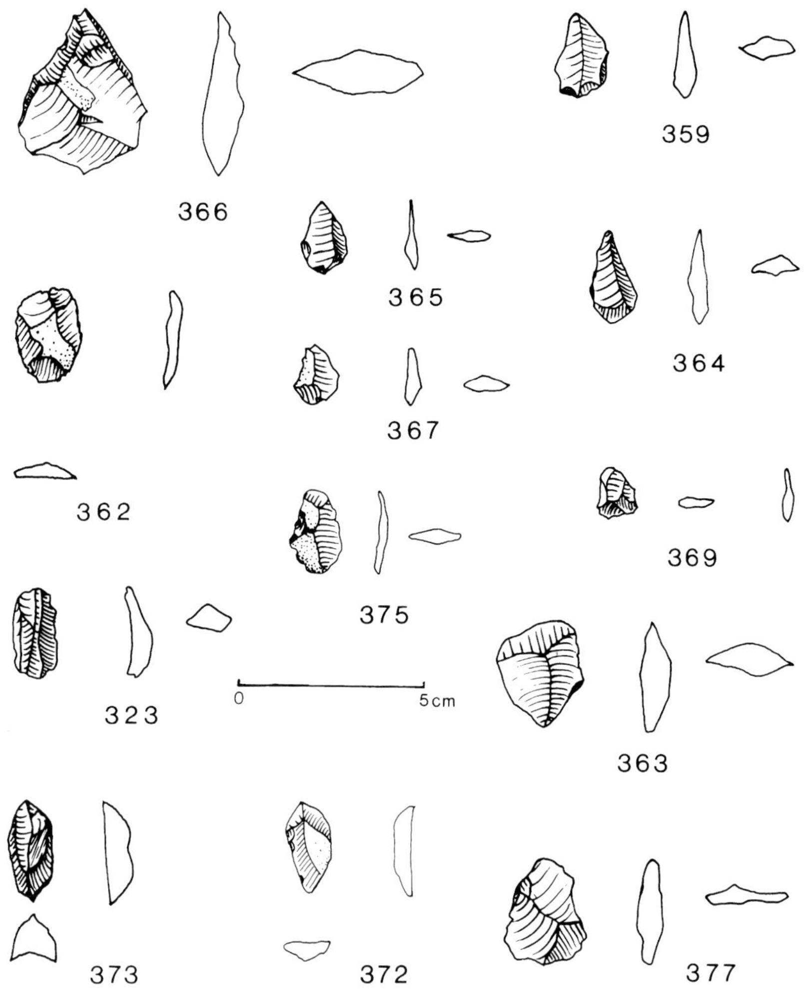

49 Cat. nos. 323, 359, 362, 363, 364, 365, 366, 367, 369, 372, 373, 375, 377.

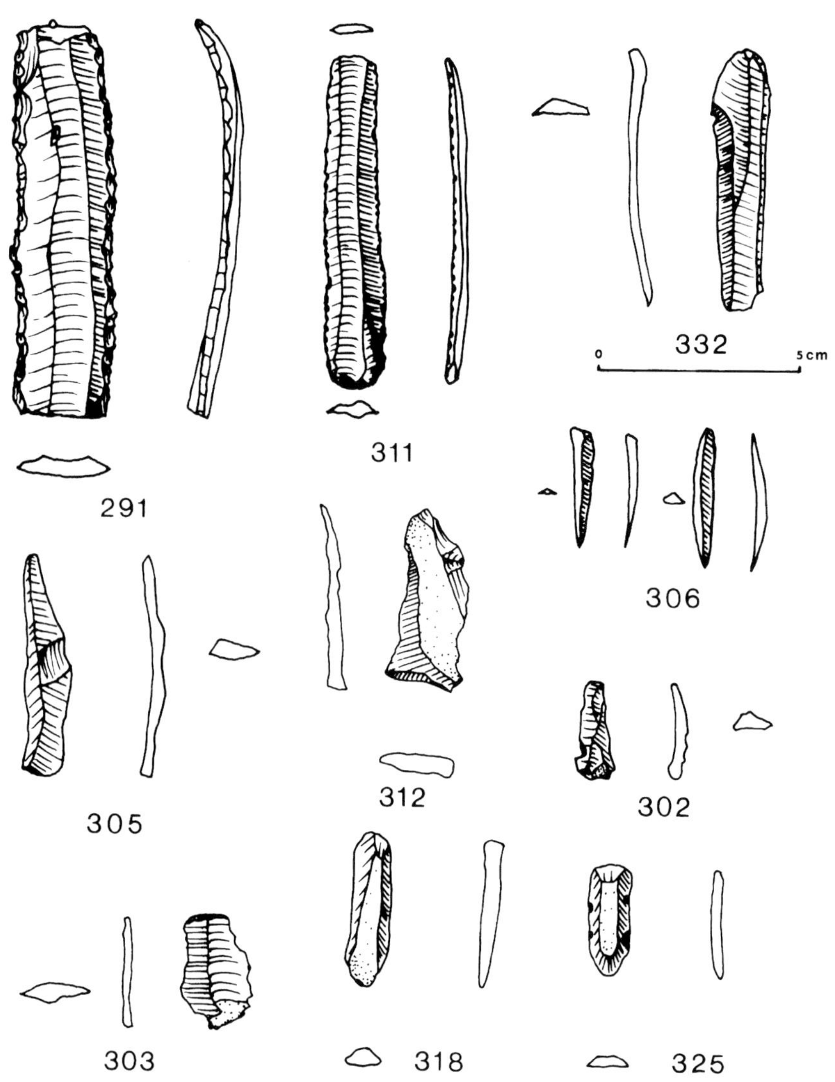

50 Cat. nos. 291, 302, 303, 305, 306, 311, 312, 318, 325, 332.

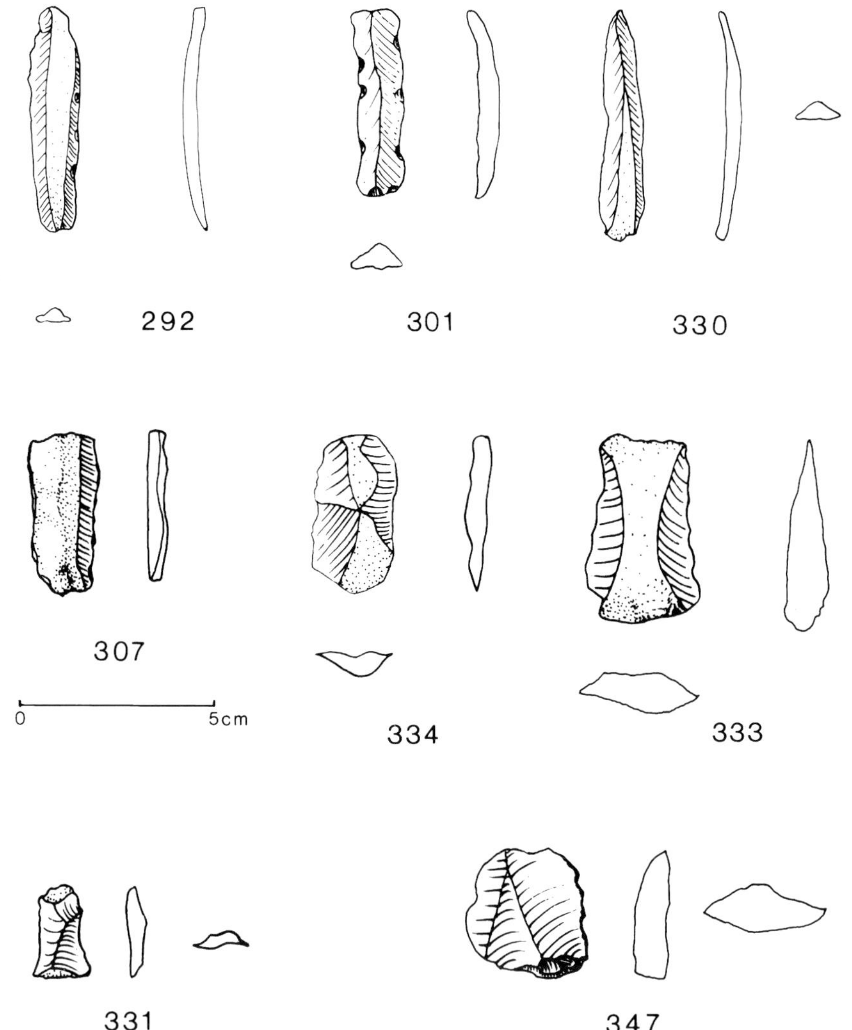

51 Cat. nos. 292, 301, 307, 330, 331, 333, 334, 347.

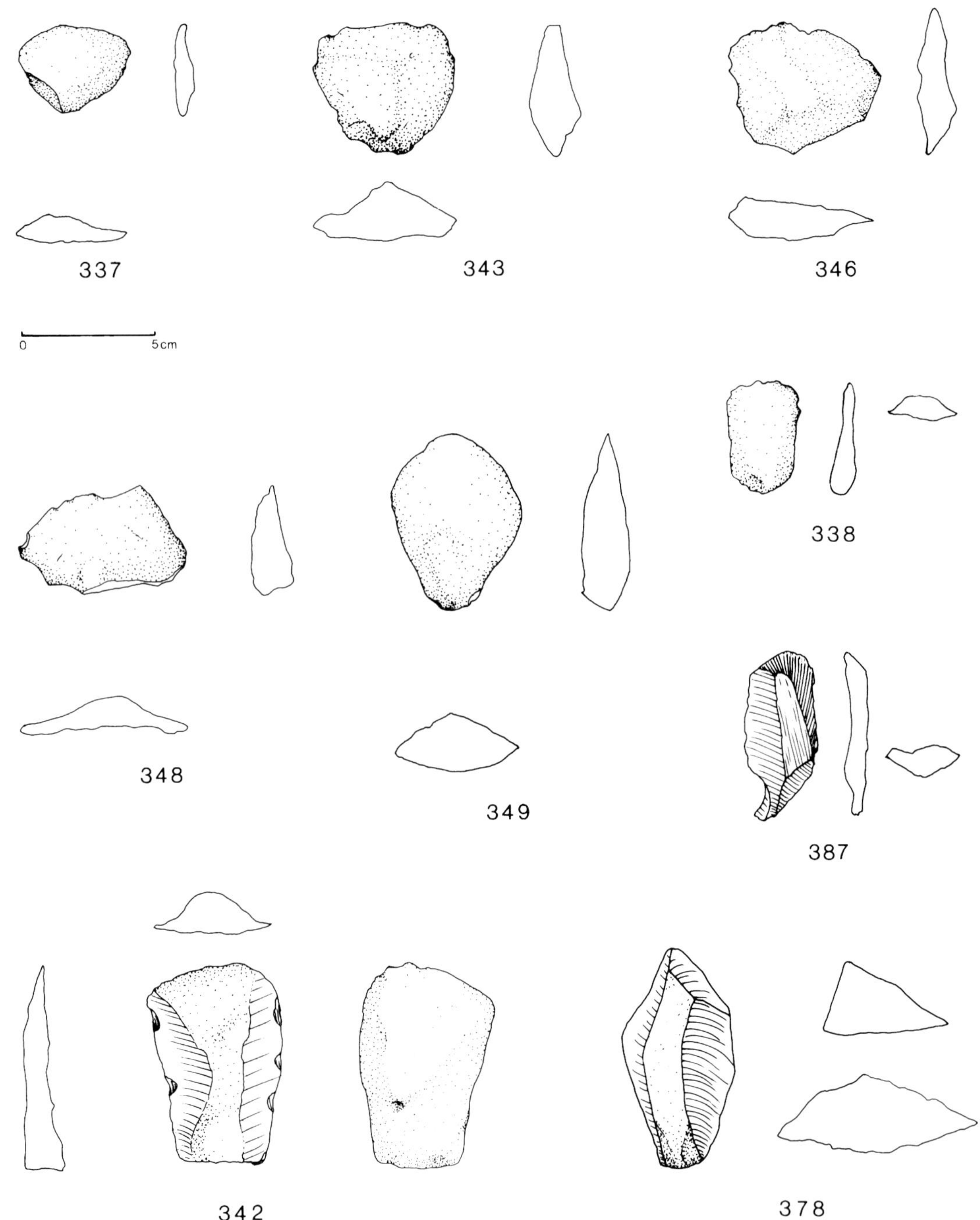

52 Cat. nos. 337, 338, 343, 346, 348, 349, 387, 342, 378.

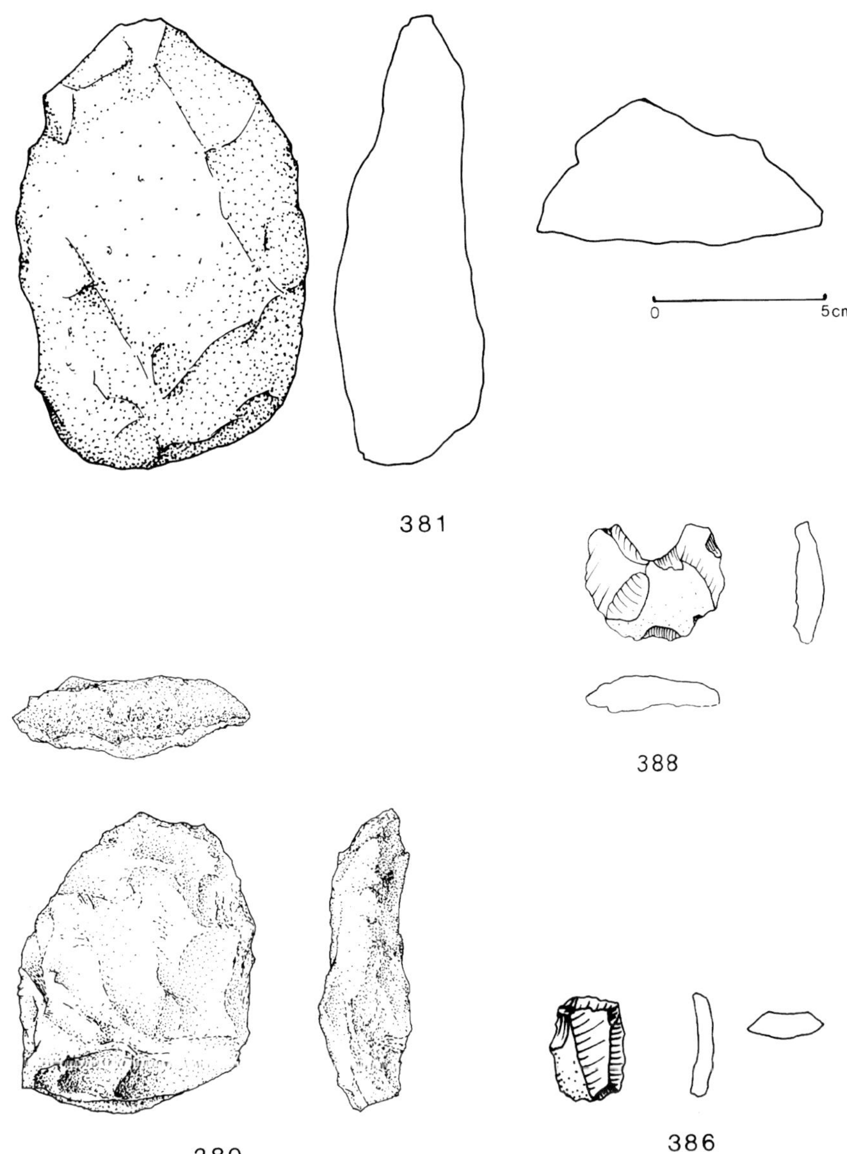

53 Cat. nos. 388, 380, 381, 386.

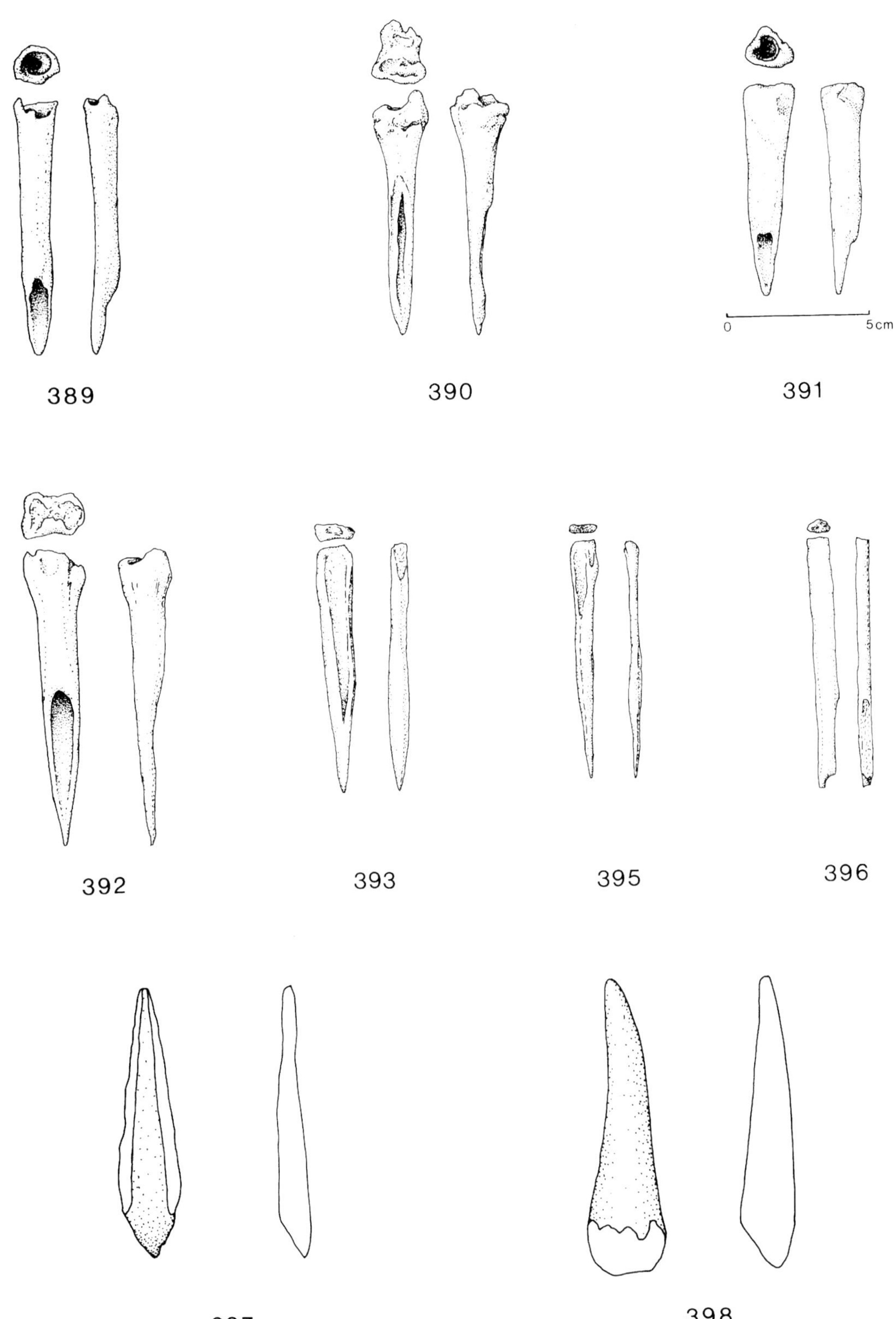

54 Bone tools: cat. nos. 389, 390, 391, 392, 393, 395, 396, 397, 398.

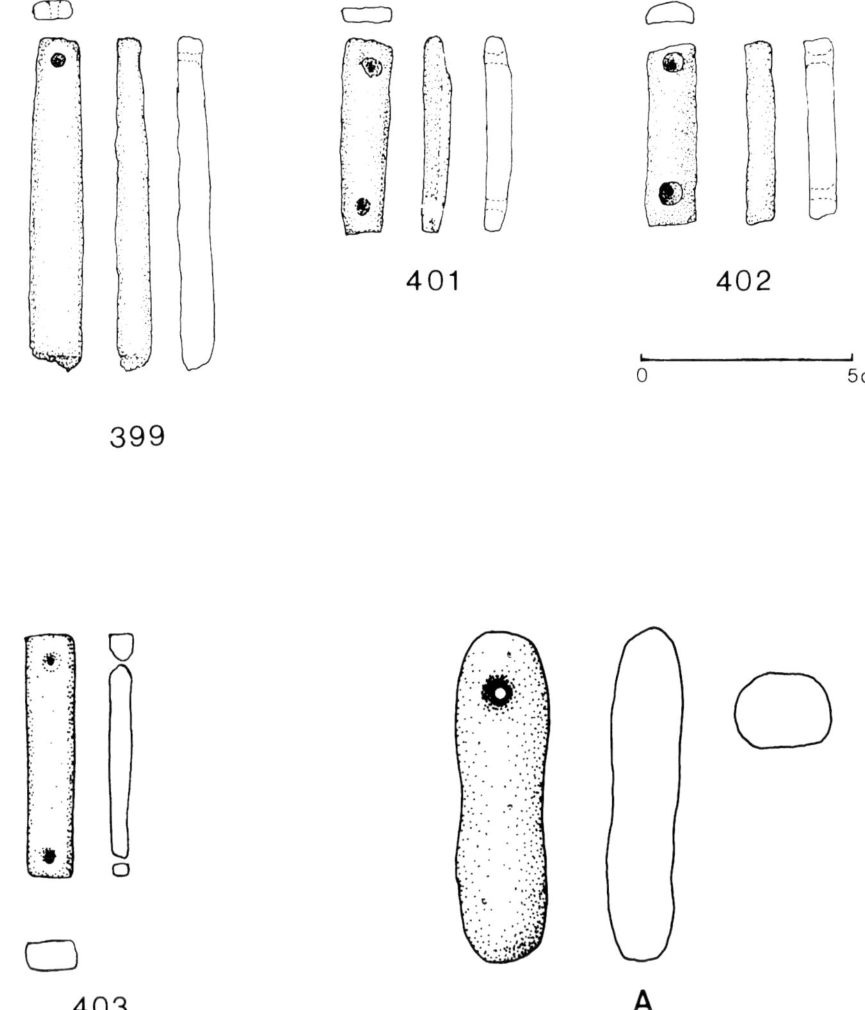

55 Pendants: cat. nos. 399, 401, 402, 403; A: large pendant from zone T.

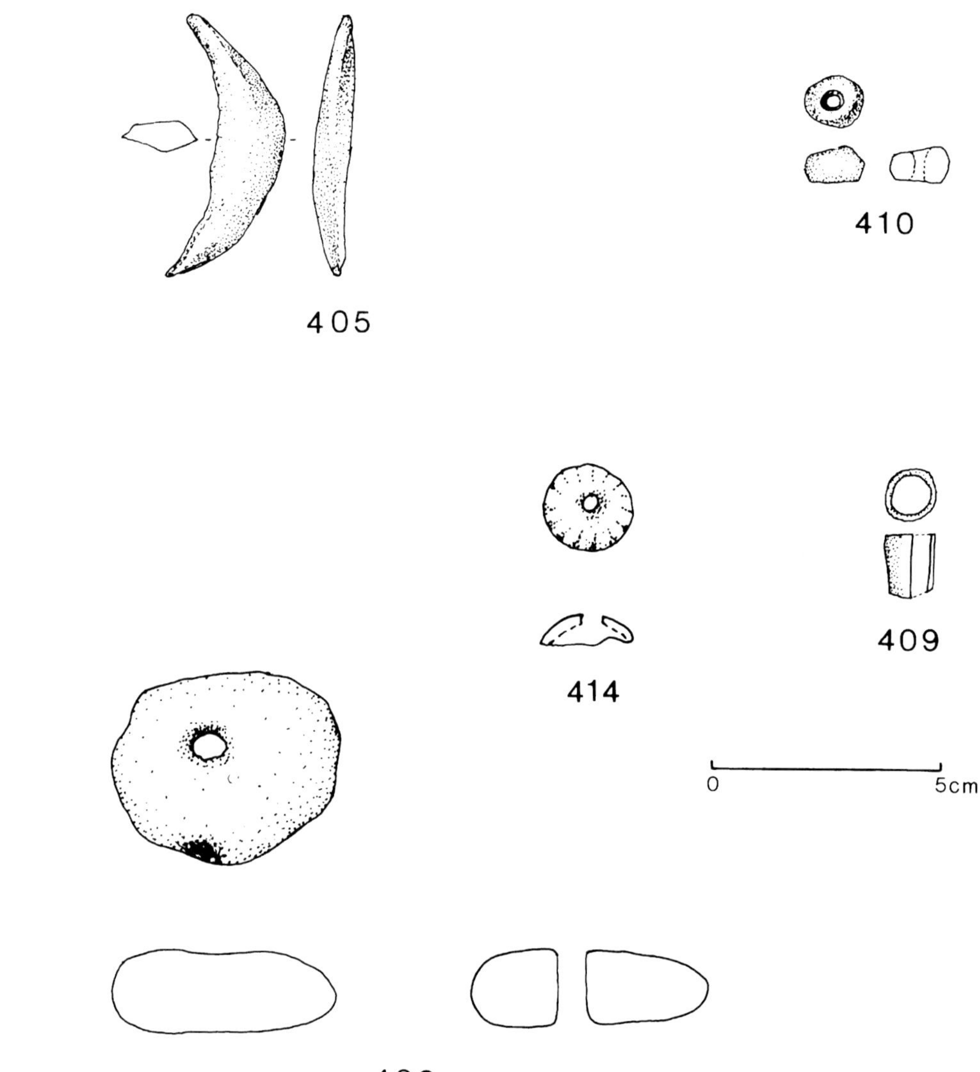

56 Pendants: cat. nos. 400, 405, 409, 410, 414.

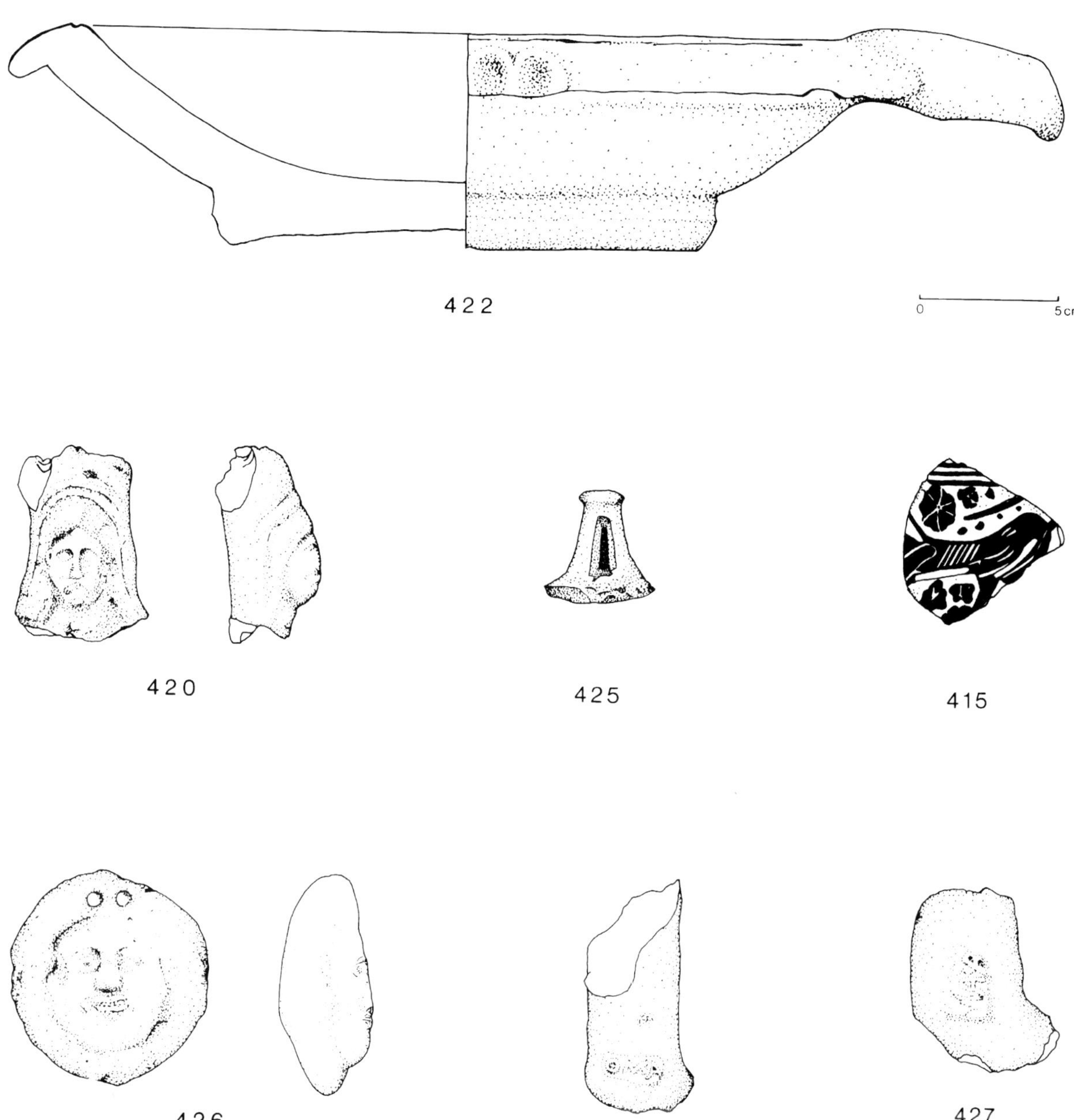

57 Historical materials: cat. nos. 415, 420, 422, 425, 426, 427, 428.

Appendix III

REFLECTIONS ON CASTELLUCCIAN MATERIAL AND FUTURE RESEARCH DIRECTIONS

Reflections on Castelluccian Material and Future Research Directions

Susan S. Lukesh

The presentation of the ceramic material from the village area at La Muculufa adds immeasurably to our knowledge of the Castelluccian culture in general and to the south-central Castelluccian in particular. And for this a great debt is owed to Drs. McConnell and Maniscalco. The full publication of La Muculufa material[1], together with the recent publication of a catalogue of Naro-Partanno material[2] and the corpus of designs on the fragments from the dump at Castelluccio di Noto[3], allows us to look at a large body of Castelluccian material from across Sicily. Before we turn to such a consideration, however, it is instructive to review what this new material from the village of La Muculufa offers to us in comparison with the prior material.

(For design motifs, see Plates E – L.)

---

[1] Muculufa I (with both material from the village and the sanctuary) and the current publication, this volume, (with additional, more recently excavated, material from the village). I include with this discussion the full corpus of design motifs from La Muculufa, which has been expanded to include the new ones revealed in the additional material from the village. The Catalogue of Motifs is presented to demonstrate the various individual motifs (and occasional composite designs) which we used to record the material from La Muculufa in the seasons up to 1985. It is clear that many of these motifs are very simple, and this was purposeful so that we could keep records of even the smallest decorated fragment. Up to five individual motifs per sherd, with their location on the vessel, were kept in our records, allowing us to study the coincidence of individual motifs. References in this Catalogue refer to published examples of material.

[2] Sebastiano Tusa and Marco Pacci, La collezione dei vasi pre-istorici di Partanni e Naro, Ceramiche dell'antica età del bronzo nella Sicilia centro-occidentale, (Palermo, 1990) hereafter Tusa-Pacci.

[3] Giuliana Sluga Messina, Analisi dei motivi decorativi della cermaica da Castelluccio di Noto (Siracusa), Università degli studi di Trieste, Facolta di Lettere e Filosofia, Istituto di Archeologia, (Roma, 1983), hereafter Sluga Messina.

The New Evidence from the Village Excavation

I am struck immediately by a small number of new motifs and composite designs. Most remarkable is the face (Plate 30, no. 93) the likes of which we have not seen on other Castelluccian material. It falls, however, well within the Castelluccian tradition. It appears here on the neck of a pitcher, or amphora, which contains a typical neck motif (albeit a variation), formed from a group of horizontal parallel angular lines, between solid bands at the rim and the neck junction. In this instance, the lines are placed close to the bottom of the neck area, leaving space for the 'face.' It is unfortunate that only part of this vessel is preserved since how the remaining neck space was treated might help us understand if this was a well-planned motif or an afterthought. Since the pattern does not appear to be centered, one could argue that this is more likely a one-handled pitcher (although one-handled pitchers commonly have a handle which rises above the rim, better to assist in pouring). And that there was slight evidence for another such face on the reverse of the pot suggests that if symmetry were maintained there was a series of faces around the neck. In any event, this motif presents new food for thought in the ongoing discussions of anthropomorphic representations in Castelluccian material[4].

Less dramatic, but also important, is the example of the sun/eye illustrated in Plate 32, no. 98. While circular motifs in the repertoire of Castelluccian material are rare, no other examples were previously found at La Muculufa which placed a fringe around the circle. Whether we read this as an eye, with the fringe denoting eyelashes, or a sun, it expands the corpus of Castelluccian motifs[5].

Another new curvilinear motif is seen in Plate 37, no. 160 where two concentric ovals are attached to a row of joined half round/ovals with a small bar at the top of the

---

[4] L. Bernabò Brea, "Eolie, Sicilia e Malta nell'eta' del bronzo," Kokalos 22–23 (1976–77) 59. Sluga Messina, 127–29.

[5] I have been struck many times by the similarity of some of the multiple angular or wavy line patterns in Castelluccian ceramics to patterns produced readily when wind blows across the sea. One could extend the interpretation and offer other examples of wavy/angular lines as indications of water. In this instance we could then suggest that the sun is setting over the water. I am, however, opposed to interpretations such as this since I believe we are too far removed from the pot painters and have too little other evidence to warrant such speculation.

join of the ovals. (This small bar resembles those used in the pattern AN, multiple, parallel angular lines; see the Catalogue of Motifs.) This pattern shows again how the Castelluccian painter often echoes one motif with another, here ovals echoed by half ovals, demonstrating, I believe, a fine sense of design. This motif may simply be a variation of one which appeared on a vessel recovered from the Sanctuary (Plate A.1). This is an unusual vessel in that it was clearly disfigured on firing, yet it had held enough importance to be brought to the Sanctuary.

Finally, I note a new pattern (seen in the fragment in Plate 33, no.133, Catalogue of Motifs, HW). I saw no examples of this among the vast number of decorated sherds previously found at La Muculufa, although I have noted other published examples. One is from Partanna on a dolio (storage jar) in the catalogue of Naro-Partanna material (Tusa-Pacci: catalog 40). As with the example from La Muculufa, this piece presents a sense of woven fabric in comparison to a related piece, also from Partanna (Tusa-Pacci, catalog 39). The pattern of this latter piece more closely resembles a series of triangles filled with lines. While the difference could be due to placement on the vessel and the curvature of the body of the vessel, I believe it is more likely that they are two differently conceived pattern systems. A second example occurs on a closed-neck, two-handled Serraferlicchio vessel, published by Tusa[6]; here, we see extensive use of this pattern on the body of the vessel. Two vessels in the Ashmolean Museum display the pattern on their handles. Unfortunately, these two have no provenience and so we derive no additional assistance from these examples[7]. In any event, this new pattern offers parallels to material from Partanna and the earlier Serraferlicchio material and may assist in placing the site of La Muculufa in the Castelluccian context.

Although not new motifs at La Muculufa (since they occurred on material recovered from the sanctuary), it is worth noting that two motifs not previously recorded from the village at La Muculufa appear in this new material. The first is the series of hatched diamonds (DH, Catalogue of Motifs). Three examples are illustrated in this

volume: Plate 24, no. 25, which is white-banded, and Plate 33, nos 87 and 88. A variation of this motif, Z5, also not found previously at the village, adds the common 'fringe' or 'feathered' motif to the central vertices of the diamonds. The second motif (FF, Catalogue of Motifs), an example of 'fringe' or 'feathering,' is seen in Plate 24, no. 25, on the handle of the pot, and in Plate 28, no. 78.

A series of fragmentary pitchers (Plate 27, nos 65–70; Plate 30, no. 90; and Plate 32, no. 106) opens up the possibilities of new understandings of the relationship between decoration and pot shape and/or function. In this instance there appears to be a set of rules which governs the decoration of the pot: horizontal angular/wavy lines on the neck, framed above and below by a solid band, 'fringe'(or short lines) or, in one instance, triangles down (Plate 32, no. 106) mark the beginning of the body decoration, and sets of vertical bands and lines which run from the neck band to the base. Where the pot is preserved, motifs appear as filler in the empty space between the vertical band/line motif: crosses or X's (Plate 27, nos. 65 and 66), opposing triangles or butterflies (Plate 27, no. 68) and vertical wavy line (Plate 27, no. 70) which echoes the vertical wavy line on the handle. This is a striking collection of pitchers whose resemblance to one another suggests, I believe, either that rules governed the decoration of one-handled pitchers, and/or that a small localized production area (e.g., a workshop) was responsible for these vessels. Either of these interpretations increases our understandings of the dynamics of pottery production in both the specific Castelluccian culture and in prehistoric cultures in general. Plate 30, no. 90, in fact, may be a fragment of an amphora (the handle does not rise above the rim), but it too follows the formula of neck pattern of angular/wavy lines and body pattern of vertical bands and lines, a common pattern from La Muculufa pottery in general. (This last fragment is reminiscent of the fragment in Plate 30, no. 93: there is a hatching pattern on the body, and the handle—in both instances not rising above the rim—is decorated with another common La Muculufa handle motif - a series of horizontal bands. Perhaps we have here (Plate 30, no. 90) a cousin to the vessel which carries the 'face' motif. Comparison of the design composition and vessel shape with the one-handled wide-mouthed cups nos. 81 and 82, Plate 29, further argues for rules governing composition and/or practice in the workshops.)

---

[6] Sebastiano Tusa, *La Sicilia nella preistoria*, (Palermo, 1983), 213, figure 9.

[7] Marco Pacci, "Nota su alcuni vasi protocastellucciani dalla Sicilia occidentale conservati all'Ashmolean Museum di Oxford," *I Quaderni di Sicilia Archeologica*, Azienda Provinciale Turismo, Trapani, n.d.: figures 16 & 22.

Of particular note is the fragment illustrated in Plate 36, no. 151. The individual design motifs as well as the combination (vertical AP between multiple vertical lines) recalls the pedestalled bowl which I have associated with the La Muculufa Master, the painter of a finely decorated amphora restored from fragments found in the sanctuary[8] and illustrated in Figure B. If this is so, it is an additional argument for the contemporaneity of the sanctuary with the village.

This presentation of new material from the village of La Muculufa supports conclusions drawn in Muculufa I and suggests additional insights into the Castelluccian culture in south-central Sicily. It is instructive to consider next how it relates, not to all material in Sicily, but specifically to the two recently published bodies of Castelluccian material from Castelluccio di Noto and from Partanna-Naro (see notes 2 and 3).

Comparison of La Muculufa with Other Bodies of Castelluccian Material

Our Catalogue of Motifs from La Muculufa provides references to published parallels from Partanna, Naro, and Castellucio di Noto, as available. This allows us to readily see some of the comparisons in the selection and use of individual design motifs. Nonetheless, this does not begin to define the relationships, or lack of relationships, since how a motif is executed, how it is placed on the vessel, and how it is combined with other motifs are much more indicative of "style." Most striking is the example of the 'new' La Muculufa motif (Plate 33, no. 133, Catalogue of Motifs, HW) on the dolio from Partanna (note 6 above) and the example of the use of 'dots' on the interior of a low pedestalled bowl from Naro. In the latter instance, we remind the reader that the use of dots was noted in the previous publication as more prevalent in the material from the village than in the material from the sanctuary at La Muculufa. An individual motif of lines and dots which occurs on two vessels from Partanna is seen also on the cup from La Muculufa illustrated in Muculufa I: figure 35. There are numerous instances of this motif from La Muculufa.

When we turn from individual motifs to more complex design patterns on whole or nearly whole vessels, we can cite parallels between the cup illustrated in the earlier publication of La Muculufa (Muculufa I, figure 40) and Partanna-Naro catalog (Tusa-Pacci, catalogue 58 and 108, both from Naro). The strong comparison between the cups illustrated in the earlier publication of La Muculufa (Muculufa I, figures 42b and c) and the vessel from Naro (Tusa-Pacci, catalog 77) was noted in that publication (Muculufa I, 36) and bears repeating here. Finally, although only preserved in a small fragment from La Muculufa, the correspondence between the pitcher illustrated from Naro (Tusa-Pacci, catalog 78) and the fragments illustrated here in Plate 33, nos. 87 and 88 must be considered.

The recent publication by Sluga Messina of the material from the dump of Castelluccio di Noto (see note 3) does not illustrate the actual sherds but rather the decorative motifs from a number of them. Nonetheless, the publication affords us an opportunity to review a large body of Castelluccian motifs from the eponymous site of this culture. Many of the motifs illustrated by Sluga Messina have no direct parallel among the motifs recovered at La Muculufa (e.g., Sluga Messina: inventory no. N.37, p. 32) but even so are remininiscent of La Muculufa motifs (in this case D1). Another example in the inventory (Sluga Messina: inventory S.66, p. 64) is virtually identical to La Muculufa motif D1 as is another one from Noto illustrated by Tusa[9].

Four motifs from fragmentary pots (Sluga Messina, inventory S.61-S.64, p.64) use individual motifs not seen at La Muculufa. Where enough of the pot remains to see vessel shape, we note that the shape (a straight-side slightly conical cup) is not common at La Muculufa, especially for painted ware. Here the shape was generally reserved for unpainted, coarse ware.

In some instances (Sluga Messina, inventory S.15, p. 40), we see two well-known individual motifs from La Muculufa (AH and CK) combined in a fashion not seen at La Muculufa. The motif AH, in fact, an angular band filled with hatching, is quite common among the material illustrated from the dump of Castelluccio di Noto (e.g.,

---

[8] Lukesh, S. S., "The La Muculufa Master and Company: The Identification of A Workshop of Early Bronze Age Castelluccian Painters," Revue des Archeologues et Historiens d'Art de Louvain, 2 (1993), 9–24.

---

[9] Sebastiano Tusa, La Sicilia nella preistoria, Sellerio editore, Palermo, 1983.

Sluga Messina: inventory S.72—S.76, S.768, S.84, S.85), as it is among the material recovered at La Muculufa.

The decoration painted on handles seem to be drawn from a small repertoire of motifs. In addition to sets of horizontal bands and lines, the La Muclufa pattern H1 is common from Noto. Many examples are illustrated (e.g., Sluga Messina: inventory S.146-S.162).

Sluga Messina's inventory number S.71 offers us the possibility of viewing the design composition on an amphora. Here we see that the familiar neck pattern of angular line has the hatched-filled triangle motif above it; the body appears to be a series of hatched crosses (motif HC). Once again the Castelluccian painter has balanced the hatching on the neck with hatching on the body. With the exception of the horizontal bands delimiting the rim and the break between neck and body, the painter has reflected the horizontal angluar line on the neck above and below with different patterns which produce the same angluar effect. Fragments S.72 and S.73 from Castelluccio may come from the same pot. While these motifs are each individually found on pots from La Muculufa, the specific combination had not been recovered.

The Catalogue of Motifs from La Muculufa indicates, as mentioned, correspondence to published illustrations of Naro, Partanna and Castelluccio di Noto material, and it is not necessary to discuss all such correspondences. It is instructive, however, to consider one or two other points. In the first place, Sluga Messina finds parallels to many of the motifs in the eastern Mediterranean, especially, she concludes, in the interior regions of Greece and Asia Minor, rather than in material from the coasts or outlying islands. She traces specific motifs to Iran and Asia Minor, for example the 'sun' or 'eye' (La Muculufa motif SN) and the hook (La Muculufa motif HK). I agree with Maniscalco that the "very expanse of the area" and the lack of precise chronological connections keep us from drawing any significant conclusions.

In addition, I suggest, the common use of simple motifs around the world need not indicate a common origin. Sluga Messina suggests that the 'Castelluccian' motifs used by modern day Algerian potters on their pots trace their history back through the millenia although the significance of the symbols has been lost. While this is possible, unless we can demonstrate an unbroken history of use, we may have to accept that similar motifs do not necessitate a similar origin. Just as I would not argue that the

pattern of a row of filled triangles below a horizontal band on the rim of a Pueblo pot from the 15th-16th c A.D.[10] derives from those same Castelluccian motifs (on a pot of similar shape), so I am unwilling, on the basis of evidence to date, to ascribe all the correspondence noted by Sluga Messina to direct origin in the eastern Mediterranean.

Muculufa I, figure 27 demonstrated how many Castelluccian motifs could easily arise from transformation of the simple angular line. Plate D here shows a similar possible development of many of the motifs from the simple triangle. This is not to say that this is how they developed but how simple geometric motifs can be used to develop more complex elaborate motifs without outside influence. As an inveterate 'doodler', I often find myself tracing a pattern (illustrated below) of four lines, moving from point 1 to 2 to 3 to 4 and back to point 1. When filled in this pattern becomes La Muculufa motif DT, or the 'butterfly.' It is a very easy pattern for the wrist to make and I think we needn't insist on eastern Mediterranean influence for its use in Sicily.

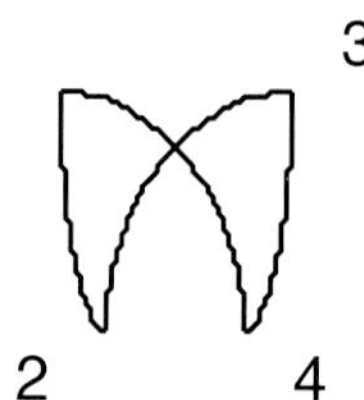

While Greece and the Near East are often cited as the homeland for much in the ancient world, I suggest that some, if not many, of the designs and complexity on Castelluccian ware originated in Sicily. The bone plaques of the Castelluccian period, interestingly enough, support this idea, since those found outside Sicily are the ones devoid of decoration, while most recovered in Sicily carry hatching and circular motifs reminiscent of the pot decoration[11].

Although there is clearly a use of similar motifs on the material from the site of La Muculufa with those of material from the sites of Partanna, Naro, and Castelluccio, the comparisons are not overwhelming; in fact, the material from these sites which does not find close correspondence

---

[10] John W. Berry, *American Indian Pottery*, Books Americana, Florence, Alabama, 199: figure 371.

[11] R, Ross Holloway, *Italy and the Aegean: 3000–700 B.C.*, Archaeologia Transatlantica 1(Providence and Louvain, 1981) 17–19.

with La Muculufa is far more plentiful. The comparisons noted are not restricted to fine ware and especially not to fine ware cups (or dippers). We see from the catalogue of material from Partanna and Naro, that the Naro corpus includes cups which are rather crudely painted (e.g., Tusa-Pacci: catalog 52), cups whose shapes are not in strict comparison with those La Muculufa (e.g., Tusa-Pacci: catalog 54), and pitchers which have few if any correspondences (Tusa-Pacci: catalog 76, and 78, compared with catalog 77 mentioned above). The pedestalled bowls in Tusa and Pacci's Partanna-Naro catalog are low-footed for the most part, and the few on higher feet bear little resemblance to the group from La Muculufa, either village or sanctuary (see particularly the tall footed examples illustrated in the first Muculufa publication, Muculufa I, figure 33a-c). In short, a close study of the catalogue of material from Naro-Partana suggests that the term "Naro Style" is an abstraction of little independent value. The same may be said for the term "S. Ippolito style." Moreover, I would be reluctant to assign any chronological value to these terms especially when, in the case of the "Naro Style," the term is restricted to a group of fine ware dippers and pedestalled bowls. In fact, the absence of any Castelluccian material throughout Sicily from well stratified sites which can show a clear demarcation between early and late styles hinders our attempt to put too fine an emphasis on the chronological horizons proposed.

What we do see, from both collections of material recovered from La Muculufa, is that in addition to the simple style there exist ceramics we can categorize as of finer and finest quality—these include not only cups/dippers but also pedestalled bowls and amphora (the name vase of the La Muculufa Master is the classic example, Plate A.2). While this body of fine material has some parallels to material from Naro (and perhaps Partanna with the motif in Plate 33, no. 133), there are far clearer parallels to material from other sites in the Salso River Valley (Xiboli, Monte San Giuliano, Canticaglione, and Casalicchio-Agnone) and neighboring Canicatti[12]. The great mass of fragmentary and reconstructed pedestalled bowls from La Muculufa (both from the sanctuary and the village) do not belong, in my estimation, to the 'finest' tradition. The amphora, cups and pedestalled bowls by the La Muculufa Master and his circle[13], however, belong here. Nonethe-

less, there may well be what I would term a 'finer' tradition to which material belongs. Here I would include the vessels in Muculufa I, figure 32a,b, 33a-c; and this volume, Plate 22, no. 14; Plate 23, nos. 17,20,24; and Plate 24, nos. 11 and 22—as well as the material in Plate 35, no.146 and Plate 36, no.147. Plate 36, no. 151 may well fit the 'finest' tradition. The 'finest' material has no close comparisons with the published material from Naro. In fact, throughout the material from La Muculufa, as with that from Naro, we see great variation in quality of potting and painting. There are a number of possible explanations for such variation. One may ascribe such variation, for example, to individual styles or horizons; or to function and use (everyday vs ritual/special occasion); and/or, finally, to maker (domestic creation in the home or village or creation by specialized craftsmen). Explanations drawn from the second and third possibilities can easily coexist and, in fact, we might see that special use vessels (for religious rituals, marriages, etc) may well be purchased from specialized craftsmen rather than made at home. What this means to me, however, is the difficulty of using the terms S. Ippolito and Naro to describe material which does not have close correspondence with either S. Ippolito or Naro. At one point in our developing understanding of the Early Bronze Age material from Sicily these were useful descriptive categories. The material recovered from excavations to date suggests that the situation may be more complex. To me, the published material demonstrates that neither term properly describes the material recovered at La Muculufa.

The Significance of the Craftsmen

Variation, we indicate above, may be ascribed to individual craftsmen. If this is so, it opens up possibilities of new understandings of the relationships displayed by the ceramics and their chronologies. In a recent paper, I have argued for the identification of an individual Castelluccian painter and his workshop, the La Muculufa Master (see

---

[12] Muculufa I: 36.

[13] Note 8. I use the term 'his' advisedly as a collective noun. In a private communication, Dr. McConnell asked of the possibilities of discussing gender of maker, presence of workshop and whether or not pots were prepared for the painter or he made them himself. While I believe it is possible to identify individual makers, identification of gender or specific role (painter vs potter) is beyond our capabilities without further evidence.

note 8). It is useful, for the further discussion of La Muculufa ceramics and their contribution to our understanding of Castelluccian culture, to include some of these arguments here.

Archaeologists who study the similarities and differences among recovered artifacts are intent not only on identifying the meaning of these similarities and differences but also on understanding the relationship of them to the network of communities from which the objects were drawn. On one hand, archaeologists may see ceramic variability as a measure of community variability, as does Wobst, who sees ceramics as playing an important role in information exchange, and for whom "style reacts with great sensitivity to changes in other culture variables and, of itself, actively supports other cultural processes, such as cultural integration and differentiation, boundary maintenance, compliance with norms and enforcing conformity[14]."

On the other hand, archaeologists may be reluctant to ascribe enormous relevance to ceramic variability, as Hodder, who, while considering ceramics as symbols of social and economic relations, prefers to see the extent of their interaction dependent on the strategies and intentions of the interactive groups and on how they use, manipulate and negotiate material symbols as part of their strategies[15].

At whichever end of this spectrum of interpretation one's own viewpoint falls, most archaeologists continue to find ceramic variability an important component in the understanding of the communities responsible for its creation. Frank Hole, who views much of the mental process behind pot-making as subconscious, sees pottery as a true information exchanger, believing that it can be characterized in a way analogous to language dialect[16]. If this is so, then the more we understand about pottery manufacture and distribution, the more informed we are about the culture in general. And the recognition of individual craftsmen leads to more clearly understanding patterns of manufacture and dissemination. The question, then, is

how do we identify individual hands in prehistoric material?

Within the last two years, three papers have addressed the attribution of individual craftsmen to prehistoric material[17]. Gill and Chippindale, in their discussion of cycladic figurines, consider how the goals of the archaeologist and the connoisseur conflict when we seek to attribute prehistoric material to an individual. They demonstrate this clearly with the entry from Christie's catalog which shows how the buyer (connoisseur) is appealed to on the basis of attribution to an "accomplished sculptor with an individual style, by the same hand as a figure in the Goulandris collection[18]." It is understandable that if the purpose in identifying the individual craftsman is to increase the monetary value of a prehistoric artefact archaeologists should all be dismayed. Gill and Chippindale write that "the material consequences of the connoisseur's esteem, as we have been able to document them, are calamitous to the archaeological interest, because they have led to many Cycladic figures being taken out of context that many roads to a secure knowledge of the prehistoric Cyclades, as once available in the archaeology of these figures, have been closed[19]."

Archaeologists, I have suggested, see other values in the attribution to individual craftsmen, and will continue to seek this identification to further their understandings of the culture(s) involved. Regardless that Jiri Frel wrote, as quoted by Gill and Chippindale[20], "Instead of anonymous marble figures, we can see real people at creative work, communicating in spite of the passage of time and

---

[14] H. Martin Wobst, "Stylistic behavior and information exchange," in For the Director, ed. Cleland, C.(Anthropology Papers, No. 61, 1978), 335.

[15] I. Hodder, Symbols in Action, (Cambridge,1982), 185.

[16] Frank Hole, "Analysis of structure and design in prehistoric ceramics," World Archaeology, 15 (1984) 334.

[17] David W.J. Gill and Christopher Chippindale, "Material and Intellectual Consequences of Esteem for Cycladic Figurines," American Journal of Archaeology, 97 (1993) 601–660. John F. Cherry, "Beazley in the Bronze Age? Reflections on Attribution Studies in Aegean Prehistory," Aegean Bronze Age Iconography: Shaping a Methodology, Proceedings of the 4th International Aegean Conference/ University of Tasmania, Hobart, Australia, 6–9 April 1992, edited by Robert Laffineur and Janice L. Crowley (Université de Liege, Histoire de l'art et archelogie de la Grece antique, 1992). Christine Morris, "Hands Up for the Individual! The Role of Attribution Studies in Aegean Prehistory," Cambridge Archaeological Journal, 3, (1993) 41–66.

[18] Gill and Chippindale 659.

[19] Gill and Chippindale 658.

[20] Gill and Chippindale 639.

different ways of life," many of us who see individuals among the anonymous craftsmen of prehistoric material, seek to establish a more precise chronology and better understandings of manufacture and distribution. This is in direct contrast to Redman's contention, also quoted in Gill and Chippindale, that "all too often it seems as though scholars who study the behavior of particular individuals do so at cost of more general investigations[21]." Cherry and Morris offer a different perspective.

J. F. Cherry, writing before the publication of Christine Morris'paper (above, note 17) but with the knowledge of her work, brings up an important point—self-awareness on the part of the artist[22]. In his discussion, he moves back in time, pointing to Renaissance artists who were supremely confident of their own worth as special individuals, to the Greek potters and painters, who he argues were clearly conscious of themselves as artisans. While he doesn't take sides, he cites the efforts of some scholars to discredit any idea of individual artisans in the Mycenaean period[23]. Lack of signature as we recognize it, and lack of mention in the Linear B tablets of individual artisans, is not sufficient argument, to me, to conclude that those who created the works were not conscious of their efforts as individuals. Whether or not we agree that these artisans were 'self-aware,'I do agree completely with Cherry's conclusion that identifying hands need not be governed by the producers' own awareness of themselves as artisans. Morris continues this thought, with references to Berenson's statement that attribution is more successful when the artisan is conscious of him/herself as the creator, arguing to the contary that the identification of individual artisans is dependent rather on the existence of a discernable style[24]. She convincingly illustrates her point with an example drawn from 20th c Pueblo artists.

Attributes critical to the identification of individual artisans, which both Cherry and Morris discuss, are the selection of individual designs and design sets and the characteristic methods of producing the specific designs. Cherry argues that the "primary focus, and the most important criterion of individuality, must be variation below the level of design element[25]." He uses the example, especially pertinent to Castelluccian ceramics, of hatching—not the predilection for hatching, but how the hatching is executed. This is tantamount to the arguments of motor skill, which Hill has convincingly demonstrated is uniquely attributable to individual people (see discussion below and note 33).

Nonetheless, I am still persuaded, as is Morris, of the value of the selection of individual designs and the composition of design sets in the identification of individual artisans. Morris discusses the character of the design sets and the choice of individual details, concluding that "the choice and location of subsidiary or filling motifs is also an important aspect of microstyle and overall style[26]." This is similar to Berenson's arguments that we should look to habitual or conventional patterns in the work of the artist when painting unimportant items. In the comments following Morris'paper, Dyfri Williams warns against too heavy dependence on the design set, since it can be learned or imitated, unlike motor habits[27]. The material from La Muculufa has shown that when one artisan is familiar with another's design sets, it is still often easy to discriminate between them. In my discussion of the La Muculufa Master (note 8), I discussed and illustrated a second large amphora. In this instance, while there is the same selection of overall design and individual motifs, we can easily refuse to attribute the second vessel to the La Muclufa master.

Finally, Morris identifies a third point which has direct bearing on the efforts to identify individuals among the artisans of Castelluccian pottery—the culture of the craftsmen themselves. She sees, not regional variation, but a "continued sharing by different artisans of many conventions, some found only on pottery and not in other media, in the execution of complex elements and themes. This strongly suggests interacting individuals working within a common tradition and awareness of each other's work[28]." I suggest, in fact, that we may be able to identify workshops based on sets of structural rules which guide the design compositions and that the Castelluccian mate-

---

[21] Gill and Chippindale 638.

[22] Cherry 125.

[23] Cherry 126, n. 12.

[24] Morris 43.

[25] Cherry 139.

[26] Morris 50.

[27] Morris 62.

[28] Morris 51.

rial from La Muculufa provides us with a first opportunity to do so. Michael Graves, working with the Kalinga potters, found a similar phenomenon. He wrote that "attributes that comprise the structure of a design system on vessels of the same shape and size appear to be shared across communities of interacting potters who learn their craft at approximately the same time[29]."

While these recent studies have discussed the problems inherent in attribution (the development of expectations for monetary gain in the antiquities market, the need to identify individuals and their life stories, for example), I believe that the identification of individuals among the prehistoric potters and painters serves a much more important purpose—that of helping to understand the patterns of interaction among the peoples of the place and time. How do these arguments on the identification of individual artisans assist us in better understanding Castelluccian ceramics? Let us review briefly the evidence for painted pottery from La Muculufa, especially from the sanctuary.

As the original La Muculufa publication noted, an enormous quantity of pottery was recovered from the sanctuary at La Muculufa; of over 20,000 decorated fragments recorded, 75% were recovered at the sanctuary. Most were elaborately decorated and carefully executed and one of the vessels recovered, the name vase of the La Muculufa Master, is a masterpiece of Castelluccian ceramics. Much of the material recovered represents cups or dippers, amphorae, and pedestalled bowls.

The fragments reconstructed into the vase in Plate A.2 were recovered over the course of three seasons of excavation. The design filling the body of the amphora, parallel angular bands connected by vertical lines, is otherwise unknown from Castelluccian material, although the pattern of parallel angular bands is quite common. Both because of the quality of the executions of the design on this amphora as well as the introduction of a new pattern, as we recovered sherds to this vessel we called the artist who executed the pot the La Muculufa Master, the name attributed to his work today.

While decorated pottery accounted for 38% of the finds in the sanctuary, only 22% of the fragments from the village were decorated (percentages through the 1985 season only). Fine, thin-walled, one-handled cups were more common in the material from the sanctuary than in the village, and the character of the decorated pottery in the two areas was different: originally eight decorative motifs were found exclusively in the sanctuary area (now, apparently only six, in light of the new material), and eight others appeared there in overwhelming proportion[30]. Furthermore, as noted, pottery from the sanctuary has connections with material found at other sites in the Salso River Valley (Xiboli, Monte San Giuliano, Canticaglione, and Casalicchio-Agnone). It is difficult to believe that the village of La Muculufa manufactured pottery for all sites in the Salso River Valley and neglected to keep some varieties of production for its own use. Instead, it seem far more likely that those who visited the sanctuary brought pieces of decorated ware made by their own potters.

Although the Castelluccian culture is known and recognized chiefly through its pottery, to date no examples of kilns have been published and, until recently, no temper studies of the wide range of ceramic material has been undertaken. This makes the identification of a common hand and workshop, at this stage, completely dependent on eye recognition[31].

As Morris and Cherry and others contend, the identification of individuals responsible for the manufacture of particular art objects has a substantial history. It has been addressed with Euoprean material by Morelli and Berenson[32] as well as with the American material[33]. In the American discussions, different levels of variability can be isolated: attributes reflecting behavioural or use variability, those reflecting style, and those reflecting individual variability. It is within the last two levels that I focussed in order to identify individuals in the material recovered from La Muculufa. Based on the work of Berenson, Beazley, Graves, Hill, Hole and others, it is possible to identify three points relevant for the assignment of individual responsibility. These are essentially the same criteria used by Morris:

1. The design composition or structure, including the number and shape of partitions, the basic symmetry and the juxtaposition of specific motifs.

2. The selection and interpretation of specific motifs (form or morphology).

---

[29] Michael W. Graves, "Ceramic Design Variations Within a Kalinga Village: Temporal and Spatial Processes," in Ben A. Nelson, ed., Decoding Prehistoric Ceramics, (1985) 32.

[30] Muculufa I: p.23, Table D.

3. Technique or the execution of specific motifs including the level of ability and attributes of motor performance.

[31] This volume discusses the petrographic analysis of sherds, chosen from Maniscalco's S. Ippolito and Naro groups, which demonstrated that the sherds were made from the same types of clay and that the vessels were prepared in the same manner. This leaves us with a few possiblities: the different sherds were all made at the same location, either by the same people or by different persons (itinerant potters, for example) or they were made at different locations which had the same types of clay. It is important to have this analysis, although no strong conclusions can be drawn from it yet. The scarcity of find-spots of pottery-making is not unique to Castelluccian material, as London relates: "For various reasons relatively few ancient pottery production locations are known. Where to look and what to expect are problems exacerbated by the emphasis to excavate non-industrial areas at many sites. ...even the larger, heavier material correlates of the pottery industry will not always be preserved in situ for several reasons: the seasonality of the industry; the multifunctional use of space; and the reuse or recycling of broken pottery, kilns, and by-products." Gloria Anne London, "On Fig Leaves, Itinerant Potters, and Pottery Production Locations in Cyprus," in Cross-Craft and Cross-Cultural Interactions in Ceramics, Volume IV, Ceramics and Civilization, ed. P.E. McGovern, M.N. Notis, and W.D. Kingery, (The American Ceramic Society, 1989). Finally, as discussed by Reents-Budet, anthropologists working with contemporary potters in the Yucatan and Guatemala have identified paste recipes specific to potters "and thus their ceramic products can be distinguished chemically from those of other pottery producers in the respective areas. Applying these data to an archaeological situation, pottery that shares a distinct paste compositional profile should represent the output of a group of potters working closely together within one community and possibly even within one workshop." Painting the Maya Ceramics: Royal Ceramics of the Classic Period, Dorie Reents-Budet (Duke University Press, 1994):167–68. Similar analyses on Castelluccian sherds might enable us to group precisely pottery from workshops and/or individual potters.

[32] B. Berenson, Rudiments of connoisseurship: Study and Criticism of Italian Art, New York,1962. (Published in 1902 as The Study and Criticism of Italian Art.) See the discussion of Berenson in Muller (below n. 32): 24–25. Giovanni Morelli, Italian Painters: Critical Studies of their Works, translated by Constance Foulkes, 2 vols., London, 1892–93.

[33] Michael W. Graves (above n. 29): 9–34. James N. Hill, "Individual Variability in Ceramics and the Study of Prehistoric Social Organization," in James N. Hill and Joel Gunn, ed., The Individual in Prehistory, (New York, 1977) 55–108. Jon Muller, "Individual Variation in Art Styles," in James N. Hill and Joel Gunn, ed., The Individual in Prehistory,(New York, 1977) 23–40. Frank Hole, "Analysis of structure and design in prehistoric ceramics," World Archaeology, 15 (1984) 326–347.

While many of us are comfortable identifying particular motifs and recognizing individual design configurations, few of us are conversant with the relevance and identification of individual motor performance characteristics. For this reason, Hill's article, "Individual Variability in Ceramics," is particularly pertinent[34]. He presents much of the relevant recent discussions of individual variability and motor performance, the evidence of a number of experiments he and his students conducted, as well as his own studies of prehistoric pottery. I summarize a few points which, I believe, assist in understanding the identification of individuals in the assemblage of Castellucian material here.

Handwriting analyses have shown that handwriting is largely subconscious and that essential motor-performance characteristics of an individual cannot be taught to others. Additionally, an individual's handwriting cannot be copied nor can an individual consciously alter or disguise his own handwriting to the degree that it cannot be recognized. Furthermore, all this is generally true regardless of tools and inks, speed or carelessness of execution, and almost all other conditions. Finally, "the more expert a writer is, the less variability is exhibited in his motor performances, and thus the easier it is to distinguish his work from that of others[35]." Hill believes, and I concur, that these characteristics are equally true of the motor performance of painters, and, in fact, he demonstrates this in studies presented in his article.

In a hand writing experiment of his own, Hill was able to demonstrate that while "early and latter samples could be discriminated, the discrimination was not as good as it was for the individuals themselves[36]." This suggests that differences reflecting the change in individual motor performance over time is not as great as difference in motor performance between individuals. That is, the handwriting of one's older self is more like that of one's earlier self than it is like anyone else's.

I have argued that ceramic material recovered from La Muculufa as well as related material recovered from other sites in the Salso River Valley allow the identification of

[34] Hill (here n. 33).

[35] Hill (here n. 33), p.101 drawn from Wilson R. Harrison, Suspect documents, their scientific examination, (London, 1958).

[36] Hill (here n. 33) 90.

individuals responsible for the manufacture of particular pieces and that this identification can be made based on these three critical points : design composition (structure), selection and interpretation of particular motifs (form), and execution of particular motifs (technique)

My discussion examined in detail a number of reconstructed pots from La Muculufa, including the name vase of the La Muculufa Master, and fragmentary vessels and sherds from other sites. These include material from Xiboli, Monte San Giuliano, and Casalicchio-Agnone. The material reviewed permitted, for the first time, the identification of distinct hands among painters of Castelluccian pottery. Beginning with the name vase of the La Muculufa Master, I identified fragmentary examples of pots which reflect the same selection of motifs, the same overall comprehension of balance in the design composition, suggesting a common set of structural rules, and even the same technique or execution of motifs. Plate B illustrates an amphora, partially reconstructed from a number of fragments, whose motif selection and design composition strongly argue for the same workshop if not the same artisan. In addition, a group of fragmentary cups (Plate C) is discussed in this article which, while not currently used to identify distinct hands, reinforces the close relationship among painters of pots found at La Muculufa, Casalicchio-Agnone, Xiboli, Monte San Giuliano, Canticaglione, and Canicatti. At the least, those responsible for the pots (Plates A and B) were from a group of interacting artisans. I suggest, then, that we can identify a group of artisans among the material recovered from the sanctuary at La Muculufa whose work is similar enough to suggest a 'workshop,' one in which there was at least one set of structural rules for design composition.

Craftsmen and the Study of the Castelluccian Culture

The identification of individual hands and a group of artisans whose work is strongly related opens up new understandings of the Castelluccian culture. It also brings into sharp relief some of the problems that exist with the traditional approach to organizing and ordering Castelluccian ceramics. In the first place, it is clear that there is a long history of survival of a basic repertoire of elements. We see this from the motifs on the Serraferlicchio material, which, while painted on vessels of clearly different shape, carry hallmark motifs of the later Castelluccian (hatching,

white-banding, for example). This long survival makes it difficult, in the absence of other fixed points, to present a securely defined chronology. An impressionistic ordering of stylistic traits to create a stylistic sequence is not enough. That we can readily find parallels to motifs across Sicily, as Maniscalco has done in reference to the La Muculufa material discussed above (e.g., hatch crossing bands at Naro and Partanna, 'butterflies' or opposing triangles at Mizzebbi and Adrano), and as others have done in discussions of different collections, only underscores the problem. What do these appearances of similar or identical motifs mean? Must we assume close connections or simple acquaintance? That the Castelluccian ceramic material belongs to a time when a large portion of southern Sicily was using a similar repertoire of design motifs on similarly shaped pots is clear. That the Casteulluccians then, perhaps over a long time horizon, were in contact and knowledgeable about each other's craft is also clear. But can we carve the area into three different groups on the basis of this ceramic material, and further can we propose meaningful chronological successions among such impressionistically defined groups?

The S. Ippolito material, as Maniscalco points out, is difficult to define as a cultural *facies*. I believe there is too little material and related evidence to call this a separate *facies* or horizon let alone establish it as defining an earlier Castelluccian phase. Maniscalco uses the term "Naro style", which although found together with material of the "S. Ippolito" type at La Muculufa, is, in her view, slightly later. I am less sure than she that there are the strong Naro conections in the material from La Muculufa. There is, instead, material which is less finely made ("S. Ippolito") and material which is more finely made ("Naro") and material which, I have proposed, is very finely created and which represents an individual artisan and his/her workshop. Maniscalco has defined a broad area within which La Muculufa fits—from Naro on the west to Caltagirone and Gela (where the S. Ippolito style is attested) on the east. I prefer to focus on a narrower area whose material is very clearly related, as I discussed above, believing that we can ultimately derive more information about the Castelluccian culture in this fashion.

And it is the potential identification of individual workshops which holds the key to the next stage in our growing understandings of Castelluccian material in Sicily. Before I discuss this further, however, I would like to turn briefly to the idea of the level of manufacture complexity one may assume at La Muclufa and the assumptions which one can or cannot make about the industry. Sinopoli[37], drawing from Van der Leeuw, discusses four levels of pottery manufacture or industry: household production, household industry, workshop industry, and large-scale industry. The difference between the first and second, she indicates, is that at the second level while ceramics are still produced at the level of the household, some production is oriented toward trade. In the third level, specialists work almost full-time and the production may involve wheel- or mold-made vessels, and permit production of large quantities of vessels over short periods of time. The fourth is characterised by factories which employ large numbers of people. The ethnographic evidence for the first two levels indicates that the potters are generally women, and in the second level, widowed or unmarried women with more time on their hands. The production levels defined by ethnographic research certainly help us to better understand the possibilities for production in Sicily 4000 years ago, but we should not, I suggest, insist on adopting them literally.

Thus, while I would prefer not to identify our potters by gender and I do not believe that we need a potters'wheel for any industry-like production, I do believe that we see in the La Muculufa material and the identification of hands evidence for pottery industry (manufacture and distribution) in the Early Bronze Age. There is no doubt that a great deal of the material is created for utilitarian purposes, most likely in household industries for personal use. Some potters with more skill create better made pieces, perhaps again, initially only for personal use[38]. Additional time (a seasonal variant) and demand from others may well turn some of this production toward trade, most likely, within a well-defined, easily reached area. It is clear that multiple modes of manufacture must

have existed simultaneously. The evidence from southern Sicily to date indicates that this 'trading' area for ceramics in the Early Bronze Age may have been primarily limited to river valleys (in this case, that of the Salso River). The river valley is thus the area of closest and normal contact. The geographical situation of La Muculufa in the center of the Salso Valley favored exchange of pottery and ideas about its creation from the area of Caltanissetta at the head of the valley in the north to Casalicchio-Agnone at the edge of the coastal plain near the Salso River's mouth at Licata. The mechanism of exchange of goods and ideas was further favored by the existence of the sanctuary at La Muculufa and its role in drawing the people of the valley together at this site. The pottery recovered at the sanctuary exhibits strong similarities to material recovered from other sites within the Salso River valley, suggesting that the makers, as Graves saw among the modern day Kalinga, were interacting potters who learn their craft from each other (here, note 29).

In addition to offering insights into manufacture and distribution, attribution studies offer another important piece of information, and one that is not yet easily found, I have argued, among Castelluccian material. This is the support for chronology. Susan Sherratt, in her response to Morris'paper, articulates this well.

> From an archaeological point of view, the great advantage of attribution studies is that the grounds on which pots or other objects are grouped together are made quite explicit, with the conversion of stylistic into chronological classification thus given some tangible rationale. In this respect, attribution studies—particularly in the hands of a sensible and sensitive practitioner—are infinitely preferable to the way in which minor stylistic similarities are reified into rules of chronological classification without any attempt to consider underlying connective mechanisms. The attribution of a group of pots at least gives us a reason for putting their creation, if not their deposition, in a limited time-band, and unravels much of the mystique which pottery classification for chronological purposes has tended to create for itself[39].

It should be clear that I see the importance of the recognition of individual hands among the material of La Muculufa neither in connoisseurship nor in understanding

---

[37] Carla M. Sinopoli, Approaches to Archaeological Ceramics, (New York, 1991). She cites S.E. van der Leeuw, "Toward a study of the economics of pottery making," Ex Horreo, ed. by B.L. Van Beek, R.W. Brandt, and W. Goeman-van Waateringe (Amsterdam, 1977) 68–76.

[38] A colleague of mine at Hofstra University, anthropologist Cheryl Mwaria, observed the same phenomenon among the Kamba from Kitui, Kenya. While baskets were made in all the households, those who made the better ones were sought out for special occasion or special use.

[39] Morris (above n. 18): 62–63.

individuals. Rather the value lies in our growing understanding of socio-political organization in Early Bronze Age Sicily and the Salso River Valley and in the potential for well-defined chronologies[40]. These possibilities suggest we focus our efforts not on identifying widely defined horizons, but on more narrowly defined communities of Castelluccian sites, which may be identified by the pottery and the 'workshops' responsible for them (see discussion of the support of chemical identification of paste recipes in note 31). The site of Monte Grande, for example (currently under excavation by Giuseppe Castellana) suggests itself as another gathering place, commanding the drainage area east of the Naro River[41]. Recognition of such communities across southern Sicily will help us better see the networks of manufacture, distribution and interaction. This in turn will better help our understandings of the dynamics of the broader Castelluccian culture.

[40] In the area of socio-political boundaries, the world of the Maya, though far removed from that of the Castelluccians, brings us important insights. In her seminal publication, Painting the Maya Ceramics: Royal Ceramics of the Classic Period, Dorie Reents-Budet (Duke University Press, 1994) describes the role painted ceramics played in the Maya world. Unlike the Castelluccian, the Maya used hieroglyphs to describe pottery function on the vessel, as a lidded jar from Rio Azul, Guatemala, testifies—its contents are cacao (p.75). Further evidence from the ceramics shows how they function as social currency and, more significantly, demonstrate that the "correlation between the development of myriad painting styles and the complex political scenario [was] not coincidental because the painted pottery functioned as an integral component of the social politics of the time (p.91)." The Maya ceramics have shown that "when art becomes a commodity that circulates as social currency, it is increasingly important to create 'additives of prestige' that enhance the objects' value. …one of the recurring additives is the recognition of the works of master artists (p.92)." Finally, Reents-Budet suggests that "if styles send messages of social, political and economic group affiliation…it should be possible to identify sociopolitical ties among archaeological sites based on the presence of specific styles of painted pottery (p.96)." While the Maya were significantly more advanced than the Castelluccians, I suggest that the lessons of socio-political organization and pottery manufacture, distribution and use which they demonstrate have much to tell us. As with the lessons of ethnographic studies, we should keep the various functions of pottery in the Maya world in mind as we consider the role of Castelluccian pottery.

[41] G. Castellana, "Monte Grande" in Un decennio di ricerche preistoriche e protostoriche nel territorio di Agrigento, (Agrigento, 1990): 32–38. The lengthier discussion, "Il santuario di Monte Grande presso Palma di Montechiaro…" appeared in vol. 5 of Quaderni dell'Istituto di Archeologie della Facoltà di Lettere e Filosofia, Università di Messina. Although dated 1990, this volume was not published until 1995.1

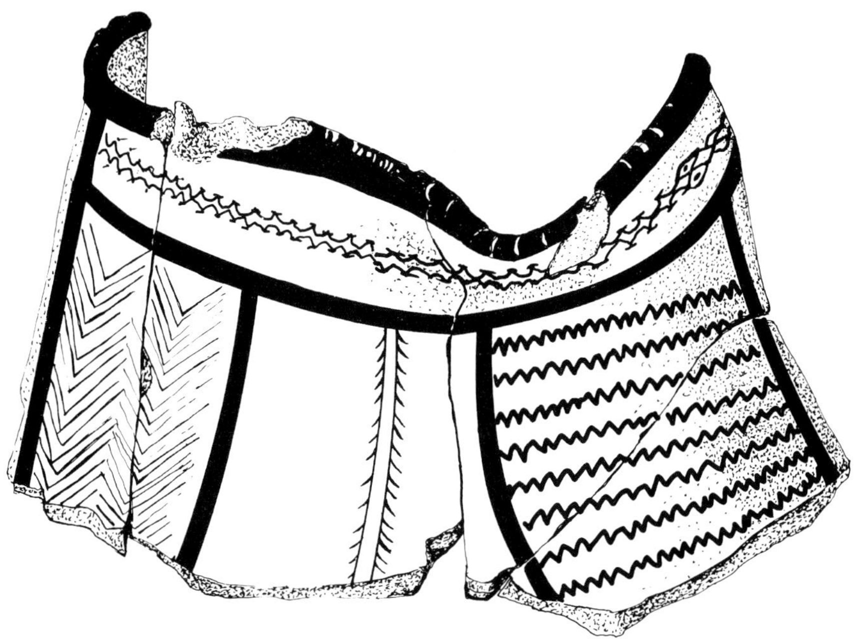

A.1 Excavation zone T (Sanctuary area) deformed vessel fragment; shown also in plate 19.2

A.2 Excavation zone T (Sanctuary area) name-vase of the La Muculufa Master.

B Excavation zone T (Sanctuary area) fragmentary vessel attributed to the La Muculufa Master.

C.1 Excavation zone T (Sanctuary area) cups.

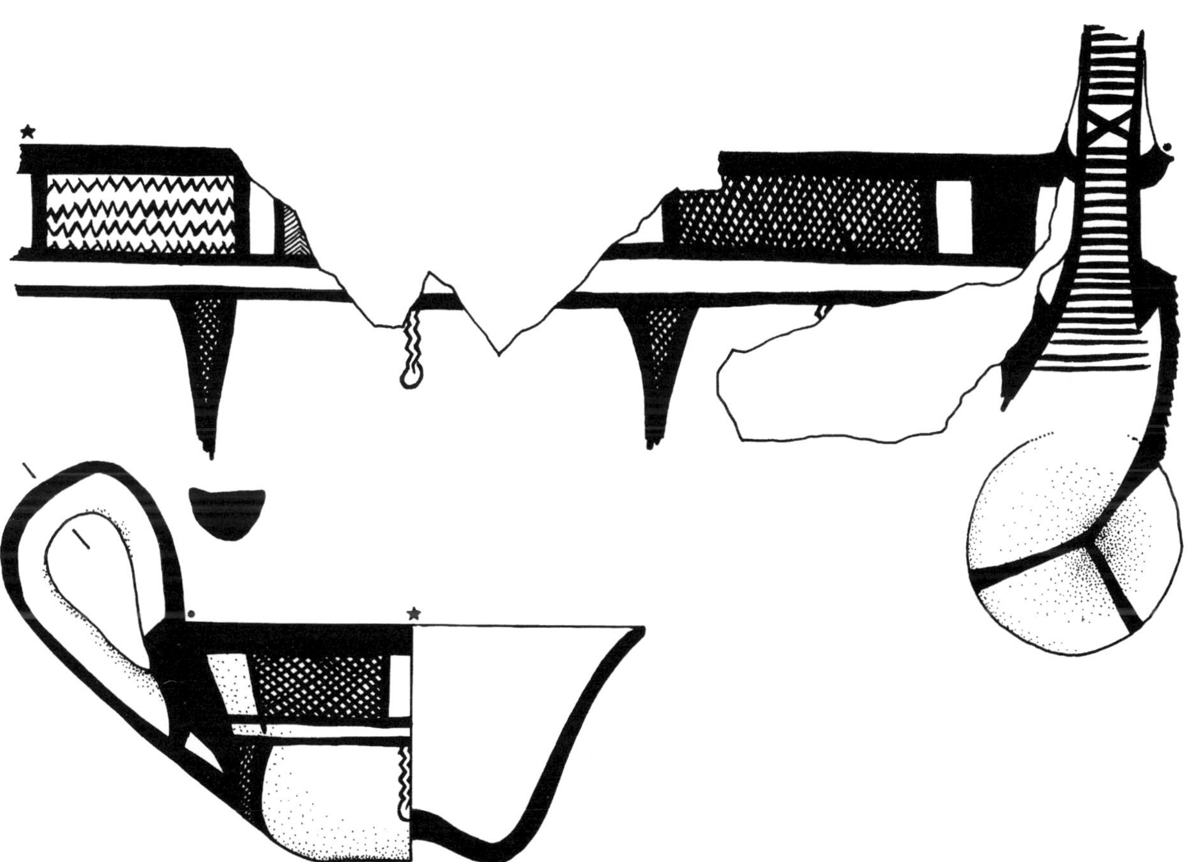

C.2 Excavation zone T (Sanctuary area) cups.

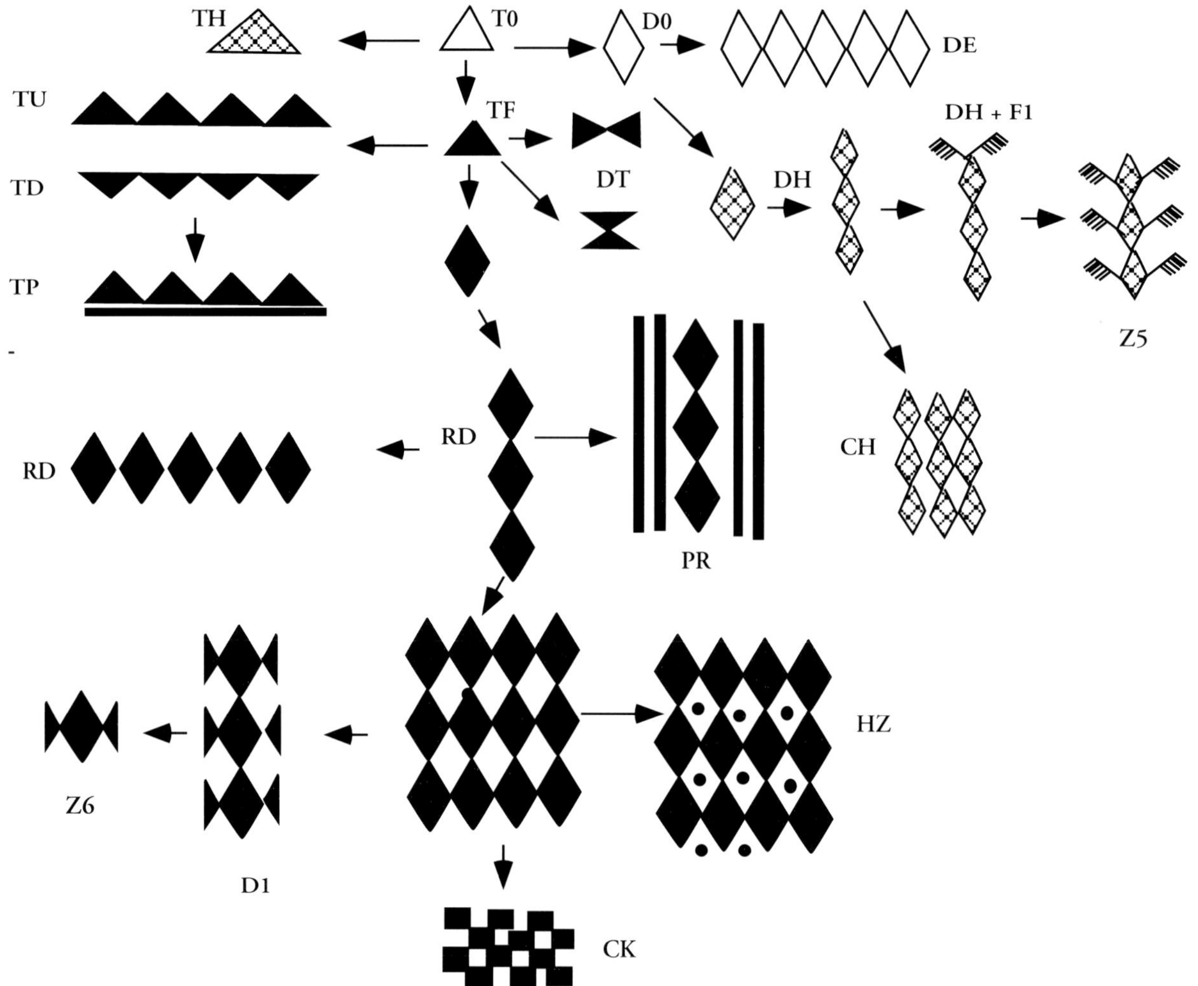

D Castellucian design motives.

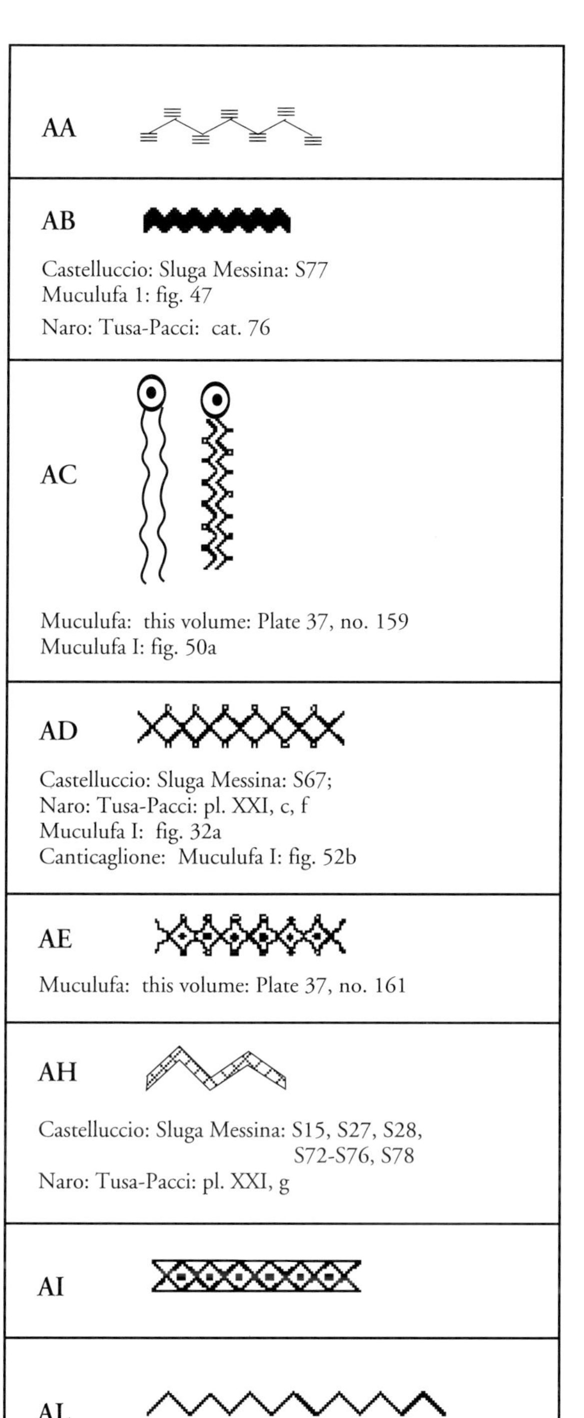

AA

AB

Castelluccio: Sluga Messina: S77
Muculufa 1: fig. 47
Naro: Tusa-Pacci: cat. 76

AC

Muculufa: this volume: Plate 37, no. 159
Muculufa I: fig. 50a

AD

Castelluccio: Sluga Messina: S67;
Naro: Tusa-Pacci: pl. XXI, c, f
Muculufa I: fig. 32a
Canticaglione: Muculufa I: fig. 52b

AE

Muculufa: this volume: Plate 37, no. 161

AH

Castelluccio: Sluga Messina: S15, S27, S28,
                              S72-S76, S78
Naro: Tusa-Pacci: pl. XXI, g

AI

AL

Muculufa I: fig. 43a
Canticaglione: Muculufa I: fig. 52c
Mufulufa: this volume: Plate 24, no. 11

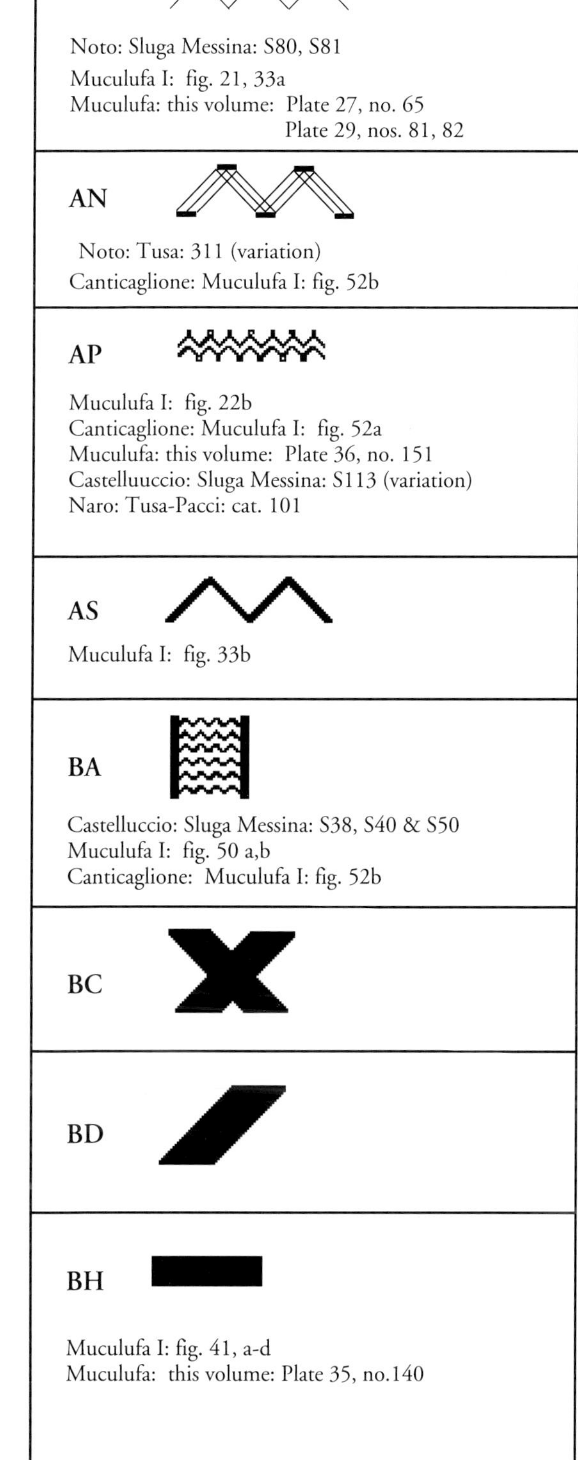

AM

Noto: Sluga Messina: S80, S81
Muculufa I: fig. 21, 33a
Muculufa: this volume: Plate 27, no. 65
                        Plate 29, nos. 81, 82

AN

 Noto: Tusa: 311 (variation)
Canticaglione: Muculufa I: fig. 52b

AP

Muculufa I: fig. 22b
Canticaglione: Muculufa I: fig. 52a
Muculufa: this volume: Plate 36, no. 151
Castelluuccio: Sluga Messina: S113 (variation)
Naro: Tusa-Pacci: cat. 101

AS

Muculufa I: fig. 33b

BA

Castelluccio: Sluga Messina: S38, S40 & S50
Muculufa I: fig. 50 a,b
Canticaglione: Muculufa I: fig. 52b

BC

BD

BH

Muculufa I: fig. 41, a-d
Muculufa: this volume: Plate 35, no.140

E Design Motifs.

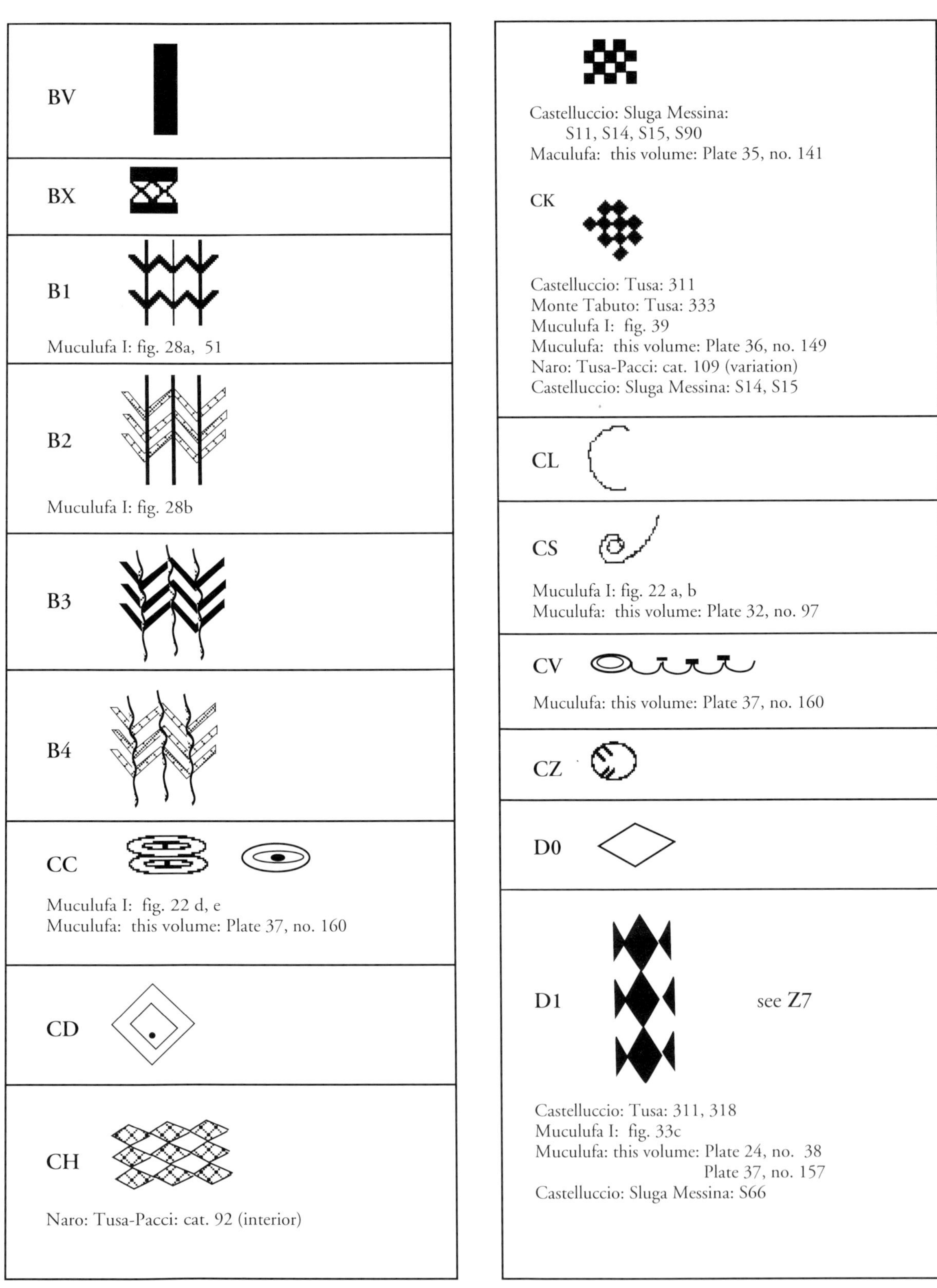

BV	
BX	
B1	Muculufa I: fig. 28a, 51
B2	Muculufa I: fig. 28b
B3	
B4	
CC	Muculufa I: fig. 22 d, e Muculufa: this volume: Plate 37, no. 160
CD	
CH	Naro: Tusa-Pacci: cat. 92 (interior)

Castelluccio: Sluga Messina:
    S11, S14, S15, S90
Maculufa: this volume: Plate 35, no. 141

CK

Castelluccio: Tusa: 311
Monte Tabuto: Tusa: 333
Muculufa I: fig. 39
Muculufa: this volume: Plate 36, no. 149
Naro: Tusa-Pacci: cat. 109 (variation)
Castelluccio: Sluga Messina: S14, S15

CL

CS

Muculufa I: fig. 22 a, b
Muculufa: this volume: Plate 32, no. 97

CV

Muculufa: this volume: Plate 37, no. 160

CZ

D0

D1   see **Z7**

Castelluccio: Tusa: 311, 318
Muculufa I: fig. 33c
Muculufa: this volume: Plate 24, no. 38
                Plate 37, no. 157
Castelluccio: Sluga Messina: S66

F Design Motifs.

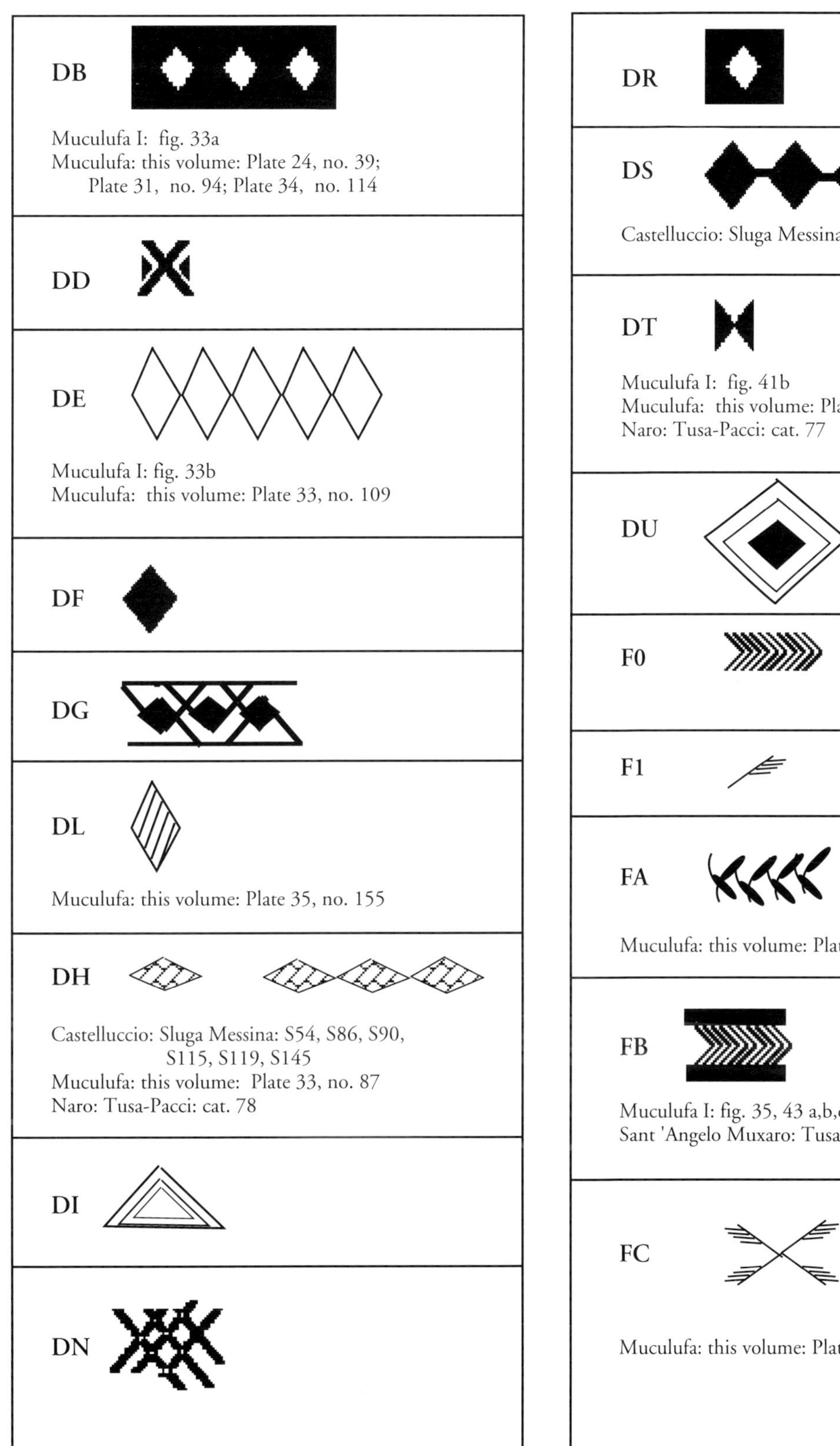

DB	Muculufa I: fig. 33a Muculufa: this volume: Plate 24, no. 39; Plate 31, no. 94; Plate 34, no. 114
DD	
DE	Muculufa I: fig. 33b Muculufa: this volume: Plate 33, no. 109
DF	
DG	
DL	Muculufa: this volume: Plate 35, no. 155
DH	Castelluccio: Sluga Messina: S54, S86, S90, S115, S119, S145 Muculufa: this volume: Plate 33, no. 87 Naro: Tusa-Pacci: cat. 78
DI	
DN	
DR	
DS	Castelluccio: Sluga Messina: S66 (variation)
DT	Muculufa I: fig. 41b Muculufa: this volume: Plate 25, nos. 26, 28 Naro: Tusa-Pacci: cat. 77
DU	
F0	
F1	
FA	Muculufa: this volume: Plate 36, no. 153
FB	Muculufa I: fig. 35, 43 a,b,c Sant 'Angelo Muxaro: Tusa-Pacci: fig. 22, p. 87
FC	Muculufa: this volume: Plate 36, no. 147

G Design Motifs.

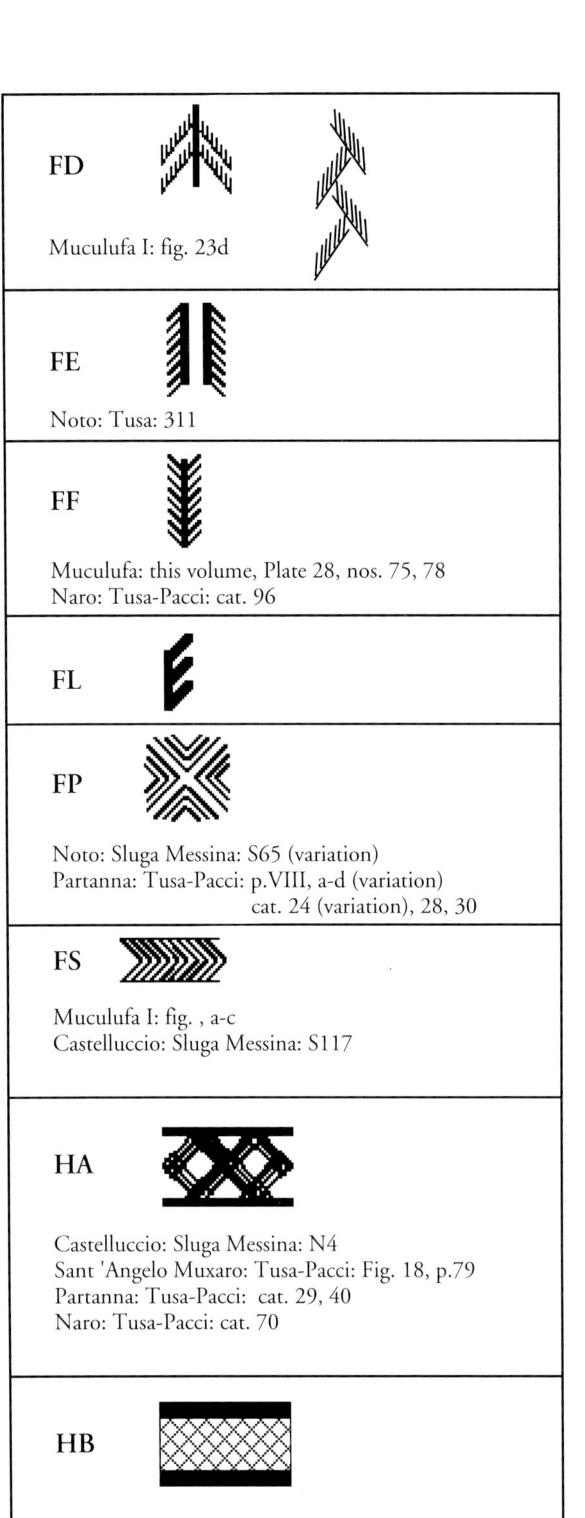

FD

Muculufa I: fig. 23d

FE

Noto: Tusa: 311

FF

Muculufa: this volume, Plate 28, nos. 75, 78
Naro: Tusa-Pacci: cat. 96

FL

FP

Noto: Sluga Messina: S65 (variation)
Partanna: Tusa-Pacci: p.VIII, a-d (variation)
        cat. 24 (variation), 28, 30

FS

Muculufa I: fig. , a-c
Castelluccio: Sluga Messina: S117

HA

Castelluccio: Sluga Messina: N4
Sant 'Angelo Muxaro: Tusa-Pacci: Fig. 18, p.79
Partanna: Tusa-Pacci: cat. 29, 40
Naro: Tusa-Pacci: cat. 70

HB

Muculufa I: fig. 21, 23a
Canticaglione: Muculufa I: fig. 52 a,c,d,e

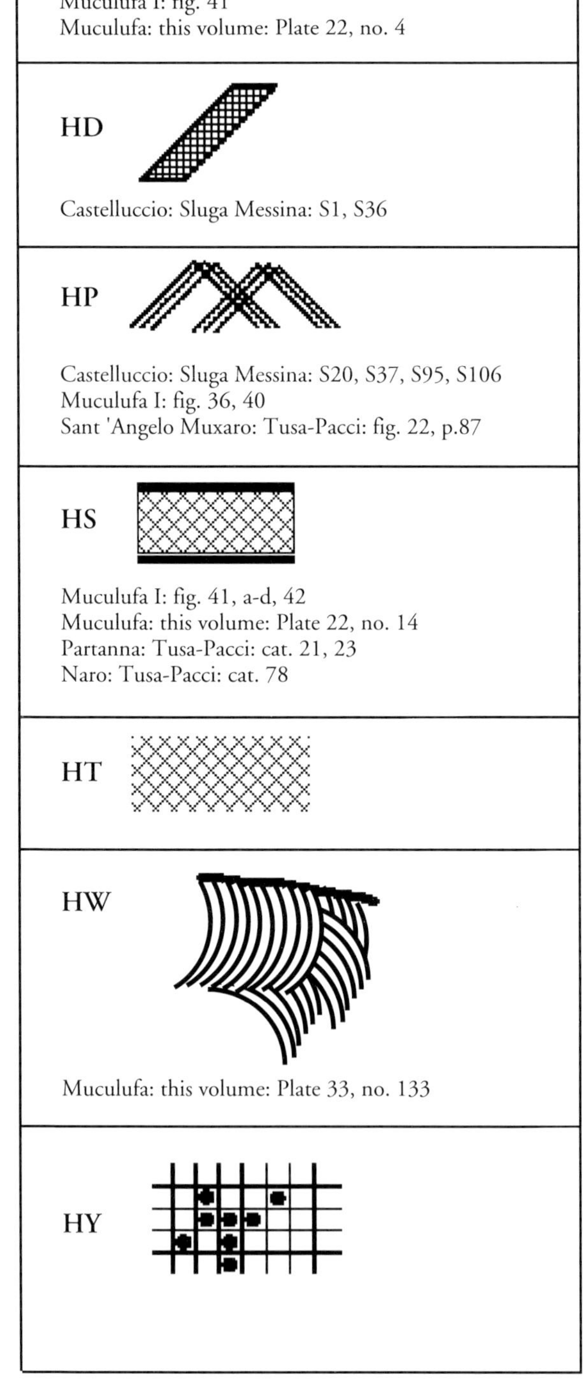

HC

Castelluccio: Sluga Messina: S3
Muculufa I: fig. 41
Muculufa: this volume: Plate 22, no. 4

HD

Castelluccio: Sluga Messina: S1, S36

HP

Castelluccio: Sluga Messina: S20, S37, S95, S106
Muculufa I: fig. 36, 40
Sant 'Angelo Muxaro: Tusa-Pacci: fig. 22, p.87

HS

Muculufa I: fig. 41, a-d, 42
Muculufa: this volume: Plate 22, no. 14
Partanna: Tusa-Pacci: cat. 21, 23
Naro: Tusa-Pacci: cat. 78

HT

HW

Muculufa: this volume: Plate 33, no. 133

HY

H Design Motifs.

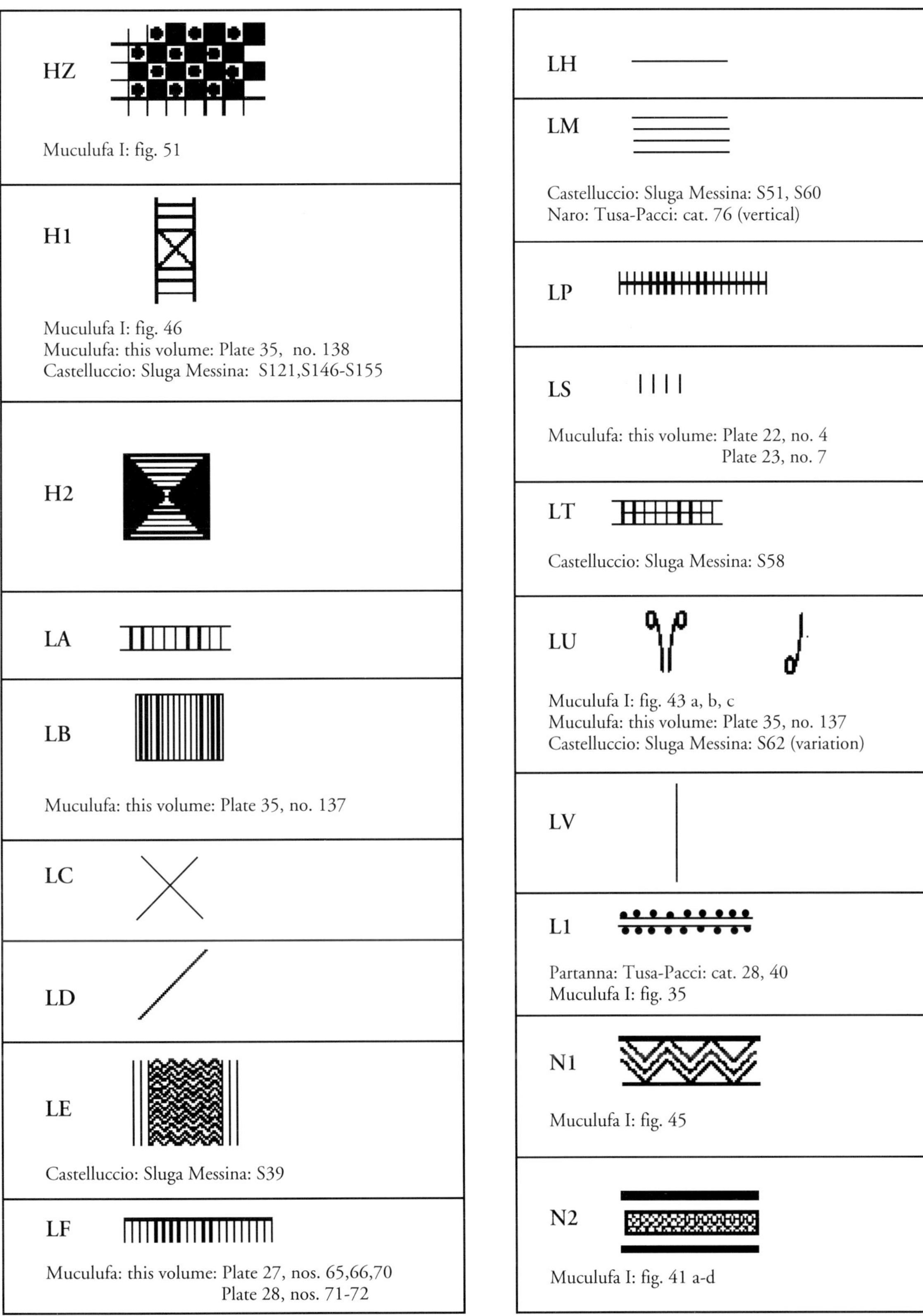

I Design Motifs.

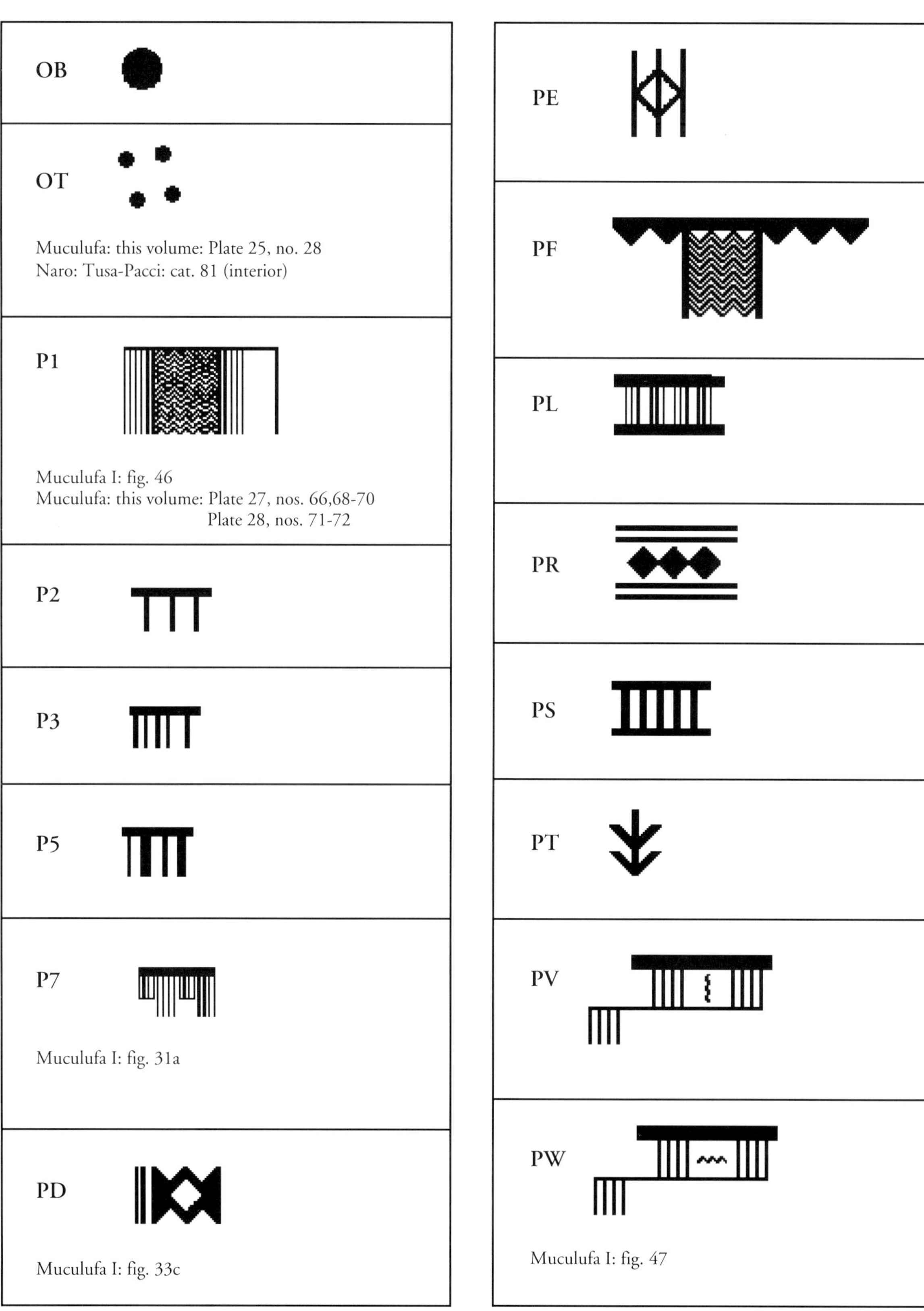

J Design Motifs.

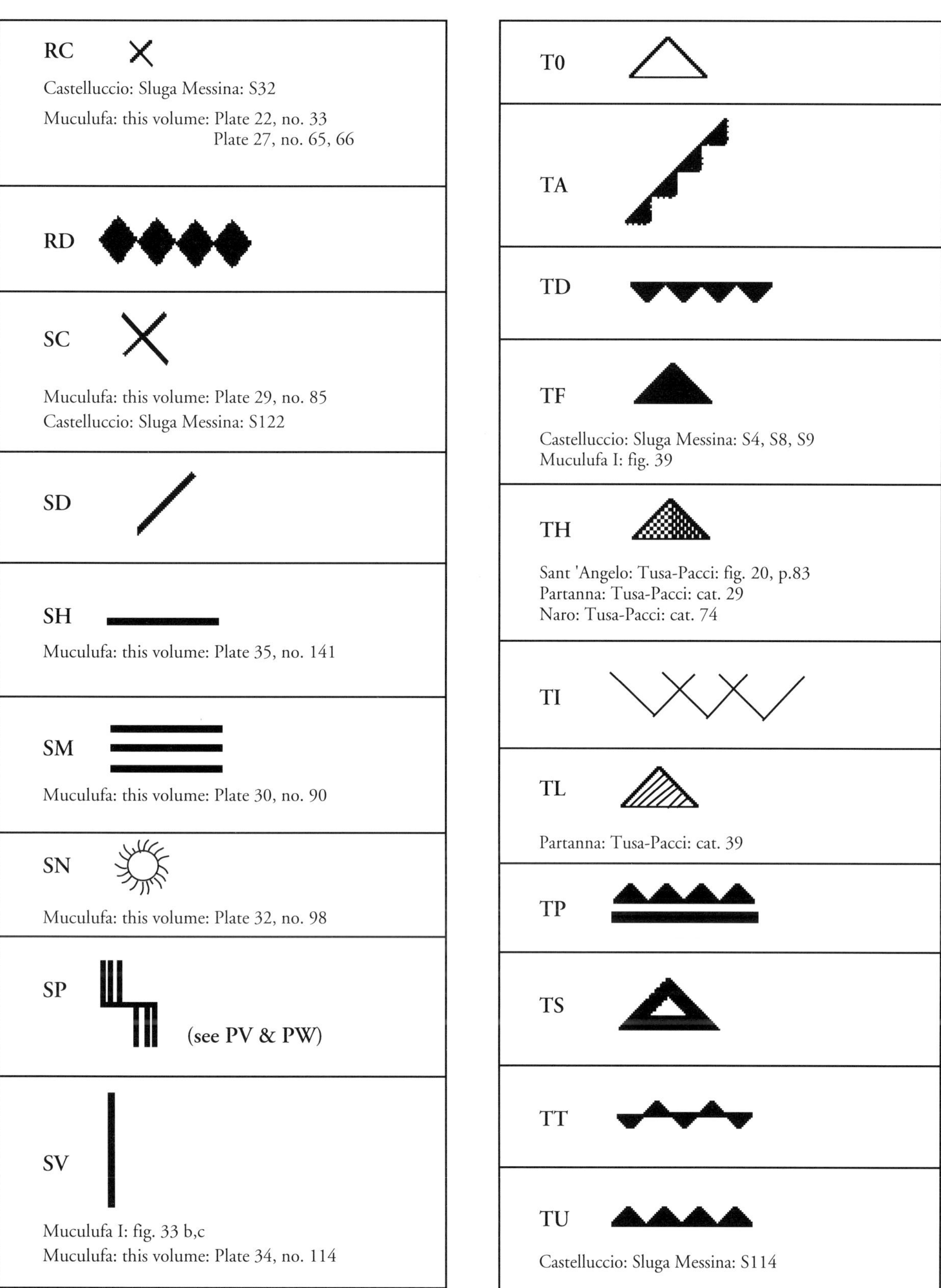

K Design Motifs.

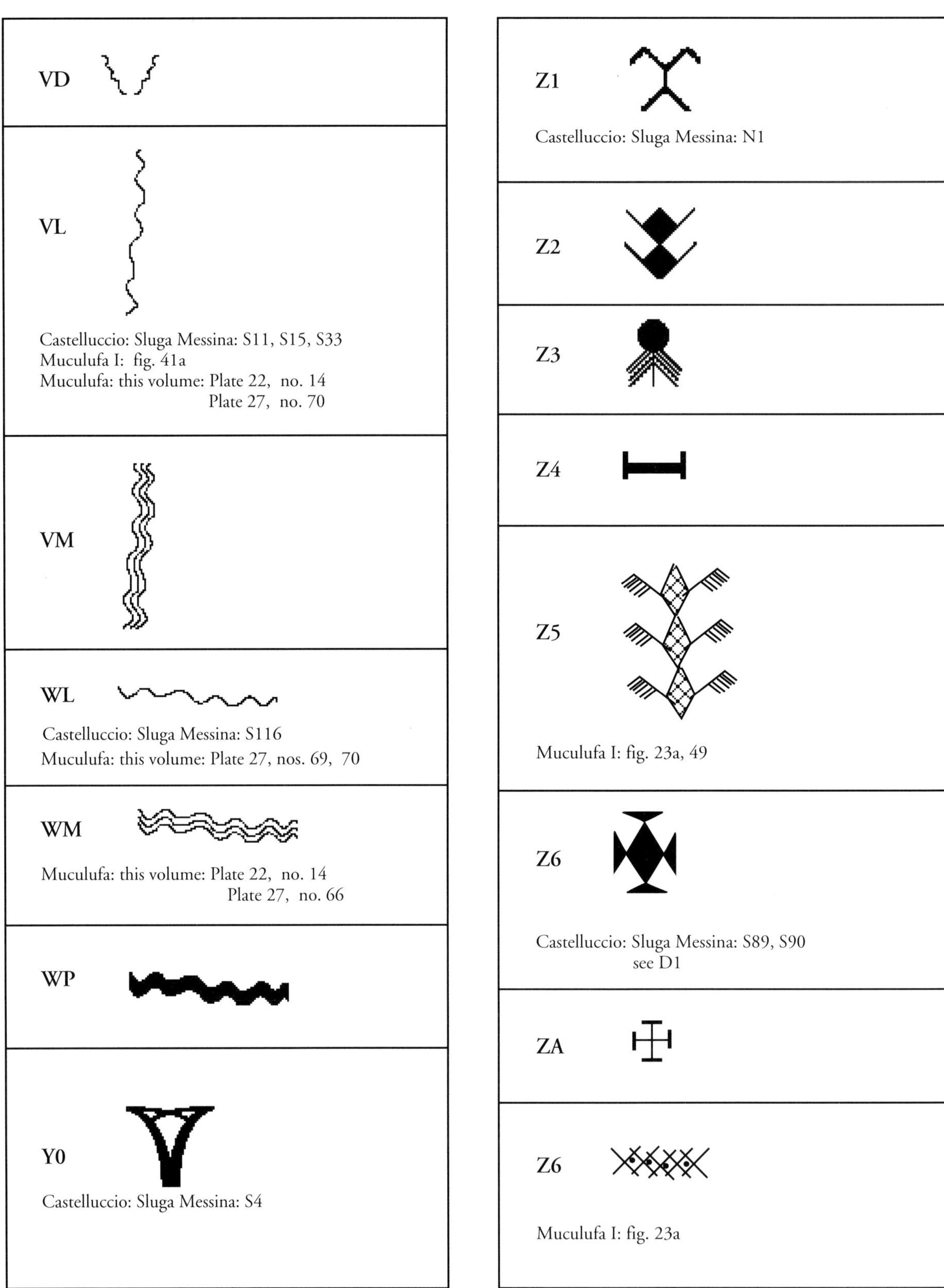

L Design Motifs.